Paul Bourget

Outre-mer

Impressions of America

Paul Bourget

Outre-mer
Impressions of America

ISBN/EAN: 9783337187521

Printed in Europe, USA, Canada, Australia, Japan

Cover: Foto ©ninafisch / pixelio.de

More available books at **www.hansebooks.com**

OUTRE-MER IMPRESSIONS OF AMERICA BY PAUL BOURGET

MEMBER OF THE FRENCH ACADEMY

WITH FRONTISPIECE PORTRAIT

LONDON PUBLISHED BY T FISHER UNWIN PATERNOSTER SQUARE 1895

CONTENTS

OUTRE-MER

I

AT SEA

ON BOARD THE ——, AUGUST, 1893.

THE enormous ship — it has three funnels, a displacement of ten thousand tons, and an average speed of five hundred miles a day — is ploughing the broad ocean under full headway. An August afternoon sky broods over the Atlantic with its autumn clouds. It is like a flat gray lid, beneath which, tirelessly, monotonously, the waters heave and swell. The dull gray waves, opaque as the sky, rise up, tower aloft, and then come crashing down. For a second, as each uprears itself, the thin ruffled crest shines green, a fringe of foam plays along it, white and undulating. Then the wavering crest gives way, the emerald wall crashes down in a heavy mass of brackish water under the swelling of another wave. There are thousands upon thousands of them, heaving, raging, clashing in a frenzy as of a resounding battle; over it sometimes a bird flies with outspread wings, black against the gray sky, seeking its prey in the wind and tempest. The mighty ship ploughs through the terrific heaving of the sea, without either pitching or rolling. So steady is the deck that it would seem like a weird nightmare but for the ceaseless quivering of its metal frame.

This is one of the five or six steamers that sailors call "ocean greyhounds." It deserves the felicitous epithet as much by its proportions and the elegance of the lines which define the slender contour of its colossal hull as by its prodigious speed. Only a few hours ago, we started, and already the coast of Ireland is fading away, losing itself in the leaden rim of the cloudy dome which encircles the horizon. A few more turns of the double screw, and for a whole week we shall have around us only the unfathomable waves, and beyond them the New World.

How it draws me — that New World, and for reasons no doubt far enough removed from those which are attracting my fellow-travellers. The flag that floats above us bears upon its white field the spread eagle of the United States. The ship is American, and so are most of my fellow-travellers. Having decided once again to quit France, I preferred to cut the thread at once, and here I am already in Yankee land. I hear only English on this deck, — a nasal English in which the word "well" takes the place of the word "yes," and recurs continually. It has already behooved me to change my French money and to learn without delay that the unit of expenditure has leaped from the franc to the dollar; in other words, is quintupled. These are the first two evidences of expatriation, and the next is the indescribable insolence of the ship's servants, or rather of the help. For have I not long known that there are no servants in the United States? Not one of my neighbors, who to the number of a hundred or so are enjoying the air on long folding-chairs, has probably observed these trifles; but for the foreigner they are like the little shiver that thrills through the swimmer as he makes the first plunge. However accustomed one may be to what the tragical and restless Maupassant used to call "the errant life," there is in the sudden leap from any "home" a vague sensation of melancholy. Or rather — for that is a pretty large word for a simple contraction of the nerves — it is rather an involuntary impulse to draw back. The thousand inconveniences of the uprooting rise up before you, and you ask yourself, "Why this new journey? What am I crossing the ocean to seek, far from my friends, my books, the familiar scenes of the land where I grew up?" Alas! it is no longer *that* land that is fading away yonder into the mist, for the name of this coast is Cape Clear Island. Never mind, that Irish island belonged to Europe, after all. That lighthouse which has just been kindled is no doubt heralding the arrival home to other travellers, who for one reason or another have already gone through the experience upon which I am entering. When, eight or ten months hence, if God wills, I see again that point of land, that light flashing out against the sky, shall I have brought back from beyond the sea a rich harvest of ideas and memories? Shall I be telling myself then that I was wrong in again exiling myself for so long a time, or shall I say that I was right?

To the two questions of *afterwards* I cannot yet make answer, but I see clearly my reply to the two former, the questions of *beforehand*. What America has to give me I do not know. What I expect from her I know very well, and I should like to sketch in a few lines upon the opening pages of my journal a sort of programme, an intellectual self-examination.

When I come to revise my notes, it will make the best of prefaces for them, I think; and it is also the best way of beguiling the weariness of the steamer, that sensation of days at once long and empty, which from the experience of eastern sea-faring I know only too well. There is no such thing as time at sea, — no distribution of hours, no small divisions of life. One is as if cradled, rocked by a mighty power which suppresses you, in which you will melt away. The infinitely littles of sea-faring life, vague dreams of things seen only in their large outlines, are all that come to help you to while away these mornings and afternoons of languid vegetation. I shall try two remedies, and I begin with the second, which accords only too well with the dominant passion of my mind, with my fancy — my mania, almost — for gathering thousands of scattered facts into the brief limits of a formula. Well, the wolf will always show himself wolf, saith the sage. That is just a way of thinking, of looking at things, and it must have its uses as well as its limitations. In any case, it is my own particular kind of impressionism, and I can be sincere only by yielding to it, begging, in advance, the reader's pardon for this abuse of abstract reflection.

"Expatriation," I wrote just now. How harsh the word is, and how false it rings! In all my journeyings I have felt, and I feel still more strongly now, that one can never be expatriated. However far he may be from his native land or from any land, he has only to retire into his innermost consciousness to find himself citizen not of the world, but of that little corner of it from which he came. What draws me to America is not America, but Europe and France; it is the disquietude of the problems in which the future of Europe and France is hidden. Three powers are at work to-day to hew out that future; three divinities, with hands as stern and inexorable as those of the Parcæ, whose sovereignty over all the interests and enterprises of the Old World it behooves us to recognize. The first is Democracy; the second is Science; the third, the last to appear and the least easy to name, is the idea of Race. Turn to whatever remotest corner of the continent you may, from St. Petersburg to London, from Rome to Paris, you shall find these three powers at work, busy in moulding the lineaments of a new world, — so at least their devotees assert, — busy in destroying, piece by piece, the antique edifice which for ages has sheltered human life, and, say their adversaries, without building up anything to replace it. And the latter have no difficulty in showing us what sort of a Europe these new divinities have made, how sinister it is, how different from that of which our fathers dreamed, when, at the close of the last century, they hailed with a shout of confiding hope the dawn of the Revolution. Universal suffrage, — that is to say, the imbecile tyranny of numbers, the reign of force in its blindest and most unjust form, — this is the régime which Democracy has established wherever it has triumphed. To this it has added the clamorous awakening of the lower appetites, a universal discontent with one's lot, and the constant menace of a revolt of the fourth estate, of poverty and envy, against a civilization which promised to give liberty, equality, and fraternity, and which has gone bankrupt of all its unrealizable promises.

The positive benefit bestowed by Science is a more adroit treatment of nature, known at last with precision; but it is dearly bought, if it be true that philosophical nihilism is the last outcome of this gigantic attempt to ask questions that have no possible solution. Brought face to face with the Unknowable, and constrained to acknowledge that its method is powerless ever to reach the causes that lie back of phenomena and the substance that lies behind accidental circumstance, what aliment can Science give the soul, except the bread of bitterness and the waters of death? Developing to the highest degree in the man of to-day the spirit of experiment and of criticism, it has made faith in the supernatural almost impossible to an innumerable multitude of average consciences, and it is the sum of the average consciences that makes what we call the national conscience. Hence, what a loss of the Ideal in contemporary Europe! What uncertainty of conviction, and, as a natural consequence, what incoherent feebleness of will, what weakening of character, what ill-regulated energy, what moral maladies, forever recurring in ever-new complications, in these last years of this end of a century, which has so longed to do well!

And, finally, the idea of Race, which amid the gun-flashes of Solferino seemed so generous, so logical,— into what a menace of barbarism it has resolved itself, now that the very Europe which gave herself to progress is only a succession of fortified camps, where thousands of men wait beside their loaded cannon for the hour of such an extermination as history has never yet known!

Yes, this is the evident task of these three direful and merciless toilers, whom it is nevertheless vain to ban. For in the grand, irresistible forces of society, as in those of nature, there is a character of fatality which is just so far sacred. Lying beyond the foresight and control of man, they appear to us as mysterious emanations of the very principle from which all reality flows. All that is irresistible and illimitable in them commands our acquiescence, as birth and death command it, as day and night, or as this sea, whose waves beat upon this vessel on which I write these lines. In presence of such a necessity despair is impossible, until one has calculated all the chances of a happier future; that is to say, until one has made certain that the effects produced by these implacable causes are always the same.

Now one country has been found where these three forces, so destructive in our old world, have been called upon to construct, out of whole cloth, a new universe. This country was a democracy from the very beginning, and a scientific democracy, because to conquer this virgin soil it was necessary to make use of the most modern machines and methods of industry. It was a country upon which the race problem was forced at its very origin, and against which it still continually brings up, being formed of the alluvium of all the nations of Europe, Asia, and Africa, and forced to make it possible not only for Englishmen to live with Irishmen, and Germans with Frenchmen, but yellow and black men with men of white skins.

Up to the present time it appears to have succeeded. Every

year its population augments, its riches increase, its cities
grow, with the energy of tropical plants.   Forty years ago,
what was St. Louis, or St. Paul, or Minneapolis? what was
Chicago itself?   To-day, the inhabitants of those cities of
yesterday are counted by the hundred thousand, two hundred
thousand, five hundred thousand; and this year the most
surprising one of them all has opened an Exposition to which
the whole world was invited — and the whole world has gone!
An army of twenty-five thousand men suffices this people, who
yet, less than thirty years ago, proved that military energy was
as abundant among them as all other forms of energy; and
then, the struggle ended, they returned to the occupations of
peace with the same rapidity with which they had organized
the formidable machinery of war.   How can one know of the
existence of such a nation, and not be curious to study the
conditions of its existence elsewhere than in books?   How
lose an opportunity to estimate upon the spot the worth of
this society, which claims to be that of the future, and which,
in any case, is one of the possibilities of the future?   I believe that I am aware in advance of all that will shock me in
this country, where the poetry of a past is wanting, — I who
have so loved Italy, Greece, Syria, and their soil, half formed
of the dust of the dead.   I know that I shall not find among
them those of my own mind and heart.   But where would I
not go, or to whom, in the hope of getting back a little faith
in the future of civilization, which, among us, seems upon
the point of sinking into irreparable ruin?

I have let five days pass since the afternoon of our departure, when I tried my powers at that sort of mental balance
sheet, which it is good to draw up in the first and last hours
of a long journey.   During the journey itself, one must give
oneself up to the present sensation.   The writer must make
use of his general impressions, in the way that the painter

utilizes the walls of his studio. He hangs upon them the studies which at once hide and are sustained by them. During these five days, therefore, I have done my best to forget my theories, as I hope to forget them during the months to come; and I have given myself up to steamer life, which is always the same in all climates and on all seas. Nevertheless, looking at it more closely, this ship is already a bit of America, and one who is keen-sighted in manners could easily distinguish here, as elsewhere, the national tone, that ineffaceable little sign which every people imprints upon its own physiognomy. Who has ever quitted a steamer of the Peninsular Company, the classic P. and O. of Egypt and India, for a vessel of the *Messageries*, without feeling that all England is in the one and all France in the other, just as all Italy is in the between-decks of one of the *Florios*, which coast from Genoa to Patrasso? But one discerns these shades of difference only when one already knows the peoples.

Here, at all events, is a sketch of some of the pictures which I shall carry away with me from this voyage, now so soon to end. We have made such good time that, having left Southampton on Saturday afternoon, we shall be in New York to-morrow — Friday — evening, notwithstanding that the sea has rudely assailed us at certain times, notably at that middle point of ocean which sailors call the "devil's hole," and although, at the very moment when I resume my journal, the fog is thickening over a sea so smooth that it barely shows a ripple. A ground swell lifts it in a large, slow undulation, while the ship is veiled in a soft, white mist, so dense that from one end of it persons and things at the other seem to melt together in a vague, spectral shimmer. Moment by moment the whistle rends the fog with its strident call, but the speed of our course is not lessened by a single knot.

"It is safer," says one of my table companions. "In case of collision, the swiftest vessel always cuts down the other."

And first this upper deck, on which I have passed so many hours, while the waves, beaten by the wind, sprinkled it with their salty spray; let me once more bring before my eyes the two passages along the cabins, with their lines of close-crowded steamer chairs. There men and women passed their days, reading, conversing, lounging, sleeping; the colors of their plaids, the intermingling of green and yellow, red and black, bringing out the brightness or the blemishes of their faces. To my fancy, these faces, young and old, which every morning I found in the same place, were like enigmas of race, in which, with a singular curiosity, I amused myself with searching the not-to-be-attested heredities, all the various elements which have been fused together in that Corinthian brass, the American race. In all this crowd there was nothing of the clean-cut outline which distinguishes the physiognomy of almost all Englishmen, clear, heavy, distinct, like their printing. Instead of this were countenances so dissimilar, and physiques so contradictory, that one could easily detect in them all the different atavisms of which the United States is the synthesis. This square-shouldered personage, with hands heavy as beetles and feet like the base of a column, who smokes great cigars with a strong inspiration of the breath, and whose small eyes flash through their spectacles with an expression at once shrewd and kindly, do I need to be told that his name ends in *mann*, and that he is returning to Chicago, before I can be sure that he is German, or a son of Germany? This other, with the nervous gayety of his deep blue eyes, his red beard, his excited gestures, the evident all-but of his dress, how can I doubt that he is Irish, or a son of Ireland? This third, with his too black eyes, set in a spare, thin, olive-tinted mask, how indisputably Spanish, the living silhouette of some Californian adventurer!

And then, beside these faces, with their clearly defined character, there are others in which five or six different types

have blended,— faces heavy and colorless, deeply marked
with lines that tell of struggle. They smile, and in the very
act of smiling they remain austere, almost bitter, as if the
labors and pains of more than one generation had left their
impress upon them. Many of the women, and very pretty
ones, talk familiarly with both classes. Among them are
several actresses, returning to their native country after a tour
in England. I picture to myself the gallantries, actual or
prospective, which such travelling intimacies would imply on
a boat belonging to a Latin country. In the present case, the
contrary impression prevails; here are crude manners on a
basis of energy and determination, as ours are based on pleasure or wit. It is all symbolized in the courage, hardihood,
persistence with which, ever since setting sail, and whatever
the mutations of the sea, many of the young women have per-
sisted in pacing the deck with steady steps; while a group of
young fellows and older men played cricket on the forward
deck, in driving spray or drenching rain.

"My brother is not comfortable if he has not two hours of
hard exercise every day," a young girl said to me, looking up
from her diligent reading of a review article on *Physical Culture*.

The dining-room, also, rises up before my eyes, with the
barbaric luxury of its new gilding and the humming of voices
around the tables. From the hour of our departure the abundance of food has kept pace with the barbaric luxury, with its
twenty-five dishes for breakfast, luncheon, or dinner. I had
often heard of American wastefulness. I became aware of
it three times a day, in face of this prodigality of food, which
conjured up visions of oxen, sheep, and pigs hanging up by
the score in refrigerating rooms between decks, heaps of fish
in other ice-boxes, and a provision of milk products and fruits
enough to last through a siege.

The distance between me and the land of the vine was evident enough merely from seeing how those who devoured these things washed down their food. Whiskey, ale, soda, tea, lemonade, port, sherry, dry champagne, brandy, apollinaris, appeared on all the tables, attesting that voluntary habit of diet so characteristic of Anglo-Saxon countries. There is no type of food with them, as there is with us. Each stomach obeys its own caprice. And in the semi-hallucination caused by the rocking of the sea, I always seemed to see hovering over this assembly the smile of a certain singular personage, a New York dentist who lives in Rome, but whom I met again on this ship, on his way to a congress in Chicago,—one of those indefatigable artists in gold who, with all the daring and dexterity of an engineer, dig tunnels in the teeth of their clients, and build metal bridges in the most devastated mouths. At times he seemed to my eyes to be clothed in the dignity of host at this travelling table, so plainly, from the very first breakfast, did the boon companions show that animal avidity which characterizes a predatory race, to whom the preservation of a great masticating implement has of necessity become as important as talons to the vulture or claws to the lion.

I see that dining-room again, quiet, decorous, solemnly resonant with the voice of a minister reading prayers. It is Sunday morning, and of two hundred passengers more than one hundred are present at this service! These very faces which I saw yesterday, and shall see to-morrow, flushed with much eating, are bent over Bibles, with the seriousness of sincere personal conviction. All these people travel with their own prayer books. I watched them through the skylight, with the feeling that, in spite of the prodigious afflux of immigration, the soul of those Pilgrim Fathers who set sail in the Mayflower in 1620 is not yet dead, and I pictured to myself that setting forth, preceded by a day of solemn humiliation, "the pastor having taken for his text this verse from Ezra: 'Beside the river Ahava I proclaimed a day that we might humble ourselves before our God and receive of him direction in the right way, we, our children, and all our substance.'"

This is the profound feeling that still stirs in the "revivals" of America, with their emotion so intense that, even in this nineteenth century, new sects are forever springing up. You could feel the throbbing of it between the gilded walls of this gaudy saloon, with which in my mind it will ever be associated. I shall always see there yet another and very different scene — a concert arranged by a theatre manager who is making a starring tour as far as San Francisco. The proceeds of the concert were to be given to the hospital for poor sailors. A former minister of the United States to one of the first courts of Europe had accepted the presidency of the affair. All the humor of a nation of debaters, of men accustomed to be always talking, in private and public, spoke in the tone with which he began, alluding to his unhappy cabin experiences: "*I present to you a very poor sailor.*" If I had not known to what part of the world I was going, I should have learned from the absolutely simple manner of the umquhile diplomatist. It was enough to make amends for a sentimental ditty that will long ring in my ears, which began, "Two lambs in the field, not dreaming of mint sauce," and the painful vulgarity of a singer who mimicked an Irish chambermaid about to become an actress. Shaking her fist with the vigor of a professional boxer making ready to give a "punishment," she howled, "I want to be a Hactress! a Hactress!" in such formidable tones that the glasses trembled at them as they had not done at the raging of the sea.

What a course of international psychology was that lower smoking-room, about nine o'clock in the evening, especially yesterday, when they drew the numbers of one of the last pools, on the speed of the ship. Fifty people, perhaps, in an atmosphere redolent at once of the steamer, of tobacco, of toilet water — for the barber's shop is next door, and he was occupied, with the door open, in shampooing a client's hair — and of alcohol! There is a bar at the end of the room, where the alchemist to whom is intrusted the cocktails manipulates one of those corrosive mixtures with which Americans delight to burn themselves up. Poker-playing goes on all night long in this room, with its lining of yellow wood and its electric lights, shaded by globes of blue and rose color, that shed a fairy-like radiance. The players are reading the points on the corners of their huge playing-cards; their impassive faces, schooled for a bluff, betraying only that cold fever of the gambler, which now rages around the numbers of the pool. A cadaverous, thick-lipped actor has put them all in a bag, and is drawing them out and allotting them to the different passengers who in the course of the day have inscribed their names on the sheet of paper hung up against the smoke-dimmed mirror. Next, they will be put up at auction, and the fat man will run up the bidding, descanting on the merits of number with the glibness of a commercial traveller, though with sinister prediction. Thus he will say, "481, . . . there will be a terrible fog; 480, that is the lowest, and the best. We shall slip along like the Victory. 480, who wants enough to pay his insurance? 504, that is the highest and the best. This is all halcyon weather. We shall make 506." And the bids go up, one dollar, five, ten, twenty, a hundred, until — "One, two, three, *gone!*" to the Honorable Mr. ——.

The faces of these stick most in my memory, with their hard, restless eyes, and the firm, half-cruel movement of their mouths. Almost all of them are gray rather than brown-haired, their complexion poisoned by the abuse of the formidable alcoholic drinks. Their faces inevitably bring up before me those western legends where a cocked revolver is always within reach of the player. Two faces, especially, appear clearly before me: one, square cut and open, with a sailor-cap drawn down over the brows, a short, straight pipe in the corner of the mouth, and a mocking smile as he raised the bid; the other, sharp and insolent, with an expression at once sly and vulgar. The voices which issued from these two mouths, as each grew more intense in this strife for dollars, betrayed a hatred almost like that of two different species, as if there were, in the background of this play, or more properly this deed, the display of a force almost animal. And no sooner was the strife over the number of miles brought to an end, than it began again over the number of the first pilot we should meet.

That first pilot boat, how tiny it was as it came flying before the wind to meet us, with all sails spread, the waves at times threatening to engulf it! We were six hundred miles from port, and it was a matter of three hundred dollars for the pilot. That evening we met another, who had made his five hundred miles for nothing, in the fearful wind of these last few days. For one second the steam is shut off. A tiny bark puts out from the schooner, bearing a rower with the pilot. The latter catches the rope ladder thrown to him from the deck. He has not overleaped the bulwarks before the machinery is at work again, and the steamer once more at full speed. Five minutes more, and the brave little sail-boat is only a white speck in the vast expanse, continually engulfed in the enormous hollows of the waves through which we cut, with the uniform speed of men who are determined to "break the record." That is the untranslatable expression by which Americans so well express that which, from the very first, has been the foundation of their character; to hold it possible to do anything which has once been done, and to exceed it. Is this pride? Is it the madness of battle? Is it yet another instance of atavism — since these men are sons or grandsons, within three or four generations, of desperate men, who crossed this same ocean with the fixed idea that this was their last resort. I do not know; but I do know that I shall not soon forget the frantic speed of the ocean greyhound, during that last day cf heavy fog, nor that first approach to the land of all audacity in the audacity of a speed great enough to cut through an ironclad, if we had happened to meet one. But who except myself thinks of such a thing? Every one is already absorbed in the newspapers which the pilot has just brought. "It is hardly worth while, though," says some one; "they are two days old."

The seventh day we arrive in sight of New York, on a summer morning at once burning and overcast. We could not come up to the wharf yesterday, because of the lateness of the hour, and I am glad of it, in view of the incomparable beauty of the approach. The steamer is passing up the mouth of the Hudson, which forms the harbor of this great city, with a motion as measured as twenty-four hours ago it was rapid. This sensation, so unexpected and profound, would alone repay the whole voyage. The enormous estuary frets and plashes, upheaved by the last surges of the Atlantic ; and on either shore as far as the eye can reach,— on the right, where New York stretches away, on the left, where Jersey City huddles,— is a long succession, indefinite, indeterminate, of short wooden wharves, broad and covered over. There are names inscribed upon them, here a railway company, there a steamship line, then another railway, and then another steamer company; and so on indefinitely, while from one wharf after another gigantic steamboats come and go, carrying away or pouring forth passengers by the hundred, scores of carriages, vast trains of loaded trucks. I count five, six, of these ferry-boats,— fifteen, twenty. Enormous, their two tiers of white and brown cabins overhang the green water, their iron wheels churn the heavy waves, and over all a gigantic walking-beam beats off their rhythmic motion. They meet, touch lightly, and pass one another by without a shock, so sure is their motion. They seem like colossal beasts of labor, each performing its task with sure fidelity. Numberless little vessels, stout and nimble, dart across their course. They are the tugs. The swells break rudely on their small hulls, and you hear the harsh puffing of their engines, those robust and almost over-large lungs of steel, which quite fill their little bodies. You realize how strong they are by their forward motion, so accurately directed that without ever slowing down they dart between heavy vessels, the impact of which would be shipwreck. Trailing in their wake are the most fragile kind of barks, carrying two, three, four masts. The slight little craft, trembling, almost disappears in the sea-green track cut deep in the laboring water, lashed into combing waves. Now and again one of these tugs sends forth a piercing and piteous whistle, which mingles with the hoarse bellow of the ferry-boats. They are all threading their way on the breast of this vast river, among half a hundred great, slow-moving steamers like our own,— vessels from Europe, from South America, from North America. With tranquil strength the high red hulls cut the heaving mass, freighted with so much of human toil, so many human lives. Their forms are blurred in the warm haze, their outlines melt away, phantom-like. Behind them other steamers come into sight, barely outlined, dimly seen; and still farther in the background looms up a mighty forest of masts and yards, while high over all this gigantic moving mechanism, which might well be the mart of the entire world, towers the statue of Liberty, tall as a lighthouse, outlined against the foaming clouds. On the right and on the left the two cities stretch away, like the perspective of a dream, far as the eye can reach — beyond the reach of thought.

Leaning over the ship's rail on the side toward New York, I succeed in distinguishing a mass of diminutive houses, an ocean of low buildings, from the midst of which uprise, like cliff-bound islets, brick buildings, so daringly colossal that, even at this distance, their height overpowers my vision. I count the stories above the level of the roofs; one has ten, another twelve. Another, not yet finished, has a vast iron framework, outlining upon the sky the plan of six more stories above the eight already built. Gigantic, colossal, enormous, daring, there are no words, — words are inadequate to this apparition, this landscape, in which the vast outlet of the river serves as a frame for the display of still vaster human energy. Reaching such a pitch of collective effort, this energy has become an element of nature itself. To deepen this impression, history adds the ferocious truth of figures. In 1624, not much more than two hundred and fifty years ago, the Indians were selling to a Westphalian the extreme tip of Manhattan Island. He founded this city which lies here before me. It is the poetry of Democracy, and these sproutings forth of popular vitality are a poem, where the individual is lost sight of, and personal effort is only a note in an immense concert. Verily, this is not the Parthenon, — that little temple on a little hill, in which the Hellenes summed up their Ideal, with hardly anything of the material, and of the Spirit enough to animate it with measure and harmony down to its smallest atoms. But it is the obscure and tremendous poetry of the modern world, and it gives you a tragic shudder, there is in it so much of mad and wilful humanity in a horizon like that of this morning — and it is the same every day!

c

II

THE FIRST WEEK

I HAVE passed a week in New York and have hardly seen one of the persons to whom I have brought introductions. During the burning heats of an August as stifling as that of Madrid, they are all in the country, at the seashore, in Europe. I myself am about to set out for Newport, the Deauville of America, that I may see society at close range. I have therefore had leisure during these seven days, to ramble about the city as a mere tourist, and to receive a first impression of it — a first shock, as the agreeable Professor Charles N. of Cambridge said to me, advising me to name this book of travels *American Shocks*, by way of contrast to my *Italian Sensations*.

I wish I might put down here the journal of this week; not that I overestimate the importance and interest of these quite superficial hotel and street experiences. They warrant no general conclusion, and yet they have their value. It is, so to speak, a rushing sense of the foreign, which a longer sojourn will tone down, will do away with, to make room for a more quiet, perhaps more exact, observation. These almost instinctive perceptions of the difference of atmosphere between the country we are in and that from which we come, no longer deceive us when they have once been interpreted. I already foresee that certain very general theories are nearing the limit of their existence. It is probable that these hypotheses are very inadequate, and that I shall change them more than once before leaving this continent. Let me at least fix the surprises of these first hours before they are quite effaced — if it were only by way of memorandum.

Saturday. — Henry J. said to me when we parted in London, "I am looking forward to your impression of the wooden docks of New York. You will want to return by the next steamer, as C—— did."

The latter is a young Frenchman of rare mental superiority, who like myself determined to visit the New World for a course of treatment of activity and democracy. He landed upon a wooden wharf, as I did, found his way to some hotel, as I have done, presented his letters of introduction, as I shall present mine. Five days later he boarded a vessel about to sail for Europe. "I could not endure the blow," was his only reply to the surprise of his relatives.

In truth, the blow of the landing is severe, at least to a Frenchman accustomed to that administrative order whose delays he curses when he is subjected to them, whose conveniences he sighs for in this crush of the Anglo-Saxon crowd, where the struggle for life has its humble and vexatious symbol in the struggle for baggage.

No sooner is the steamer docked than you find yourself in an immense shed crowded with people who come and go, jostling and being jostled. Gigantic policemen, rotund under their tight girdles, stand firm in the sea of people, like columns against which they must break. Custom-house officers in uniforms unbuttoned because of the heat, their cheeks distended with tobacco, deface with long jets of brown saliva the place destined for the trunks; and the trunks are no sooner brought up from the hold and set down there, than around them swarm expressmen offering checks, and carpenters armed with hammer and chisel to open and nail down the boxes. Custom-house officers plunge their arms into the open trunks, turning and overturning linen and dresses with all the rough heedlessness of men in a hurry. The trunks at last closed and checked are seized by porters, and sent spinning down to a lower story by a long wooden incline, at the risk of crushing them, while a pungent, sickening odor of perspiring flesh mingles with the confused din. Such is the entrance to the great American city — as swift and brutal as a round in the ring. All the time there are sharp-eyed little men running about in the chaos of people and trunks. They are reporters on the lookout for an interview. I see the ship's dentist struggling with one of them, who is asking him about the cholera in Italy. The dilapidated hack in which I finally seat myself seems like a wheeled Paradise, as it bears me away from the tumultuous crowd, though it is jolting over a wretched wooden pavement, and the quarter that lies between the wharf and Fifth Avenue, where my hotel is to be found, is abominably ugly.

Rows of red houses stretch out before me to an indefinite extent, all precisely alike, with sash windows and no blinds. Other houses appear hideous with signs, their ground floors occupied either with liquor saloons or with stalls set out with miserable wares, cheap fruits, and withered vegetables. The foul pavement is covered with a sticky mud, compounded of rubbish rather than of earth. Not a tree before these houses, not a grass plot ; but rails laid along the streets for tramways, poles for telegraph wires, and presently what seems to be a long double tunnel supported by iron pillars. It is the aerial railway, the " elevated " as they say. There are four of them which stretch the whole length of the city, and carry two hundred million passengers every year. During the short time that our way follows this tunnel I count the trains that pass overhead, three going down town and three up. The strong framework which supports them trembles under their weight and the fleetness of their passage. What can be the life of those inhabitants of this city whose windows open upon this incessant mad flight of locomotives and cars ?

The hack passes through two quieter streets and reaches an avenue, where a succession of cable cars rushes by in the same mad haste. An endless chain runs underground, carrying along the heavy cars upon rails, over which our carriage jolts. Their automatic movement would terrify you like a nightmare but for the man standing in the front. His clenched fingers work the handles of the lever that by turn grips and releases the chain, which moves invisible below the long fissure that lies like a third rail between the other two. There are so many of these cable cars, they go so fast, they so compactly block the avenue, that vehicles drawn by horses hardly find room to pass along. The latter are, therefore, becoming so rare that the aspect of the streets is not like any part of any European city. There are no *fiacres* such as are the gayety of Parisian streets, no hansoms such as make the animation of those of London, none of the *botte* which roll through Rome to the nimble trot of their horses. You at once perceive that that darling of the middle class, the private hired carriage, has no reason for being. The laborer and the business man have the elevated road or the street car that goes faster than the best horse. Those who are neither laborers nor business men are rich men and have their own carriages.

One open place with trees and turf, dominated by a tower like the Giralda of Seville, is Madison Square, the point where commercial Broadway crosses fashionable Fifth Avenue stretching endlessly away without cable road or elevated railway. The tower is surmounted with a statue, in whose outlines I recognize the Diana of the great sculptor, St. Gaudens, photographs of which I have seen. The slender figure of the goddess stands out finely against the blue sky. It is the first evidence of beauty that I have seen since I set foot outside of the ship. Below the Diana, all up and down the tower, is stretched in huge iron letters the announcement of a bicycle exhibition. Between the noble creation of the artist and the contiguous advertisement the contact is as close and the contrast almost as great as between the New York of labor, which I have just passed through, and the New York of wealth, which at this moment I am entering. Is there a cause for this total absence of transition? Does it betray a complete absence of that sense of harmony which we call — which we used to call — taste? Is it simply that the city, having grown too rapidly upon a territory too narrow, finds space lacking for its growth, as it is also lacking, it would appear, for the posting of bills? I leave the solving of these problems to a time when I have not to install myself in a new hotel, and when I am not wearied with seven days at sea. A negro in livery, with smiling face and white teeth, in which sparkle bits of gold half as large as my finger-nail, has just opened the door of my carriage. I have barely time to speak to the clerk when another negro opens the door of an elevator, which mounts with dizzy rapidity to the seventh floor; and now behold a third negro entering the parlor in which I am hastily scratching down these notes, to bring me a jug of filtered water, overtopped by a lump of ice almost as big as his head. I gaze upon him in amazement; but he, much offended with my absence of mind, while waiting for my orders draws a key from his pocket, takes a second from a secretary, and a third from the door, and begins to jingle them to attract my attention.

"What are you doing?" I ask him.

"I thought you might want to send a telegram," he replies, with a familiar mendacity that would disarm a slave-dealer. I send him for a newspaper, which he brings me. It is marked three cents, but he asks me ten, adding philosophically, by way of excuse, —

"You know, on the other side everything is cheaper."

Sunday. — Mass this morning in a little church at the corner of Thirtieth Street. One of the facts best known and most remarked upon in France is the vitality of Catholicism in the United States. The names of the three great authors of this renascence — Cardinal Gibbons, Archbishop Ireland, and Monsignor Keane — are as familiar to us as to Americans themselves. What is the secret of this vitality? I shall try some day to find out. At present I can only grasp the too apparent contrast between our own churches and this one.

On the outside, its walls of gray stone, with their fluttering Japanese ivy, are not very different from the other buildings in the block. To enter, you cross an anteroom, where you must pay fifteen cents, — a little more than seventy-five centimes. For that matter, what would the poor do in the vast hall of polished wood, which serves as chapel? Each seat is covered with leather cushions, the entrance to them barred by red silk cords, hanging between hooks of copper. The entire floor is carpeted ; the pictures on the walls are covered because it is summer. It gives one the impression of a prayer club. Everything is brand-new, opulent, comfortable, and yet religious, for the worshippers follow the service without a whisper or a wandering glance. Recognizing copies of certain pictures, behind their green gauze coverings, — a Madonna of the impassioned Andrea, a Virgin of the lucid Raphael, Allori's tragic Judith, — the churches of Italy rise up before me in sudden contrast, — ruinous, unclean, sullied by superstition ; and yet so beautiful, because they have endured, because everything in them moves the heart with the profound emotion of the past — a long, long past !

But the worshippers who are gathered in this church have precisely such a building as suits them. They are men of the present, and for them religion is neither a reverie nor a longing. The sermon, which the priest bases upon the gospel for the day, — the incident of the Good Samaritan, — still farther reveals the close presence of things actual. He speaks of the descent from Jerusalem to Jericho in precisely the terms with

which he would speak of going from up-town to the Battery.
He refers to St. Paul, and his conversion as the apostle was
riding near Damascus corner. In his illustrations, the word
dollar continually recurs: " If you had made a thousand
dollars " . . . " If you had paid a hundred dollars for such a
thing ; " and his severe, large-featured face grows sarcastic, his
voice vehement, as he pours invectives upon the clergy of
Europe, " with their prelates who live like princes." When
he raises his arm, I see that the red vestment which he has
put on for preaching shines with a brilliant newness which
harmonizes well with this church, these seats, this carpet, these
people, this sermon. But I ask again, at what hour and where
do the poor folk pray?

By carriage up Fifth Avenue and through Central Park,
which is the *Bois de Boulogne* of New York. Two hours of
the afternoon ; and I paid four dollars — say twenty francs —
for a drive that would be worth a hundred sous with us, or five
shillings in London. One of my steamer companions, who
recommended this drive to me, gave me several reasons for
its costliness. The first and most evident, I have already mentioned. A carriage is a luxury, and all luxuries are expensive
here, while the necessaries are cheaper than elsewhere. This
is why America still tempts our laboring people, and why so
many of its own rich men go to Europe that they may have
these luxuries, and better ones, at a fifth or a sixth the price.
The second reason is that the hackmen, like all other laborers,
are bound together in an impregnable Union.

Besides, it is but too evident that money cannot have much
value here. There is too much of it. The interminable succession of luxurious mansions which line Fifth Avenue proclaim
its mad abundance. No shops, — unless of articles of luxury,
— a few dressmakers, a few picture-dealers — the last froth of
the spent wave of that tide of business which drowns the rest
of the city — only independent dwellings, each one of which,

including the ground on which it stands, implies a revenue which one dares not calculate. Here and there are vast constructions which reproduce the palaces and châteaux of Europe. I recognize one French country seat of the sixteenth century ; another, a red and white house, is in the style of the time of Louis XIII. The absence of unity in this architecture is a sufficient reminder that this is the country of the individual will, as the absence of gardens and trees around these sumptuous residences proves the newness of all this wealth and of the city. This avenue has visibly been willed and created by sheer force of millions, in a fever of land speculation, which has not left an inch of ground unoccupied. This rapidity is again shown in the almost total absence of life-like figures in the sculptures with which the windows and colonnades of these impromptu palaces are decorated. An artist needs time to observe and patiently follow the forms of life ; and if the whole United States had not found means to get along without him, where would they have been? They have made up for it by feats of energy. That is something to triumph over in the industrial world. The world of art requires less self-consciousness, — an impulse of life which forgets itself, the alternations of dreamy idleness with fervid execution. Years must pass before these conditions are possible on the banks of the Hudson.

Is the Park also a hasty and arbitrary production? However that may be, the virginal vigor of the soil there bursts forth in foliage of surprising opulence. It seems to me — but is this a just view? — that there is a degree of disproportion between this prodigal leafage and the branches themselves, as if these fine trees had slighter trunks and a more nervous ramification than ours. Have they grown too fast, like the houses?

The extent of the Park is enormous, and you stand amazed when, having followed paths embowered in verdure, others winding around a lake, still others bordering immense fields where

sheep are feeding, you perceive above the thick green of the
clumps of trees a train flying over a track of red metal, thirty
feet up in the air, and the city beginning all over again.

This Park is simply a garden bisecting one of the avenues of
the city, — the Seventh. A whole people throng its paths this
Sunday afternoon, a veritable nation of working folk at rest.
I have not met two private victorias on these roads, swarming
as they are with vehicles. They are all pleasure carriages,
packed full with women and children, or tilburys driven by
their owners. I observe a sort of cart which is new to me, —
an oblong box with a bellows top, which at need might shelter
two persons. It is almost hidden between four enormous
wheels of startling fragility. A horse which goes like the wind
is attached to it without a collar, entirely free in his slight network of flexible straps. As these carriages fly past, you might
fancy a race of huge demented spiders, so large and at the
same time so slight is their iron framework. The people who
pass you by in these vehicles and on the sidewalks are substan-
tially dressed and without elegance, — not a single workman's
blouse, and on the other hand not a rag nor anything which
would betray poverty. The men are rather small, thin, and
nervous in action. The women are small, too, and without
much beauty. In the dress of the latter there is a visible
abuse of high colors and of trimming. It is like an immense
walking emporium of ready-made clothes. Nevertheless, an
air of social health and good humor breathes from this crowd.
The mounted policemen who occasionally pass appear as little
to be watching as to be themselves in need of watching.
What I feel most strongly, without being able to give a positive reason for the feeling, is that I am terribly far away, and
in a terribly different country.

Monday. — At what time of day do they die here? At what
time do they love? At what time do they think? At

what time, indeed, are they men, nothing but men, as old Faust said, and not machines for work or locomotion? This is the question I keep asking in spite of myself, after a day spent in the cable cars, the elevated, — the L, to borrow the New Yorker's abbreviation, — the electric cars, the ferry-boats, seeing the city. One succeeds the other so rapidly, you are so quickly transferred from tramway to tramway, from train to train, that the stranger, one who is not up to the times, feels a stupefaction something like that of the honest citizen at one of Hanlon-Lee's pantomimes. This, be it said in parenthesis, is probably the origin of this device in America. The acrobats had only to hurry, to make haste, to excite to frenzy that fever for getting there which has led the people of this country to the singular invention of making the street walk.

For that is what this cable tramway, this railway on the level of the street, these electric tramways, really are — it is the street which walks — which runs indeed. You miss a car — another is here; so full you could hardly drop a dollar on the floor. You get in none the less, glad of a chance to stand inside on the platform, on the step, while ragged urchins, frightfully thin, but all nerves and energy, manage to jump aboard of a car between two street corners, into an elevated car between two stations, crying the daily paper — no, not even that, the paper of the hour, of the minute. Edison began life that way, legend says.

What faces I have met in the vagaries of this aimless journey; what thousands of faces which I shall never see again! What strikes me most in these innumerable countenances is the absence of interest. The contrast is extraordinary between the good-fellowship of the omnibus that is *complet* with us, where all the neighbors take notice of one another, where the merest nothing starts a conversation. Here each eye seems fixed upon the inner thought — upon some business — whatever it may be, which will not wait, and which is the reason why, when they leave the car, men and women run, as they ran to catch it, as they run up and down the stairs of the elevated road.

Mr. ——, a brother journalist who has served me to-day as guide, says that they are no more pressed for time than any Parisian.

"They hurry so," he said, "from mere habit, interest, nervousness. With it all they have curious streaks of laziness. You will see them buy a paper in a hotel, at a restaurant, and pay three cents more than the marked price, because they are too indolent to go into the street for it."

I begin to understand how this negligence and this activity belong together as I remark the rude finish of these very cars, the want of care in the attire of the people. But these are individual cases; and you have only to come in contact with things as a whole to receive again that impression of a Babel with a splendor all its own, an impression which — shall I avow it? — I have felt most strongly in connection with a building devoted entirely to business offices, and a bridge over which runs a railway !

The building is called the Equitable, from the name of the insurance company that built it. It is a gigantic palace with a marble façade, rising up almost at the end of Wall Street, the street of the milliards, and very near Trinity Church cemetery, where, hushed by the frantic tumult of life and the grating of the cable car, reposes the printer of the first newspaper published in New York, — William Bradford. What a tomb for a ' journalist !

Figures alone can give an idea — not, indeed, exact but approximate — of this human beehive with its thousand offices. Mr. —— tells me that ten thousand persons a day use the elevator of which we availed ourselves for going up to the roof. The hum of life in the enormous building, the swarms of comers and goers, the endless ramifications of the corridors, reduce your mind almost to a stupor of admiration, such as you also feel when looking from above upon this great city.

Far as the eye can reach it stretches away, between the two rivers which girdle the island, and through innumerable columns of smoke one is still able to distinguish the practical simplicity of its construction — broad, longitudinal avenues cut at right angles by streets, thus distributing the blocks of houses in equal masses. You are acquainted with the city as soon as you understand it. Given the number of the street, with the usual East or West, showing that it is on the right or left of Fifth Avenue, and you know within ten yards how far you have to go, all the blocks being of uniform size. This is not even a city in the sense in which we understand the word, we who have grown up amid the charm of irregular cities which grew as the trees do, slowly, with the variety, the picturesque character of natural things. This is a table of contents of unique character, arranged for convenient handling. Seen from here it is so colossal, it encloses so formidable an accumulation of human efforts, as to overpass the bounds of imagination. You think you must be dreaming when you see beyond the rivers two other cities — Jersey City and Brooklyn — spread out along their shores. The latter is only a suburb, and it has nine hundred thousand inhabitants.

A bridge connects New York with Brooklyn, overhanging an arm of the sea. Seen even from afar, this bridge astounds you like one of those architectural nightmares given by Piranesi in his weird etchings. You see great ships passing beneath it, and this indisputable evidence of its height confuses the mind. But walk over it, feel the quivering of the monstrous trellis of iron and steel interwoven for a length of sixteen hundred feet at a height of one hundred and thirty-five feet above the water; see the trains that pass over it in both directions, and the steamboats passing beneath your very body, while carriages come and go, and foot passengers hasten along, an eager crowd, and you will feel that the engineer is the great artist of our epoch, and you will own that these people have a right to plume themselves on their audacity, on the *go-ahead* which has never flinched.

At the same time you ask yourself what right they have to call themselves, as a people, young. They are recent, their advent is so astonishingly new that one can hardly believe in dates in the face of these prodigies of activity. But recent as is this civilization, it is evidently *mature*, at least here. The impression upon me this evening is that I have been exploring a city which is an achievement and not a beginning. Its life is not an experiment ; it is a mode of existence, with its inconveniences as well as its splendors. For the *go-ahead*, the tireless *forward*, is not confined to trains and machines. I have been called from this paper to reply to fifteen applications for autographs and six requests for interviews. This eagerness would make me vain if I did not know that it is the lot of every foreign visitor. Let but the press announce your arrival, and if your connections are in the slightest degree public — though you are here merely to avoid a scandalous lawsuit — you must pay your entrance fee, sign your name hundreds of times and proclaim aloud what you think of the country — before you have seen it ! A reporter has even come this evening to ask my opinion as to love in America, after a sojourn of forty-eight hours !

Tuesday and Wednesday. — Matters of business have called me again to the neighborhood of the Equitable and the Battery, with the effect only of renewing and heightening my first impressions. The less prosaic duty of securing a suitable shelter for a somewhat prolonged winter sojourn has led me, in the course of these journeyings, to examine several hotels.

Such visits give only the most superficial impressions.

And yet, in every country, hotels have this documentary value, that they give what the people of the country ask for. Every one who establishes a lodging-house or a restaurant is, in his way, a psychologist, whose talent consists in securing guests. And how, if not by perceiving and ministering to their tastes? A simple inn, once it is successful, resembles the imagination of those who frequent it, and who enjoy themselves there because they frequent it.

In the French provinces, for example, the hotels are indifferently furnished, with tiny wash-basins and water jugs, battered furniture, and threadbare carpets; but the food is nearly always excellent, and the wine cellar stocked with intelligence. This is indeed the taste of the middle-class citizen of our country, whom boarding-school and barracks have taught to do without comforts, who are hostile to useless expenditure on any large scale, economically making things last indefinitely. On the other hand, his sensations are acute; he is a high liver, knowing in wines. He likes to talk, and he willingly lingers over the table, in the good fellowship of the coffee cup and the liqueur glass. So in Italy, the grand dismantled palace, which so often does duty as *locanda*, with its frescoed ceilings, the great pictures on its walls, ill-warmed from a badly constructed chimney, with servants in tattered dress-coats, intelligent and familiar, with fried fish, a *risotto* and *fiaschi* of home-made wine scattered over the table — how well it suits the travellers of Tuscany, of the Romagna, and Venice! Not one of these features but its counterpart is to be found, in the man accustomed to a poverty-stricken life in some setting of magnificence, naturally kindly to his inferiors and indulgent as to their personal appearance, son of a country where money is scarce and industrial activity still more infrequent, and where parsimony governs even food. So, again, the English hotel, with the abundance of its little rooms, its distant and active servants, its copious morning breakfast, the great pieces of roast meat for its cold lunch, and its dinner served at separate tables, that by themselves alone reveal the love of home and the reserve which are the ground-work of nineteen Englishmen out of twenty. They have a word for it for which neither Frenchmen nor Italians have a translation, so little have they the thing; ,it is *privacy*, that which a gentleman is bound to respect in the private life of another gentleman, and the right to make respected in his own life. Even in a transient *caravanserai* they find means for having this law observed.

These various pictures and reflections followed me as I crossed the threshold of certain New York hotels which had been pointed out to me as most recently built. They are all edifices of the kind which, in Chicago, they call "sky scrapers" and "cloud pressers." One is ten stories high, another twelve, another fourteen. The last and newest has seventeen.

First comes the marble hall, more or less splendid in deco-ration, upon which frequently opens a restaurant or bar, a cloak-room, a book-store, and other shops. An index points you to the fact that the barber shop is in the basement. Behind a grating are the elevators,— four, five, six,— ready to mount up with the rapidity of an electric despatch. Yes-terday I felt as if the Americans made the streets walk; to-day I feel as if they made the floors of their houses fly.

These hotels, foolishly sumptuous, have carpets only on the passageways. The stairways show their naked marble, on which no one ever sets foot, unless, haply, the servants; who also have their own elevators. And all along the walls of the passages, as on those of the smallest chambers, are fan-tastic appliances for keeping up this chase of the stories, and giving you, if you live on the fifteenth floor, the sensation of being on the first. Upon a box in each corridor are written these words: "United States Mail Chute." I ask their mean-ing, and my guide shows me a long glass channel, down which a letter thrown into this opening will descend to the box to which the postman has access. My attention is attracted by a mysterious disk covered with printed characters, to which a needle is attached by a pivot. My guide explains to me that by pressing a button the traveller can order to be brought him the thing to whose name he has directed the point of this needle. I glance at the curious list, and perceive that I may thus procure for myself, within five minutes, the whole series of cocktails and champagnes, all the newspapers and reviews, a one- or a two-horse carriage, a doctor, a barber, a railway ticket, all sorts of cold or warm dishes, or a theatre ticket. The only wonder is that the machine has not been so far perfected as to offer the means of being married or divorced, of making one's will, and of voting.

While awaiting these necessary improvements, it is proper to add that these niceties of refinement are merely complementary to others more appreciable. You can count the bedrooms which have not their private dressing-room, with bath-room, where hot and cold water run at will at all hours of the day and night. And with this, a meaningless luxury of woodwork and draperies. As I transcribe these notes, I see again a tiny parlor on the ninth floor of one of these hotels, at the corner opposite to and at precisely the same height as the clock in the tower of a neighboring church. With its sofa and armchairs of Havana silk, its narrow bands of soft white silk on the tables and the backs of chairs, the light mahogany of its woodwork, the fine quality of its wicker chairs, and the etchings on the walls, one would never believe it to be a hotel room, to be let for the day or night. And there are two hundred of these bedrooms and parlors in this immense building.

Look at it now from without, and consider that all these apartments are warmed by an apparatus of metal tubes, through which hot water passes up or down at the turn of a

D

wheel; that electricity lights its uttermost corner and keeps everything going, from the bells to the clocks; that gas is laid on everywhere alongside of the electric lights, in case the latter should give out. Think then of the innumerable quantity of pipes which perforate this sort of living creature of brick and iron. It does not move, indeed; but at an incredible distance overhead it breathes out a column of black smoke, thick as that of a steamer. Think what human ingenuity is required for the adjustment of so many small pieces! I counted, in my visits to these five hotels, five different systems for emptying the wash-basins and bath-tubs. Translate this humble detail into concrete reality. It means that five subtle intellects, at the service of five men determined to make a fortune, have studied this apparently childish problem, in the hope, justified by the result, of meeting with capitalists who will patronize the invention, and architects who will adopt it. Is it thus from the small to the great? Very probably; and this genius of novelty is evidently in its youth. But, seeing what a travelling American requires for his occasional shelter, recognizing how much money is necessary for the satisfaction of so complicated a desire for comfort, measuring the degree of ingenuity here attained in making matter subserve to the needs of man, how can we admit that this civilization is only a first sketch? It is at once clearly manifest, to him who reviews it without prejudice, that these are signs of maturity far rather than of experiment and beginning. But New York does not sum up the whole United States, any more than Paris sums up France, and we must see.

Thursday.—Two oases in the tourist existence which for four days I have been leading here. A luncheon at the Players' Club, with men of letters connected with a great review, and an evening at the theatre with another literary man, who manages an important newspaper. I jot down my impressions, without being careful to connect them with those that have gone before, quite understanding that, though it is always legitimate to set down physical things, one must exercise great care when it comes to moral things. I hope to remain in the United States for several months, that my judgment of these things may be accurate.

This club has a singular history, and confirms what I have often heard of the peculiar position of comedians in America. It was founded by the actor Booth. He bought the house and furnished it. He adorned it with precious collections, gathered by his own care, and entirely composed of objects which have to do with the theatre. He then gave it to the club, reserving the right to occupy one apartment, and there he died. I was struck by the extreme decorum of the surroundings. The square before the windows, Gramercy Park, looks like a bit of Kensington. The respectability of the artist is written everywhere, and a thousand details attest that it is not personal to him; I mean that it is the comedian's art itself, of which this house reveals the worship.

Two fine portraits, one of Booth himself, the other of Jefferson — by the painter Sargent — show faces deeply moulded by thought and will, almost too intellectual for a profession which demands more of instinct, of unconsciousness. All the other actors whose pictures adorned the walls have this same expression, grave even to severity. I seemed to see in them the energy of the race applied to culture. One must hear the Americans utter the word *art*, all by itself, without the article, to understand the intense ardor of their desire for refinement; and this word *refined* also recurs continually in the conversation of the members with whom I visited the club.

You hear few or no anecdotes of private life in the conversations suggested by the portraits. On the other hand, I am astonished to observe how carefully they guard the remembrance of the slightest shades of expression observed by these actors in their play, and especially how the interpretation of such or such a part in Shakespeare fires their minds. Once again I perceive the national strength of this poet's genius, and how all literature derives from him in every English-speaking country. Molière has no such position with us, nor Goethe in Germany. Their work does not radiate that unique and continuous influence which Dante also exerts over the Italian mind. Perhaps Americans feel a more passionate attachment to Shakespeare than even the English. It is their way to cling fast to a tradition, and I have already fancied more than once that I perceived the sense of need of a more distant background in this country, where all is present and actual. I gained a new proof of this, though a very slight one, while walking out with one of my companions of this morning, who directed my attention to two lanterns planted before a house.

"They were put there," he said, "during the time when the master of this house was the first magistrate of New York. It is the custom. He died, and they were left there. You cannot understand that,—you who live in a country which has a history,—but I like to look at them because they have been there for twenty-five years, and it is good to find a little of the past in a city so new."

Nothing, on the other hand, can be more exclusively and absolutely local or less Shakespearian than the play to which another brother journalist took me in the evening.

"It is not very good," he said, "but you will see what suits our public."

We found ourselves in a little theatre, which possessed the peculiarity of having almost no boxes. No New York theatre has more, except the Opera. Is it due to want of skill, or haste in the construction of the halls? Is it the wish to increase the number of sittings? Is it a sign of democratic manners? Or is it simply the ever-present precaution against fire? However this may be, men and women without distinction, and of almost all classes, are crowded together in the orchestra and balcony. They follow the drama with passionate interest, though they already know it, for it has been given an incalculable number of times. Its name is *The New South*, and the mere title of the piece suggests curious differences, not only of manners but of laws.

A Northern officer, stationed in the South a few years after the war, finds himself involved in a quarrel with the brother of his fiancée, a Georgian planter. This man snatches his sword from him and threatens him. The officer defends himself with the scabbard. He strikes his adversary upon the head, and the latter falls. The victor hastens to seek for succor, and during his absence a negro whom the planter had formerly insulted, and who sees him lying unconscious, cuts the planter's throat with the officer's sword. The latter, convicted of murder, is sentenced to perpetual imprisonment. His fiancée believes in him. She appeals to a law peculiar to that State, which authorizes any citizen, with the authorization of the governor, to choose a convict for a servant. She releases from prison the supposed murderer of her brother and takes him into her service, that he may prove his innocence. The character of this girl, so extraordinary in the eyes of a foreigner, arouses tempests of applause. When she says to her father, "Go you your way; I will go mine," the enthusiasm of the public exceeds all bounds.

The personal force of will, the impelling power of conscience in the being who acts according to its dictates, this, doubtless, is what these people were applauding. By contrast I picture to myself how a French audience would receive this girl's attitude toward her father. I must believe that these spectators do not look upon family relations precisely as we do; for péals of laughter greeted another scene which would rudely shock a Parisian audience. The heroine's sister — in love with a doctor, to whom she first makes a mock declaration in the course of a consultation in which she puts out a tongue a foot long — surprises her father in the act of asking the hand of an old lady in marriage.

The insolent girl's boisterous outburst of laughter, as she cuts a caper, shaking her finger at the old gentleman, appeared highly gratifying to the audience, who evidently found this absolute equality between parents and children the most natural thing in the world. My companion, to whom I made some such remark, admitted that the family is much more united with us than in Anglo-Saxon countries, and notably than in America.

"But," he said, "you have this evil, that with you a girl cannot live her own life apart from her family. Her parents love her too much and she loves them too much. She never learns to depend upon herself. She has no 'self-reliance,' as we say. This independence of ours has the advantage that a young woman without fortune expects to earn her bread honestly and courageously, like a man. She becomes a doctor, a professor, the secretary of a company, no matter what, — and she is happy."

Can he be right on the last point? Neither he nor I will ever know. As I make my way homeward, I recall to mind, as bearing out his assertion, the few minutes after luncheon which I spent in visiting the offices of the Review with which my hosts of the Players are associated. I see again the various women there engaged, in all departments of the work; one, especially, young and graceful, seated before a type-writing machine, copying a manuscript. Her taper fingers played upon the keys of the instrument as upon those of a piano. It was a suitable work, dainty, not too fatiguing, and I could read upon her charming face a deep serenity of con-

science, a calm will, a dignity that was touching in a creature
so young and evidently so poor. Must we believe that the
active independence of such a woman necessarily results in
a relaxation of family ties? It is possible, after all; for the
continuance of the family appears to be entirely conditioned
upon the right of primogeniture, or at least upon freedom of
bequest, and upon that inequality which appears to be, of all
others, most unjust,— that of inheritance.

Friday. — I resume my journal on the train between New
York and Newport, very comfortably settled in one of those
Pullman coaches which bear the pretentious name of *palace
car*. By way of parenthesis, let me say, that though I have
not yet been a week in the United States, I can bear witness
to the habitual excess of metaphor, which seems to be an
American instinct. The most insignificant production is
advertised as "the best in the world." A victorious pugilist
becomes "the world's champion." I happened to open the
annual report of the West Point Academy, and there I read,
"Science and art, in which the cadets excel."

Where does naturalness end? Where does that charlatanism begin, which is so well defined by the three well-nigh
untranslatable words which we are beginning to adopt and
practise, the *puff*, the *boom*, and the *bluff?* Certainly, the
splendors of a real palace have nothing in common with the
lavish elegance of these long carriages. Such as they are,
their luxury puts to shame the best European railway carriages.

They are so connected as to form a covered vestibule from
one end of the train to the other. A buffet is attached to
them; and, if the journey is to be not of six hours but of
several days, bath-rooms, a barber's shop, and a reading-room
will be added. It can hardly be called extravagance to travel
in them; for there is only one class in the United States, and
the supplement which gives a right to seats in these cars is

insignificant. I paid only a dollar for my Pullman chair from New York to Newport.

Here again are fifty signs of that singular bent toward complexity which has struck me every moment since I landed. Everything is fitted, planned, compressed, so as to get the greatest number of adjustable articles into the smallest possible space. The arm-chair in which you are seated turns upon a pivot, and may be tipped to any angle that pleases you. If you want your window open, a negro brings a metal screen which he slips into grooves cunningly devised between the ledge of the window and the raised sash. If you desire to take luncheon, play cards, or write, he places before you a table which rests upon the floor by a single movable foot, the other end being fitted into the side of the car. Boys are continually passing along, offering newspapers and books. I distinguish among them Alphonse Daudet's *Sappho*, with a second title added, *Or, Lured by a Bad Woman's Fatal Beauty !* Everywhere is a profusion of rugs, draperies, carved mahogany, and nickel-plated ornaments. The very negroes who pass back and forth, now in uniform and now in white jacket and napkin, seem like ornamental animals, a whim of the company, who have provided for my benefit this outlandish display. Armed with a sort of feather brush, which they wield with simian agility, they move about as we approach the stations, impartially dusting passengers and furniture, and equally without consulting their wishes. I just now saw one of them whisk off the hat of an old gentleman who was reading the paper. He brushed it, and replaced it upon the sufferer's head, without saying with your leave or by your leave. The old gentleman did not so much as raise his eyes.

Town and country succeed one another. The train passes at full speed over low bridges, spanning broad rivers which flow between forests, — remains of forests, rather,— violated, massacred forests, whose vigorous vegetation still bears witness to the primitive splendor of this country, before "the pale-faced destroyer of forests " had set foot upon it. Rows upon rows of cottages, without gardens, without a single one of those little, open-air drawing-rooms in which the French citizen loves to saunter, pruning-shears and watering-pot in hand. But where shall Americans find the time to saunter, the time to watch the budding rose trees, to let themselves live? Their rose trees are those vast, ever-multiplying factory chimneys. Their gardens are these houses, so rapidly built that a single generation sees them increase fivefold, tenfold, and more. In 1800, New Haven, through which we have just passed, had five thousand inhabitants; to-day it has eighty thousand, and its commerce is valued at more than a hundred and fifty million francs a year. A little way back it was Bridgeport, which last year put out a hundred millions worth of sewing-machines and carriages; or Hartford, where insurance companies have an aggregate capital of seven hundred millions of francs. These figures become, as it were, concrete in view of this landscape, which they explain and with which they blend, so many are the steamboats in the most insignificant ports, the electric railways in the city streets, the factories in the country towns, and the advertisements, advertisements, everywhere. I had taken out paper to make a general summary of the impressions of this first week. I cannot do it, so much is my attention absorbed by the medley of primitive scenery — so little removed from aboriginal wildness — and exaggerated industrialism.

There is hardly any motion of the car, notwithstanding our great speed. A pamphlet by one of our most distinguished engineers, M. de Chasseloup-Laubat,[1] which I read before leaving home, had already explained this to me, pointing out the wisdom with which the builder had placed the long car

[1] *Travels in America, chiefly to Chicago*, by the Marquis of Chasseloup-Laubat, Paris, 1893.

upon small, six-wheeled trucks, in such a way as to bring the seats outside of the axis of trepidation. Through this pamphlet I also made acquaintance with the locomotive, that strong and beautiful engine of speed, here built very high and so arranged that through his cab windows the engineer can see the track, as it lies ribbon-like before him. All the mechanism — cylinders, valves, levers — is exposed, and within easy reach. The forward part rests upon a small guiding truck, which admits of shorter curves, and a more slightly built track. Who invented all these improvements? Who thought out all the strangely complicated details of these cars?

The answer is always the same; everybody and nobody, a will always under control, an ever-watchful eye, an intrepid search for novelty, and an insatiable longing for improvement, which, so far, seems to me the most marked feature of American civilization, and the one least expected. Nevertheless, if I were obliged to return to Europe to-morrow, it is in this thought that I should sum up the impressions of my first rapid contact with this people. They seem, in fact, to have triumphed over time, since this extreme attainment of luxury touches so closely the barbarism of the West, and still more undisguisedly that of the popular quarters of New York. I am curious to know whether I shall find the same contrast, the same astonishing differences of atmosphere, in the watering-place where I shall be this evening, and of which all the Americans who have spoken to me of it seem a little proud and a little ashamed.

"There is only one Newport in the world," they say; invariably adding, "But Newport is only a clique of millionaires, only a 'set'; it is not America."

"Why not ?" I have several times asked.

"You will understand when you have been there," they reply, no less invariably. "There are more millions of dollars represented in the small tip of that little island than in all London and Paris together."

III

SOCIETY

·I. *A Summer City*

I came to Newport for a few days. I have remained here a whole month, taking my part in this life which has indeed no counterpart, at least, not to my knowledge. Neither Deauville nor Brighton nor Biarritz resembles it, nor Cannes, although the last approaches it in the splendor of its villas and the almost total absence of the lower middle class. But Cannes is a *Cosmopolis* like Rome or Florence, perhaps more so, while Newport is exclusively, absolutely American. A few European visitors have passed through it this summer, on their way to Chicago and the World's Fair. Usually they may be counted by six or seven. The French know nothing of Newport. The English — a very few of them — come here for the yachting; but they prefer the Isle of Wight, with Cannes and the convenient Solent.

The small number of travellers, explained by its remoteness and the shortness of the season, gives this watering-place an inveterately national character. No; this elegant coterie, or, as the detractors of Newport scornfully call it, this "set," is not America, but it is American society; and social life, empty and artificial as it may appear to be, is always bound by deeply-lying secret fibres to the country of which it is the flower — a flower sometimes insipid, more often poisonous. Even when its standards, as in France, are totally different from the standards of the country in general, it reveals in its adherents the spiritual faults and virtues which are peculiar to the race. The idlers bring the same susceptibility, the same temper, the same intelligence, to their amusements, or their attempts at amusement, which the industrious bring to their toil.

In the upper circles of Parisian life, for example, all the strength and all the weakness of the French nature are found devoted to the arts, to luxury, to amusement. Extreme vivacity of thought, with its subtle variations, criticism with its startling destruction of illusion and its unexpected betrayals into enthusiasm, a mad hardihood of irony, with bondage to public opinion, an indescribable mediocrity of human nature, an air of good taste even in folly, above all, a charm, a spirit of sociability, pervade the atmosphere of our clubs, our salons, our restaurants, theatres, promenades. National character has always its own shades of individuality in its vices and its virtues, its frivolities and its toils. This national physiognomy is what we have to discern ; and every datum is of value, from the hall of a casino to a church, from the prattle of a woman of the world to the utterances of a revolutionary laborer.

I am very sure, therefore, that any one who has eyes to see may discern the American spirit — the real interest and the chief reason of my journey — behind the ostentation of Newport. But have I these eyes? At any rate, here is a bundle of sketches from life taken on the spur of the moment in response to the first questions which one naturally asks in making a study of people of the world. How are they housed, and with what furniture do they surround themselves? How do they recruit their numbers? How do they amuse themselves? How do they converse? More general inquiries will come later, if they are to come at all.

How are they housed? Detached villas, very near the street, with greenish, most velvety lawns and bronze figures under the trees amid clumps of blue hortensias; porticoes before the doors, over which flutters the Japanese ivy, rapid growing, not evergreen like the other, but fading every season; graceful symbol of the American impatience which cannot wait. There are twenty, thirty, forty different styles of construction, almost as many as there are dwellings; some square and squat, others tall and slender, others slender and long; all with guillotine and bow windows, almost all of painted wood, which clothes them, as it were, in a thin dark sheath of elegant cleanliness — and so on indefinitely along Bellevue Avenue, Narragansett Avenue, all the streets of the new Newport which, within a few years, the caprice of millionaires has built upon the cliff; for this part of the town has only yesterday become fashionable.

The other, the real town, is down near the shore, with modest little houses of white wood which have a grace all their own. Somehow they suggest the cabin of primitive times, the frail rustic shelter built by the colonist's own hands, in this land of forests, with its rough-hewn beams and ill-matched boards. To this day stone buildings are rare in the United States. Brick and iron have succeeded to wood. To quarry and dress stone requires too much both of time and labor.

Between old Newport, where the quiet homely life keeps on all through the winter, and the other, the summer Newport, fashionable and transient, there is no intermediate. Nothing suggests the rough draught of a watering-place; first efforts corrected, worked over and over, a gradual encroachment of fashion. The same outbreak of individuality which reared the palaces of Fifth Avenue in New York, almost as by Aladdin's lamp, created in a flash of miracle this town of cottages. The only difference is in the complicated architecture where the rich have vied with the rich as to who shall excel the others. The " go-ahead " American spirit is seen here in a costliness of construction very significant, when one reflects that these dwellings do duty for six weeks, perhaps for two months, in the year, and that each one takes for granted such accessories as a four-in-hand, a yacht, or perhaps two, for cruising along the coast, a private car for railway journeys, a New York house and another country house!

One of these men has spent some time in England, and it has pleased him to build for himself on one of these Rhode Island lawns an English abbey of the style of Queen Elizabeth. It rises up, gray and stern, so like, so perfect, that it might, without changing a single stone, be transported to Oxford on the shores of Isis, to make a pendant to the delicious cloister of Magdalen or the façade of Oriel. Another man loves France, and he has seen fit to possess in sight of the Atlantic a château in the style of the French Renascence. Here is the château; it reminds you of Azay, Chenonceaux, and the Loire, with its transparent ribbon of water winding idly in and out amid the yellow sand of the islands. A third has built a marble palace precisely like the Trianon, with Corinthian pillars as large as those of the Temple of the Sun at Baalbek. And these are not weak imitations, pretentious and futile attempts, such as in every country bring ridicule upon braggarts and upstarts. No. In detail and finish they reveal conscientious study, technical care. Evidently the best artist has been chosen and he has had both freedom and money.

Especially money! Caprices like these take for granted such quantities of it that after a walk from cottage to cottage, from château to abbey, you half fancy that you have been visiting some isle consecrated to the god Plutus, whose most modern incarnation is the god Dollar. But this is a Plutus who yesterday sat at the hearthstone of Penia, the untamed goddess of poverty; a Plutus whom neither wealth nor luxury has enervated or enfeebled; a Plutus who, being no longer obliged to work, wills that his gold shall work, that it shall make itself manifest, spread itself, " show off," to use the real Yankee word.

And this gold makes itself so manifest, it shows off with such
violent intensity, that it impresses you like the deploying of an
army. Flaubert wrote to one of his pupils : " If you cannot
construct the Parthenon, build a pyramid." All America seems
to be instinctively repeating to itself in other words this stern
but stimulating counsel. As in the harbor and streets of New
York you are dismayed at so much activity, so in these Newport avenues you are amazed at so much wealth. It either
revolts or charms you, according as you lean toward socialism
or snobbery. The psychologist who looks upon a city as a
naturalist looks upon an ant-hill, will recognize in it the fact
which I observed at the very first, — something indescribably
extravagant, unbridled. The American spirit seems not to
understand moderation. Their high business buildings are too
high. Their pleasure-houses are too elegant. Their fast trains
go too fast. Their newspapers have too many pages ; too much
news. And when they set themselves to spend money, they are
obliged to spend too much in order to have the feeling of spending enough.

How do they furnish their houses ?
I have in mind, as I write these words, the interior of some
fifty of these villas, perhaps more. From the week of my
arrival, upon the presentation of my letters of introduction, I
was caught up in the whirlwind of luncheons, coaching-parties,
yachtings, dinners, and balls, which for several weeks sweeps
over Newport like a simoom. " Be in the rush," says an advertisement in the electric car which runs between the beach and
the lower town. A recommendation of a special brand of
yeast accompanies this eloquent appeal, this " all aboard "
which the Americans speedily force you to act upon.
Their energy extends even to their hospitality, which bestirs
itself in your behalf, multiplying its " five-o'clock teas " and its
" to meets." It is a warm spontaneity of welcome of which we

have no notion in Latin countries. With us the foreigner may
get into society if he settles down and does us the honor of
preferring our country to his own. As for him who is simply
passing through not to return, it takes us some time to overcome a certain distrust; we do not, without a thorough acquaintance, pass over from formal courtesy to intimacy. The
American throws his house wide open to you as soon as you
are duly presented. He wants you to know his friends; he
wants all his friends to treat you as he does.

Slanderers say that there is no merit in this; that their large
way of living prevails in all Anglo-Saxon countries where children are many, needs complicated, incomes proportionately
large, and economy unknown. One more guest hardly counts
in such a home. This is true. Still I think I perceive here a
feeling more complex than that opulent and indifferent hospitality which is still that of wealthy Orientals.

The American, who lives so fast, carries to the highest pitch
a fondness for seeing himself live. It seems as if he looked
upon himself and his surroundings in the light of a singular
experiment in social life, and as if he hardly knew what he
ought to think of it. He makes it a point that you, a European, shall be correctly informed before judging of this experiment, and he helps to inform you. "You see such or such a
one," he will say to you. "He is an American of this or that
type. Read such a book—you will find there a true picture
of the American of that State." If he knows that you are
travelling for the purpose of taking notes, he is disturbed, and
yet he finds pleasure in it as an act of homage. He wants
your notes to be taken from life. If he sees in you a simple
tourist, he wants your reports when you return home to be
something other than the erroneous legends of which, to his
exasperation, he finds traces in our newspapers. There is a
curious mixture of doubt and pride in the pleasure which he
feels in escorting you from one end of his house to the other,

showing you in a breath the picture gallery and the linen closet, the drawing-rooms and the bed-chambers. One of their best novelists, Howells, has sagaciously noted this peculiar trait of character, this facility of offering oneself as a lesson of things.

"We men of the modern world," says March, in *A Hazard of New Fortunes*, "are inclined to take ourselves too objectively, to consider ourselves more representative than is necessary."

Meanwhile, to the professional observer this turn of mind lightens half his task. It is so difficult in Italy, Spain, Germany, in France itself, to picture to oneself the "home" of those we know the best, and yet the witness that tells the most is the objects which we gather around us according to our own whims. A drawing-room, a bed-chamber, a dining-room, have a physiognomy, almost a countenance, in the likeness of our tastes, our needs, the things in ourselves which often we ourselves do not suspect.

A first impression emerges from the homes of Newport. It ought to be correct, so much does it accord with the rest of American life, even outside of villas like these. This is a new evidence of excess, abuse, absence of moderation. On the floors of halls which are too high there are too many precious Persian and Oriental rugs. There are too many tapestries, too many paintings on the walls of the drawing-rooms. The guest-chambers have too many *bibelots*, too much rare furniture, and on the lunch or dinner table there are too many flowers, too many plants, too much crystal, too much silver.

At this moment I can see in the centre of one of these tables a vase of solid silver, large and deep as the pot of a huge plant, too small, however, for a bunch of grapes, a prodigal bunch with grapes as large as small cannon balls. I see again a screen made of an Italian painting of the school of the

E

Carracci, cut into four parts. The canvas has not been much injured and the work was well done, but what a symbol of this perpetual extravagance of luxury and refinement!

This excess has its prototype in the rose so justly called the "American beauty," enormous bunches of which crown these tables. It has so long a stem, it is so intensely red, so wide open, and so strongly perfumed, that it does not seem like a natural flower. It requires the greenhouse, the exposition, a public display. Splendid as it is, it makes one long for the frail wild eglantine with its rosy petals which a breath of wind will crumple. For the eglantine is a bit of nature, and also of aristocracy, at least in the sense in which we Europeans understand the word, for with us it is inseparable from an idea of soft coloring and absence of pretension. It is certain that this excess reveals in this people an energy much more like that of the Renascence, for example, under divers forms, than that meagreness of individuality which we moderns disguise under the name of distinction. That vigor of blood and nerves which has enabled the men of the United States to conquer fortune, persists in him through all his fortunes and manifests itself by splendor within the house as it was first manifested by splendor outside of it. You find vigor everywhere, even in the senseless prodigalities of high life.

Yet, these millionaires do not entirely accept themselves. This is the second impression forced upon you by a more attentive observation of these "halls" and drawing-rooms. They do not admit that they are thus different from the Old World, or if they admit it, it is to insist that if they chose they could equal the Old World, or, at least, could enjoy it.

"We have made money enough to be artists now," said an architect to me, "and we have no time to wait. So I am studying the French eighteenth century; I intend to build houses of that type, with every modern improvement,—water, light, electricity."

His patriotism is perfectly sincere, very intense, and he makes
it consist in the conquest or at least the loan of a foreign style !
The furnishings of the Newport houses betray a similar effort,
—a constant, tireless endeavor to absorb European ideas. One
might count in these villas all the articles made in America.
It is in Europe that the silk of these stuffed chairs and these
curtains was woven; in Europe that these chairs and tables
were turned. This silverware came from Europe, and this
dress was woven, cut, sewn in Europe; these shoes, stockings,
gloves came from there. "When I was in Paris;" "Then we
go to Paris;" "We want to go to Paris to buy our gowns."

These expressions continually recur in conversation, and it
was certainly a Parisian salon which served as model of the one
in which you find yourself. These toilettes are surely modelled
on the same pattern as those of the elegant Parisian women.
Only, drawing-room and dresses alike have, like everything else,
that indescribable something too much. The fashion of these
gowns is not of to-day but of to-morrow. The dressmakers
have a very expressive way of noting this almost indescribable
shade of difference. They say, "We will try the new designs
first on the foreigners — then we shall weed them out for the
Parisian women."

Thus is explained this characteristic of the excessive; this
art of being on dress parade, which these women — often so
beautiful — still further heighten by a profusion of jewels worn
in daylight. At noon they will have at their waists turquoises
as big as almonds, pearls as large as filberts at their throats,
rubies and diamonds as large as their finger-nails. Yes, it is
indeed Europe, but overgrown, exaggerated; and this inordinate imitation only accentuates the difference between the Old
World and the New.

Among the freaks of decoration thus borrowed from our
country, one has become singularly changed during its passage

of the Atlantic.　I speak of the taste for old things — the fancy for bric-à-brac and *bibelots* so characteristic of our age.　It has become hateful to us, because universal competition has so raised the prices that very few European fortunes are large enough to permit it.　Counterfeiting has followed, and second-rate articles are especially abundant.

The Americans have come to market with their full purses. With us a millionaire is a man who has a million francs.　Here a millionaire is one who has a million dollars; that is, five million francs.　They have brought to market that universal knowledge which comes from the constant habit of having seriously undertaken collecting and looked at it in the light of a true lesson in things.　For the last thirty or forty years, thanks to their full purses, they have laid hands upon the finest pictures, tapestries, carvings, medals, not only of France, England, Holland, Italy, but also of Greece, Egypt, India, Japan. Hence they have in their town and country houses a wealth of masterpieces worthy of a museum.　In some Newport villas which I could name, is an entire private gallery, which has been transported thither bodily; its original owner having spent years in collecting it from among the rarest works of the early German school.　And they keep on in this way !　The other day I heard an amateur say sadly, alluding to the financial crisis which happens to bear heavily upon Italy and the United States at once : —

"The Italians are rather low down just now, and there are things to be had *sub rosa*.　But at present nobody can profit by it."

One asks oneself where they would put these Italian things, so completely covered by paintings is the Cordovan leather which covers the walls of their houses.　And then there are the glass cases under which treasures of cut stones await the magnifying-glass, with enamels, engraved armor, ancient books, medals, especially portraits.　In two adjacent villas, a quarter of an hour apart, I thus saw the portrait of a great Genoese seigneur, a Venetian admiral, an English lord of the last century, that of Louis XV. by Vanloo, with the inscription "Given by the King," that of Louis XIV. by Mignard, with the same inscription, that of Henry IV. by Porbus. F——, who does not like the Americans, said to me with irony : —

"Yes ; they have the portrait of the great King, but where is their grandfather's portrait?"

And he attributes this love of old pictures to a vague and awkward attempt to make a false gallery of ancestors. In my opinion he does not recognize the sincerity, almost the pathos, of this love of Americans for surrounding themselves with things around which there is an idea of time and of stability. This sensation, so difficult for us to conceive, and which my companion of the Players artlessly expressed to me in New York, is intelligible to me, and after these few weeks of the United States I feel it myself. It is almost a physical satisfaction of the eyes to meet here the faded colors of an ancient painting, the blurred stamp of an antique coin, the softened shades of a tapestry of the Middle Ages. In this country, where everything is of yesterday, they hunger and thirst for the long ago. We must believe that the soul of man is possessed by an indestructible desire to be surrounded with things of the past, since these extravagances of luxury subserve such a desire. They do not discern it in themselves, but they feel it all the same. Last week one of these men ordered his carriage to turn back that he might show me the statue of a Newporter who was a friend of his grandfather.

"One likes to think of a time so far away," he said.

This desire for a deeply prepared soil is just what a tree would feel on being transplanted to a new place with its roots too near the surface. This unconscious effort to surround themselves with the past, to ennoble themselves by it, is what saves these homes of millionaires from being coarse, so formed by sheer force of money, and for the purpose of showing that they were so formed. It is an unexpected bit of poetry in what but for that would be merely "the apotheosis of the check and the *chic*," to repeat a low pleasantry of a very low song of a former day. It consoles one for seeing strewed about among these magnificences a few inexpressibly vulgar and childish ornaments such as an outrageous toy,—a moon-faced doll with an eyeglass and a tall hat, smoking a lighted cigarette, while a music box hidden in its body plays a vulgar air. Written below it, to the shame of those writers who first made use of the expression, are the words, "*Fin de siècle.*" What a mosaic is the taste of this race which takes everything pell-mell from our civilization, the excellent and the bad, our finest works of art and our most deplorable caricatures!

How do they recruit their numbers? By a single method and from a single class. In this respect, when we compare this summer Newport with our Deauville, or with Brighton on the other side of the Channel, there is a never-to-be-forgotten difference. There is here no upper class, as in England, no aristocratic Olympus whose customs are followed by all "tuft-hunters"—the picturesque word with which Oxford students banter those of their comrades who are trying to get into the smart set, hypnotized by the golden tassel that dangles from the caps of the students who belong to the nobility. There is not here as in France that irrational but potent survival of an ancient order in the very midst of a vigorous democracy, whose most expressive sign is without doubt our notion of the "club." With us the "circle" has ceased to be the natural, almost the necessary, sphere of those who keep up a certain style. It has come to be a sort of brevet, almost a rank, in an undetermined social regiment, the staff of which lives at the Union, the Jockey, or the Rue Royale.

In America all men in society have been and still are busi-

ness men. They were not born to social station; they have
achieved it. They did not find it ready made and handed
over to them. They made it themselves, because it suited
them to add such a refinement to their wealth, by way of cop-
ing to their edifice. The result is a profound equality among
them, a singular uniformity of habits, thought, tastes, which
speak their absolute similarity of origin. The attempt has
indeed been made, of late years, to break up this uniformity,
to establish an artificial Olympus, that of the "four hundred,"
which are drawn from the families of oldest traditions and most
wealth. This whim could not be carried out, because the true
foundations of all these great fortunes are too recent, too well
known; and besides, they could not be kept up without a continuance of the toil which produced them. Such a one became
rich through the discovery of a gold mine twenty-five years ago.
A railroad built in 1860 made such a one a millionaire. Behind
each of the names which appear in the newspaper reports of
social functions, any American can see this or that factory,
commercial house, bank, land speculation, and generally the
factory is at full blast, the wickets of the commercial house and
the bank are always open, the speculation is still going on.
Democrats may say that such titles to a place in society are
worth quite as much as a coat of arms crossed by bastardy or
doubtful marriages, or a historic celebrity which has no counterpart in those that inherit it. Certain it is that the foundations of American society are frankly evident. Their immediate results are no less so.

First among them is the almost total absence of adventurers
and adventuresses in a watering-place like Newport. It is easy
to deceive a composite society, but not a society of business
men. A family whose revenues are doubtful may make a figure
in a circle where the authentic nobility must needs resort to
expedients for its support, in which reigns that spirit of shifti-
ness in money matters which is habitual with those who earn

nothing. In America, every one knows what his neighbor is "worth," and besides, society life is here a luxury, while the minor daily expenses are so great as to be unsupportable by an ill-balanced budget.

French novelists since Balzac have often painted the type of the ambitious poor young man who keeps himself in the full current of high life by the superior management of very modest resources. Here a presentable evening suit costs a hundred and fifty dollars, — seven hundred and fifty francs, — a carriage to go to dinner costs three dollars, and five if you also return by carriage. A woman pays fifty per cent duty on the evening dress she brought from Paris. The New York dressmakers' and milliners' bills come up to about the same figure. It is hardly an economy to have a seamstress in the house to copy the models of the great dressmakers, — that resource of the prudent Parisian woman, — in a place where a clever maid has forty dollars a month and a good dressmaker three dollars a day. This sort of abuse of wealth, not peculiar to Newport but found all over America, is at once a folly and a purifying process. We may rail at the frivolity of this existence, condemn its extravagance. It may deserve many satires. It is at least very upright and very sound.

(It is all that, in this summer sojourn; witness the total suppression of the element which in Europe adorns and corrupts so many watering-places — I refer to the *demi-monde*.) As American society is principally drawn from business circles, the men have but little leisure. They are all absent several days in the week, occupied in making the money which it is the function of their wives to display. It follows that if they have relations outside of their own homes, they are not to be found here. Those who remain in Newport the whole week round are few in number, and for the most part old, since they are "out of business," or very young and not yet in it. A few diplomatists on their vacation and a few flying visitors complete the masculine part of society, the smallness of whose number would compel them to good conduct if, indeed, their inherited puritan morality, always present in a country of Anglo-Saxon traditions, — at least under the form of hypocrisy, — did not make all scandal impossible.

For that matter, by what diplomatic processes would the most adroit member of the *demi-monde* succeed in brushing up against the real society, in offering a facile imitation of it, as with us, in a circle where all forms of pleasure are organized into a club and one must have an admission, a presentation, patronage, in order to take a cup of tea here, to play a game of tennis there? More than this, the race is not old enough for the courtesan to have become the petted but refined creature, scoffing and witty, who amuses a man and little by little makes her way into his daily intimacy. Simply to recognize how entirely she is absent from a city which elsewhere would be her favorite field of operation is to see that she is here reduced to the condition of a mere instrument of pleasure. Theo, who has lived ten years in the United States, said to me, —

"Women are not necessary to Americans as they are to us. A man only goes with them here when he is slightly drunk and wants to keep it up."

It is possible that the sentimentality which gives a touch of tenderness to gallantry in France is in certain respects more human. Socially the American is right ; I mean that the sharp line of demarcation between the women of his own circle and the others makes him look upon the former with quite other eyes. He respects them more in his imagination and in his conduct. He may be a profligate ; he is never or very rarely a libertine. The distance between the two words is great. The proof is found in the conversation of young men at the clubs. They talk of sport, of play, of business, but the name of a woman is never uttered.

The common origin of the social forces, if I may so call it, has also this result, that social life finds its end and aim in itself. All the families included in it being rich, and aspiring to nothing else to which it can help them, the result is that the atmosphere is more simple, happy, innocent, than any we know. There is less secrecy in personal relations, because they are not nor can be the means of self-advancement. The wealthy classes of America having no sort of influence over the elections, an ambitious politician has no use for society. There is no Institute toward which the favor of a social set may advance a writer or an artist. Nor is there any group of salons whence literary reputations may radiate. It is only exceptionally that daughters are dowered, so that the number who seek fortune through marriage is limited to ruined foreigners of title, and these generally disappear after a season. They quickly discover that old Europe is still the safest field for this sort of speculation.

As on the other hand morals appear to be especially good and an acknowledged *liaison* is a phenomenon here, social life cannot serve as a screen for the complications of amatory experience. Thus reduced to its true basis, social life turns its efforts into the line of public pageantry and outward display, and as it must always have a genuine aliment, a positive occupation for its vigorous activities, society life in this country tends to give itself up entirely to sport. Here, again, that which is essentially a fault becomes a source of health, so true it is that with strong races everything ministers to their strength, while among a decaying people even culture and refinement lead to nothing but disease and decay.

How do they amuse themselves? That I might answer this question with some sort of correctness, I have amused myself with following, hour by hour, for several days together, the way in which those of the women who are what is called "leaders in society" employ their time. I transcribe one of the sketches I thus made, taking it at random from twenty others. They are all pretty much alike in respect of the powerful physique, which they take for granted, the fondness for the open air and exercise. This way of amusing themselves explains why these women of the world, instead of having a ruined digestion, pale cheeks, "an old-glove air," — to quote a wicked humorist,— like so many of their sisters in European capitals, still retain their brilliant complexions, their supple motions, their strong vitality. They know this, and are proud of it.

"What pleases me in the fact that I am an American," said one of them, "is the thought that I belong to a fine, healthy race."

I remember, too, with what contempt another, speaking of an actress of the Odeon, who was in New York for a month, described her as "That little woman with a wishy-washy complexion." They are inexhaustible in their criticisms of Parisian women. I remember that another of them, deploring the change in one of her countrywomen recently married to a Frenchman, said, "She was so plump, with so good a complexion, and now she has become thin and quite sallow."

They smile when thus speaking, with that gratified smile of theirs, so difficult for us to understand in its respectable animalism, with their polished teeth, in which the dentist has put bits of gold that shine so brightly as not to appear in the least like a blemish.

The young woman whose striking image I now invoke was in the saddle before nine in the morning, after one of those hearty breakfasts which the Anglo-Saxons find necessary, the meal at which they gain strength for all the demands of the day. She has trotted and galloped for two hours in the salt air, returning at eleven, in time to change her gown and go to the Casino, where there is a tennis tournament. Two of

her friends, a girl and a young woman two years married, are
to take part in it.   This is the fashionable place of meeting
in Newport,— this square of turf framed in with buildings
of tasteful architecture, clothed in the temporary ivy of the
Japanese vine.   Around the players are gathered a concourse of
women, for the most part in light-colored costumes, with that
profusion of dainty ornament which makes their toilette as
evidently perishable as costly.   Their costumes look as if
made to be worn a single hour, with nothing to individualize
the beauty of the women who wear them.   A saying recurs
to my mind, in reference to this sort of impersonality of con-
summate elegance, so delicate, so romantic, and which so
well explains the difference between this sort of elegance and
another sort.   In one of those pen portraits with which people
amuse themselves as a parlor game, a Frenchwoman wrote,
describing her own character: —

"I never dressed myself for a ball without knowing whom
it was that I was going there to see."

American women dress themselves that they may be beautiful, because they are "fine, healthy women," like others of
their race, and at the present moment not one of them is
thinking of exciting admiration, so absorbed are they in the
game, in which the newcomers immediately become as much
absorbed as the others.   Trained by their "physical culture"
lessons, they can judge of athletic feats wherever they see
them, with an almost professional intelligence, just as in a passage of arms a fencer measures with a single glance the quickness of the champions and their recovery.   At one time one
of the young men, who had just served a ball, held up his
foot for an attendant to clean the mud from the rubber sole
of his shoe.   His attitude during this very commonplace
action was so graceful that I heard a young girl exclaim: —

"Oh, I hope he will win!   He is so nice looking!"

The artless expression betrayed the American woman's profound admiration of "looks,"—physical beauty considered after a pagan sort of way. This admiration is carried to such a point that one of the most celebrated gymnasts of the United States invited a number of women of the best society to his private room, after one of his exhibitions, and gave them a lecture on muscular action, illustrating by his own person. The photograph of this torso, with muscles indeed like that of the Vatican over which the aged Michael Angelo passed his hands, is sold in all the shops, and more than one of these women who are now looking on at the tennis tournament has it in her own sitting-room.

"Some people think it is terribly indecent," said one of them, showing me this singular witness to the independence of her ideas. "I don't. It is just something Greek; that's all."

Half-past twelve. — Tennis is over for to-day. The beautiful horsewoman of this morning, who has taken her rest by looking on at this game of strength and skill, breathing in the air like a great plant, has left the Casino for a yacht, where she will take luncheon. I see her get into her carriage, a very high *duc*, take up the reins, and go off at the full speed of her horse, guiding him with her supple and firm little hands, bravely, deftly, in her elegant costume and her jewels. She is a "whip," as they say here, one of the five or six women who can best drive a coach, and to whom four horses offer no more terrors than this single chestnut.

Half an hour later I find her in the electric launch which plies between her yacht and the wharf. The machinery of this frail bark has been improved after the invention of another yachtsman, the owner of one of the pleasure boats which I see anchored in the harbor. Th—— was speaking to me of the ignorance in which some of the children of the rich are brought up. If they have good minds, they gain by it the ability to retain the truly American gift of direct vision; they see things

and not the ideas of things.   Furthermore, their ever-active life
develops in them the virtue of an immediate relation with reality.
The number of yachts in this roadstead is a sufficient demonstration of the degree to which the love of a life of activity and
movement is a national characteristic.   They form a little fleet,
some of them almost as large as a transatlantic steamer, and
capable of a cruise around the world, though that included
the enormous ground swells of the Pacific and the heavy seas
of Cape Horn.   Others are small toys of ships equal to a
voyage from Bar Harbor to New York if they keep close in-
shore, doubling all the capes and entering all the creeks.   And
then there are sail-boats, decked cutters which remind me of
the *Bel-Ami*, poor Maupassant's floating work-room.

The one which we board is of medium dimensions, but fitted
up with a magnificence which again gives me the impression of
the want of restraint of this strange country.   The sleeping-room,
with its hangings of old rose damask and its furniture of white
enamel; the drawing-room, also in light colors decorated with
plants and flowers, with its book-shelves, its piano, its deep armchairs, its ancient rugs, its water-colors by well-known artists;
the dining-room in its dark mahogany, with the table laid, on
which the soft brilliancy of orchids mingles with the harsher
brilliancy of crystal and silver; the glazed upper saloon with its
embroidered cushions on the wide sofas, where negroes are
stationed banjo in hand; finally the deck with its rocking-chairs
set among palms, and an aviary of exotic birds with flashing
wings, — all this represents an extreme attainment in luxury
which touches upon the realm of fancy.

Imagination looks backward twenty five — fifty years.   It
sees a pioneer plodding over the Western plains, a poor Irishman landing in New York from an emigrant ship, a German
seated at the desk of some hotel office.   These were the
fathers or grandfathers, or at most the great-grandfathers, of
the company gathered here, already so accustomed to these

refined splendors that they are as much at their ease as princes of the blood. It takes generations to make a real nobleman, one who feels and acts as such. But a single generation suffices to make a man of high life who shall have all the easy assurance in the midst of elegance of one of the innumerable indolent lords who swarm in the clubs of London and Paris. Even half a generation is often enough.

Half-past four. — Lunch, where again the inevitable dry champagne has flowed without stint, has given place to conversation upon the deck. Other women have come, two girls alone, two others accompanied by two Yale students not even related to them, four or five bachelors, veritable citizens of *Cosmopolis*, spending their incomes between Paris, London, Cannes, and this corner of the world, whenever the care of their property recalls them to the United States. Already the electric launch is beginning to carry passengers back to the shore. The whole "party" gathered on the boat is about to disperse. Most of them, and among them is the young woman whose day I am describing, are going to look on at a polo match. I am going with her. A quarter-hour upon the always-troubled waters of the harbor, twenty minutes in a carriage, and we are at the boarded enclosure in which this admirable and redoubtable game is to be played. A side hill commands it, and a dense mass of people are gathered there with intent to see the match from the outside. This game is so national, its energy and danger are so well suited to the race, that humble working-women, washerwomen for example, begin their day at four o'clock in the morning that they may the sooner be through with their work and spend their afternoon here.

"They are right," said the American who told me this fact. "It is a magnificent game. . . . Twenty years ago our young men thought of nothing but drinking. Now that they have cultivated a taste for sports, especially this one, they are obliged to be temperate so as not to grow stout. They eat little ; they do not drink ; they go to bed early. Without this regimen they could not keep it up a week at a time."

The fact is that, once having set foot upon this green lawn and seen the two bands of players riding their horses at full speed, their bodies bent forward, their long wooden mallet balanced in the free hand, it is difficult to associate with drunkenness or dissipation the enthusiasm such a virile exercise necessarily takes for granted. There are eight of them galloping along on fleet and nimble ponies. With their yellow boots, their knickerbockers, and their shirts and caps of the colors of their side, they follow in compact mass the white ball which rolls over the green turf. The horses, lathered with foam, follow it of their own accord, with the fine intelligence of an animal bestridden by a horseman so well trained that he seems like a part of his horse.

The ball leaps forward under a blow of the mallet more accurate than the others, and the two bands are off on a gallop. They defile close in front of the line of carriages drawn up along the boundary. You hear the horseshoes pound along the trampled turf. The sound is at once muffled and clear, and accompanied by the louder sound of their breathing. The same little shudder thrills through the lookers-on that they feel in Seville when watching the duel of the cuadrilla and the bull. Perhaps there is more real danger here, although the setting seems less ferocious. I was on the field only an hour, and in that time one of the riders had fallen from his horse. Another took his place, and ten minutes later received a blow of the mallet full in the face. I saw him fall from his horse blinded with blood. He fainted, then revived, and left the field supported by two friends, without attracting much attention from any one. The chief regret was the interruption of the game.

The necessity of dressing for the evening offered some consolation. For this long day of comings and goings will close, like all the others, by a dinner party followed by a ball at the Casino or elsewhere : unless the open air and so much exercise have got the better of the fashionable woman. The fatigues of the day explain why evening receptions are so rare in Newport, with the exception of these balls. Dinner parties break up at half-past ten or even earlier, the departing guests sometimes leaving their hosts so weary that they would feel some hesitation at remaining a quarter hour later.

"It has often happened," said Miss L——, the most beautiful " lioness " of this season, " that having ordered my carriage a little late I have remained in the dressing-room and gone to sleep upon a bench, so tired was I, rather than return to the drawing-room, knowing as I did that my poor hosts were tired too."

How do they converse ? This is the last question and the most important which can be asked with regard to the men and women who constitute society. All the rest is only trappings and gesticulation : the art of conversation is society itself. When good, it is its best reason for being ; when bad, silly, and empty, it is its greatest weariness, and always, good or bad, its chief characteristic. But how describe the peculiar character of a conversation without setting down a whole series of real dialogues, which would be at once incoherent and in bad taste ? We must seek for its true tone in the romances of those writers who have known and loved society, and from this point of view Mr. Henry James's earlier novels appear to me to be the most trustworthy witnesses. I say his earlier ones, because this very acute observer has of late more particularly studied his compatriots as they appear in foreign lands. Those on this side of the water find fault with him for this, and I recently read in a newspaper this astounding epigram, the metaphor being borrowed from the electric railway : —

" He has so much talent it is to be regretted that his trolley does not run on an American wire ! "

F

None the less is it true that no one else has so accurately reproduced the distinguishing characteristics of conversation as heard in a drawing-room or at a dinner table in Boston or New York.

As to the more strictly contemporary talk, that color of the present and the actual which Gyp so happily renders for us, it seems to me that no one has given a better idea of it than the distinguished woman who has made the pseudonym Julien Gordon famous. I refer to her novels the European reader, who, without crossing the ocean or leaving his easy-chair, may be curious to verify the few features which to my mind most distinctly mark American conversation. For Americans love to talk much more than the English, if not so much as the Gallo-Romans ; especially is this true of those in whose veins flow a few drops of that excitable Irish blood, which is no more able to be silent than to forget.

The first of these features is somewhat hard to reduce to a formula. I venture one nevertheless, helping it out by comment. I call it *point of view*.

You converse with a Frenchman; if he is bright and animated, after ten sentences the subject will have changed. He lets himself be carried along by the association of ideas so that in the course of an hour you will have touched on all subjects, without method, without profit, but with pleasure. He leaves you with the impression of an alert and ready mind which, to use correctly an old word that is very French, is illumined on many things. You have not felt that which nine times out of ten you will feel with an American man or woman, — an energy which never relapses even in the trivialities of social intercourse, a mind which has its own standpoint from which to look upon life, and which holds to it, compels you to accept it, utilizes you.

This is because, under the outward semblance of the

woman of the world who is talking with you in a drawing-room amid lights and flowers, there is a resolute creature who, from the time she came *out*, began to mould her own personality after some chosen model. Such a one has resolved to be a great lady after the English type. She has lived much in London, and has had the wit to fit herself to her surroundings. You find it impossible to draw her away from this position, or to elicit from her any "references" that are not British and of London. A second is pleased to be a Parisian, and her conversation shuts you up in a round of ideas which forever and ever presuppose Paris. For her there is nothing but our books, our pictures, our plays, our actors. A third has taken it into her head to be an actress. She has taken lessons in elocution and speaks well. Her conversation turns wholly upon the theatre. A fourth is by way of being literary. Within a quarter of an hour you discover that in the midst of the whirlwind of society she had found time for a wide reading, and she keeps it up by talking to you with that singularly vigorous precision and particularity with which people here are endowed. One of my French friends who was sought for as the husband of a very rich girl, renounced the half-formed engagement because the girl, being extremely interested in science, spent a whole evening in explaining to him a newly invented locomotive. "I can't marry an engineer," was his only reply to the reproaches of the person who had introduced him to her.

In general, it must be admitted, the point of view is less severe, less uncompromising, and you will find in the conversation of Americans, especially of the women, a second characteristic which saves them from stiffness and pedantry. This is vivacity. In their lightest words there is a distinct flavor of reality; there is also animation, action. Nothing abstract or vague; the words always make pictures, the terms

always reveal experience. They have not in the slightest
degree that motive of personal effacement which gives to
manners their highest polish, but which robs conversation of
so much individuality. They never hesitate to speak of themselves, to tell of their journeys, their adventures, of what
they call their "experiences." With little feeling for the
spirit of words, they easily come thus to have what we may
call the spirit of things, a picturesque speech which, when
mingled with gaiety, produces an original and novel "humor."
Here again, under the rich woman or the stately man, you
feel "the people" close at hand.

You feel it also in a certain general artlessness of conversation. Broad innuendo is absolutely absent from it, and
scandal is seldom cruel. The imitation of aristocratic imper-
tinence, that scourge of underbred society, finds no place
here. Ridicule is incessant, but it is a ridicule that never
wounds. It is carried on chiefly by lively anecdotes. Personal characteristics are its principal object; after that social
blunders, lack of taste in "lion-hunting," that is, the pursuit
of celebrated or titled people. Anecdotes of this class generally come from Europe, and go to prove that the usual result
of the passage from the New to the Old World is not to correct the faults of the American, but to make them more pronounced. At home, in his natural surroundings, he is more
simple, more cordial. In short, hearing him talk you esteem
him, you feel him to be "good-natured," to use his own expression, without many dislikes or many desires, and easily
amused. Forain said to me after a few days in Newport,
"They are children." This sort of spirit seemed flavorless to
that keen observer, who has entered so deeply into the old
age of our decadence. It has a flavor, but so different from
the Parisian acridity that it is perhaps impossible to taste
them both.

However, the Americans are doing their best in this line.

They enjoy repeating this most admirable of Forain's stories, though with the same effort of understanding which they apply to the reading of Verlaine and Mallarmé. For another note of their conversation is a frequent reference to French writers of the extreme Left. This taste has reached even the women by the medium of the painters who have gone to Paris to study and have been pleased to enter into the current, make acquaintance with things. One of the unintended pleasures of conversation with these women is the amazing contrast between certain names and the lips that utter them, and that go on to apply to them with surprising frankness the same words, "lovely," "enchanting," "fascinating," that equally describe all paintings and all natural landscapes, a horse and a musical phrase, a bonnet and a statue.

Two classes of subjects appear to me to be entirely excluded from conversation; one is politics, the other religion. This silence is the more significant when we reflect that these are the two unfailing interests of America, and that in no country do political and religious life appear to be more intense. This phenomenon may be attributed to various causes. For my part, I see in it a proof that Americans possess in a very high degree that distributive faculty which in itself is only a particular manifestation of their strength of will. You never hear a business man speak of business outside of his office. They excel in fixing the stopping-point. The same energy which permits them, having embarked in an undertaking, to give themselves entirely to it, permits them, the matter being finished, to give themselves with equal thoroughness to a new one. They make a certain use of the verb "to have" which shows this. They say that they *have* a drive or a ride, as they would say that they have a bottle of wine to drink, a book to read. It is as if, a portion of the day being theirs, an hour, two, three hours, their first concern is to use it — to make the most of it, to make it an almost isolated whole.

They no more mingle their sentiments than their occupations. These are pigeonholes which they open and close at will. Politics is one of these pigeonholes, religion is another, society is a third; and then, politics here are not, as with us, left a prey to the hazard of popular fancy or passion. They are ordered like any other business, and the parties are governed by the "machine" in a way which permits no chimeras either of general ideas or of petty intrigues. As to religion, absolute freedom has so multiplied sects, and shades of difference in the sects, that all discussion has come to be impossible. It would be a clashing of opinions so vast and continuous that as a natural consequence they have agreed to a mutual tolerance. This absence of the two great principles of irritation which exist in this world has resulted in giving conversation an air of harmlessness, almost of benignity, as of a most cordial simplicity. So, at least, it impresses me, for all these travelling impressions ought to carry with them the corrective of a "perhaps," since they can never be entirely verified even after a second, a third, or even a tenth experience.

IV

SOCIETY

II. *Women and Young Girls*

I HAVE a quantity of notes made in the course of months after those first ones, upon that American "society," of which at Newport I had at once the most complete and most striking experience. I have seen it again under all aspects, at Boston, at Chicago, at New York again, and at Washington.

These notes were hastily set down day by day, like a painter's sketches, destined one day to be blended in some special final picture. I have run them over more than once, with the idea of classifying them, of summing them up in a few somewhat clear statements. The difficulty which I have found in making such a synthesis arises less from their abundance than from a process of metamorphosis which my own mind has undergone in the course of this long journey and these many experiences.

Just as the words "the United States" now translate themselves for me by thousands of concrete and distinct pictures, while at my arrival they brought up before me a confused and indeterminate mass, so these other words, "American Society," have ceased to express for me the unique thing of which I had a prevision at Newport.

There is no American society as there is a French society and an English society. In the United States there are as many social systems as there are cities, and as not one of these cities has succeeded in establishing a supremacy of fashion like that which Paris exercises over our provinces, it results that there are all sorts of social centres, each one of which deserves a monograph. Certain novelists are working in this field; among them I may cite Mr. Chatfield Taylor, to whom we already owe such curious sketches of fashionable Chicago; and common speech itself furnishes proof of these differences in social circles, with the extravagances peculiar to proverbial expressions. How many times in the course of this journey have people said to me : —

"In Boston they ask you what you know; in New York, how much you are worth; in Philadelphia, who your parents were ! "

This epigrammatic remark is not entirely accurate. It seemed to me that in New York, for example, painters, sculptors, writers, and theatrical artists were assured of as cordial a welcome as in the ancient and learned citadel of Puritanism, — the "Hub" of Massachusetts. It remains none the less evident that the ardor for culture is more general and more intense in Boston, the mania for luxury more violent in New York, and that in Chicago there is more imitation, more uncertainty in the endeavor after the fitting. In that city I saw ladies rise from their seats in the theatre at the suggestion of one of their escorts, to visit an actor in the green room. But when a lady from New England who was with them in their box refused to join them in their incursion behind the scenes, they sat down again, their eyes betraying the thought, "So it is not proper ! "

They long after Washington. "It is a delightful place," a lady said to me. "The men are not busy as they are here. They are in politics or something. They have plenty of time for afternoon teas ! "

This abundance of time for five-o'clock teas does, in fact, give to the city on the banks of the Potomac something of the effect of Dresden or Weimar. Walking along these streets, with their border of private houses, with no suggestion of business or commerce, you might fancy yourself in some *strasse* of a German capital. And the easy flexibility of social life is in singular contrast with the overweighted condition of the other cities. I fancy that 'Frisco — as the contemptuous East insists upon calling San Francisco — has also its very distinct, very special, very original social circle ; and St. Louis also, and especially New Orleans.

It results that the traveller has, after a little while, some difficulty in recovering the first impression of unity, which is yet the true one ; for these different " societies " are merely varieties of a single species, or as groups within a group. They have, at any rate, one trait in common, with regard to which it is so impossible to be mistaken, that the most superficial observers have remarked it no less than the most profound, the two weeks' tourist as much as a Bryce, or a Claudio Jeannet. All these forms of social life, however different they may be, are entirely, absolutely, the work of " woman." It is by woman and for women that these social circles exist, so that, in order to understand them in their birth and development, it is necessary first of all to study and understand the American woman. Such a task is difficult in any country : how much more when it has to do with creatures at once so complete and so complex, each one of whom has her own will, a small universe of ideas, sentiments, ambitions !

At all hazards, here are a few reflections, a few sketches chosen from among a couple of hundred, as in some respects the most representative.

A first problem forces itself upon you, — a historic problem, the solution of which will, at least, explain how this supreme product of this civilization has been made. How does it come to pass that the men of this country — so energetic, so strong-willed, so dominating — have permitted their wives to shake off masculine authority more completely than in any other part of the world? It would seem as if these sturdy conquerors, accustomed to see everything bend before their daring and often their severity, would be more incapable than others of tolerating in· their homes a will, an energy, an activity, a personality in fact, equal to their own, existing by itself beside them and confronting them.

The contrary fact appears, inscrutable, and, if social life is more closely observed, every slightest detail of manners makes it equally evident. Not a hotel, not a bank, not a public building, which has not its ladies' entrance by which they go in and out as independently, as much a law to themselves, as men can be. One of them enters those electric or cable cars which abound in the United States. The seats are all occupied, but nineteen times in twenty a man gets up to give his place to the newcomer, who accepts it without thanks, so entirely natural does the courtesy appear. If this rule has any exceptions, it is because certain women deem it a reproach and humiliation to be treated differently from men. That the young girls of the best families go out alone on foot, or in a carriage, is a social custom so well known that one would be ashamed to cite it, except for the sake of interpreting its meaning more accurately. This proof of their freedom of action is also a proof of the respect which men in America profess for them. A man who should too boldly stare at a woman who was alone would be so discredited that the most ill-bred person would not venture to do so. What do I say? He would not so much as think of it, so fixed is the habit of equality between the two sexes.

This equality extends from small things to great. You visit a public school ; you will there see girls working with boys, and the teacher a man or a woman as it happens. You enter a laboratory of the university. There are young girls bending over the microscope side by side with the students. You permit the entrance of a reporter, who comes unannounced in the name of a great newspaper; it is a woman who asks to interview you. You ask the address of a doctor; you ascertain that there are as many women doctors as men, or if not as many, that they are so many as to cease to be exceptional. You go into the courts of law; the secretary who draws up the warrants is a woman. There are women lawyers. There are women pastors in certain churches. At the head of a volume containing the census of the occupations of women in the United States, one of them, a poet of high standing, Julia Ward Howe, has placed this proud sentence. It explains better than whole commentaries that passion for activity which characterizes the claims of women in this country.

" The theory that woman ought not to work is a corruption of the old aristocratic system. . . . A respect for labor is the foundation of a true democracy."

Who can be surprised if creatures possessing this pride, this consciousness of individuality, having conquered the right of taking upon themselves occupations most foreign to their sex, reign uncontested in the realm most fit for them, — the management of social life? The very origin of the social life of America, as I have already pointed out, makes this necessary. In this country the women who belong to society have not, as with us, and in England, received a different education from those who are not of it. Their birth is not different; their family is not different; nor is their nature. They bring to it the same strength of resolution, the same power of realism, the same independence of personality. It remains to inquire why men permitted this independence to be born and to grow up.

This phenomenon has complex reasons, as excellent observers have pointed out. And first, it is precisely that fever of democracy, that idolatry of the doctrine of equality, which for a hundred years was one of the passions and the prides of the American. To this day, though in certain Eastern cities an invasion of old European prejudices has introduced a few pretensions which that Jacobin Stendhal energetically called the "aristocratic virus," this idolatry of equality remains very much alive in the middle class. I have seen a theatre audience spring up frantically at this word of a laboring man as he entered a liquor saloon: —

"I am a freeborn American citizen, and I will go where I please."

Such theories have their logic. The equality of the man and the woman was on similar terms. The religious sects have contributed to this end, by giving to woman the possibility of preaching like a man, and consequently of considering herself, and making herself to be considered, his equal in reason, eloquence, and authority. There are women in the origin of many of the religious confessions. Ann Lee founded the Shakers. Barbara Heck reformed the Methodists. Lucretia Mott gave their faith to the Hicksites, — to the "Friends," — who, like Tolstoi, preach "obedience to the light within." You will continually find in the newspapers notices like the following, which I copy from an Albany journal: —

"The Rev. Anna H. S—— will address the men's mass meeting at German Hall, at four o'clock: no boys under sixteen admitted."

Thus granted entrance to offices, women necessarily held in their homes a place which the conditions of the conquest of the vast continent contributed to make all the more important. Women were few in those frontier settlements which, advancing continually westward, marked the stages of the great democracy, in its progress from Atlantic to Pacific. They were most necessary to the maintenance of this half-savage life, in which men were called to struggle at once against nature and against men. Treated without sufficient consideration, the women could not have lived through it. They would have died, as Lincoln's mother did, seized with that mysterious prairie malady, that "milk sickness," which never yields its hold. It was necessary to be careful and considerate of them.

A singular sort of chivalry is thus developed, the signs of which are found in the local character studies which the Americans are so fond of writing, setting on the stage, and playing. One type continually recurs in these pieces, that of the Westerner, rough and loyal, who chews, drinks, and talks a frightful dialect through his nose, but who, where a woman is concerned, is capable of the most remarkable flights of honor. I have nowhere found this singular hero better represented than in Boston, in a comedy entitled *In Mizzoura*, and by an actor named Goodwin. This cross between a cowboy and Don Quixote saved the life of a rival, who was on the point of being lynched by a mob. With his facetious and intent features, his tobacco distended cheek, his far-streaming jets of saliva, his harsh voice, his hat on the back of his head, and a sort of automatic passivity of manner, the comedian was the very incarnation of the sentimental and kindly countryman; and I found an amazing contrast between the applause with which the public greeted his generous deeds and the ease with which they accepted the idea of lynching. Both these things are a part of their customs.

By all sorts of influences like these that special creation, the American woman, is elaborated. These are the roots by which the frivolous and capricious independence of the millionaire's daughter sinks deep into the springs of the national life. In the strangely perplexing relations between American men and women there is a still deeper reason, at least so it appears to me, and one which is wholly physiological. But when we have to do with the laws which rule the mutual relations of the sexes, we always have to come back to physiology.

If, for example, the Orientals have reduced their women to a frightful state of slavery and degradation, it is because their love for them is strongly sensual, and in all sensuality there is a basis of hatred, because there is a hidden taint of animal jealousy. If the Latin races, while according a greater liberty to women, yet instinctively revolt from the idea of their independence and personal initiative, it is because, under all our refinements, we are a little like the Oriental. Sensuality and the despotism of jealousy are at the foundation. If, on the other hand, the English accord more liberty to their women, it is because climate, race, religion, have more tamed the ardor of their natures. The *sera juvenum Venus* of Tacitus is as true of young Oxford men as it was of the young Germans of the first century. All who have closely studied the young men of America will say, with one consent, that in this respect they are like young Englishmen, or still more cold.

Merely to reflect upon the conditions under which the country has grown up, is to see that it must logically be thus. The incessant toil into which these men must have thrown themselves, in the effort to wrest the land from nature and from the Indians, the nervous tension due to the stress of competition, bad cooking, the absence of wine and the use of intoxicating liquors, religious fervor and political ardor, and a score of other causes, have checked the development of this people on the side of the senses. Art and literature are recent things ; neither, then, has the emotional imagination been fed. A trifling fact is singularly significant. I am assured that in all the United States there is not an entirely nude statue. Only yesterday the Bostonians, so cultured, so liberal, so in love with art, refused to accept for the façade of the Public Library two children done by the powerful sculptor St. Gaudens, because they were not clothed! The municipality of Chicago forced another sculptor to put clothes upon a Hebe designed for a fountain, which he had left undraped.

These circumstances combined have brought about this result, that woman's charms have been given the second place in the interest of men. This sense of charm, though lulled to indifference, has become neither morbid nor unhappy! That species of cruelty which grows out of too great desire is the true principle of the great inequalities of legislation in which was manifested the secret desire of the male in defiance of the female. In American sensibility, it simply does not exist. It even seems as if this relative diminution in the prominence given to the life of the senses has modified — only slightly indeed, but none the less truly — the difference of appearance between the two sexes.

I remember that at Cambridge, visiting the "Hasty Pudding," one of the students' clubs, where they give amateur theatricals, I had an opportunity to examine the photographs of those of the young men who had taken women's parts and wore their dress. There was a surprising similarity — almost identity, indeed — between these portraits and those of their sisters or cousins, tall girls, with narrow chests, falling shoulders, straight backs, who have practised gymnastics and "high-kicking," who can lift their foot as high as their head, and jump from their own height without injury. It seems as if the type of manhood, while taking on a finer nervous organization, had lost something of its primitive weight, and, on the other hand, that the type of womanhood, vigorous, energetic, and impulsive, had taken on a more resolute charm, firmer, less voluptuous, and delicately masculine.

These are but suggestions, but they help to a better understanding of what makes, not the whole of a people, but its real and permanent basis, — the physical existence of the race. And though the social life be luxurious, artificial, and overloaded, such a race gives a basis of reality to the nation, or, to make a more accurate comparison, it is the web upon which may be embroidered the flowers of life.

This apotheosis of woman, which is the most characteristic feature of "society" in America, is in the first place and especially the apotheosis of the young girl. The words are simple, yet they need to be explained; for it is probable that on every point — except indeed that of honor — they express precisely the contrary in the United States and France.

That which first strikes the foreigner, who has heard so much about American girls, is the absolute impossibility of distinguishing them from the young married women. The much-commented fact that they go in and out entirely unattended does not sufficiently account for this perplexity. Their identity is much deeper than that. They dress in the same way, wear the same jewels, have the same freedom of speech and of smile, they read the same books, do the same things, possess the same full-blown beauty, and, thanks to the invention of the "chaperon," there is no theatre, or supper party, or tea where they cannot be present all by themselves upon the invitation of any man of their acquaintance. The character of this official surveillance may be estimated by the companion fact that the young girl, in whose honor the "bachelor" gets up a party, usually chooses the chaperon herself. The younger the chaperon, the better she suits. The young widow and the "grass-widow," whether separated, divorced, or simply apart from her husband for the time being, is an ideal person for this duty. It may also be said that the young girls whom you see around a table at Delmonico's, in company with these young men and the said chaperon, are as much at liberty as if they had no one to answer for them but themselves.

This habit of unchecked self-government is manifest in the singular serenity of their countenances. One of the most charming men in New York, a poet of reputation, conceived the clever idea of making a collection of miniatures in which, with their permission, should be included all the noted beauties of the city. I remember that when I passed a magnifying-glass over the glass behind which smiled a hundred refined and inscrutable faces, I sought in vain to distinguish those who were married, and I could not. What more, indeed, can marriage bring a girl when it comes? Duty; a husband to submit to, children to bring up, a house to look after. The young girl feels the weight of none of these chains to-day. She knows it, and that she is enjoying her best days. Once married she will not have one whit more freedom, and she will have fewer opportunities to amuse herself. Therefore, more often than not, she will marry late. If it is not entirely the end of things for her, as for the young man in Paris who decides to give up his bachelor life, it is the entering-wedge of abdication. And many of them do not shut their eyes to this fact.

" We must amuse ourselves before marriage," one of them said to me, with a smile. "Who knows what will come afterward? "

The divorce cases reported from time to time in the newspapers prove this young woman's good sense to be equal to her beauty. For my part, after having closely studied human conditions in Europe and here, I think that a young man from twenty to twenty-five has the best chance of happiness by being an Englishman of good family, studying at Oxford ; and a young girl by being born an American, of a father who has made a fortune in mines, railroads, or land speculations, entering New York or Washington society under good auspices.

At the first glance this absolute freedom makes all the young girls look alike. They are the model after whom many authors —some of them very distinguished, but none of whom has taken the trouble to come here — have composed the type which has become classical with us, — the American woman of the romance and the theatre. Our writers manufacture her of the simplest possible materials, — very bad manners upon a background of simplicity; there you have the walking doll.

G

Nevertheless, it is only a doll, and the two elements of which it was made appear to me to be equally false.

The American girl, when we see her in France, may often appear to us ill-bred, because we compare her with our own conventional type of young girl, which, let me whisper, is not very close to the truth either. Seen near at hand and in her own home, you are better able to understand that this freedom of action may quite as probably be associated with a good, as with a bad, education. After a very few weeks, you learn to distinguish quite clearly between those who are " fast," as they say, and those who are not ; between her who takes pleasure in arousing the interest and awakening the desire of a man and her with whom moral familiarity is impossible, still less physical familiarity.

As for simplicity, when we Frenchmen apply the word to young girls we always take it for granted that there is only one question in the world for them, — that of love. We implicitly admit that that is the essential fact of their existence, as of all women's existence. We ask ourselves, what they think about it, what they know about it, and our measure of their innocence, of their virginity of soul, if I may so speak, is entirely based upon the answer. It is always understood that their acquaintance with the things of real life accords with this single answer. Such a test is not applicable to the American girl, because with her as with the American man of from twenty to thirty years, the question of love is relegated to the background. The question whether or not she will be married in accordance with the desires of her heart, whether or not her life will be a love story, has very often not the slightest place in a girl's thoughts. Even for those who seem the most intent on pleasing, and who make the most of their personal attractions, — there are fewer of them than Frenchmen suppose, more of them than Americans will admit, — it is still true that nine times out of ten their relations with a man are merely a fact of social life. It is simply a way of gratifying their self-love, of becoming what the newspapers call "Prominent people in society" by the number of their adorers. This love of admiration has not the danger here that it would have elsewhere, because, on the one hand, of the reserve of men in America; on the other, of the girl's thorough understanding of the masculine character. They began at so early an age to be on intimate terms with men, that, so far as they are concerned, they are in the position of the children of a circus rider with horses. One girl, speaking to me of a common acquaintance, a Spanish woman married in Rome and very unhappy, said : —

"She does not know how to manage her husband."

And she told me how this woman's rival had gone to work to attract and retain her unfaithful husband. The sort of intelligent innocence which such remarks take for granted is not very intelligible to us. A diplomat who spent several years here, and to whom I repeated this conversation by way of ascertaining its precise import, summed up his own impression of them — which is severe — in the words, "They have a chaste depravity." He supported his epigram by anecdotes concerning "engagements," as they say here.

"I have known," he said, "many young girls engaged to men whom they had not the slightest intention of marrying. They liked them as lovers, but they did not want them as husbands. I have known others who for months have kept secret a serious engagement, in order to retain the attentions which are denied to an 'engaged girl.' A girl's engagement is, nine times out of ten, what an interesting situation is to a wife, — something to be concealed as long as possible, and admitted only when it can be concealed no longer."

For my part, I see in these little facts, which I have reason to believe true, nothing which proves either profligacy or perversity. They are a sign that the American girl is, before all things, a reasoning creature, fitted both by nature and education for self-guidance.

"What is the matter with you?" one of my compatriots, who had stopped in New York on his way to Chicago, asked one of these young girls. He had sat beside her at two successive dinners, and had found her very singular the second time; quite different from the evening before.

"I am a little nervous," she replied. "Some one came to see me at five o'clock, and acted in a way I don't like. I shall be obliged to give up my flirtation with him and I am sorry. He is such a bright fellow!"

How shall I translate this word "bright," to which the Americans give so much of meaning, to which they add so much of quick adaptability and effective power? How, also, shall I understand the mental processes of a modest girl who extends such confidences to an acquaintance of yesterday? Frankness like this appears to me precisely a proof of a simplicity which we are ill-fitted to understand. To recur to the comparison lately used, I am sure this child attached little more importance to the "bright fellow's" lack of breeding, than she would have attached to the stumbling of a pony which she had "badly managed." He has broken his knees and can't be used again. What a pity! "He was such a bright pony!" A girl who, corrupt or impassioned, would attach an extreme importance to love matters, either does not speak of them or speaks in another tone.

Precisely because the American girl's imagination does not play around sentimental problems, she has far more shades of variety in her character than her compeers in Europe. The latter do not expect their true development until their heart has spoken, and the influence of a man has begun to mould them. The American girl exists by herself. She knows it and wills it so. She is proud of it. She has nothing in common with the Galatea of the pagan myth who receives all from Pygmalion, from the embodiment of her beauty to the fire of her soul. Her individuality is already complete when she arrives at marriage — at the latest possible moment, as I have already said, if her parents have ever so little fortune. She proposes to choose a husband who will take the place of these convenient parents, in the matter of indulgence and also of wealth. She only half counts upon the generosity of her father, who is not obliged to dower her, and who, once she is married, may reduce her allowance to an absurd figure. One girl, a blonde with great half-mocking blue eyes, — blue eyes which are both tender and tantalizing, and a delicately-formed nose, at once sensitive and scornful, told me between smiles that showed beautiful teeth, in which there was not a speck of gold : —

"Mamma says that love is like a toothache. So far I have no need of a dentist. I shall never marry any but a rich, a very rich, man. The rest may come as it may, or not at all. At this moment I have a suitor who is worth five millions. So there is no hurry."

And then she added, thoughtfully : —

"I should like, above all things, to be a widow. I have always thought how nice it would be to lose my husband on my wedding-day. I should have less reason to mourn as I should know him less. I should like to see him struck with lightning as we come out of the church. It is so nice to be a young widow ! "

This lively little creature — she was nineteen years old, — libelled herself with all the charm of a witty girl posing before a French novelist. " French novelist," the two words have always had a vague aroma of scandal here. But her paradox only lent weight to her real thought; namely, that she would do well to take time before she bartered her present lot for one more uncertain and more dangerous. Many of her companions think as she does. It is for this reason that they willingly remain single till they are twenty-five or twenty-six years old, and in these long years of unchecked independence, each one follows her own tastes, each her own fancy, her own nature, indeed, oppressed by so little constraint. Hence it results that the individuality of each nature is amply developed. Innumerable types also work themselves out, which a traveller of a few months' experience is utterly unable to distinguish in even the most general way. Those which I am about to sketch are, perhaps, not the most happily chosen. They have at least the merit of having been studied from life.

The most artless of these young-girl types, and to my mind the most touching, for reasons which I will explain, is the *Beauty*. There are two or three in every city, and their supremacy is so well recognized that you are continually receiving such invitations as " Pray come to tea to-morrow afternoon, to meet Miss ——, the Richmond beauty." I say Richmond at random ; in its place put Savannah, Charleston, Albany, Providence, any city north or south that you please. To merit her title, the Beauty must indeed be lovely with that radiant brightness which extinguishes all other women at a ball, a dinner, or the theatre. She must be very tall, very well formed, the lines of her face and figure must lend themselves to that sort of reproduction of which the newspapers and their readers are so fond. She must also know how to dress with magnificence, which here is inseparable from elegance.

Once recognized, though she may not be more than twenty years old, she enters upon a sort of official, almost a civic, existence. In the newspaper columns devoted to " Social Gossip," the types spontaneously form her name, so often have the compositors set it up. She is as necessary a part of every grand dinner and ball as the roses at a dollar apiece, and the champagne *brut*. Her own city cannot suffice to her, or, rather, she would not be fulfilling her mission if she did not represent that city in New York, Washington, Newport, at the races, the regattas, all the events where, as on a stage, American society displays itself. She is, in fact, a social actress and a champion of her order, like a master of billiards or chess. ˌLet us be more ambitious, — like a pugilist, like Jim Corbett the Californian !

For her successes to be perfect, she must compete for her place "abroad," and play her part as leading social lady in Paris, London, Rome. When she returns from Europe with her crop of laurels, she still does not lay down her arms. She has a *record* to hold, and the day when she shall be assuredly, incontestably, excelled by a rival, it will be with her as with the Boston boxer, the hapless J. L. Sullivan, who no longer counts since he has been once beaten, — as with the *Teutonic* and the *Majestic* since the *Campania* has made the passage from Europe in five days sixteen hours and a few minutes. It is all over — they belong to the past.

Behind the Beauty, to keep up the insane expenses of a life always in full dress, in the most senselessly luxurious circle in the two hemispheres, is a father who most likely is never seen, who divides his life between his office, his club, and sometimes, in certain cities, the bar of the best hotel. His daughter, to whom he makes an allowance which would suffice for the trousseau of a princess, is dear to him by a complex sentiment into which enters less of affection than of pride. He sometimes passes entire seasons, not to say years, without seeing her when she crosses the ocean. Even when she is in the United States and at home, the meals which he takes with her could be counted. Nevertheless he loves her, but by such a displacement, such a projection of his personality as Balzac described, with the blemish of his habitual extravagance, when he pictured the friendship of Vautrin for Lucien de Rubempré.

"He was *myself*, young, and brilliant," said the convict. "From the depths of my cell I put on his coat. I drove in his tilbury ; I entered drawing-rooms with him."

Probably the business man, laboring over railway plans and manufacturing projects, accompanies his daughter by a similar imagination. His money goes about in this young girl ; that is

to say, his will, his labor, all that is most personal to himself.
Whether he marries her to some noble Italian, Englishman, or
Frenchman, or whether he refuses her to the nobleman, — the
American father's vanity may take on either of these forms, —
she serves to prove to him his power. He has this daughter just
as he has a twenty-story " building " which bears his name, a
picture gallery mentioned in the guide-books, as he has his
stocks. " I know my social value," said one of these girls.
She spoke of herself as of a certificate of New York Central, or
Chicago, Burlington, and Quincy stock. Social value, — this is
probably the best definition of this singular creature, whose
existence consists — in the heart of a democracy — in under-
going as much representative etiquette as if she were maid of
honor to a princess, or herself a princess in a court that was
always making festival. Speaking of one of these girls, whose
health was failing in the midst of her social victories, and who
has since died of them, a very acute woman dropped this
word, to which I shall add nothing, so perfectly does it seem
to me to express that which must be the last calamity of such
a lot : —

" I always longed to condole with her upon her toilettes ! "

A second type, less rare than the professional beauty, but
still less common than many others, is the young girl with
ideas. This class may be divided into two groups, — the
convinced girl and the *ambitious girl*. Like the Beauty, this
girl lives in society with that sort of extravagance so difficult
to avoid in America. She also figures in the daily procession
of the fashionable carnival ; only she is not, like the other,
at the head of the procession. She has not attained to this
incontestable and somewhat mechanical success. For that
matter, she does not desire it. She is a girl who has laid
down for herself a special programme, and is occupied in carrying it out with a regularity and perseverance that she allows

nothing to interrupt. Sometimes this is the case of the *con-vinced* girl. This programme is in the purely moral order, and of a very high type. For example, she has said to herself that marriage being a contract, the man ought to bring to it the same loyalty as the woman, the same pure past, the same innocence ; and that she will not engage herself to any one who has more past experience than she herself. This puritan rigor of conscience would seem strange in a setting of such frivolity, if you did not recall to mind that a never-failing current of religious ardor flows in the veins of these descendants of the exiles of the *Mayflower* or the companions of Penn.

Or, again, the girl with ideas decides to take part in politics. For this two things are required, — that some person nearly connected with her shall hold some high position or be working to that end ; and that she herself have time to direct or aid that person ; she also is working for that. Such is the thoroughly American peculiarity of her character. She is a realist and insists upon having the reality of that power of which she will have the semblance, through a father, a brother, a husband. She strains every nerve to make the two former senators, members of Congress, ambassadors ; she will endure the same toils to enable the latter to occupy a similar situation, perhaps to bring him to the White House ; and at the same time she labors that she may be, when the time arrives, a perfect instrument for the service of this ambassador or president, making herself familiar with politics and administration, attending the sessions of legislatures, watching the workings of the electoral machine, following the complications of the European chess-board.

Such a one is both earnest and ambitious. There is another type that is ambitious only. This girl has made up her mind that her name shall be written in the golden book of the English peerage, that she will marry a lord. For many years she has been preparing herself for this, losing no opportunity of

gaining entrance to the upper circles of English society, meanwhile occupying herself with overcoming the obstinacy of her
father, whose opposition to international marriages is a matter
of principle, — of *jingoism*, to use the Anglo-Saxon equivalent
of our French *chauvinisme*, — and also a matter of judgment.
So many of these unions have turned out badly! None the
less, the young girl will succeed at last in joining the small pha-
lanx of American peeresses; the nervous tension of her expression is my warrant for that, and so is the decided curve of her
lips, with the vigorous little chin. And once having attained ·
to the British Olympus, she will need to be taught nothing
either of people or of customs — she, whose grandfather began
life in a little restaurant in Chicago, before the fire!

An ambitious girl who is less gifted, especially if she is
less rich, cheerfully becomes a "bluffer," to borrow once
again a significant term of the national game of poker. She
went to Europe last year with the idea well fixed in her pretty
brown head to play the same game with some rich man over
there that so many European adventurers have come over
here to play upon rich girls. What could be fairer? She
knows that her father's fortune will not endure investigation,
and she knows, too, that every one else knows it and that the
brilliant parties given in their mansion on Fifth Avenue
deceive no one. The "bluffer" has told herself that her
beauty will make a sensation in London and Paris; that she
will easily turn some simple head; that her would-be husband
will take her luxurious life, her fine clothes, above all, the
fact that she is an American girl abroad, as authentic witnesses of millions. She has had before he illustrious examples
of successful bluffs of this sort. Unluckily, she has chanced
upon a young man who, though very elegant and well-con-
nected, has come to the end of his own resources, and being
reduced to expedients has resolved to "bluff" some rich
foreigner. The two actors are mutually deceived, and the

young man, coming to New York to press his suit, has departed, after explanations which must have been most deliciously amusing! Unhappily, comedies of this kind are played without spectators.

Another character more frequently assumed is that of the tomboy. She has generally been to Europe — for that matter you must always ask this question with regard to every American girl. She there became conscious of her individu-ality, as a philosopher might say. She knows that she is "the American girl," and she wants to be even more so than she is. She makes game of you in her own character by exaggerating it beyond all bounds of probability. She will tell you how, in Paris, in the Rue de la Paix, a gentleman took her for what she was not and followed her. She found the adventure "great fun."

You feel it incumbent upon you to excuse the indiscretion of your compatriot?

"Stupid thing!" she replies; "he didn't so much as speak to me."

This is the girl who opens her doors to a class in "high-kicking," the art of lifting one's foot as high as possible. She holds the record of six feet three inches, none of her friends having been able to excel her.

"What a pity that you can't see me kick!" she says to you; "without bending the knee, you know."

This is the girl who, dining with a young married friend, without her mother, asks you for cigarettes, smokes four at a time, — and exclaims: —

"To think that I have to come to Jessie's to get a few puffs of straight-cut."

She has the street-Arab in her make-up, but the American street-Arab; not Gavroche, but Gallegher. I refer the reader to Mr. Richard Harding Davis's clever story, that he may appreciate the difference between the innocence of Parisian and the coarseness of American blackguardism. Compare one of their pantomimes with one of our street singers. The American girl when she undertakes to be masculine is disconcertingly daring in her speech.

"What do you think of the little trousers with which the virtuous women of Philadelphia and Baltimore have clothed their statues?"

I saw one of my French friends start at this question suddenly put to him in a drawing-room of virtuous New England. Another of them found himself growing interested in one of the innumerable Mays whom you meet at all the balls and afternoon teas. One of May's friends — it happened to be the smoker of cigarettes — said to him saucily: —

"Well, when is the marriage coming off? She is very nice, you know, very nice! It is a pity that she has nothing pretty but her face. Yes," she went on teasingly; "we slept in the same room a whole week in the country," and a minute description followed — "hollow chest, projecting shoulder-blades, thin legs, no hips — nothing but hair — hair — up to there."

And she bends her leg and points to the bend of her knee with her mocking laugh like a schoolboy who should describe to you some creature whom he had met on the Boulevard Saint-Michel on a holiday evening.

Another, feeling bored one evening at a formal dinner, wrote a few lines on the back of her menu, folded the card, and sent it to an officer of our marine on his way to Chicago, whom she had known just three days.

"I love you," she wrote. "What more will you have?" She went into fits of laughter over the expression of the man's countenance at the absurd joke of this make-believe declaration.

Another, invited to tea by Miss May's lover, and not succeeding in getting her mother's permission, wrote to him,

"If I were a French girl they couldn't treat me worse. That is all the good it does to be an American," and then by way of postscript, "You know that if you insist, I will come all the same." And this was not a mere mode of speech.

The tomboy is a sort of young woman who in general excels in all sports, wears tailor-made gowns, walks erect, plays billiards, and finds much less pleasure in being courted than in devising some new excitement, such as a ride at full speed on the cow-catcher of a locomotive. I have met the daughter of a director of a great railway, of whom this was the favorite amusement. She had covered miles upon miles of the prairie — squatting on the metal platform above which puffed the machine, and by the expression with which she exclaimed "How exciting!" I could see how her nerves must have thrilled with the rush of speed and danger.

This is the physical tomboy, if one may so speak, in contrast with whom arises the more serious face of the intellectual tomboy; the girl who is up to the times, who has read everything, understood everything, not superficially, but really, with an energy of culture that could put to shame the whole Parisian fraternity of letters. The trouble is that nine times out of ten this mind, which is capable of assimilating everything, is incapable of tasting anything. It is an iron stomach, like that of Didymus, the commentator of the decadence, whom the Alexandrians called the Scoliast, with entrails of brass — with no palate. Though like all the others she gets her gowns from the best houses of the Rue de la Paix, there is not a book of Darwin, Huxley, Spencer, Renan, Taine, which she has not studied, not a painter or sculptor of whose works she could not compile a catalogue, not a school of poetry or romance of which she does not know the principles. She subscribes impartially to the *Revue des Deux Mondes* and the gazettes of the latest coteries of the Latin Quarter or Montmartre. Only she does not distinguish between them.

She has not an idea that is not exact, and yet she gives you
the strange impression as if she had none. One would say
that she had ordered her intellect somewhere, as we would
order a piece of furniture, to measure, and with as many
compàrtments as there are branches of human knowledge.
She acquires them only that she may put them into these
drawers. This is the most striking illustration of the misdi-
rected effort from which this civilization suffers, and the proof
that effort can replace nature only to a certain point. I
remember that as we were leaving the palace of one of the
Chicago millionaires, Forain said to me in a voice fairly
quivering with the frantic longing of a sensitive artist for a
glimpse of simple human nature: —

"Oh, for a concierge's lodge! What would I give to see a
concierge's lodge!"

Before the intellectual girl one longs to cry: —

"Oh, for one ignorance, one error, just a single one. May
she make a blunder, may she prove not to know!"

In vain. A mind may be mistaken, a mind may be ignorant, but never a thinking-machine!

A new type now comes into view, that of the coquette, for
she too exists — the feminine and compliant coquette, who is
somewhat like what we know in Europe, though with decided
shades of difference.

First there is the *collector*, she whose wiles are exercised
upon several persons at a time, usually four, for a variety in
jealousies, — two somewhat elderly adorers, and two very young
ones. In a parenthesis I may observe that it is a striking characteristic of the United States that a man's age appears not to
have the same importance to the American as to the French
girl. Arnolphe need not here envy Horace the charm of his
twenty-five years, so far as Agnes is concerned. The proof is
the readiness of young girls to marry rich old men, and the
usual happiness of such unions.

My diplomatic friend insists that calmness of temperament alone explains this anomaly. This hypothesis is scarcely to be reconciled on the other hand with that admiration of "looks," of the physical beauty of man, which, on its part, explains certain elopements of which the papers occasionally speak. I think it more correct to recognize that an American woman's love of admiration is no more than other things a matter of impulse. Will is her guide here too, and leads her to as much satisfaction in turning an old head as a young one. The proof of this element of intention is found in her way of going to work. She almost always uses compliment, but so obvious, so terribly downright, that you know not how to take it. It is a way of asking you for as much in exchange which, those say who know, you may make as extravagant as you like. They will not believe much that you say, but they will like it.

"I do love the French so!" said one woman in my presence. "They know so well how to pay compliments! They go at it in such a way that you believe that they really mean it." And they readily add: "Write to me. Tell me what you think of me."

It is this admiring interest that the "collector" desires to arouse and keep alive. It is enough for her; she is always ready enough to be displeased if the correspondence thus suggested should go so far as a declaration, or if this admiring interest became bold enough to risk a caress — unless indeed the "collector" herself becomes equally interested. For, unhappily, my friends assure me, there is a type of young girl who still is modest, who yet permits herself to receive trinkets, jewels, even pairs of horses, from the admirers whom she keeps on a footing of Platonism! She does not go often so far, but contents herself with summer flirtations with men who are rich enough to give her the use of their carriages during the season.

This singular variety. this virgin nature which remains pure by calculation, while still taking advantage of her beauty for the benefit of her own whims, appears less odious here than elsewhere.

The financial relations of man and wife are very singular in this country, where the wife most frequently bears to her husband the relation of disbursing agent, hardly ever seeing him, receiving from him a profusion of money, which she lavishes by herself alone upon luxuries which her husband never enjoys.   He is never there, unless in the form of checks!

The species, happily, is rare, so rare that I speak of it only by hearsay, while, on the other hand, I have often met the sentimental coquette, her who has the excuse of believing herself to be "desperately in love" with the man with whom she flirts.   The extravagant speech, so characteristic of America, makes use of such expressions to designate the mild *passion-ettes*, which are at least so far original that they are indulged in by these romantic persons with a self-possession in which all the energy of the race is revealed.   When the American girl has been attracted by a young man, she does not content herself, as our schoolgirls do, with timidly dreaming about him.   She always has some obliging friend whom she despatches to him.

"Miss N—— is very anxious to make your acquaintance. Come, and I will present you to her."   It is regularly another girl who thus plays the part of go-between.   She goes farther. "Why don't you pay attention to Nannie?   She is charming, I assure you.   I think you would please her."

She doesn't think it — she knows it; for Nannie has made her her confidante and entrusted her with this message.   But Nannie, with her romantic daring, is a reasoning child.   Who has said that the Americans are like pins, always held by the head?   After a certain time she will perceive that she was mistaken as to the intensity of her feelings, especially if a marriage which pleases her becomes possible.   Once married to another and quite happy, if she ever meets the young man of her little passion, she will say to him:—

"How foolish I was! But how I loved you!"

And in this reminiscence there will be so much of frank good-fellowship that the idea of resuming with the married woman the interrupted romance begun with the young girl will not occur a second time to the man who is the object of this singular confidence.

With respect of these types, which nearly all lend themselves to satire, it is only just to sketch another figure, which is also to be found in this country of the "always too much," that of the well-balanced girl. The charming personality of the young girl who is all propriety and harmony is of all countries and all times. Molière modelled his Henrietta after her, Dickens his Agnes, Zola his Denise. That which distinguishes her in America is the precocity and universality of her experience. Usually, in London as in Paris, the very well-balanced girl is, above all things, a child who has been well cared for, closely watched, whose life has been carefully regulated, whose education is narrow. She has either made the best of very painful circumstances, or else has undergone a very rigid discipline.

Here, on the contrary, she has preserved her natural poise in the midst of the most lavish, unrestrained, and complicated life possible. But neither her father's wealth, nor the luxury in which she is wrapped, nor the world-fever by which she is swept along, have been able to prevail against her judgment and reasoning faculty. By herself, she has distinguished between all the sensations born of her surroundings, recognized those which are sound and those which are unsound, chosen the former and repelled the latter. She has moulded for herself a character entirely in accord with her social position, and yet individual and peculiar to herself.

To a girl like this, we know by instinct, no test would prove

H

dangerous, no accident of fortune find her other than she ought to be. So clearly do we perceive her to be energetic, clear-sighted, and gentle, that we understand that the vigor of her race, so unrestrained in every one else, is in her kept under control, in her reaches its limit. The absolute freedom of feminine manners in this country has not destroyed in her a single one of the graces of her sex, and these graces multiply with such vigor as will convince her husband, not alone of her irreproachable fidelity, but that she will be a support in trouble, of whatever nature. Like all the others, she is a highly finished person, self-made, and sufficient to herself, but with enough of intelligent good-nature to understand another person who is near her, to receive him, help him, and associate herself with him.

That this young girl is not very rare in the United States proves that, if the principle of unrestrained freedom of action has produced grave faults, it has also produced new shades of moral beauty and charm. This creature, a mixture of feminine delicacy and virile will, attracts, surprises, entices, comforts us. We respect her, and she moves us. We are grateful to her for existing, as for one of the noble things of the world; and we could dream — so perfect is she — of having her as a part of our lives, as confidante, counsellor, friend,— I was about to say, and I am sure that it is the best eulogy,— as comrade.

Well or ill balanced, coquettish or sentimental, learned or reckless, designing or simple, the young American girl is before all things else a whole little universe, formed and developed entirely apart from masculine influence. It would seem as if the difference of spirit, of habits, almost of species, between her and her father, which I have already noticed, so entire as to be incredible, must inevitably result in some terrible moral catastrophe. If such are rare, it is because here, more than anywhere else, they practise the sensible and humane maxim, "Live and let live." Nevertheless, this extreme liberty is saved from friction only by the avoidance of familiarity; with the natural result — of great importance for the young girl, and still more for the young wife — that home life is less known in the United States than in any other country.

A thousand signs indicate this sort of disintegration of the domestic hearth; in the first place, the singular facility of travelling, and especially the number of rich people who lead that hotel life which is so nearly unintelligible to Europeans, and especially to the French.

"We call Rochester our home, but we have spent ten winters here," said a much-admired young woman. As these ten winters spent in New York correspond with ten summers at Newport, as many autumns at Lenox, and probably several springs in Paris, it may be imagined how much of a place the real home has in the life of such a family. This singularly movable manner of life becomes more pronounced as one travels westward. The story goes that some cities in the far West are entirely composed of wooden huts, grouped around an immense hotel.

It is in the hotel, that caravansary furnished with the extravagant luxury which newly made rich people delight in, that is sketched the first rude outline of that social life which you will find in all its glory in the great centres on the Atlantic seaboard. The family live in a hotel with their private drawing-room, which they adorn with pictures and draperies, and often with their own furniture.

One must have sojourned in one of these hotels and dined with these people to be able to realize how entirely the members of these families live side by side rather than with one another. They eat, indeed, at the same table, but no one ever waits for another. The wife or the daughter is getting up from the table when the father or the husband comes in to breakfast, lunch, or dinner.   It is a very commonplace, but very expressive token of that which is the basis of American family life, — every one for himself and by himself.

The young girl has this principle written on her innermost heart.   Everything conspires to impress it upon her, and she has too fully accepted it not to know, when she marries, that this rule is to govern her own household as it did her father's before her. She is far enough from expecting, as our girls do, to find in the man she marries one with whom she will share every thought, a friend who will train her mind, her heart, her whole being. For that matter, one cannot say of her, as we say in French, that in marrying she becomes a woman (*femme*).   She was that before she married, in her ideas, her character, her freedom, her habits.   The difference is that on the one hand the possibilities of the future will be fewer for her, and on the other, that she will be of less account.   With us the passage from girlhood to wifehood is an event.   Here it is quite the other thing ; it is a resignation.

Why is the young married woman less courted than the young girl in the United States ?   This is the first question that forces itself upon the foreigner after a few weeks' residence.   Is it that Americans respect marriage more than we do ?   Is it that, their manners being simpler and purer, the young man's heart revolts at the bitter emotions, the cankered sadness, of unlawful love even in the moment of happiness ?   Is it because time is wanting for the deep-laid, far-reaching processes of seduction ? Is it the hatred of falsehood, so strikingly characteristic of the Anglo-Saxon ?   Certain it is that in society you almost never hear an allusion to such connections as abound in Paris, and even in London.   American conversation always avoids the line of demarcation between coquetry and intimacy, between the surroundings of a fault and the fault itself.

"Such things do not exist in the United States." So said
one and another of my women friends here, and when I de-
murred, adducing the conduct of such and such women with
such and such men, as appearing to me to be indisputable evidence, they would answer : —

"These women only want to be talked about, because that
is the way people do in Europe. Only, instead of going on
secretly, they make everything as public as possible, precisely
because there is nothing serious."

The foreigner can only reply by the favorite word of doubt
of the most sceptical and least American of people, "*Sara*."

Two reasons, very different in character, however, make it
evident *a priori*, so to speak, that the married woman must
be more carefully guarded here than in the Old World. The
first, which should neither be exaggerated nor underrated, is
the reserve capital of puritanism which, in the past fifty years,
has declined from year to year, almost from month to month,
but has not entirely disappeared. One of the most eloquent
magistrates of Massachusetts, Judge Oliver Wendell Holmes,
has said in one of those brief and impressive speeches in which
he excels : —

"Even though our mode of expressing our wonder, our
awful fear, our abiding trust in face of life and death and the
unfathomable world has changed, yet at this day, even now, we
New Englanders are still leavened with the puritan ferment."

This is true in New England, which still continues to be the
moral leaven of America. Now we must bear in mind that for
two hundred years the Mosaic law, which punished adultery
with death, was written in the codes of New England. The
first mitigation of this stern law was simply to brand with the
letter A the persons convicted of this crime. Such ferocities
of legislation may be done away with, but they leave behind
them, in public opinion, traces not to be lightly effaced. The
campaign of Dr. Parkhurst, last winter, against the prostitutes

of New York, and the raids carried out at his instance upon these dwellers in the "Tenderloin," — the name given to the disreputable part of Broadway, — attests that the harsh, reforming spirit of ancient times is not yet dead. It suffices to prove that the easy Parisian custom of accepting, while ridiculing, the triple family alliance, is not yet that of the United States.

The second reason is less historic and less ideal. It inheres in that extraordinary facility of divorce which rigid moralists groan over. If they are right from the point of view of the greatest good, they are surely wrong from the standpoint of the least evil. Here, again, the Americans have obeyed their instinct for seeing things as they are, and are guided by facts, which they admit without discussing them. They start out from this perfectly simple idea, which, however, our Latin minds have not yet admitted, that divorce offers no menace to happy unions, and that it is greatly to public and private interest that the more quickly and easily the unhappy ones are broken the better.

This ground taken, there was as it were a rivalry between the States as to which should do most to facilitate divorce. It is a standing joke, that the brakemen used to cry, at the stations in Chicago, "Twenty minutes' stop for divorce!" It is a truthful charge that in certain Western codes the rupture of the marriage tie is not much more complicated than the purchase of a piece of ground. In most of them a six months' residence enables you to take advantage of their divorce laws; in a few, North Dakota for example, ninety days are enough.

Intemperance, a sentence to prison for two years, voluntary absence for one year, adhesion to an adverse religious sect, on the part of either husband or wife, — these are a few of the grounds of divorce which I select at random from the various articles of these codes. Not a week passes but you may read in the papers that Mr. X—— or Mrs. Z—— has gone to such or such a State to pass the time necessary to establish a resi-

dence, after which they will be free to return to their former
condition and form new ties. These *villégiatures* for the purpose
of divorce are among the gayeties of the more advanced spirits.

"I used to know Mrs. V—— well," said a Washington girl to
me. "When we had a box in the New York Opera, we were
always meeting on the train. It was just the time when she
was going every week, for a few days, to the house in Dela-
ware that she had hired for her divorce!"

From this facility of freedom from ill-advised bonds, it
results that those unions which remain appear to be highly
irreproachable, as do also those which are made after the rupture of a first marriage. There is, indeed, no reason why an
ill-assorted union should continue. This is not ideal, to be
sure; but when you look carefully into it, you come at last to
the conclusion that this flexible legislation does not create
an unwholesome social system. Men and women become
accustomed frankly and openly to start over again when they
have made a mistake, and that is always better than the
organized falsehood so common with us, which equally degrades husband, wife, and lover. But perhaps all three of
them would find the solution offered by the United States
cruelly inconvenient in its so-called convenience.

With the door to liberty thus ajar, ready to fly open at a
push, how shall the young wife, so developed, so sufficient to
herself, so energetically trained both to will and to do, how
shall she submit herself to the moulding influences of the
companion whom marriage has given her? She was independent before; she is independent still. I mean, thinking
for herself, directing her life according to her own ideas, and
continuing her self-development with the same determination
that was hers before, without letting herself be moulded under
the imprint and according to the ideas of her partner. That
is the true epithet for marriage, — not indeed always, but very
often. It is a social partnership, to which the man brings for

capital his labor and his money, and the woman her beauty, her art of dress, and her social talents.

Then come the children, who, with us, are the vital question of a household, its final reunion, its salvation. It is not thus on Anglo-Saxon soil. The idolatry of father and mother, which are the key to the French family — its weaknesses, the equal division of the family inheritance, its warmth also and its unity of interest, — this idolatry, a little morbid but very tender, is replaced in English and American countries by a more virile and colder vigilance, which does not stir the inner fibres of the heart, or at least which stirs them with a different thrill. My French friends of this part of the world are very severe on this point. They tell me that the hope of motherhood is carefully concealed as long as possible by the young wife, who blushes for it as for some animal function almost humiliating and to be concealed. They repeat as very characteristic the remark of an old lady who, when told that one of her young friends had just given birth to twins, exclaimed : —

" How vulgar ! "

They tell me of this and that society woman who has spent ten months on a stretch in Europe, without distressing herself about her children, left to the care of relatives or friends. I do not know whether such desertions are the exception or the rule, and in any case I put little faith in anecdotes. In history they are all false, in literature all calumnious, and where social life is in question they are almost all exaggerated, without those shades of individuality which explain the anomalous or those circumstances which justify it. But, on the other hand, I believe in statistics, and those of divorce appear to me more conclusive. Fathers and mothers who are not brought together by their children cannot love them much, and, on the other hand, if the direct education of the child by its father and mother were more frequent, the independence of the young man and the young girl would not be what it is.

As the American marriage appears to be above all a partnership, so the American family appears to be more than anything
else an association, — a sort of social camp, the ties of which
are more or less strong according to individual sympathies,
such as might exist between people not of the same blood.   I
am certain, not from anecdotes but from experience, that the
friendship of brother and brother, or sister and sister, is entirely
elective.   So it is with the relations between father and son,
mother and daughter.   A young Frenchman much in love with
a New York girl said to me in one of those moments when
the coldness of the woman you love drives you to be cruelly
frank : —

"She has so little heart that she went to the theatre five
weeks after her mother's death, and no one resented it."

I knew that he was telling the truth.   But what did it prove ?
What do the inequalities permitted by the laws of inheritance
prove?   Nothing if not that our natural characteristics, instincts, sensibilities, are not the same as those of the people of
this country.   They have much less power of self-giving, much
more of personal reaction ; and especially a much stronger will.
Their will rules their hearts as well as their minds.   This seems
to us less tender.   But are we good judges?

We must continually keep in mind this general want of
association in family life if we would in any degree understand
the sort of soul celibacy, if we may use the term, which the
American woman keeps all through her married life.   No
more in this second period of her life than in the first, does
love bear that preponderating part which seems to us Frenchmen an essential characteristic of the lot of woman.   When
a Parisian woman of forty reviews her life, the story that memory tells her is the story of her emotions.   To an American
woman of the same age, it is more often the story of her
actions, of what she calls, by a word I have before cited, her

experiences. She gained, between the ages of eighteen and twenty-five, a conception of her own self, which was imposed upon her neither by her traditions — she has none — nor by the instructions of her parents — they never gave her any — nor even by her own nature; for it is characteristic of these easily " adaptable " minds that their first instincts are chaotic and undetermined. They are like a blank check, which the will undertakes to fill out. But, whatever the will writes upon it is written in letters that will never be effaced. Action, action, always action, — this is the remorseless, but unchanging, devise of such a woman. Whether she seeks for a place in society, or is ambitious for artistic culture, or addicts herself to sport, or organizes " classes," as they say, for reading Browning, Emerson, or Shakespeare with her friends, whether she travels to Europe, India, or Japan, or remains at home to have some young girl among her friends " pour " tea for her, be sure that she will be always and incessantly active, indefatigably active, either in the lines of " refinement " or of " excitement."

With what impressiveness these women utter both these words, which we must not weary of returning to; for they, perhaps, sum up the entire American soul. They are bandied about in conversation like two formulæ, in which are revealed the persistence of this creature, which, born of a stern race, and feeling herself fine, wills to become finer and ever finer; who, reared amid democratic surroundings, wills to become distinguished and ever more distinguished; who, daughter of a land of enterprise, loves to excite continually in herself the sensation of overstrained nerves.

When you see ten, fifteen, thirty, fifty like this, the character of eccentricity which you first found in them by comparison with the women of Europe, disappears. A new type of feminine seduction is revealed to you, less affecting than irritating, enigmatic and slightly ambiguous by its indefinable blending of supple grace and virile firmness, by the alliance of culture and vigor, by the most thrilling nervous sensitiveness and the sturdiest health. The true place of such a creature in this society appears to you also, and the profound reason why these men, themselves all action, leave these women free thus to act with total independence. If it is permitted to apply an old legal term to creatures so subtle, so delicate, these women are the delegates to luxury in this utilitarian civilization. Their mission is to bring into it that which the American has not time to create and which he desires to have : The flower of elegance, something of beauty, and, in a word, of aristocracy. They are the nobility in this land of business, a nobility developed by the very development of business, since the money which is made in the offices comes at last to them, and manipulated by their fingers is transfigured, blossoming into precious decorations, made intellectual in plays of fancy,—in fact, *unutilized*.

A great artist, foremost of this epoch by the ardor of his efforts, the conscientiousness of his study, and the sincerity of his vision, John Sargent, has shown what I have tried to express, in a portrait which I saw in an exhibition, — that of a woman whose name I do not know. It is a portrait such as the fifteenth-century masters painted, who, back of the individual found the real, and back of the model a whole social order. The canvas might be called "The American Idol," so representative is it.

The woman is standing, her feet side by side, her knees close together, in an almost hieratic pose. Her body, rendered supple by exercise, is sheathed — you might say moulded — in a tight-fitting black dress. Rubies, like drops of blood, sparkle on her shoes. Her slender waist is encircled by a girdle of enormous pearls, and from this dress, which makes an intensely dark background for the stony brilliance of the jewels, the arms and shoulders shine out with another brilliance, that of a flower-like flesh,—fine, white flesh, through which flows blood perpetually invigorated by the air of the country and the ocean. The head, intellectual and daring, with a countenance as of one who has understood everything, has, for a sort of aureole, the vaguely gilded design of one of those Renascence stuffs which the Venetians call *sopra-risso*. The rounded arms, in which the muscles can hardly be seen, are joined by the clasped hands,— firm hands, the thumb almost too long, which might guide four horses with the precision of an English coachman.   It is the picture of an energy at once delicate and invincible, momentarily in repose, and all the Byzantine Madonna is in that face, with its wide-open eyes.

Yes, this woman is an idol, for whose service man labors, which he has decked with the jewels of a queen, behind each one of whose whims lie days and days spent in the ardent battle of Wall Street. Frenzy of speculations in land, cities undertaken and built by sheer force of millions, trains launched at full speed over bridges built on a Babel like sweep of arch, the creaking of cable cars, the quivering of electric cars, sliding along their wires with a crackle and a spark, the dizzy ascent of elevators, in buildings twenty stories high, immense wheat-fields of the West, its ranches, mines, colossal slaughter-houses,— all the formidable traffic of this country of effort and struggle, all its labor,— these are what have made possible this woman, this living orchid, unexpected masterpiece of this civilization.

Did not the very painter consecrate to her his intense toil? To be capable of such a picture, he must have absorbed some of the ardor of the Spanish masters, caught the subtlety of the great Italians, understood and practised the curiosities of impressionism, dreamed before the pictures in basilicas like Ravenna, and read and thought. Ah, how much of culture, of reflection, before one could fathom the secret depths of one's own race.   He has expressed one of the most essential characteristics of the race, — the deification of woman, considered not as a Beatrice as in Florence, nor as a courtesan as at Milan, but as a supreme glory of the national spirit. This woman can do without being loved. She has no need of being loved. What she symbolizes is neither sensuality nor tenderness. She is like a living object of art, the last fine work of human skill, attesting that the Yankee, but yesterday despairing, vanquished by the Old World, has been able to draw from this savage world upon which fate has cast him a wholly new civilization, incarnated in this woman, her luxury, and her pride. Everything is illuminated by this civilization, at the gaze of these fathomless eyes, in the expression of which the painter has succeeded in putting all the idealism of this country which has no ideal; all that which, perhaps, will one day be its destruction, but up to the present time is still its greatness, — a faith in the human Will, absolute, unique, systematic, and indomitable.

V

BUSINESS MEN AND BUSINESS SCENES

Back of the social and feminine world, as a support to its independence and individuality, in America, as everywhere else, stands man. But one feature distinguishes this civilization; the men of this country belong to a single category. In the United States, where there is no nobility, no squire-archy, almost no military, no diplomatic corps, and the smallest possible administrative body, society, in both senses of the word, belongs to the business man, an immense class, which includes the hotel manager and the politician, the former sinking his eight hundred thousand dollars in the furnishing of his hotel, the latter managing his own election, and adopting or rejecting laws with the methods of a contractor. At the present time, the business man has even drawn the rural population under his control, and forced them into the whirlwind of his activity, far apart as the two classes are in all other countries. The extent of the territory, and the arrangements for railway transportation of cattle and grain in immense quantities, have brought them under the domain of companies of all sorts who, for their part, have "undertaken" to feed all America.

One of the most significant proofs of this particular fact is the daily disappearance of the New England farmer, that delicious local personage, whose simple and genuine manners has furnished an inexhaustible object for the studies of so many romance writers, male and female. Incapable of struggling, isolated and single-handed, against the strong competition of the West, these farmers emigrate toward the prairie, and you continually find advertisements in the newspapers, offering for sale their modest homesteads, with descriptions like the following, which I transcribe without changing a word.

"S——, Massachusetts. For sale. A farm of sixty acres: mowing, eight acres; pasture-land, eighteen; forest, thirty to forty; tillable ground, twelve. Almost all the hay crop can be cut by machine. One-story house, five rooms, somewhat out of repair. Small barn, in good condition. Good well, near the house, and running stream back of the barn. Twenty apple trees, twelve fruit trees of different varieties. Railway station at L——, six miles distant; postoffice at S——, one mile. Price, four hundred dollars; one hundred cash, the balance at four per cent interest."

What a drama of rustic ruin may be descried back of these modest figures! and behind the details of this humble inventory what a laborious and almost idyllic existence! I have met analogous conditions far away in the South, among the survivors of those colonies of non-slaveholding whites, whom the blacks contemptuously call "crackers." I have before my eyes as I write the picture of a wooden house in the depths of the pine forests of Georgia. It is inhabited by an old man of seventy, with his daughter, his sons, and his sons' children; boys with legs as muscular as their arms, running about barefooted among the horses.

These people had the proud courtesy of families who have never known any superior, having had neither vanities nor needs. The old man remembered having heard that his great grandfather came from France — from Brittany, he thought. The Christian name of René, handed down among them, attested to this far-away origin. Their light blue eyes, Celtic eyes, shone with the light of honor. On their table was nothing which was not the product of the soil and of their own labor.

" We have everything except coffee and tobacco," they said ;

"even wines." And they produced, with the pride of a Robinson receiving the Spanish captain, a pale red liquid, — grape juice, sweetened with cane sugar, and poured, in the absence of bottles, into a tin sauce-pan. Cows, goats, pigs, pastured freely around the house. The guns, hung over the door, had the lustre of weapons often used.

It seemed as if I saw before me the primitive pioneer of the sort that abounded a hundred years ago. It is with them as with the bisons, the last head of which is jealously guarded in the Yellowstone Park. He has disappeared, and is being replaced by the agricultural laborer, who is nothing but an instrument in the hands of business men, whom, from one end of this vast country to the other, you will find busily occupied in changing and developing its character. In the upper station they give it a peculiar elegance by the luxury of their palaces and villas, their wives and daughters. In the lower, they feed the nation by enrolling men in their service.

"I assert," said one of them the other day — Mr. Chauncey Depew, an orator of the highest ability, who would perhaps be president, if the democracy of America did not set itself against this plutocratic system — "I assert that a railway president renders an enormous service to the community. He has twenty or thirty thousand men under him, representing with their families from one to two hundred thousand souls ; and their welfare, not physical only, but mental, social, and moral, depends almost absolutely upon him."

A packing business like that of Armour in Chicago, for example, furnishes daily employment to eleven thousand employees. The generalissimo of this industrial army is often a man who at twenty years old was living in a "lean-to," that is, a hut of planks leaning up against a rock or a wall. He is not forty years old and he is "worth" five millions of dollars. In a few years more he will be worth ten, fifteen, and so on, till he dies of heart disease in his yacht cabin, or his private car,

father-in-law of a lord or grandfather of young Italian princes ;
but under his nickname of Jim, Tom, or Billy, familiarly regretted or cursed by his workmen according as he has made
himself loved or hated by them.

This is a truly new type of personage, impossible to find anywhere else, and whom one must picture to oneself from small
to great, — for the series is infinite, — in order really to understand what there is most original in this strange people. In
the vigorous natures of these business men there is a vein of
technical genius which no observer, however penetrating or
imaginative, would hardly have expected.

They tell me that another portrait painter — for the Americans have an extravagant passion for portraits and busts —
was commissioned last year to paint one of the most celebrated
of Wall Street speculators. Despairing of ever obtaining a sat-
isfactory sitting, so full of business were his model's hours, the
painter finally took his material to the business office of this
gentleman, whom he painted in his characteristic attitude, with
the paper strip of the "ticker" in his hand, upon which second
by second were automatically inscribed the fluctuations in the
value of stocks. It was an accurate symbol of what we men
of art, or of abstract thought, succeed in getting when we study
one of these builders of enormous fortunes. We see a gesture,
an absorbed countenance, the tension of a prodigious energy, and
that is all. What the manipulator of money feels while looking
at his figures, the particular action of a mind of this quality in
travail of combinations, why one triumphs and another comes
to shipwreck, are all problems which so far remain insoluble.

I have just mentioned the name of Mr. Chauncey Depew.
In a collection of his speeches, published this very year, I
find a singular expression on the "unequalled genius" of the
first Vanderbilt, the celebrated Commodore. The few instances
which the orator brings to his support of his assertion manifest,
indeed, such a superiority that no one thinks of being surprised

I

at the epithet.   We admit with the speaker, that an intellectual
force has been at work there, as remarkable as that which wins
battles, governs Parliaments, makes or unmakes treaties.   But
he understands this force, because he has worked beside it,
under it, with it.   To us who have not done so, who cannot
have that practical vision, his professional talent remains undefinable and unattainable.

A single resource is left us : to gaze with all our powers,
through the ideas awakened by the sight, upon the work produced by these business men, the scene amid which their
activities are carried on, the plans which they executed ; and
venture a few conjectures upon the sort of human nature which
this work, this setting, these plans, must take for granted.   Many
a time in the course of this journey I have tried this experiment, particularly in a too short Western trip, or at least to
what was lately the West, Chicago, St. Paul, Minneapolis ; for
every five years the frontier of civilization draws farther westward, and the time is approaching when the people of Colorado
will be offended at not being considered Eastern people !   What
does it all matter — East, West?   These are but words.   The
prodigious reality is the growth of the three cities whose names
I have just written, the added ages of which do not amoun'
to more than a century and a half !   When you reflect that
behind this inordinate growth, this almost instantaneous passage from a desert to a city of two hundred thousand, five hur-
dred thousand, eight hundred thousand inhabitants, one always
comes face to face with the energy of the business man, the
prejudices of the man of letters cease to influence you.   I
hope that there will not be too many traces of it in these
sketches taken from my journal, and the two or three psycho
logical theories which they comment upon.

*Chicago in an autumn morning from the tower of the
Auditorium.* — It is two hundred and seventy feet high, and

it crowns and dominates a chaotic cyclopean structure which connects a colossal hotel with a colossal theatre. One's first visit on arriving should be here, in order to get the strongest impression of the enormous city, lying black on the shore of its blue lake.

Last night, when the conductor called out the name of the station at which I was to leave the train, a frightful storm, such as one experiences nowhere but in America, was deluging the whole country with cataracts of water, and between the station and the hotel I could see nothing but the outlines of gigantic buildings hanging, as it were, from a dark sky streaked with lightning, and between them small wooden houses, so frail that it seemed as if the furious wind must scatter their ruins to the four quarters of the tempest-tossed city.

This morning the sky is clear, with a soft, warm clearness, washed clean by the rain. It brings out all the more strikingly the dark coloring of the city, as it is reflected back from the deeper azure of Lake Michigan, ploughed with steamboats like a sea. Far as the eye can reach Chicago stretches away, its flat roofs and its smoke — innumerable columns of whitey-gray smoke. They rise straight upward, then stoop to heap themselves into vapory capitals, and at last meet together in a dome above the endless avenues.

It needs but a few minutes for the eyes to become accustomed to the strange scene. Then you discern differences of height among these levels. Those of only six or seven stories seem to be the merest cottages, those of two stories are not to be distinguished from the pavement, while the "buildings" of fourteen, fifteen, twenty stories, uprise like the islands of the Cyclades as seen from the mountains of Negroponte.

A mighty murmur uprises from below like that of no other city. There is an incessant tinkle of locomotive bells, that seem to be sounding in advance the knell of those they are about to crush. They are everywhere, crossing the streets, following the lake shore, passing over the river which rolls its leaden waters under soot-colored bridges, meeting and crossing each other's tracks, pursuing and overtaking one another. Now you distinguish an elevated road, and there, beside the railways on the level of the street, you see other trains on the avenues, three or four cars long, but without locomotive. It is the cable system. And there are steamers lowering their yards and coming to anchor in the harbor.

Yes, the scene is strange even to unreality, when one reminds oneself that this Babel of industry grew out of a tiny frontier post, — Fort Dearborn. The Indians surprised it and massacred the garrison about 1812. I am not very far beyond my youth, and yet how many men have I known that were alive then, and how near that date is! In 1871, that is to say, later than the Franco-Prussian War, there was fire writhing around this very place where I am standing this bright morning. The irresistible devouring force of one of the most terrific conflagrations mentioned in history transformed this entire plain into a burning mass which still smoked after many days had passed.

"Where this tower now stands," said my Chicago guide, concluding the epos of that awful event, "you might have stood in a bed of ashes, with not a single house between the lake on your right hand and the river on your left."

I looked from one to the other, the river and the lake, as I heard these words. That month of October, 1871, was more than near to me; it seemed as if I could touch it, as if I were still in it. I could tell the names of the books that I was reading then, the articles that I was writing. I could remember how I spent almost every day. I realized with an almost physical accuracy the length of the years since that date, — twenty-two. How few hours that makes, after all! and I leaned again over the balustrade of the tower, gazing down upon this prodigy, stunned with the thought of what men have done!

Men! The word is hardly correct applied to this perplexing city. When you study it more in detail, its aspect reveals so little of the personal will, so little caprice and individuality, in its streets and buildings, that it seems like the work of some impersonal power, irresistible, unconscious, like a force of nature, in whose service man was merely a passive instrument.

This power is nothing else than that business fever which here throbs at will, with an unbridled violence like that of an uncontrollable element. It rushes along these streets, as once before the devouring flame of fire; it quivers; it makes itself visible with an intensity which lends something tragical to this city, and makes it seem like a poem to me.

When, from this overhanging tower, you have gazed down upon this immense volcano of industry and commerce, you go down to look more closely into the details of this exuberant life, this exhaustless stream of activity. You walk along the sidewalks of streets which bear marks of haste, — here flag-stones, there asphalt, yonder a mere line of planks crossing a miry swamp. This want of continuity in road material is repeated in the buildings. At one moment you have nothing around you but "buildings." They scale the very heavens with their eighteen and twenty stories. The architect who built them, or, rather, made them by machinery, gave up all thought of colonnades, mouldings, classical decorations. He ruthlessly accepted the speculator's inspired conditions, — to multiply as much as possible the value of the bit of earth at the base by multiplying the superimposed "offices."

One might think that such a problem would interest no one but an engineer. Nothing of the kind! The simple power of necessity is to a certain degree a principle of beauty; and these structures so plainly manifest this necessity that you feel a strange emotion in contemplating them. It is the first draught of

a new sort of art,—an art of democracy made by the masses
and for the masses, an art of science, where the invariability of
natural laws gives to the most unbridled daring the calmness
of geometrical figures. The portals of the basements, usually
arched as if crushed beneath the weight of the mountain which
they support, look like dens of a primitive race, continually
receiving and pouring forth a stream of people. You lift your
eyes, and you feel that up there behind the perpendicular wall,
with its innumerable windows, is a multitude coming and going,
— crowding the offices that perforate these cliffs of brick and
iron, dizzied with the speed of the elevators. You divine, you
feel the hot breath of speculation quivering behind these windows. This it is which has fecundated these thousands of
square feet of earth, in order that from them may spring up
this appalling growth of business palaces, that hide the sun
from you and almost shut out the light of day.

Close beside the preposterous, Babel-like building extends a
shapeless bit of ground, undefined, bristling, green with a scanty
turf, on which a lean cow is feeding. Then follows a succession of little wooden houses, hardly large enough for a single
family. Next comes a Gothic church, transformed into a shop,
with a sign in great metal characters. Then comes the red and
pretentious ruin of some other building burned the other week.
Vacant lots, shanties, churches, ruins,— speculation will sweep
over it all to-morrow, this evening perhaps, and other "buildings"
will spring up. But time is needed, and these people have
none. These two years past, instead of completing their half-
finished city, they have been amusing themselves in building
another over yonder, under pretext of their exhibition. It is
entirely white, a dream city, with domes like those of Ravenna,
colonnades like those at Rome, lagoons like Venice, a fair of the
world like Paris.

They have succeeded, and now the most composite, the
most cosmopolitan of human mixtures fill these suburban and

elevated railways, these cable cars, coaches, carriages, which over-flow upon these unfinished sidewalks before these wildly dissim-ilar houses. And as at Chicago, it seems that everything and everybody must be larger, more developed, stronger, so from block to block in the middle of these streets are posted, to maintain order, enormous mounted policemen, tall as Pome-ranian grenadiers ; gigantic human barriers against which break the seething eddies of this multitude. Most of them are Ger-mans ; their red faces are unformed as if hewn out with a hatchet, as if hastily blocked out, and their bullock-like necks and shoulders make a striking comment on divers facts of the daily papers, which continually tell of some " hands up " performed in the taverns, the gambling-houses, or simply in a carriage, or on the tramway.

"Hands up!" It is the classic command of the Western robber, as he enters, revolver in hand, his first business to make sure that you have not yours. How many times has it been uttered in the suburbs of this city, the meeting-place of the adventurers of the two worlds? How many times will it yet be uttered? But the spirit of adventure is also the spirit of enterprise, and if the size of the policemen of this surpris-ing city attests the frequency of surprises attempted by these ruffians, it completes its complex physiognomy; different, surely, from every other since the foundation of the world, a mosaic of extreme civilization and almost barbarism, a savage existence only part discerned through the abruptness of this industrial creation. In short, it is Chicago, a mira-cle that would confound the dead of seventy years ago, if they were to return to earth and find themselves in this city, now the ninth in the world as to population, which when they were alive had not a single house.

One of the enormous branches of traffic of this city is in meat. The Chicago folk are a little ashamed of it. In earlier days they would talk to you of their packing-houses, with that artless pride which is one of the charms of great parvenus. It is the simplicity natural to an elemental strength, which knows itself strong and loves to exercise itself frankly. They are tired now of hearing their detractors call them the inhabitants of Porkopolis. They find it a grievance that their city is always "identified," as they say here, with that brutal butchery, when it has among its publishing houses one of the vastest marts of books in the world, when its newspapers never let any incident of literature or art pass without investigating it, when it has founded a university at a cost of seven millions of dollars, when it has just gathered together representatives of all forms of belief, at its remarkable Parliament of Religions,— a phenomenon unique in the history of human idealism! Chicago aspires to be something more than the distributor of food, although last year a single one of its firms cut up and distributed one million seven hundred and fifty thousand hogs, a million and twenty-five thousand beeves, and six hundred and twenty-five thousand sheep. Its enemies seek to crush it under figures like these, omitting to remember that the Chicago of the abattoirs is also the Chicago of the "White City," the Chicago of a museum which is already incomparable, the Chicago which gave Lincoln to the United States.

On the other hand, these abattoirs furnish material most precious to the foreigner who desires to understand the spirit in which the Americans undertake their great enterprises. A slaughter-house capable of shipping in twelve months, to the four parts of this immense continent, three millions five hundred thousand dressed cattle is worth the trouble of investigating. Everywhere else the technical details are very difficult to grasp. They are less so here, the directors of these colossal manufactories of roast beef and hams having discovered that the best possible advertisement is to admit the public to witness their processes of working. They have made a visit to their establishments, if not attractive,— physical repulsion is too strong for that,— at least convenient and thorough. On condition of having your nerves wrung once for all, these are among the places where you shall best see how American ingenuity solves the problems of a prodigiously complicated organization.

I therefore did like other unprejudiced tourists, and visited the "stock yards" and the most celebrated among the "packing-houses," as they are called,— cutting-up houses, rather,— which is here in operation; the one, indeed, the statistics of whose operations I have but now quoted. This walk through that house of blood will always remain to me one of the most singular memories of my journey. I think, however, that I owe to it a better discernment of the characteristic features of an American business concern. If this is so, I shall have no reason to regret the painful experience.

To reach the "Union Stock Yards," the carriage crosses an immense section of the city, even more incoherent than those which border on the elegant Michigan Avenue. It stops before the railways, to permit the passage of trains running at full speed. It crosses bridges, which immediately after uprear themselves to permit the passage of boats. It passes by hotels which are palaces, and laborers' houses which are hovels. It skirts large plots of ground, where market-gardeners are cultivating cabbages amongst heaps of refuse, and others which bear nothing but advertisements. How shall I deny myself the pleasure of copying this one, among a hundred others: —

"Louis XIV. was crowned King of France at the age of five years (1643). X——'s pepsin had been crowned with success as a remedy for indigestion before it had been publicly known a single year."

The advertising fields give place to more houses, more railways, under a sky black with clouds, or smoke,— one hardly knows which,— and on both sides of the road begin to appear fenced enclosures, where cattle are penned by the hundred. There are narrow lanes between the fence, with men on horseback riding up and down. These are the buyers, discussing prices with the "cowboys" of the West.

You have read stories of the "ranches." This adventurous prairie life has taken hold upon your imagination. Here you behold its heroes, in threadbare overcoats, slouch hats, and the inevitable collar and cuffs of the American. But for their boots, and their dexterity in guiding their horses by the knees, you would take them for clerks. They are a proof, among many others, of the instinctive disdain of this realistic people for the picturesque in costume. That impression which I had in the park in New York, almost the first day, as of an immense store of ready-made clothes hurrying hither and thither, has never left me. And yet, nothing can be less "common," in the bad sense of the word, than Americans in general, and these Western cowboys in particular. Their bodies are too nervous, too lithe, under their cheap clothes. Their countenances, especially, are too intent and too sharply outlined, too decided and too stern.

The carriage stops before a building which, in its massiveness and want of character, is like all other manufactories. My companions and I enter a court, a sort of alley, crowded with packing-boxes, carts, and people. A miniature railway passes along it, carrying packing-boxes to a waiting train, entirely composed of refrigerator cars, such as I saw so many of as I came to Chicago. Laborers were unloading these packing-boxes; others were coming and going, evidently intent upon their respective duties. There was no sign of administrative order, as we conceive it, in this establishment, which was yet so well ordered. But already one of the engineers had led us up a staircase, and we enter an immense hall, reeking with heavy moisture saturated with a strong acrid odor, which seems to seize you by the throat. We are in the department where the hogs are cut up. There are hundreds of men hard at work, whom we have not time so much as to look at. Our guide warns us to stand aside, and before us glides a file of porkers, disembowelled and hung by their hind feet from a rod, along which they slip toward a vaulted opening, where innumerable other such files await them. The rosy flesh, still ruddy with the life that but now animated them, gleams under the electric light that illuminates those depths. We go on, avoiding these strange encounters as best we may, and reach at last, with feet smeared in a sort of bloody mud, a platform whence we can see the initial act of all this labor, which now seems so confused, but which we shall shortly find so simple and easy to understand. There are the pigs, in a sort of pit, alive, grunting and screaming, as if they had a vision of the approach of the horrible machine, from which they can no more escape than a doomed man whose head lies on the guillotine. It is a sort of movable hook, which, being lowered by a man, seizes one of the creatures by the cord which ties its hind legs together. The animal gives a screech, as he hangs, head downward, with quivering snout and a spasmodic agitation of his short fore legs. But already the hook has slid along the iron bar, carrying the hapless victim to a neighboring recess where, as it slips by, a man armed with a long knife cuts its throat, with a slash so well aimed and effective that there is no need to repeat it. The creature utters a more terrific screech, a stream of blood spurts out, jet black and as thick as your arm. The snout quivers more pitifully, the short legs are agitated more frantically, but the death struggle only quickens the motion of the hook, which glides on to a third attendant.

The latter, with a quick movement, cuts down the animal.

The hook slides back, and the carcass falls into a sort of canal tank filled with boiling water, in which an automatic rake works with a quick vibratory motion. In a few seconds it has caught the creature, turned it over and over, caught it again, and thrown the scalded carcass to another machine, which in a few more seconds has shaved it from head to tail. In another second, another hook has descended, and another bar carries that which, four minutes ago, was a living, suffering creature, toward that arched opening where, on coming in, I had seen so many similar relics. It is already the turn of another to be killed, shaved, and finished off. The operation is of such lightning quickness that you have no time to realize its atrocity. You have no time to pity the poor things, no time to marvel at the cheerfulness with which the butcher — a red-headed giant, with shoulders broad enough to carry an ox — goes on with his horrible work.

And yet, even in its lower forms, life is something so mysterious, the death and sufferings, even of a creature of the humblest order, are something so tragic when, instead of carelessly picturing them you look them thus full in the face, that all spectators, and they are many, cease to laugh and joke. For my part, before this coarse slaughter-house scene I felt myself seized with an unreasoning sadness, very short but very intense, as if, for a few minutes, the spirit of Thomas Graindorge had passed before me, — the philosophic dealer in salt pork and oil, so dear to my master, Taine. It suddenly seemed as if I saw before me existence itself, and all the work of nature, incarnated in a pitiable symbol. All that I had often thought of death was as if concrete before my eyes, in the irresistible clutch of that hook lifting those creatures, as the overpowering force of destruction which is in the world will one day seize us all, — sages, heroes, artists, as well as these poor unconscious brutes. I saw them rushing, writhing, moaning, their death agonies following fast on one another, as ours follow one another, only a little more rapidly,—how little more, considering how fast 'time flies, and how small a part remains for all that must be done! And the way that we looked in at this ghastly scene, my companions and I, was in nothing different from the way with which others will one day look on at our entrance into the great darkness, as on a picture, a something exterior, whose reality, after all, concerns only the being who undergoes it!

We went into the department reserved for the cattle. Here the death struggle is different. No outcry, almost no blood; no terrified expectation on the creature's part. And the scene is all the more tragic. The animals are penned by twos, in stalls like those of a stable, though without the manger. You see them trying, with their intelligence and their gentleness, to accommodate themselves to the narrow space. They gazed with their large, soft eyes — upon whom? The butcher, standing in a passageway a little above them. This man holds in his hand a slender bludgeon of steel. He is waiting until the ox is in the right position. You see him gently, caressingly, guiding the animal with the tip of his bludgeon. Suddenly he uplifts it. It falls upon the creature's forehead, and it sinks down in a lifeless heap.

In an instant a hook has lifted it up, blood pouring from the mouth and nostrils, its large glassy eyes overshadowed with a growing darkness, and within another minute another man has stripped the skin from the breast, letting it hang down like an apron, has cut open the carcass, and sent it by the expeditious method of the sliding bar, to take its place in the refrigerating-room. Thousands of them await here the time for being carried and hung up in other rooms, also of ice, but on wheels, ready to be despatched. I see the closing of the last car of a train on the point of departure. The locomotive whistles and puffs; the bell rings. On what table of New York or Boston, Philadelphia or Savannah, will at last appear this meat, fattened on the prairie pasture-lands of some district in some Western State, and here prepared in such a way that the butcher will have merely to cut it into pieces? It will arrive as fresh, as intact, as if there had not been thousands and thousands of miles between the birth, death, and dismemberment of the enigmatical and peaceable creature.

If there was nothing but killing to be seen in this manufacture of food, it would hardly be worth while to go through so many bloody scenes for the sake of verifying, in one of its lower exemplifications, what the philosopher Huxley somewhere magnificently calls "the gladiatorial theory of existence," the severe law that murder is necessary to life. But this is only a first impression, to experience before passing to a second, that of the rapidity and ingenuity of the cutting-up and packing of this prodigious quantity of perishable meat. I don't know who it was who sportively said that a pig that went to the abattoir at Chicago came out fifteen minutes later in the form of ham, sausages, large and small, hair oil, and binding for a Bible. It is a witty exaggeration, yet hardly overdone, of the rapid and minute labor which we had just seen bestowed upon the beasts killed before our eyes; and the subdividing of this work, its precision, simplicity, quick succession, succeeding in making us forget the necessary but intolerable brutality of the scenes we had been witnessing.

An immense hall is furnished with a succession of counters placed without much order, where each member of the animal is cut apart and utilized without the loss of a bone or a tendon. Here, with a quick, automatic blow, which never misses, a man cuts off first the hams, then the feet, as fast as he can throw them into caldrons, which boil and smoke them before your eyes. Farther along, a hatchet, moved by machinery, is at work making sausage-meat, which tubes of all sizes will pour forth in rolls ready for the skins, that are all washed and prepared. The word "garlic," which I see written on a box in German, "Knoblauch," and the accompanying inscription, transports me to the time of the Franco-Prussian War, when each Prussian soldier carried in his sack just such provisions, which had come from this very place. These products of Chicagoan industry will be sent far enough beyond New York!

Elsewhere the head and jowl are cleaned, trimmed, and dressed, to figure in their natural form in the show window of some American or European market. Elsewhere, again, enormous receptacles are being filled with suet which boils and bubbles, and having been cunningly mixed with a certain proportion of cream will be transformed into margarine, refined in an automatic beating machine of which we admired the artful simplicity.

"A workingman invented that," said our guide. "For that matter," he added, "almost all the machines that are used here were either made or improved by the workmen."

These words shed light for us upon all this vast workshop. We understood what these men require of a machine that for them prolongs, multiplies, perfects the acts of men. Once again we felt how much they have become refined in their processes of work, how they excel in combining with their personal effort the complication of machinery, and also how the least among them has a power of initiative, of direct vision and adjustment.

Seated again in our carriage, and rolling away over the irregular wooden pavement made of round sections of trees embedded at pleasure in the mud, we reflected upon what we had just seen. We tried to discern its intellectual significance, if we may use this word in reference to such an enterprise. And why not? We are all agreed that the first characteristic of this enterprise is the amplitude, or rather the stupendousness, of its conception. For an establishment like this to have, in a few years, brought up the budget of its employees to five million five hundred thousand dollars, that is, to more than twenty-seven millions of francs, its founders must have clearly perceived the possibilities of an enormous extension of business, and have no less clearly perceived, defined, and determined its practical features.

A colossal effort of imagination on the one hand, and, on the other, at the service of the imagination, a clear and carefully estimated understanding of the encompassing reality, — these are the two features everywhere stamped upon the unparalleled establishment which we have just visited. One of us pointed out another fact, — that the principal practical feature is the railway, reminding us that the locomotive has always been an implement of general utility in American hands. By it they revolutionized military art and created a full-panoplied modern warfare, such as the Germans were later to practise at our expense. In the great national war of 1860, they first showed what advantage could be taken of this new means of mobilization. The length of the trains they sent out during that period has passed into legend. In fact, the establishment which we have been discussing is only one particular case of that universal use of the railway, which is itself only a particular illustration of that essentially American turn of mind, — the constant use of new methods.

The entire absence of routine, the daily habit of letting the fact determine the action, of following it fearlessly to the end, — these characteristics grow out of the other, and this acute consciousness of the fact also explains that sort of superficial incoherence in the distribution of labor which we have already noticed. Extreme clearness, perspicuity of administrative order, always spring from an *a priori* theory. All societies and all enterprises in which realism, rather than system, rules are constructed by juxtaposition, by series of facts accepted as they arise. But how should the people here have leisure to concern themselves with those small, fine points of administrative order with which our Latin peoples are so much in love? Competi-

tion is too strong, too ferocious, almost. There is all of warfare and its breathless audacity back of the enterprises of this
country, even of those most firmly established, like this one.

Our guide, who listens to our philosophizing without seeming
much to disapprove, tells us that this very year, in order to
elude a coalition of speculators in grain, which he explains to
us, the head of the house which we have just visited was forced
to erect in nineteen days, for the housing of his own wheat, a
building three hundred feet square by a hundred high !

"Yes, in nineteen days, working night and day," he said,
smiling ; " but we Americans like ' hard work.' "

With this almost untranslatable word, — to one who has not
heard it uttered here, — our visit ends. It sums it up and
completes it with a terseness worthy of this people of much
action and few phrases !

I visited in detail the building of one of the principal Chicago
newspapers, just when they were printing the Sunday edition,
— a trifling affair of twenty-four pages. I had seen in New
York also on a Saturday evening, the making up of such a
number, — that of the *Herald*. It had forty pages, and pictures ! There was a matter of a hundred and fifty thousand
copies to be sent out by the early morning trains. When the
circulation reaches such figures as these, a newspaper is not
merely a machine for moulding public opinion, of a power
incalculable in a democratic country, it is also an inconceivably
complicated business to carry on. Precisely because this business differs radically from that which the day before yesterday
I was endeavoring to understand, I shall be the better able to
judge whether the general features which I there discovered
are to be found in all American enterprises. I can judge of
that more easily here than in New York, the number of copies
of the paper being somewhat less than in New York, and the
process of shipping more convenient to follow.

K

It needed not five hundred steps in these offices to make evident to me the simultaneous play of those two mental tendencies which appeared to me so characteristic the other day, — the enormous range of invention, and the constant, minute, ever-watchful adoption of new means. The American journalist does not propose to himself to reach this or that reader, but all readers. He does not propose to publish articles of this or that kind, but of all kinds. His purpose is to make his newspaper an accurate mould of all that actually is, a sort of relief map, which shall be an epitome, not of the day, but of the hour, the minute, so all-embracing and complete that to-morrow a hundred thousand, two hundred thousand, a million persons shall have before them at breakfast a compendious picture first of their own city, next of their State, then of all the States of the Union, and finally of Europe, Asia, Africa, and Australia. Nor does this ambition content them; it is their will that these hundred thousand, two hundred thousand, million of readers shall find in their favorite newspaper that which shall answer all questions of every sort which they may put to themselves upon politics, finance, religion, the arts, literature, sport, society, and the sciences. It is a daily encyclopedia, set to the key of the passing moment, which is already past.

The meaning of this colossal project is shown naturally and in every possible way in every part of the newspaper building. Workmen and editors must be able to take their meals at any hour, and without leaving the building. They have therefore their own bar and restaurant. The printing of the pictures, so dear to Americans, must not be delayed. The paper has its type foundry, a regular smelting-shop, where the lead boils in the coppers. The news must be gathered up to the last second, like water in the desert, without losing a drop. The paper has its own telegraph and telephone wires, by which it is in communication with the entire world. At the time of the last presidential election, a number of Mr. Cleveland's partisans came together here, in one of the editorial rooms which was shown me, and from there they conversed with the candidate, himself in New York, receiving his instructions and giving him information. And what presses ! Capable of turning off work which thirty years ago would have required a force of how many hundreds of men ! Two workmen are enough to-day.

I find here a press of the kind of which I saw a large size in the New York *Herald* building, which, they told me there, turned off seventy-thousand numbers in two hours. The enormous machine is going at full speed when I approach it. Its roar is so great that no voice can be heard beside it. It is a noise like the roar of Niagara, and the colossal strip of paper rapidly unrolling as it is drawn through the machine gives an effect as of falling water, or the eddying of liquid metal. You see a whiteness gliding by, bent and folded by the play of innumerable bars of steel, and at the other end a sort of mouth pouring forth newspapers of sixteen pages all ready for distribution. The machine has seized the paper, turned and re-turned it, printed it on both sides, cut it, folded it, and here is a portion of a colossal number which without undue haste a child joins with the other portions.

In presence of this formidable printing creature — it is the only expression that will serve my turn — I feel again, as in New York, a sensation as of a power which transcends the individual. This printing press is a multiplier of thought to an extent not measurable by any human arithmetic. There is a singular contrast between the extreme precision of its organs — as delicate and accurate as those of a watch — and that indefinite reach of mind projection which Americans accept as they accept all facts. To their mind amplitude calls for amplitude by a sequence which it is easy to follow in the history of journalism; having conceived the idea of a paper of enormous circulation, they invented machines which would produce copies enough, and, as their machines appeared to them capable of producing a large number of copies, their conception of circulation increased in parallel lines. There can be no doubt that in less than twenty years they will have found means of producing papers of which five hundred thousand copies a day will be sold, like our *Petit Journal,* only theirs will have sixteen, twenty-four, forty, sixty folio pages.

This is the practical aspect of the plant; there is another. In vain is a newspaper conceived of and managed as a matter of business — it is a business of a special kind. It must have a moral purpose, must take its stand for or against such a law, for or against such a person; it must have its own individuality. It cannot owe its individuality, as with us, to the personality of its editors, since its articles are not signed; nor even, as in England, to the style and manner of the articles. The "editorial," as they call the leaders, occupies too small a place in this enormous mass of printed paper. And yet each one of the great newspapers of New York, Chicago, or Boston is a creation by itself, made in the image of him who edits it, — usually the proprietor. In the same way the president of a railway company is usually the principal stockholder.

Here, again, is a particular feature of large business enterprises in America and one which explains their vitality; a business is always the property of a man, the visible will of that man, his energy, as it were, incarnated and made evident. The formula which I just now used and emphasized very happily expresses this intimate relation between the man and his work. You will hear it currently said that Mr. So-and-so has long been "identified" with such a hotel, such a bank, or railway, or newspaper, and this identification is so complete that if, on passing in a street car before that hotel or bank, or railway station, or newspaper, you ask your neighbor about it, he will always reply to you with a proper name. From this it results that in all American enterprises there is an elasticity, a vitality, a continual " Forward!" and also an indefatigable combativeness.

I recognize this latter characteristic once again as I pass through these offices, if only by the minute questions of my guide as to the French press and our methods of securing a superior literary criticism.   They feel that this is our peculiar excellence, and they long to have their own newspapers attain to it.   Every actual director of one of these great public enterprises is thus on the watch for possible modifications which may distinguish his sheet from all others, continually working it over and loading it down with more facts, more articles, enrolling more people in its service, employing them to better purpose.

Thus managed, the direction of such an enterprise becomes a work of incalculable complexity.   The power to which these dictators of public opinion attain is so exceptional and so real, its existence means so much that is dear to Americans, — immense fortune and immense responsibility, enormous labor to undergo and the continual manifestation of the. fact that the ambition of truly enterprising men continually impels them into these lines.   A city is no sooner founded than papers begin to multiply.   Some of them have their newspapers before they are even founded.   It still sometimes occurs that the government gives up a large stretch of territory to an invasion of immigrants.   At a given signal they hasten thither, fall upon it, and each bit of land belongs to the first occupant.   That very evening or the next morning, on the plain where wagons and tents vaguely indicate the outline of a city, you will always find a liquor saloon, a postoffice, a church, and a newspaper!

Who knows that these wagons and tents are not the beginning of a Minneapolis, a St. Paul, a Chicago?   Who knows that in twenty-five years this town will not have a hundred thousand, two hundred thousand inhabitants, and the news-

paper as many readers? The insignificance of a beginning
never frightens an American who is planning for business.
Just as in meditating on the future of a business enterprise,
there is no possibility of extension which does not occur to
him, so no mediocrity disheartens him. He has before him
too many examples of gigantic results attained from very small
and humble beginnings. The greatest railway in the United
States, the Central Pacific, was founded by four men almost
without resources, two of whom were small shopkeepers in
'Frisco. They built the first sections of the line, mile by mile,
without money to go forward except bit by bit. Legend has
it that in certain cases they were obliged to lay the rails with
their own hands !

While I am submitting these very general reflections to my
companion, as we pass through the halls, I observe a number
of men, nearly all young, bent over their desks and writing with
that absorbed attention which speaks again of "hard work,"
the faculty of giving all one's powers to the present duty.
Others are receiving despatches which they immediately trans-
mit on writing-machines. There is none of that club atmosphere which makes the charm of Parisian editorial rooms. At
this hour, over there, the paper is nearly ready, and even while
the last touches are being added they talk ; they smoke ; they
play cards, dominoes, cup and ball. Here in this precocious
news-factory leisure is wanting, and the power to enjoy leisure.

To appreciate the difference between the two editorial offices, one must set over against one another the two personali-
ties of the French and the American reporter. The principal
quality of the former is to be witty and clever. His articles
are signed, and, in consequence, his literary self-consciousness
is always somewhat mingled with the notes to which he makes
a point of giving his own peculiar touch. You know him as
mocking or sarcastic, caustic or pathetic. He is an artist even
in his work of ephemeral statement, and his best successes are

most generally in a sort of picturesque chit-chat. He has a certain impressionism, and you will find in his "copy" something of the methods of the best writers of the day. The American reporter remains unknown, even when he gives to his journal news, to obtain which has cost him prodigies of shrewdness and energy. As if to show him that the important matter is not the quality of his phrases, but that of the facts he brings, he is paid by the word. There is in him something of the man of action, and something of the detective. Sensational novels naturally take for their hero this personage, whose master virtue is strength of will. He must always be ready to set out for the most remote countries, where he will be obliged to play the part of explorer, and just as ready to descend to the lowest social stratum, where he will need to act as policeman.

In this strenuous school he may, if he has the gift, become a writer of the first order. Richard Harding Davis, the creator of Gallegher and Van Bibber, is a case in point. A man who is himself a judge of style, having an extraordinary faculty for language in his letters and public utterances — Bismarck — goes so far as to insist that reporting, as Americans understand it, is the best school for a man of letters who desires to picture the movement of life. The opinion is of the order of those uttered by the Emperor at St. Helena, very partial and full of misunderstanding of the character of literary thought. It was worth citing; for it is very true that those improvised, almost telegraphic, paragraphs, in which the fact appears in its strong immediate clearness, often stand out in a relief which art cannot equal. But it is an unconscious relief, over which the reporter has had no anxiety. His anxiety is to be exact, and every means is good that will secure accuracy. Many people are indignant at his methods, and sometimes they are not wrong. Last summer I was passing through Beverly, near Boston, at the time of the death of one of the most distinguished officers of the

Federal army. The corpse was to be carried to Baltimore, and a funeral service was first celebrated in the little village church. In the midst of the ceremony, a young man entered, drew near to the coffin, gently raised the pall, tapped the cover with his finger, and said softly : —

" Steel, not wood."

Then he disappeared, in the midst of universal surprise ; it was a reporter.

These ruthless audacities of research are, however, performed with a certain simplicity, almost ingenuousness. I have read many " interviews " and many personal paragraphs, and, short as has been my time in America, I could count those which have in them anything wounding or even one of those humors of the pen so habitual among the most insignificant paragrapher of the boulevards. This sort of innocence of a press so audacious in its investigations is explained, I think, first, by the professional character of the reporter, and next, if I may so speak, by that of the reader. The reporter holds it to be his duty to give the reader the greatest possible number of facts. The reader considers it his right to have these facts. In the superabundance of positive details the place reserved for each personality is too short to admit of an ill-natured insinuation. The reporter no more has time to point an epigram than the detective to whom I but now compared him has time to make a practical joke upon the one he is questioning. He is much more occupied in discovering " head-lines," a collection of which would constitute the most humorous chapter of a journey to the United States. Just now, on entering the room of the newspaper reserved for necrologies, where all the biographies of celebrated living men are ranged in pigeonholes, I saw upon the table a proof of an article prepared for a celebrated singer who, at the moment, was very ill, with this " heading " : " The crystal voice is broken. The bird will sing no more."

As the charming woman got better, the article joined the

thousands of similar paragraphs which are waiting their turn among proofs of pictures representing buildings and men.

" Buildings may burn and men may die," said my guide, philosophically.   Seeing me amused by the fancifulness of these titles, he drew my attention to one which would appear on the morrow — the most surprising one, perhaps, which I have seen — " Jerked to Jesus."   It was the account of the hanging of a negro, a " colored gentleman," for " the usual crime," as they euphemistically say here, that of having outraged a white woman. He repented on the eve of his execution and died Christianly. I am not sure that the reporter who summed up this death in these three sensational words is not himself a believer, who distinctly saw in this event the entrance of a ransomed soul into paradise.   Certainly, thousands of plain readers will do so by the mere force of this announcement.   What would be the head-lines if the matter in hand was not so vulgar an event as this, but the arrival or departure of a pugilist, or his meeting with another prize-fighter?

" That is the incident which most swells the circulation of a paper," said my companion.   " Why not?" he added; " we Anglo-Saxons love a ' fight.'   We like it in politics, and this is why we must always see two ' leaders ' facing one another. We like it in our enterprises, and that is why I can never be content until I have made my paper the first in the United States.   We like it even when it is only a question of fisticuffs. And I think our race will lose something the day when we are too nearly cured of the latter.   It will take time for that," he added, with a smile that lighted up his countenance — a smile in which I found, as among many business men of this country, a little of the square solidity of the bull-dog.   I am not far from thinking, with him, that there is, in fact, an instinctive education in the national amusements, ferocious as they seem to be.   Certainly, all that teaches the calculated ardor of attack and the invincible self-restraint of resistance is useful to

men destined to live in a country where they everywhere meet
so intense an energy that, in ten years, this newspaper building,
these machines, the very paper itself, will be things of the
past, slow, unformed, behind the times. This is what a New
Yorker replied to my utterance of apprehension with regard to
crossing by the Brooklyn Bridge : —

"It is not possible that it will not fall some day," I said.

"Well," said he, "between now and then we shall have
built another, and this one will be out of fashion."

I went by one of the great Western lines, in company of one
of the directors, to St. Paul and Minneapolis. My object in
visiting the city that bears the name of the great apostle was
to pay my respects to its archbishop, Monsignor Ireland, the
most eloquent of the prelates who in these days are turning
the thought of the Church toward social problems. There is
something of Savonarola in the long, rugged face of this priest,
who finds in every kind of assembly an opportunity for giving
the word of life to the people. He said to me one day : —

"The Americans have this advantage : that people are never
surprised to see us in any sort of gathering. You could hardly
picture to yourself Monsignor of Paris at a banquet of the
city drainage department. It would be in staying away that I
should cause surprise. Such things give us many opportunities for making Catholicism understood."

And whatever the form under which Catholicism presents
itself, with whatever large magnificence of character, one needs
still to have read one of his sermons in order to understand —
to feel, rather — its vast significance. "The Church and the
age! the age and the Church! Let us bring them together in
closest union. Their pulses beat in unison. The God of
humanity is working in the age : the God of revelation is working in the Church. It is the same God and the same spirit."

And again: "What! our Church, the Church of the living

God, the Church of ten thousand victories over heathens and barbarians, over false philosophies and heresies, over defiant kings and turbulent peoples,—the great, charitable, liberal Church, athirst for virtue, ahungered for justice,—shall she quail before the nineteenth century? Shall she fear any century whatsoever?"

What words! and those who are Christians by desire, as I am, whose name is legion, how shall they not thrill to hear them sounding forth over the modern world and over their own hearts? The time has come when Christianity must accept all of Science and all of Democracy, under penalty of seeing herself forsaken by too many souls. She must perforce construct a channel for these two springs, and who knows whether the archbishop of St. Paul is not the workman predestined to this task? Who knows whether he is not some day to utter words like these from a yet higher place? There is already one American cardinal, and why should there not soon be two? Why should not a pope issue from this free nation, in which the heads of the Church have become what the first apostles were—men close to the heart of the people, to those humble hearts in which so many irrepressible ideas are now fermenting? These people believe their ideas to be contrary to the teachings of Christ. Prove to them, prove to us, that they are not so, and that we may all retain the Ideal by which our fathers lived, without sacrificing any of those ideals which throb in us! What a work for a fisher of souls of this great race, and how this modern world, so sick of the negations that vex its incomplete knowledge, will spring to meet the Church when many of its priests speak the language that this one speaks! In the shipwreck of European civilization, in the tide of barbarity which militarism and socialism are bringing upon it, here is the light toward which to steer. It will not be a small part of this country's glory that this guiding light was kindled here.

I was destined to meet the archbishop later, in New York, and receive the same impression of his person that his sermons had made upon me. This time, while I was on the way to St. Paul to seek him, in the modest "office" which he occupies under the shadow of his cathedral, he was at Baltimore, delivering one of his fiery harangues at Cardinal Gibbons's jubilee. Still I did not regret the long excursion — I call it long, in memory of my French habits. Fourteen hours in a railway car do not count in America. I was able to feast my eyes, during this long journey, with the sight of the most psychological landscape which I have seen in my wandering life; a "business" landscape, if one may so speak, so entirely has the imprint of speculation been stamped upon all the banks of the Mississippi, the river celebrated by Chateaubriand and Longfellow.

American energy has made this vast watercourse the natural vehicle of an enormous traffic. The "Father of Waters" has become a good-natured and docile servant, indefatigably transporting the logs cut far away to the North, beyond St. Paul and Minneapolis, by woodmen who have the large blue eyes and blond rosy faces of good-natured giants. They are immigrants from Sweden and Norway, who have come, to the number of six hundred thousand, in the last ten years!

Great rafts of huge tree-trunks glide along with the flowing water, each one marked with a colored sign, which tells its destination. The water, by turns green and transparent or muddy and yellow, bears upon its bosom so many islands that you can never distinguish the other shore. One side of the stream is furrowed with lines of towboats, which are indefatigably and incessantly hastening to transport the cattle and grain of this mysterious, inexhaustible West. Yet it must one day be exhausted, and one asks oneself what will become of this people when they no longer have this immense reservoir to draw from.

Meantime it was a scene of extraordinary activity, even after Chicago and New York. The private car in which we travelled had almost immediately been given its special engine. The little extra train was perpetually obliged to switch off to let the regular trains pass by,— cattle trains almost exclusively. Our car, which is that used by the president of the road on his travels, is not ordered with special luxury, although, with its two sleeping-rooms, drawing-room, dining-room, kitchen, and bath, it is a veritable house on wheels, in which you might pass weeks and hardly know that you were travelling. For that matter, how many people never travel in any other way! While at Newport, I heard a young woman planning a similar journey. She was to take her guests in her private car, and her sole regret was that the station at Chicago was too noisy for a long sojourn. The chief object of having a private car is the avoidance of hotels. If, in the course of one of these fifteen hundred mile journeys, the inhabitant of the private car happens to fall ill, a halt is called until he gets well. This is the case with a politician of my acquaintance, whom his doctor is treating for typhoid fever, in a car of this kind, temporarily shunted on one of the side tracks of some small Colorado town. Orders have been given for the engines not to whistle when they approach the place. Private cars are so numerous that such an incident passes without notice.

The car in which I am travelling is a sort of office on wheels, intended to facilitate the labors of the president and directors, who desire to see with their own eyes how things are going on their road. Here again I perceive the same identification of the great business enterprises of America, with certain individuals, which I had already observed in the case of the newspapers. Almost all the great railroads, like this one, are under the control of a very small number of individuals. In certain cases a single man owns the majority of the stock. In other cases, the entire stock is divided between four or five capitalists. At other times, the interests represented by a group of capitalists are so great that the remainder of the stockholders prefer to leave them entirely free in the direction of the enterprise. Hence results that character of autocracy in directing boards, which Mr. Bryce so justly pointed out as the unique feature of American railways. Those who manage them are their absolute masters.

The necessity of direct supervision is another consequence of this state of things. For that matter, competition is too fierce to admit of that anonymity of routine administration of which old Europe is so fond. An American railway represents too many living interests. It is not merely a more rapid means of communication, side by side with roads and canals, for example. In nearly all the States it is the only means of communication.

It not only runs between two existing cities, connecting them by a shorter line, it is itself the creator of cities. Between Chicago and St. Paul a score of them have sprung into existence, of which the station was the natal germ. Stores were opened for the benefit of the employees, then other shops for the benefit of the first shopkeepers. If there is a mine in the neighborhood, or the hope of a mine, grazing, or the possibility of grazing, immigrants come in flocks. If any natural feature, such as a waterfall, permits a factory, industries are established. Minneapolis had no other origin. The railway passed the place. The falls of the Mississippi lent themselves to a series of incomparable mills, and this was the starting-point of one of the future capitals of the world.

One must not weary of the statistics which, as it were, make evident this astounding productiveness. Minneapolis, literally founded but yesterday, in which no man now forty years old can have been born, occupies to-day, according to population, the one hundred and twenty-first place among the cities

of the whole world.   It follows immediately after the Hague,
standing before Trieste or Toulouse or Seville or Genoa or
Florence or Venice or Havre or Bologna or Rouen or Stras-
burg.

It is not merely a fantastic paradox that brings these antique
names into juxtaposition with this name so barbaric in origin
— it is derived from a Greek and a Sioux word, and so
symbolical.   A total rearrangement of the scheme of history
is shown in such unlooked-for displacements of the centres
of human activity.   If we had not suffered the extinction
of our sense of the mystery which is hidden in all reality,—
even in coarse and vulgar reality, when it is fruitful to such
a degree as this, — we should recognize in it one of the
miracles of an epoch in which nothing except the perspective of age is wanting to thrill us through with admiration!

To the business man, the unconscious worker of this miracle, the establishment of a railway is simply a question of
speculation.   According as these seeds of cities, scattered
thus from the funnel of an engine with the cinders and the
sparks, spring up or prove abortive, the surrounding district
will bring in millions of dollars or nothing.   In most cases
the company has received its lands free, without laying out
a cent.   Thus Congress granted thirteen millions of acres to
the Union Pacific, six millions to the Kansas Pacific, twelve
millions to the Central Pacific, forty-seven millions to the
Northern Pacific, forty-two millions to the Atlantic and Pacific.   Whatever these lands may become worth, so much will
the railroad be worth.   It makes them fruitful, and they en-
rich it in return.   It overlays them with an alluvium of
humanity, and this will tenfold, a hundredfold, enhance their
value to it.

Figures like these multiply themselves in the minds of the
"magnates" — so the great "railroad men" are called here
— as they look abroad from their private cars.   They see a

new city blocking itself out, pushing out in lines of cheap wooden houses, brought out in numbered sections and set down on the surface of the ground. They ask themselves how and when this embryo will come to life, grow, develop itself; and then they return to the comfort of the "rockers" of their moving drawing-rooms, colossal plans seething in their minds the while. Each one of them is accustomed to a business sphere as wide as that of a cabinet minister. He has already made cities; he has made vast regions. All the qualities of a great diplomatist have been necessary that he should carry on the struggle, to-day against a rival company, to-morrow against the governor of a State. He has conducted battles, formed leagues. For business to go on as it does he must needs have marshalled thousands of men into ranks, chosen the most able among them, commanded them as Napoleon commanded his officers and soldiers.

It is a power by no means decorative and honorary, but real, active, working, with an immediate responsibility held in check by success or the want of success. These men are princes in the feudal sense of the word, and they may generally pride themselves on having conquered their principality for themselves. They can look back twenty years and see themselves small shopkeepers, coal-dealers, hotel servants, brakemen. Such a life has its poetry,— not indeed that which poets have sung, but poetry all the same,— and it has its beauty, of the kind that Balzac would have loved.

The locomotive keeps on its way while these reflections beset me, and the landscape unrolls before our eyes. Remains of forests border the Mississippi, brilliant now with the hues of autumn. The magnificence of the red tones, their depth, their solidity, almost warm the heart. Once, in the twilight, a part of the forest was burning upon the horizon. A colossal flame curled up, illumining a range of mountains, while the waters of the river, that reflected the sunset sky, became adorable with rose and violet. For a few moments invincible nature has its revenge and abolishes industry. In the light of this suddenly transfigured landscape, I picture to myself what this part of America must have been fifty years ago, when trappers and Indians were in conflict on these fields and in the woods along this river, which Longfellow has sung: —

"Men whose lives glided on like rivers that water the woodlands,
Darkened by shadows of earth, but reflecting the image of heaven."

It is in such scenes as this that one should read the now old-fashioned romances of Fenimore Cooper, which in our youth charmed us all, beyond the seas. I have just reread one of the most celebrated, *The Pathfinder*. Its style is indifferent, the plot is constructed of childishly improbable events. The characters lack analysis and depth. And yet the book possesses the first of all the virtues of a romance, — *credibility*. This is due, in spite of its faults, to the evident good faith with which the various characters are drawn, especially that of the guide, Leather-Stocking, who has passed into legend even in Europe.

Under all the weaknesses of style and composition, one feels, as in the Scottish chronicles of Walter Scott, the reality of local traditions collected at their very source. These things cannot be imitated, and they never grow old. Behind the imaginary story you perceive nature as it once was and the American of the last century, on the eve of the War of Independence, living all in the moral domain, with none of the industrialism which now reigns over the whole scene.

That was a unique period, when the Puritan and this wild nature came in contact, and its real hero was Washington. England was close at hand, and the blood of its sons, emigrants to this new continent, had not undergone the prodig-

L

ious intermingling which has now transformed it. Cooper's romances show the English rigidity of the American of that day, and they also show the strenuousness of the war with the Indians, side by side with the marvellous animal wealth of the country now so despoiled of its large and small game. They show the beginnings of the struggle with nature, which has now been not only conquered, but violated and brutalized.

The reading of these books shows that the United States had already exhausted an entire civilization — that of the pioneers and hunters — before producing that of to-day. This new nation has lived more in its one hundred years than all Europe since the Renascence. Between the social condition described by this *Pathfinder*, and that of which I am trying to distinguish a few elements, there is assuredly more difference than between the France of the seventeenth century and that of our day, notwithstanding the upheavals of our Revolution. The plasticity of this singular country is such that we may predict as great differences between the civilization of this year of the Chicago Exposition and that of 1993; only the sunset, the water of the river, and the sky will have remained the same as to-night and as a hundred years ago. The same stars will flash out overhead, and the same moon will rise, bathing the vast, pale river and the dark forests. But will it still light up files of trains such as rush past ours, fly-ing eastward, carrying cattle and wheat, wheat and cattle,— and money, always and ever money, to swell the enormous fortunes destined some day to be shed abroad in the form of dowry over some ruined palace of Italy, some impoverished historic castle of England or of France?

St. Paùl, where I arrive on a Sunday morning, is a huge chaotic city, in part composed of the same wooden houses squat upon the ground which are found in the infant cities along the railway. But along a sort of macadamized terrace which overlooks the Mississippi, stand out a succession of beautiful stone houses, not very high, of good architecture. They form a whole street of private houses, like those in the neighborhood of Hyde Park or the Avenue du Bois.

The mere exterior of these houses betrays in the men who built them, who are all business men of this place, that habit of ostentatious expenditure that seems to be so contrary to the greed for wealth everywhere stamped upon the hard surface of this country. The contradiction is only apparent. The American loves to "make a dollar," as they say; but he is not tenacious of it. What he most cares for in the conquest of wealth is the excitement of activity, self-affirmation, and he affirms himself quite as much, if not more, by the lavish ostentation of his expenditure.

This ostentation is sometimes very barbaric. It is often very intelligent. Of this I have convinced myself by a visit to one of the houses on "Summit Avenue," the elegant street of this rough-hewn St. Paul. The gallery of paintings which it contains is mentioned in the guide-books. It belongs to the president of one of the great Western railways, a "self-made man," if ever there was one. All who knew him twenty-five years ago remember him as a small commercial employee. After that he went into the selling of coal, and the freighting of boats. The latter enterprise made him acquainted *de visu* with the wealth of Montana and North Dakota. A railway which had been begun in these regions was on the point of failure. He bought the ruined line. To-day, thanks to con-tracts that he was wise enough to make, by a series of trans-shipments, this line has a through service from Buffalo to Japan. This is the finished type of a great American busi-ness enterprise, with its foundations laid in minute personal experience and its results expanded by bold combinations to the verge of unreality.

The interior appointments of this man's house are not less

typical. Pictures, pictures everywhere. Corots of the highest beauty, among others the *Biblis* which figured at the Sécretan sale, Troyons, Decamps, a colossal Courbet, the *Convulsion- naires* of Delacroix, and a view of the coast of Morocco, before which I stood long, as in a dream. I saw this canvas years ago. I have sought for it since in hundreds of public and private museums, finding no book which could inform me who was its present possessor, and I find it here!

It is a little narrow beach, a rim of pebbly strand at the foot of a steep cliff. Some Moors are rapidly making off with a large bark. The village, a nest of pirates, shows white, high up in a cleft of the hill. This collection of hovels huddled in this lonely cranny, the wildness of the beach, the haste of the sailors, the freedom of the great sea, intensely blue under a burning sun, all speak of adventure, surprise, danger. There is realism and romanticism, brilliant color and dramatic action in this picture by a thoughtful and enthusiastic artist, always seeking for a subject of complex beauty, in which the vagueness of a tragic mystery should be mingled with splendor of execution.

What ground has this canvas covered between the painter's studio and the gallery of a millionaire of the Western frontier! So I saw in Baltimore, in the collection of the "magnate" of another railroad, the complete series of Barye pictures, a "Christ asleep in the storm" by Delacroix, with an amazing marine piece, a sea-green surf, wild and boisterous, under a sky livid with violet hues. And Fromentins and Daubignys, other Corots, Troyons, Decamps, Bonnats, — all the glory of France! What sentiment impels these wealthy speculators to gather into their own homes art treasures most foreign to all that has been the business and passion of their whole life?

I seem to discern here, first of all, traces of that dream of culture, that longing for intellectual leisure, which always impresses me in persons thus saturated with practical energy. I also recognize in it a purpose of good citizenship. They have a very particular sort of love for the city in which they live, which they have seen growing up, which they have sometimes even seen born, and which they desire to see in possession of all excellent things. A museum is such a thing, and they give her one in their own house. Almost always the wills of these great men contain a clause which proves how deep and widespread is the idea that "millions" bring civic duty in their train. They give five hundred thousand dollars to endow a library, a university, a museum for their city. When such a one dies without having taken steps of this kind, universal blame overshadows his memory.

For this reason every one of these industrial towns is proud of its millionaires. The most ignorant coachman will point you to their houses, give you the amount of their fortunes, call them by their nicknames. It is understood that municipal solidarity unites these potentates of the dollar to their fellow-citizens of their own city. In fact, this unity of interests shows itself daily, materially. The same Mr. Chauncey Depew whose remarks I have before quoted said to a reporter these significant words: —

"A railway president in the United States is a great servant of the people. He has under his orders twenty or thirty thousand men, who represent a hundred thousand, sometimes two hundred thousand mouths to fill; he holds in his hands not merely the physical well-being, but the mental and moral well-being of this multitude. He cannot do everything, nor content everybody. But he can do much, and when he does his best you will not find another man in a ' prominent position ' who does more for the comfort and good citizenship of large communities."

This warm civic ardor is one of the virtues of the American business man of which we are least aware. With reservations on the side of truth and that of "humbug," I believe it to be the most sincere.

With eyes dazzled by the luminous poetry of Delacroix's picture, I had some difficulty, on the way from St. Paul to Minneapolis, in discerning the meaning of the landscape which lies between the two cities. It is, however, most expressive. The few miles of ground which separate them are divided off into nearly equal lots, and everywhere you may see the inscription "For Sale," indefinitely multiplied. In fifty years the suburbs of the "Twin Cities of the West"— as they call them here — will meet.

Soon the wooden houses begin to appear, then brick ones. This is Minneapolis. Although the earlier houses are scattered, like farms upon a mountain side, the streets are already laid out and numbered. An electric tramway serves these districts, which, notwithstanding the infrequent houses, conform to the ideal plan. It is like a design of a colossal city traced beforehand on the very ground, planned, imagined, estimated rather, its future needs to be served by this electricity. The sewers are dug, the fountains are playing, the ground is drained   It lacks only inhabitants.

Of these, however, there are a hundred and sixty-five thousand in the built-up quarters, which form but a very small portion of the city prospected by the business men of Minneapolis. Chicago counts more than a million souls, and they have not the slightest doubt that their city will outrank Chicago. They have taken precautions to that end, and have bought all that they can buy of the adjoining land, dividing it up for sale lot by lot. They have given the vital organ to these yet-to-be-built suburbs, — the facility of rapid transit, which permits each workingman to have his little house,— and they are waiting, with a strength of hope so peculiarly American, occupied meanwhile with other speculations, which will compensate them for the failure of this one, in the event — to them improbable — of this one making shipwreck.

One of the great speculators of Minneapolis, he perhaps who from the first day has most strongly believed in the future of this city, takes me in his electric car — a private electric car; where else shall we find a whim like this? He proposes to show me that he and his friends have foreseen not merely the material greatness of Minneapolis, but have thought of its artistic life.

The car slips along the wire with frightful speed. It has not to stop for passengers. We have left the built-up quarters, and almost immediately we pass the districts yet to be built, with their imaginary streets, and their placards of " For Sale " erected on posts. These placards are so numerous that the suburb resembles the beds of a botanic garden destined for the inhabitants of Brobdingnag. The car now skirts 'a diminutive lake, whose bluish waters shimmer between slim young trees. They have cut down, destroyed, burned, the primitive forest, and this timid attempt at replantation seems all the more to denude the landscape.

We reach a bit of better preserved woodland, which forms the green border of a second lake. On the shore is one of the most singular music halls that it has ever been given me to see. Benches rise up in tiers, facing the lake. Above they are divided into boxes; below they form a uniform parterre. Wooden tables in these boxes and on the parterre remind me that in Minneapolis the principal immigration is Germanic. This place is evidently arranged for the folk of the beer garden,— Germans, Swiss, Danes, Norwegians. A huge raft is moored opposite the theatre, bearing a rostrum for the orchestra. Concerts are given here on fine summer nights, and when the public requests it the raft puts out into the lake, to add the charm of distance to the pieces played. This democratic adaptation of the dreams of King Louis of Bavaria costs the humble folk who enjoy it ten cents for the tramway and twenty-five cents for entrance — no doubt "with expenses," as the café-concert advertisements say!

All America shows in this place. The orchestra is composed of good artists, who will be better from year to year with the increasing wealth of the city. The view is exquisite on this autumnal morning, veiled in haze above the yellowing trees and the violet water. What must it be by moonlight, on the soft nights of June? The idea is a fine one, a dainty caprice of popular enjoyment. And it all has for its first principle a tramway speculation, which in turn rests on a speculation in land!

The most humble realism, most devoted to the minute observation of facts, joined to an audacity of imagination which never flinches, which grafts projects upon projects, which continually inflates enterprises already enormous, which rises to more and more colossal combinations,— the most ardent, most implacable individualism, as of a nobler sort of beast of prey, devouring all the life around it,— or, if you will, the tremendous rush of an overflowing river, absorbing all waters, inundating all lands, sweeping over a country ravaged by its insatiable floods; and with all this a generosity that never reckons, a magnanimity of civic passion that lavishes millions in disinterested works, that expends itself in tireless sacrifices for the common country; a plebeianism of most recent origin, a modesty, often a meanness of birth, family, education, powerless, it would seem, to mitigate the necessity of bread-winning toil; and with it all the magnificence and ostentation of grand seigneurs, a taste for art, a large understanding of intelligent luxury, a natural facility in the management of the tremendous fortunes acquired but yesterday; such are the contradictory characteristics which even a superficial analysis discovers in the complex figure of the American business man.

Simply to note them in this brief summary serves to show me that these traits are also those of the whole race, and in the lineaments of the potentate who reigns master over his railway, his factory, his newspaper, his mine, I recognize the early colonist, with the moral lineaments which fortune has been powerless to change.

This colonist came here a hundred years ago, fifty years ago, to find a foothold in this still new world, and he has been forced to carry on the most open struggle, the least softened by social conventions,— a struggle against people, against nature, against himself. His flesh rebelled against the severities of the first years. The prairie was hostile. The neighbors were severe, dangerous, merciless. The necessity of action forced the man to observe and to accept no ideas that were not clear and precise. This inexorable education cured him of phrases, formulæ, prejudices, and inaccuracies. So much for the realism.

But the colonist's struggle had all possibilities before it. Expatriations of this sort are not to be explained without something of that madness of hope which desperate men find in themselves in supreme moments, when the whole soul faces about under a blow which leaves to it nothing of the past. And once at this point, everything contributed to fan the fever of hope in the exile's breast,— the incredibly fertile soil, the mysterious gold and silver mines always to be discovered, the prairie, absurdly rich in game, the indestructible forests, and the daily example of gigantic fortunes amassed in a few years. So much for imagination.

And still the influx of immigrants continued to be so numerous, the struggle for life became so violent in this horde of adventurers,— all men of poverty and energy,— justice was executed in so summary a fashion, that it was necessary indeed to have recourse to *Faustrecht*, that right of the fist which was the principle of order in the German

Middle Ages. Lynching is its last relic. So much for individualism.

On the other hand, these same colonists found in this severe existence a renewal of their personality. They made for themselves a future that had no past, and experienced a passionate gratitude to the free country which had permitted the new beginning. This is the origin of American patriotism, so different from ours. Tradition does not enter into it, since the men, except a number so small that it may be counted, have their traditions elsewhere. What they love in this new country is precisely that it is new. They themselves create its tradition. They are ancestors, and they know it. So much for the glorification of civism.

Finally, these colonists were all plebeians, or were constrained to become such, since they must work with their hands. Only, the vast extent of their domains, the fact that they were dependent on no one, their consciousness of a regenerated manhood, the habit of unchecked liberty to originate, all conspired to exalt in them that pride which the humblest American born in the country naturally manifests.

Look well at this; the business man is no other than this colonist, broadened, developed, enlarged. Never was the law of heredity more visible than here, in this sublimated transposition, if one may so speak. All the soul of the pioneer of the early days appears again in the enterprises and caprices of these millionaires; and as the same soul continues to stir in the poor American who has not conquered destiny, a moral likeness is established between the poorest and the most prosperous, a close and profound resemblance, which makes the true conscience of this country. It is by this singular identity that it remains always one, in spite of many causes ceaselessly working to disintegrate it.

These business men, who are occupied with constructing a

whole Western civilization out of entirely foreign elements, naturally make it in the image of the American character. Through them the national consciousness projects itself in towns and enterprises so entirely alike that travellers complain of it. They are all agreed in reproaching this country for its cruel monotony. Some humorist or other has compared American things to hothouse strawberries, big as apricots, red as roses, and with no taste.

If there is any truth in this epigram, it is the fault of the business men. Applying to all products everywhere the same method of indefinite increase, multiplying the workman by the machine, continually substituting hasty wholesale work for the individual and delicate task, they have, in fact, banished the picturesque from their republic. All these great cities, these great buildings, these great bridges, these great hotels, are alike. But what we have to ask of these things is not an artistic impression, but an authentic report of the profound forces of American life, and this document must be added to the others, to confirm and complete them.

The particular feature manifested by business men in all the enterprises of which these cities and landscapes are the rude symbol, is in fact the same which the women manifest in their elegance and their culture, the same that New York society manifests in its extravagance, amusements, conversation, that New York streets manifest at a first glance,—a feature so characteristic as to be national. It is a habit, unique and unvarying, a habit carried to such an extreme as to become the abuse of a single human power,—that of will. It is obviously the very pivot of the machine, to which everything else is subordinated. Observe some of these great business men, after having closely studied their work; you will soon discover that even their physical powers, usually very robust, are entirely bent in this direction. Whether they are thirty years old, or forty, or fifty, their one ideal is "hard work," intense toil, which they demand of their employees as much as of themselves. I am told that it needs months to train English workmen — and they are the toughest in Europe — to the strenuous application habitual in American shops.

The employer is himself in his office from the earliest morning hour, and does not leave it until the latest in the afternoon. Most generally his only refreshment during this long period is two sandwiches and half a dozen oysters from a neighboring bar. After years of such toil his constitution, however strong it may be, is seriously undermined. He is obliged to stop. The kind of rest which his physicians prescribe for him is a sufficient indication of the nature and intensity of his fatigue. It requires six months of travel, usually by sea, to patch up the overwrought, almost shattered, machine.

Those who do not succumb carry the marks of immense fatigue borne with immense spirit. They are giants; their square-built frames have grown heavy by long sittings in their offices, their faces are gray from exhausted vitality. The expression of their countenances reveals a mind so continually on the strain that it can no longer enjoy recreation.

Conversing with them, you find it explained why the papers are continually announcing the sudden death of some millionaire, struck down in his office, in a boat's cabin, or a railway car. The words "heart disease" usually accompany the death notice; it is a commentary that shows you the human machine utterly worn out by the incessant expenditure of nervous force. These manipulators of dollars are, in short, the heroes of modern times, in whom the power of attack and resistance is analogous, under very different forms, to the power of attack and resistance of an old soldier of the Emperor. They die of it, after having lived by it, and having lived by it alone.

This is the greatness and it is the limit of this civilization. Intellectual life is in the background, and in the background also are the sentimental and even the religious life. The life of purpose has sapped all the vigor of the individual. So much is it hypertrophied that it seems sometimes to work aimlessly and in a void. This is also the defect of the whole social system. You feel everywhere that the Americans have risen too superior to time, so that by a mysterious law they are doing nothing that is destined to endure. All the pomp of these Babel-like cities is destined to give way to something else. The vision of this is already foreseen. These machines are to give place to other machines, more simple or more complicated. In ten years these hotels, with their thousand pipes, their electric lights, their hot and cold water, their swift elevators, their extravagantly magnificent furniture, will have become "old-fashioned." Others will have taken their place.

It is thus with everything, from writing-machines to fortunes, and so on indefinitely, it would seem; unless, indeed, the America of workmen and speculators is itself to pass away, as the America of the pioneers has done, and frenzied enterprise be succeeded by a civilization in which the central power will be not the conscious and calculating will, but instinct, habit, an inherited and disciplined nature. This final change is, in any case, far distant. You understand why, on studying a map of the United States and comparing the extent of its territory with the number of its inhabitants. Americans often indulge in the justified pleasantry of saying that if all France were set down in the midst of Texas, a good deal of Texas would stick out around the edges. It would be proper to add that this immense Texas has not three million inhabitants; Florida has not four hundred thousand, and it takes fourteen hours by railway to pass through it, from Lake Worth to Jacksonville.

Thirty out of forty States are in a like condition. This is the secret of this civilization. It has not yet passed the period of conquest. Its immense originality lies in this, that its conquerors leaped with one bound to the refinement of the most advanced civilization. A like phenomenon has not elsewhere been seen, and it will never be seen again. This is the reason why the leaders in this unique conquest — the business men — do not resemble our brokers, laborers, manufacturers, engineers; the reason why Chicago is not like Paris, or Minneapolis like Florence. I love best the cities of old Europe, but I admire most the business men of the New World. The work which they do by dint of sheer, unpremeditated resolution is not equal to the work which has been elaborated with us for centuries, but the actual makers of this country are examples of a more vigorous humanity.

VI

THE LOWER ORDERS

I. *The Workingmen*

"BUSINESS is the labor of others," said a socialistic humorist, amending a celebrated witticism. The epigram is only
half true in the United States, where the millionaires themselves are overwhelmed with work, quite as much so as the
most oppressed operatives on their railroads or in their mines.
It is so far correct, that the conduct of these great enterprises requires for its first element the toil of the laborer.
Behind the capitalist, however intelligent he may be, however
active and enterprising, there stands, therefore, the workingman.

Premising that America is, above all things, a democracy,
this very personage is what constitutes its substructure. If
the civilization of this country is to be changed again, as so
often seems likely to be the case, it will change through the
workingman, as the France of '89, which rested upon the
peasant class, was changed by the peasant. From time to
time, strikes, which in any other country would be called
civil wars, seem in fact to presage one of those class conflicts
of which the issue is never doubtful. Ever since there have
been barbarians and civilized people, the more wretched have
always vanquished the more fortunate when it came to the
issue of battle.

At other times, and with the exception of such moments of
overstrained feeling, if you talk with laboring men, you will
find them evidently happy in their work, performing it well,

159

with much of the independence of free citizens in their
rugged faces. They visibly have the calmness of energy,
amidst all the to and fro of pistons, the whistling of leather
straps, the screeching of steam, the panting of fly-wheels. The
expenditure of personal force is so intelligently economized
for them, so accurately supported by mechanical help! You
know, on the other hand, that wages are much higher than in
Europe,— a dollar and a half a day, two, two and a half, four.
You know with what prudential societies the activity of these
people is surrounded. These societies are so numerous, so
well ordered, so ready to sustain the workman and his family
in so many circumstances, from loss of work to death! Thanks
to one of these societies the man owns his own house. Thanks
to endowments of all sorts, the education of his children is
ensured. The tax of blood — that monstrous abuse of our
civilization — is spared to him and his sons. You return
again to this thought, which has determined so many emigrants to leave all, that America is the paradise of the common
people.

How reconcile two points of view, both of which are based
upon indisputable though radically contradictory facts? You
turn the pages of publications issued by working men and
women. The same contradiction appears still more strikingly.
In the programme of one of the associations that pass for
being the most advanced, you read, "Calling upon God to
witness the rectitude of our intentions." In a sort of hymn
in honor of the eight-hour day, ending with the line

"Eight hours for work, eight hours for rest, eight hours for what we will,"

you three times meet the name of God, and three times find
His and *Him* printed with a capital letter. You conclude
therefrom that the natural desire for beneficent reforms is
associated, in the American workman, with a deep religious
instinct, and you decide that this characteristic fits in well

with the logic of the natural character. Wherever the dominant element of a character is will, the most highly developed sentiment is necessarily that of responsibility, and the religous life is its perfectly natural condition.

Take up another paper, also designed for workingmen, and brought to your attention as typical, and to your amazement you will find declarations in the style of the following: "Paradise is a dream invented by rogues, who wish to conceal their crimes from their victims." "When the laborer perceives that the other world, which people are forever telling him about, is a mirage, he will knock at the doors of the rich thieves, gun in hand, demanding his share in the good things of life, and this without delay." "Religion, authority, state, —all these idols were carved out of the same block of wood. We will shatter them all."

What can we think of a social class of whom such opposite accounts are equally true? That is a psychological problem far too profound for me to solve. I get a glimpse of at least a conjecture which may permit one to comprehend the co-existence of ideas so antithetical in the laboring classes of America. Much has contributed to this hypothesis,— prolonged study of conditions, visits to factories, the reading of a quantity of reports, visits to innumerable workingmen's homes, interviews with especially competent persons. I shall give from among notes taken in the course of an inquiry still too short, only those which chime in with the familiar tone of this travelling journal, which does not aspire to be a treatise on political economy.

Conversations with two of the men who have most efficiently pondered the problem of the social future of America, His Eminence Cardinal Gibbons and Monsignor Ireland, appear to me to have summed up with authority and superior clearness the optimistic view of the future. Though they occurred

M

several weeks apart, I will transcribe them in succession, as
they are complementary to one another.

All French people know the names of these two apostles,
thanks to the works of M. de Meaux and M. Max Leclerc,
thanks also to the Abbé Klein's fine translation of a few
sermons preached by the archbishop of St. Paul. These two
prelates have been very active workers in the Catholic propaganda in the United States, of which I have already spoken.
A few figures will permit us to measure it more accurately.

At the beginning of this century American Catholics were
in number about twenty-five thousand. A bishop and some
thirty priests sufficed for the service of souls. To-day they
count more than ten millions of members. Their churches
and seminaries continually increase. They have founded at
the gates of Washington a university which assures to their
teaching all the supremacy of the most modern knowledge. Monsignor Keane is its rector. One of the grandest
figures of the dignified clergy of America is this rector, with
the vigorous countenance of the man of action, with vibrating
voice, gestures at times almost rigid, and eyes of flame.

"All that we have done," he said to me, "we have done
through liberty. We have no relations with the State, and
we get along together very well. We are paid by our adherents, and we like that. If they find us too severe," he added,
"and undertake to make us feel it, we support it without
pain ; for we like that, also, to do without superfluities and
display. When I was bishop of Richmond my diocese was
very poor. I lived in two little rooms and I was happy.
What we do not like is for the ministers of the Church to
maintain the style of a prince, to form a nobility. Such vanities do not become the disciples of the Divine Master."

Such sentiments explain better than any commentary why
the clergy have gained a place against which the efforts of
intolerant fanatics like the A. P. A. cannot prevail. This is

the name of an anti-Catholic league recently formed here, which calls itself the American Protective Association. Those who compose it hate the Church with that strange hatred so common among us. They well understand that in the United States they must attack it upon the ground of liberty itself. In this method they resemble the radicals of our country. Their programme consists in representing Catholicism as incompatible with the duties of the American citizen. They cite an article in the naturalization laws, which demands the full, dispassionate renunciation of all fidelity to any foreign sovereign. They add: "Do not Catholics themselves proclaim themselves dependants of the Pope, who lives in Rome?"

Neither the dangerous quibble of this reasoning, which affects to confound the spiritual and temporal realms, nor the diffusion by thousands of false documents, where the venerated names of the archbishops of Baltimore and St. Paul appear at the end of secret instructions drawn up with most adroit perfidy, nor the astute appeal to the ancient hostility to popery, so lively in the hearts of the descendants of the Puritans,— no stratagem, in fact, has been able to prevail against the evident warmth of civic energy displayed by this truly living episcopate. Neither of these prelates has missed a single opportunity to serve the people, to show himself a man of his time and of his country. When the association of the Knights of Labor was threatened at Rome, Cardinal Gibbons and Monsignor Ireland had no hesitation in going thither at once to defend it. When the organizers of the Exposition had the idea of opening at Chicago that Congress of Religions which, in spite of some unfortunate charlatanism in matters of detail, will remain one of the noble symbols of our epoch, the same Cardinal Gibbons consented to open it with a solemn prayer.

In all circumstances their hearts beat in unison with the

heart of the nation.   There is no merit in this.   A constitution which permits them to practise their religion untram-
melled, to form associations and possess property without
check, to institute good works without opposition, and to
secure the recruitment of their clergy without sophistry,—
what more could they ask?   With what enthusiasm would the
Catholics of France accept the suppression of the Concordat
with the budget of worship, under such guarantees!   And then
the clergy in the United States are really, closely, American.
The characteristics which distinguish this robust race, and
which I noted in connection with society, as well as with
business, are found with the same intensity in these bishops
and priests.   In the first place, they have realism, the
keen positive vision of the fact.   Read the two volumes in
which the cardinal has summed up Catholic dogma for his
fellow-citizens, especially the pages referring to divorce.
They have the hardy vigor of hope, and an enormous breadth
of plan.   Listen to the archbishop of St. Paul:—

"We have an admirable opportunity.   In a hundred years
America will have four hundred millions of inhabitants.   Our
work is to make this whole country Catholic!"

Over and above this they have the great national virtue,
—determination.

"Our device," one of them said, "is *do and dare!*"

We are pretty far here from the priestly functionary whom
the State wraps in swaddling-clothes for his protection, far
from those restrictive laws which forbid the religious orders
to own property, the vestries to administer themselves, the
clergy to recruit themselves freely!   Years ago I was dining
at the same table with Gambetta.   It was shortly after the
war, and the Opportunist chief was speaking of the programme
which he should apply if ever he arrived at power.

"And the separation of Church and State?" asked one of
the guests.

"We should beware of that," quickly answered he whom his friends then called "the tiger." "It would be necessary to give too much liberty to the Church, and she would become too strong."

Here in America I have thoroughly understood the significance of this remark, which has remained in my memory from early manhood. In uttering it, Gambetta followed the true Jacobean and Cæsarean tradition. That this powerful statesman, the only one which the Revolution of 1870 produced among us, should have thought thus in perfectly good faith, proves better than many pages how widely different may be the translations of the one word, democracy, into facts, laws, customs. A constitution is nothing, except through the men who obey it.

Memory has its freaks. Going one winter's day from Washington to Baltimore, where I was to see Monsignor Gibbons, I was taken possession of by the picture of the former dictator of Tours, because of this remark, which had fallen from his eloquent lips between two whiffs of a very black cigar, in the dining-room of a little basement of the Rue Linnæus. I was asking myself what France would have become if that long-winded orator, intelligent and capable of adaptation and education as he was, had made this journey to America and seen for himself all that the Church may yet to-day represent of democratic fecundity and broad popular instruction where it is free.

Then a strangely different picture rose up before my mind, that of the brilliant and unfortunate Edgar Poe, who wrote his "Raven" half a century ago, in the capital of Maryland, which I see yonder. Although this poet's genius is spoiled for me now by his terrible abuse of the artificial, by the almost mechanical grouping of his thoughts, his sensitive nature still touches me, and, above all, his sorrowful fate. I think of the ever-new mystery of the constitution of the soul. That of the poet found its principle of despair and degradation in the society where that of the priest whom I am shortly to meet found its ample development. The spirituality of the one was its torture, the spirituality of the other made its strength, in the same circle of the same civilization.

Yet at the first white view of Baltimore, as I walk along these streets, I feel that it is indeed, of all American cities that I have seen, the one best adapted to the dreams of poesy. St. Charles Street, somewhat narrow and close between its rather low, white houses, has the charm of intimacy. It is quiet enough around the square where Washington's monument stands, and I recall the elegant Place Stanislaus of Nancy. I have the impression, so rare here, but which they assure me I shall have still more strongly in Philadelphia, of a corner in some city which has endured, which will endure. These surroundings, less temporary, less pronounced, and more delicate, harmonize with my expectation, with the approach to the American primate, as the priests in the University of Washington described him to me. A few steps farther along the quiet sidewalk of this street, which has no electric tramways or cable cars, and I find myself before a palace of the same simple style as the neighboring houses. The cupola of a church dominates it. It is the cardinal's residence.

His Eminence received me in a simply furnished drawing-room, adorned with the portraits of celebrated priests. Those of Leo XIII. and Cardinal Manning are engravings, standing on easels. Physically, Monsignor Gibbons is of the race of ascetics, of whom it seems as if mortifications had left just enough flesh to support the travail of the soul.

Though he is past sixty, he appears to be hardly fifty, so erect is his slight and supple figure. I had caught a glimpse of him the other day in Washington, in one of the galleries of the House, wearing no token of his dignity except a purple skull-cap on the back of his head. To-day, in his own house, he wore a black cassock bordered with red, a cassock irreproachable in appearance, though not entirely new. Beneath it his feet could be seen, covered with thick-soled, elastic boots. Simplicity is everywhere stamped upon the surroundings of this man of prayer and action,— upon him and around him.

The hands which project from the sleeves, with no show of linen, are thin and delicate. The face, at once very thoughtful and very calm, is long and deeply lined, with a somewhat large nose, and a projecting upper lip, rigid, like that of the portrait of Erasmus in the Louvre. It is the mouth of the writer and the diplomatist rather than of the orator. Expression is to be looked for elsewhere, in the deep lines of the cheek and in the eyes, of so clear a blue in an almost ashen face. The eyes look out with an admirable expression, very gentle and very firm, very clear and very straightforward, a look of certitude. Modern psychologists have a somewhat peculiar, but very accurate word, to designate those characters in whom all powers seem to be subordinated to a central energy, a scientific or artistic, political or religious faith, accepted unhesitatingly and without revision. They call them the *Unified*. Seneca has already said, anticipating by his discoveries as moralist our modern theories of mind:—

"If you have met a man who is *one*, you have seen a great thing."

An inward disposition is not enough to secure so even a balance. For that is required a very rare harmony between circumstances and instinct, between surroundings and inward impulse. This juxtaposition occurs in the cardinal to a singularly exceptional degree. Speaking to me of his life, he told me with the affecting gratitude of a believer who recognizes the acts of Providence behind the fashion of the passing world:—

"I have had a happiness very seldom known. I was born here, baptized here. I made my first communion here, and I was ordained priest in the same cathedral of which I am now the archbishop."

And he went on to relate his first visit to Rome, where he had a seat in the Council of the Vatican, the youngest of the thousand prelates gathered in that assembly. He was bishop of South Carolina, and had been barely five years a priest. At that time there were only forty-five bishops in the United States.

"I remember," he went on, "coming here to the first Baltimore assembly, when I was chancellor to the archbishop. There are more than twice that number now. It is with this as with conversions. They counted then. This year I have had seven hundred in this diocese alone, which is very small. The human soul needs food," he added in English, "and it finds a perfect nourishment only in Catholicism."

He speaks very pure French, hesitating a little for words. Listening to him you feel that his utterance would never be brilliant, but his speech is so free from declamation, his mind is so evidently at the service of a conscience in love with truth, each phrase reveals so steady an effort to make the expression tally with the thought, without extravagance or feebleness, that an irresistible authority emanates from his words, the same that was presaged by his countenance, gentle, firm, and true. Quite naturally when he entered upon the field of social problems, Monsignor Gibbons again changed from French to English. It would seem as if we ought to be able to use a foreign language with the greater facility the more familiar are the ideas which we wish to express. Nothing of the kind. The more we have thought of a subject, the more precise our ideas, the more we require for their expression the language in which we formulated them. Perhaps we must seek here for one of the reasons why so many superior men experience singular difficulty in using for their own thoughts languages which they understand and read perfectly.

"I never had any influence over the creation or the organization of the Knights of Labor," the cardinal replied to one of my questions. "What I said on the subject at the time of my visit to Rome was that the Church has no motive for condemning on the spot and on principle all associations of laboring men. I have always thought, and I still think, that workingmen have the right to combine to protect themselves against the tyranny of their employers. I know the dangers of these associations; to begin with, strikes; once united they are so soon tempted to enter upon this way, which is not good, and in which they have always been crushed; and then intolerance and the persecution of their comrades who refuse to join them. Notwithstanding these dangers, I believe that the Church would risk the loss of too many souls by forcing millions of these men to choose between their faith and a society of which the principles are not in themselves to be condemned."

"A revolution in the United States?" he said, in answer to another question. "No, I do not think it possible. The Americans have been often reproached for being first and above all things practical. Before they dispossess a millionaire — a billionaire, if you will — of a single dollar, they will realize that they are overturning the cornerstone of the whole edifice, and they will pause. Our workingmen are very intelligent, their ideas are daring but very just, and they are quick to see the logic of things. They already understand, in spite of the sophisms of agitators, that to attack property in one form is to attack it in all forms. When the Chicago anarchists were condemned, public sentiment, as manifested almost immediately after by a vote, was in favor of the judge who pronounced the sentence, and against the governor of Illinois, who had manifested sympathy with the anarchists. We have no such revolutionary ferments among us as are upheaving Europe. Our workingman, when he will work, gains amply the means of livelihood,— two, three dollars a day. They will come in time everywhere to the eight-hour day. More than this, they are not irreligious. There is not an instance of a public man who is an avowed atheist."

Upon my observing that I had, however, met at Harvard University a large number of minds imbued with agnosticism,—

"It is true," replied the cardinal, "that a movement of this kind may be recognized in certain very cultivated circles. But it is confined to those circles, and Christianity is still very vital, both in private and public life. Congress is opened with prayer. The President never addresses the people without pronouncing the name of God. The Sabbath rest is faithfully observed."

There was a passionate firmness in the archbishop's voice, and a warmer light in his eyes when he spoke of religious things; and he also, like Monsignor Keane, extolled the blessings of liberty.

"Our great strength," he resumed, " is in having no alliance with the State, and in the respect of the State for our independence. We can the more efficaciously take part in public affairs under these conditions, and work for the good of all. The State willingly aids us in matters of public order. For example, in Baltimore, on the occasion of the last council, the postoffice department opened a special office for the use of the bishops. But, beyond minor details of this kind, the State is not concerned with us. It is the public which takes us into consideration. They are continually coming to consult us. Thus, not long ago, in the matter of the Louisiana lottery, I was requested to write a letter for the public press. I wrote it, and I think it helped toward the suppression of that scandal. The people love us, because we are their friends."

I interposed with the question if this was also the case with the rich, and if, on the other hand, he did not foresee great difficulties arising from the accumulation of such immense fortunes in so small a number of hands.

"Yes," he went on, "that is a grave problem. We must hope that in time a better way of dividing the common wealth will be found. This is why I said just now that my sympathies are with the associations by which the workingmen protect themselves. And I am not afraid of them, notwithstanding formidable excesses, because our workingman — I cannot say it too emphatically — is profoundly, fundamentally sensible. In the first place, he has himself the chance of becoming the millionaire he so much envies. That often occurs. Besides, even apart from this hope, he is instinctively liberal and just. When the income tax was proposed, I had occasion to talk it over with many of the laboring class. I found them all opposed to the measure, and all for the same reason. They did not approve of a measure which tended to espionage and falsehood. They deemed it inquisitorial and immoral. Yes, I have confidence in the people. I have confidence in their love of truth. I had a very evident proof of it a few years ago, when I published a little book showing Catholicism as it is, entitled *The Faith of Our Fathers*. Two hundred and fifty thousand copies were sold, and Catholics were not the larger number of the purchasers."

The prelate's serious countenance lighted up at the memory. I never felt more acutely than when I saw that proud smile the broad separation between the petty self-gratulation of the professional author, counting his thousands for vanity or for lucre, and the manly joy of the champion of the faith, who measures by the success of a book the service he has rendered to the truth. Men of God give such teachings without even knowing it.

With this beneficent impression closed an interview of which

I think I have usefully preserved the most important features. As I crossed the threshold of the See House, I bore with me the feeling that I had been talking with an excellent priest. "That is really something," as an old priest said to me in the Holy Land, showing me the view of Nazareth. After saying to me, "I look every day upon this scene and I say to myself, This is where Our Lord went about when he was a little child; yes," he added, with emphasis, "that is really something."

Who was it wrote this profound sentence, in which all the sublimity of the Christian priesthood is summed up: "God gave the priest to the world. The priest's charge is to give the world to God."

A few weeks later I was in the "hall" of one of the great hotels in Fifth Avenue, New York. In the office clerks were sorting mails, talking into telephones, stamping bills. Business men were reading their letters, cigar in mouth. Others were crowded around a little table, where a keen-eyed young woman, pale from sedentary work, was playing with nimble fingers upon the keys of a type-writing machine. They were waiting their turns to dictate a letter. Others were awaiting the descent of one of the three elevators that ply shuttle-wise along the fourteen stories of the hotel. Others were passing through a door beyond which could be seen reflected in a mirror the bar counter, surrounded by persons seeking refreshment.

In the midst of the "hall" a man was conversing — a sort of giant with powerful frame, one of those men of broad shoulders, thick waists, large hands and feet, in whom nature appears to have put the most vitality, and used, so to speak, the most material. But the straight lapels of his frock-coat showed that he belonged to the Church, and his violet collar that he occupied a high place there. It was Monsignor Ireland, Archbishop of St. Paul, whom I had vainly sought the previous autumn in his diocese of Minnesota.

I should have recognized him if his name had not been spoken, so much is he the visible embodiment of his eloquence. His large, long face, with its deeply marked features, is lighted up with bluish eyes, almost too small for these strong brown features. The grizzling of his hair and eyebrows, naturally very black, betray the prelate's fifty-seven years passed. The square chin gives evidence of a strong will, the high nose of sagacity, the forehead has that slightly retreating line which marked Mirabeau and Gambetta, two other great orators. The mouth is admirably flexible and expressive. It is an eloquent and persuasive mouth, with large lips that speak of kindliness, though when at rest they are somewhat stern. Notwithstanding his valor, the archbishop has passed through too many struggles not to have sometimes longed to utter the *Nunc dimittis* of the wearied crusader. At that moment he was all attention and good nature. I was to learn from him a few minutes later that the personage with whom he was thus publicly conversing was a reporter.

"I never refuse to see a journalist," he said, after explaining this little American custom. "Only I warn them that if they report me incorrectly, I will never see them again."

The archbishop's voice is guttural, almost harsh, a characteristic common to many celebrated orators. One of his admirers had told me that the opening words of his speeches are sometimes painful to the ear, but soon it becomes accustomed to his tones. Then he himself warms up, and the gift of expression is so mighty in this man who was born to be a public leader, if not an apostle, that you end by losing even the harshness of his voice. What never-to-be-forgotten hours I spent that morning, and that afternoon, and still another day hearing him talk of America with profound patriotism, of France with touching sympathy, of Europe with lucid and high impartiality! Listening, I wondered at the flexibility of his mind, in which there is all the excitability of the Celt,

— Monsignor Ireland, as his name indicates, is of an Irish family, — all the logic of the Latin, — he was educated in the little seminary of Maximieux in the diocese of Belley, France, — and all the realism of the American laboring people. His father was a carpenter, who came from Ireland to Minnesota long before the city of which his son is archbishop had come into existence.

I listened while this versatile and vivacious discourse passed from the highest theological subjects to the humblest details of practical activity. The archbishop told me how, at one time, he had been obliged to oversee the seed-sowing of the immigrants of his diocese, who were too many and too ignorant to make the best use of the homesteads they had taken up. Then he replied to my intricate psychological questions as to the nature of American piety, in which mysticism is so promptly translated in terms of activity. He described his first visit to Rome, and the sort of terrified surprise with which the old cardinals looked upon him. Then returning to the social problem upon which I had been questioning him, as I had questioned the cardinal, he went on: —

"Our workingmen? No, I dread nothing from them. In the first place, they are well disposed, and those of them who are not well disposed have good sense. There is in America, from top to bottom of the ladder, a much more conservative spirit than Europe imagines. The dominating sentiment everywhere, in the poor day-laborer as well as in the millionaire, is respect for law. The laborer is not revolutionary. He knows too well the value of what he has, to dream of a social order which shall be absolutely different. But while he accepts the existing order, he desires to protect himself from it, — is he so wrong? And he proceeds by means of associations, — is he so wrong in that? That is in the race. Rich men amuse themselves in clubs. Why should not workingmen organize in clubs too, and especially in societies for their own protection? A great step was taken when the several trade associations formed themselves into a larger association. And again, why should they not? In this way was formed the Knights of Labor. In my opinion, this is well. Capitalists are beginning to understand that they have to reckon with these great collective forces. What is the result? They confer, and conference is the surest means of coming to an understanding. For instance, this year the directors of a Western railway, the president of which I know, felt obliged to lower wages; the profits of the company had fallen too low. This is what took place. First of all the president entered into conference with the representatives of the engineers. These conferences lasted four days. The men asked the reason of the reduction. They examined the balance-sheet of the company. They learned what were the figures necessary to the maintenance of their present wages. These conferences with the president ended, they conferred with their comrades. Finally, this body of workmen having accepted the reduction, it was the brakemen's turn. You would need to have been present at one of these interviews to be able to appreciate the deep sense of equality that pervades this country. But, you see, the American business man is too little removed from the time when he was himself a workingman not to know, when he talks with his workmen, with whom he is talking and what he ought to say to them. These people do not deem themselves of two different races, and that is much."

The archbishop was silent. He was about to touch frankly upon a painful subject. In every word I had felt the thrill of the plebeian apostle. By his origin the neighbor of the humble, like the business men of whom he had been speaking, he rejoices in the progress of the laboring people, and suffers in their mistakes. He went on: —

"Nevertheless, our workingmen are touched by two grave

faults. The first and greatest is intemperance — unhappily that of alcoholic liquors. For they drink practically no wine. We have carried on and we are carrying on an unwearied campaign against this vice. We have not yet conquered. The second fault is extravagance. Our workingmen go too fast. They spend their money as fast as they earn it. They want their daughters to be ladies. Go into their houses: you will find carpets, pianos. It is not that they care for luxuries; it is the profound feeling of equality that urges them to make a show. It seems to them natural, almost necessary, that luxuries should be within the reach of everybody. Then when hard times come they are poor and they suffer. Insurance is correcting this a little. Side by side with the extravagant are the prudent. Many come at last to buy a bit of ground on which to build a house, and then they immediately buy the next lot for speculation. This is why envy of capital does not exist among us. More than this, our working people are chaste and they are religious. I am told that in Europe concubinage is the scourge of the poorer classes. There is nothing of the sort among our people. I can sum up their virtues in one word: the hope of the Church is in the working people. All who are Catholics practise their religion. You will see them all communicate at Easter almost without exception. This fervor of the people is what gives us the magnificent opportunity of which I am always speaking.

"Yes," he went on, "this immense country is new, free from prejudices, and it increasingly feels the need of that order in unity which is the distinctive mark of the Catholic Church. The great problem in order that this unity shall be manifested, that there shall truly be an American Catholic Church, is that of language; there must first be one speech. But many of our members are immigrants, Germans, Poles, French Canadians. They come here speaking their own lan-

guage, led by priests who speak no other language.   Here is
a real peril.   If we insist upon the English language in our
dioceses, these priests will be left without a flock and these
people without priests.   And yet it is necessary to compel
both people and priest to learn English, in order that our
Church be not dissipated in a series of local bodies and also
that we leave no ground for the accusation that we remain as
foreigners in the country.   But what then! it is an effort to
require it of the first generation, but the second will be composed of true American Catholics.   Here again we have had a
struggle.   The Germans have petitioned Rome that the bishops
here should be of different nationalities in proportion to the
nationality of the immigrants.   Now of ten million Catholics,
more than three millions are Germans.   A third of the bishops
would then be Germans.   That would be the end of the unity
of our Church.   Happily, the petitioners mingled politics
with their request.   That touched the patriotism of American
citizens.   They bestirred themselves and we won.   Ah, our
future is vast, very vast, if only we will be profoundly, reso-
lutely American and democratic.   We have need of three
things: morality, and we have it; adherents, and immigration
is unceasingly bringing them; knowledge, and our universities
and seminaries are going to give it to us more and more.   But
mark well, it is not the culture of yesterday that we need, but
that of to-day, of to-morrow, of the twentieth century."

And while the archbishop appeared already to see with his
clear eyes the triumphant morrow for which he has given his
life hour by hour, I called to mind his utterance in the cathedral of Baltimore, of which all our conversation had been only
a commentary: —

"Christ made the social question the very basis of his teaching.   For this is the proof he gave of his divinity: The blind
see, the lame walk, the lepers are healed, *to the poor the gospel
is preached!*"

N

One of my French friends, to whom I read the report of these two conversations, shook his head. For ten years his duties have kept him in New York. He knows the United States well, and he believes the country to be threatened, if not with a catastrophe, at least with tremendous disturbances. I should add that he is naturally a pessimist, very hostile to democracy, and that he lives in a state of permanent rage against the positivism and the impenetrability of American society.

"I should like to have them here, your two archbishops," he said, after a few petulant and mocking exclamations; "I should just like to lay a few of these documents before their eyes." And running through one of the cases on his desk he brought out several files of papers.

"These are not ideas and phrases, here; these are facts and figures which I have collected for a great work, which I shall perhaps never write, and as they are all taken from reports published by the Labor Bureau in the last ten years they are incontestable. It is now January, 1894. Well, at the end of last December, not twenty days ago, the official investigation stated that, in the States of New York and New Jersey, the number of men out of work amounted to two hundred and twenty-three thousand two hundred and fifty. In Pennsylvania, the number reached a hundred and fifty-one thousand five hundred. Calculate, and you will not be beyond the truth, that there are thus in this country more than eight hundred thousand unemployed, as they call them. Add the two million women and children who compose their families, and you will reach the conclusion that at the present moment, in this terrible winter, the Great Republic has upon its soil three millions of human beings who are literally dying of hunger! And they would have me not believe in an approaching revolution, when such armies of desperate folk are here ready to follow the first agitator who knows enough to arouse them!

"Add to this that all these starving people are enrolled in some association, and that beside them swarms another army, almost as wretched, — the workmen whose pay is little by little reduced, and whose work is made almost intolerable by the universal business depression.   Here are more figures from the same official list.   You will find them, and others as conclusive, in the book which Madame Aveling — Karl Marx's daughter, I think — and her husband have published, under the title *The Working-Class Movement in America.*   In Fall River, for example, in the large cotton manufactories, the average wage of the workingman is nine dollars a week; that gives him a dollar and a half a day, while in New Jersey the average comes down to a dollar and a quarter, and in the rest of the United States to a dollar.   At a first glance, these figures seem rather high, and it is by bringing them forward that certain economists boast of the superior condition of the laboring classes in America.   But to appreciate what these six or seven francs a day are really worth, you must make a comparative table of the cost of living in different countries.

"The average rent of the American laborer is sixty-six dollars a year, while the average rent of the Swiss laborer is twenty-five dollars, and that of the German laborer twenty-two dollars. The American laborer spends for fuel nearly thirty dollars, while the Swiss laborer spends twenty, and the German ten. Everything is in proportion.   The wages which appear sufficient from a European point of view do not represent the support of a family.   The labor of women and children results from this state of things, and here the conditions are still more severe.   See, here are other figures.   In Philadelphia, the making of women's chemises brings sixty cents a dozen, nurse's aprons thirty-five cents.   A woman can make nearly a dozen chemises or two dozen aprons in a day, working from half-past five in the morning till seven in the evening.   Better educated women, employed in what they call "clerical work," in stores and offices, earn from five to six dollars a week. Out of this they must pay their board and washing, and dress well in order not to lose their positions.

"As to the children, these are the heart-rending statistics. In Connecticut, of seventy thousand laborers, five thousand are under fifteen. Of every hundred employed in cigar-making in New York City, twenty-five are children. Now the work in cigar factories is ten hours a day. In the cotton-mills it is eleven. In Detroit, the small boys in the factories work nine hours sixteen minutes, the little girls nine hours and ten minutes. Observe that these figures are taken in the States where labor legislation is a prominent feature. And now," he added, folding up his papers, "if you want these statistics to become alive for you, you have only three very simple experiments to make, none of which will keep you from your hotel more than a few hours. Ask a newspaper editor to detail one of his reporters to accompany you into the lower quarters of the city: the first visit during the day, the second at night, the third to the penitentiaries on the Islands. You will see the refuse of this civilization, the pomps of which have so dazzled you, and perhaps you will conclude that I am not wrong in protesting against the optimism of two great bishops, whose ideas about the working classes in the United States you have sought. Like many good men, the dreams evoked by their good wishes hide from them the hideousness of the real."

I have followed my compatriot's counsels, although the documents which he cited made no very profound impression upon me. I have studied social problems too much to attach great importance to official investigations. They are the same as revolutionary inquisitions, and that is saying all. Both proceed by extreme figures and, when all is said, the proof that existing social conditions are endurable is that men continue

to endure.   They permit frightful wretchedness, which springs
from causes too complex for the remedy for this refuse of
civilization, as my friend expresses it, ever to be formulated
with exactness.   Whenever men have tried to apply radical
measures of reform to this infinitely complex organism, they
have added the injustice of disorder and its misfortunes to the
injustice of destiny.   None the less, the revolutionaries are
right in dwelling with emphasis upon the too odious facts and
the brutal oppressions which constitute the social sin, the sin
of all of us.   They prevent wretched egotism from sleeping,
either by terrifying us in the midst of our security, or by
awakening our humanity, and they urge us to remedies of
detail, the only ones which have even a little mended the lot
of the victims of a too severe competition.

I do not therefore regret the three excursions into the lower
strata of New York, undertaken in consequence of this conversation.   Although such experiences are very superficial, I think I
have gained from them a more accurate view of the conditions
among which the future of this unparalleled country is being
worked out.   The hours spent in these three visits were short,
and the details which I was able to grasp were limited.   The
reader will judge by the pages in my journal, to which I con-
signed each of these " experiences " on the spot, whether I am
mistaken in attaching some importance to their significance.

January 13. — Toward noon on a cruelly cold winter's day,
Mr. K—— and I boarded one of the green cars on Broadway,
which are still drawn by horses.   In twenty minutes we had
quitted the New York which I know for a New York which I
do not know.   Blocks succeed blocks, built after a still more
incoherent manner in this part of the town than in that in
which I disembarked five months ago.   We changed cars at
the corner of First Avenue, and after twenty minutes got out
again, and went on foot down a long street of dilapidated

houses.   The cellar of one of them has a steep stairway, which leads us to a sort of little "office," divided into two rooms by an unpainted, unpapered board partition.   One serves as waiting-room, the other as office.

This is the central office of one of the workingmen's associations, which abound in the United States.   This one has recently been founded by a young man, who happens at the moment to be within.   I shall call him *Bazarow*, after the nihilist student in Turgenieff's novel, *Fathers and Sons;* it will not be in contradiction with the remarks which we exchanged during this strange afternoon.   He is a Russian Jew, from the part that borders on Poland, who came to New York six years ago,— an agitator by profession.   He is rather good-looking, with long, very light hair, which curls around a very pale face.   His prominent eyes are sea-green, the whites dashed with minute threads of blood.   His thick enunciation has less of a foreign accent in French than in English.   He has but recently acquired the latter language, but he speaks it with the extreme facility which belongs to his double origin, —Slav and Semite.

This disturbing personage asked us to be seated, after having looked at us with that searching glance which takes for granted a possible spy, — the glance of all militant socialists. However, he is all right with the law, and the certificate which authorized him to found his association is displayed upon the wall above the table, beside a small notice printed in Hebrew, and marked with a death's head and crossbones.   Apparently he saw nothing in us to justify suspicion, for he continued to sort the voluminous morning mail; but this time with the ostentatious air of the over-busy official.   He would read names, dictate appointments, express surprise at not recognizing this or that one, consult his secretary.

The latter, a man of forty, sordid of dress and sorry of mien, was occupied with counting out fifty cents to a workingman,

who meekly, with a sort of dogged passivity, held out a red
pass-book.   The secretary exchanged a few words in German
with his gloomy client, then spoke in Russian to his chief.
I became aware of a pile of pamphlets on the table, destined
for the propaganda.   They were the English translation of
a work by the Italian Mazzini, — *The Duties of Man.*   I
opened it haphazard, and found a chapter upon God.   This is
the point from which the revolutionary party sets out!   To
arrive where, their newspapers tell too clearly!   What they do
not tell clearly enough, that which such a place as this makes
perceptible and, as it were, concrete, is the international mixture, the astounding fusion of races, which this company represented.   I found here a corner of *Cosmopolis*, one of the
quarters, a suburb, rather, of this city of cities, whose founders
were exquisites like the Prince de Ligne, Lord Byron, Madame
de Staël, Beyle, and Heinrich Heine.   These great artists and
noblemen sought in expatriation and travel that which would
make them the better enjoy the composite charm of the vast
modern civilization.   It is one more proof that our habits and
our surroundings have precisely the meaning and value of our
souls.

Bazarow finished with his mail, and set out with us for the
police station.   We were there to take a detective to accompany us on our visit to the lower districts of the city.   The
agitator himself expressed the desire that we should be thus
protected, and himself with us, against dangers which proved
to be entirely imaginary.   But the slight detail showed better
than all the discourses how essentially this party of social
destruction, which to us conservatives appears to be so united
in its hatred of the established order, is at bottom divided
against itself.   Our guide was afraid of being maltreated by
workingmen of another school of opinion.

His gait alone was enough, in this city of haste, to betray

the foreigner.   It was the gait of the lounger, who walks without aim, without haste, without directness.   He wore a sack
overcoat, longer in front than behind, because of the books
with which his pockets were crammed.   With his soft, shapeless hat, his flannel shirt, his shiny trousers, he reminded
me of the Bohemians of literature who haunt the cafés of
the Latin Quarter and Montmartre, with their indifference to
the external world, their aggressive thoughtlessness, and their
infatuation for ideas, and especially for words.

During the half hour which we spent going first to the police
station and then, the chief of the said station being absent, to
a bar for luncheon, Bazarow talked, talked, talked.   His gar-
rulity was not without eloquence.   Like all revolutionaries
whom I have known, he kept to generalities.   He was lavish
of unverifiable, and therefore indisputable, theories of a vast
regeneration, continually interrupting himself with a "that is
my belief," enough to arouse an assembly of idiots to
frenzy.   He announced certain precise opinions upon the
French peasant, whom he compared with the Russian peasant.
That he understood them both shows the extent and the
penetration of this revolutionary work, in its prepara-
tions for attacking the farm laborer, after corrupting the
factory hand.   The name of Jerusalem having come up in
the conversation relative to the farm colonies which some
benevolent Israelites are undertaking in Palestine, Bazarow
exclaimed: —

"Jerusalem!   My father wanted to send me there!   But my
Jerusalem is here.   My father," he continued with a sneer,
"would have made me a saint.   I have become an infidel."
His large green eyes shot forth the strange glance peculiar to
some of his race, in which there is an infinitude of mystification
and of lost illusions.   When you have seen the Jews weeping
at the foot of the Temple wall in Jerusalem, on Fridays, you
can understand what must be the scepticism of those who have

hoped for ages, whenever they cease to believe in the promised Messiah, who, for them, has never come.

And, as if this man had heard my thought, he went on : —

"There is a deep gulf between us and the men who believe in the Bible, I know. There are those who pretend to be socialists, especially Catholics, Archbishop Ireland, for example. But Catholics, Jews, or Protestants, priests, rabbis, or pastors, they all tell the people that they must accept the will of God, that they must be resigned, *satisfied*. Well! socialism consists in teaching precisely the opposite, in demonstrating that he ought to be in revolt, *dissatisfied*."

He uttered the profound remark at the very moment when we were crossing the threshold of the restaurant, into which Mr. K—— invited him, saying, with the incisive irony of a true American,—

"We democrats like aristocratic public houses, don't we?"

We entered a dining-room, pretty sumptuously decorated, indeed, with mirrors and colored glass. Business men, almost all Jews, were taking a hasty lunch. One of them recognized Bazarow and shook hands with him. It was one of the manufacturers for whom he had worked on his first arrival in New York, and whom he had well-nigh ruined by a strike.

"He fought me quite openly," said the agitator, "and I fought him openly. That is not a reason for not recognizing one another."

He smiled, remembering the strike, episodes of which he related to us while eating some fried oysters. He saw in it a glorious campaign in favor of ideas which I hope he at least believed to be true. He forgot the men it made more hungry. For that matter, those are things that revolutionaries never think of. When you investigate their mental make-up, you always find that these are minds given to the abstract, for whom human woe is simply the starting-point for a course of

reasoning. The theorists who talk of it the most are those
who have felt it the least!

We returned to the police station.   Our companion remained
at the door, and wisely, for the celebrated Mr. Byrnes, whom
we found at length, spoke of him in terms which would have
made the visit very painful if he had been present. This
superintendent of public safety, the best that New York has
ever had, is a sort of stern-faced giant, with firmly closed
mouth, and penetrating, almost compelling, eye. It is a
strange impression thus to exchange in a few seconds the
company of a declared revolutionary for that of a professional
officer of justice.   You feel the necessity that every civilized
person shall take part in the implacable and incessant duel
of order against disorder, and, at the same time, the legiti-
macy, in a certain sense, of both sorts of people. I was
destined to feel this impression still more strongly. To escort
us in our tour through the land of poverty, Mr. Byrnes detailed
one of his best officers, whose real name I have promised to
conceal.   I shall call him Clark, as I have called the Slavonian
nihilist Bazarow.

A man entered, short and thick-set, with the face of a mus-
tachioed Molossian, and a tenacious jaw beneath a square-cut
nose.   His little black eyes seemed to be burning away back
near his brain, like those of beasts of prey. He was an
animal all muscle and all pursuit, his slightest movements
betraying the agility of a savage. Merely in looking at his walk
I understood why American romance-writers have a fancy for
taking detectives as the heroes of their sensational novels.   In
a creature of this race, physical and moral energy are in a state
of perpetual ebullition, as among soldiers on a campaign.
Audacity, presence of mind, capacity that would suffice to
itself in all dangers, address, and art, showed themselves present in this athletic policeman, and, with it all, the joviality of
a soldier.

We took leave of Mr. Byrnes, whose sharp eye softened as he looked on "his man," and were soon downstairs. Mr. K—— and I introduced Messrs. Clark and Bazarow to one another. All the antagonism of two social species was suddenly revealed, in the accidental meeting of these two men. The prominent eyes of the revolutionist became insolent, with a sort of ironical and terrified insolence, while the policeman's little short nose wrinkled and shrivelled, like the muzzle of a bulldog about to spring. The "Very glad to see you, sir," with which he greeted the other, sounded like a growl. Then walking side by side, their backs alone continued to call up the thought of two worlds in conflict, the one with his trooper's figure, his military overcoat, brushed and buttoned, his hat shining like metal, his feet encased in strong boots, walking with a singular firmness, while the other, by instinct and bravado, emphasized his carelessness of attire, with his uncertain steps, his irresolute hands stuck in the pockets of his torn and soiled trousers, his indifferent, mocking, and indomitable air under his ragged headkerchief. And yet they began to converse, with the good-natured familiarity which seems to float in the air of this vast democracy, and to be breathed in at every pore.

"It is astonishing that we should not have met before, Mr. Clark," said Bazarow.

"And that I have not arrested you, my boy," replied the other.

"Oh!" said the Pole, "we know that Mr. Byrnes and his men are not fond of men who are engaged in organizing labor, and those men are not fond of Mr. Byrnes and his men, either."

There was pride and defiance in the foreigner's thick utterance. We foreboded a dispute, and I asked Mr. Clark about his life and profession.

"Well," he said, after a few words about his age and his family, "my profession has the merit of always holding out the hope of some little excitement. Last week, for example, I had the muzzle of a desperate burglar's revolver in my mouth. If he had fired, I should not have had the pleasure of making your acquaintance and that of this gentleman."

He looked again toward Bazarow. I felt his muscles swell under his overcoat. They tingled at feeling their prey so near and not being able to fall upon it. His little eyes shot forth a wicked gleam. For the moment the excitement of his profession consisted in protecting the enemy upon whom he could have pounced with such good will. Mastering himself, he laughed and offered him a cigar.

While conversing thus, we had reached the heart of the district the New Yorkers call the Bowery, from an old Dutch word meaning farm. The street which we had entered might, with all its sordid houses, have been a suburb of Rome or Naples; for it was inhabited only by Italians. After having walked for a few moments between these buildings, all whose signs and notices were in Italian, we entered the first abode. It consisted of two rooms on the level of the street, as small as a boat's cabins.

Men and women, to the number of eight, were working there crouched over their work, in a fetid air, which an iron stove made still more stifling, and in what dirt! Not one of them spoke English. I put a question to them in their own language, and learned that they were from Catanzaro, in Calabria. Four years ago, at this precise date, I was visiting that lovely city, perched aloft where one can see the sea, and which one reaches by climbing a hillside planted with cactus. Why did not they stay there, pasturing their flocks and eating the wild fruits that grow along the edge of the thorny green leaves of the prickly pear?

Invincible hope brought them here, to this hole, for which they pay eight dollars a month, the price of a year's rent in their own country! Instead of their window opening on the wild, purple mountain, the deep green ravines, and the free blue sea, they open their window, when they want to renew the air, upon a court, cold and noisome as a sewer, into which rain down the pestilent microbes from the linen of all the neighbors, hanging overhead from ropes.

It is like this, indefinitely, all along this street, and how many others? We visited a second house, where lived a second family, composed of nine persons. This one came from Caserta. The women and children are shivering in their rags, in spite of the stove, always at white heat. With their Southern faces, yellow — almost greenish — from the heat of their natal sun, with their brilliant black eyes, these exiles move you to pity. Two steps away, in the open air, — if this harsh, pestilential cellar-fog can be called air, — girls from Abruzzo, wrapped in thick shawls, are tacking coverlids. Thin, and already worn out, in spite of their twenty years, they look at you with a smile that is hungry and cold, — above all cold, cold to the marrow of their bones, cold to their blood, — and curse *questa brutissima terra*, this hideous land.

We recognize the emigration enterprise, the exodus of entire villages, the voyage from Naples to Gibraltar, then from Gibraltar here, at cheap rates, in the hold or on the deck, according to the season, on board of one of the vast steamers the colored picture of which was displayed in the windows of the wine shops along the street. Above it flaunts the announcement of the company, which is German. On the front of another liquor saloon is the Savoyard cross. There is a symbolism in the juxtaposition. Is it not to the work of the Triple Alliance and their military folly that we must attribute the flight of these unhappy wretches from their beautiful but impoverished country? Even between these two wretchednesses, the *agio* does not let them alone. The sufficiently ironical inscription, Banca Popolare, appears at a corner. Blue bills of a hundred or fifty lire are displayed in a glass case, tempting the hand. Our companions pause.

"Do you not think," said the socialist, emphatically, "that it would be better to give all this money to the wretches whom we have just seen?   Besides, what if they should take it?"

. "They will not," said the policeman, philosophically. "The habitual crime in this ward is not theft.   It is first of all knifing, and prostitution also.   They sell their women to the Chinese over in the neighboring district.   The law forbids yellow women to live in the United States.   But John" — this is the American nickname for the natives of the Celestial Empire — "John has a great liking for white women, and he buys as many as he can with the money he earns or steals. For theft is his crime, as drunkenness is that of the Irish. Here is their street," he concluded.

Italian signs had given place to illegible signs in characters of the extreme Orient, and on the narrow sidewalk, which here was clean, I heard the clicking of the thick wooden soles of the yellow men.   Short and fragile, with smooth faces under their round hats, with black braids of hair rolled up underneath in an oily chignon, they come and go silently. Their bodies have no visible form under their wide-sleeved blue blouses, and their small feet have still less under the flapping of their loose pantaloons.   This sort of delicate-featured dwarfs, with their loop-shaped eyes, so black in their copper-colored skin, their high cheek-bones, the triangular framework of their faces, and their flat noses, gives the impression of an invasion of beasts that would spread over all the city, gain and gain and destroy everything.   There is something of the serpent in their flat faces, and an enigmatic endurance in the expression, that seems to receive nothing from the surrounding world.

Since we had left the Italian street, Bazarow appeared to have himself become as impassible as these casual foreigners. The revolutionary could not but hate them, for they are more dangerous enemies to socialism than the most ferocious capitalist, working for almost nothing, with a result always uniform, ever repulsed, never wearied, fifteen and sixteen hours on a stretch.   In them labor feels itself disgraced; and it is constantly necessary to protect them from the wrath of their competitors of the white race, whom they would ruin if they were left free to do it.   In proportion as the agitator grew gloomy the detective became more jovial.   He found these people "great fun."   He went into all their shops, handled all their wares, clapped them all on the shoulder with his broad hand, bursting into roars of laughter.

The little yellow men winked their black eyes with sly humor.   They offered us their wares,— tea enclosed in dainty boxes, lacquers, stuffs, porcelains, all worthy of a bazaar of the twentieth order.   But they asked exorbitant prices, and kept on smiling when we discussed them, without emotion and without insistence.   It is not commerce by which they live in New York, it is laundry work.   They undertake it at such low prices that they have monopolized it; they need so little!

To observe their diet we went into one of their restaurants. Prepared dishes, which showed minute handiwork, were waiting on high round tables; stuffed oranges, first peeled and then reclothed in their protecting skins, dressed onions, hashes in green leaves, strange crudities betokening entirely different stomachs, the gastric juice accustomed by a heredity of a hundred centuries to dissolve other foods.   Everywhere the long straight pipes with their little metal furnace betrayed the traditional vice,— the terrible taste for opium.

"You should come back at night to see them smoke; they work by day.   Between the two they have not much time for mischief.   If they alone were in New York, Mr. Byrnes would not be so busy."

While the watch-dog of the police thus muttered, looking again at Bazarow, the countenance of the latter cleared and brightened.   His ironical mouth began again to speak.   We were now in the midst of his adherents, for we had passed from the Chinese to the Jewish quarter.   These are mostly Germans and Poles.   Ah! the invincible, the indestructible race, which I find just like itself, just what I have seen in the lanes of Tangier and Beyrout and Damascus, and on that height of Safed, where, in the synagogue, the old rabbis comment on the Talmud and proclaim the Liberator.

Whence came the poor Jews of this quarter?   Through what abominable Odysseys of persecution have they come, to set out in this quarter of New York such displays as only they and the Auvergnats have the secret of,— these stalls, where the merchant finds a way of selling the unsalable,— old iron, old buttons, old bits of wood, old rags?   These indescribable shops, with their refuse of refuse, encroach upon the sidewalk.   The signs are now in Hebrew.   Newsboys are offering papers, also in Hebrew.   There are swarms of children, attesting that fruitfulness which the Book promised "as the sand of the seashore."   Many of these little ones have eyes of magnetic Oriental brilliancy, and we see it also in the eyes of the women who are living in all this poverty.

Now Bazarow is at home.   He moves among smiles and salutations.   He knows every one and every one knows him. The uncertain steps of an hour ago become firm to guide us. We follow him into several workshops, as much of men as of women, where they work with the needle.   We find there, ranged under the oversight of the chief, the "boss," thin, patient, masculine faces covered with hair, with enormous noses, poor, hollow, feminine chests, shoulders sharpened by consumption, girls of fifteen as old as grandmothers, who have never eaten a bit of meat in their lives,— a long, lamentable succession of forms of poverty.

We could hardly endure the air of these shops, where the odor of ill-cared-for bodies mingled with the odor of spoiled food, both being exasperated by the heavy odor of the stove. We asked these slaves as to the wages they earned. Here the figures given by the partisans of revolution became sadly correct, a correctness which, thus certified, wrung the heart. For a dozen of these little children's trousers, over which these hunger-hollowed faces were bent, the contractor pays seventy-five cents. The worker cannot make eighteen in his best days, by not losing half an hour. Twelve shirts, that consumptive women are hurriedly stitching, with needles held in feeble hands with bent finger-nails,— yes, twelve of these shirts,— bring thirty-one cents, and the worker must pay for the cotton! And even these prices are not sure. Within a year wages have been lowered one-half. Who can say what they will be to-morrow? Meanwhile, they must sustain life, but how? Plates scattered over the tables make reply, filled as they are with scraps that would disgust a famished dog. These embittered lips bite into them with an avidity that appals you. We saw a twelve-year-old girl lay down her work to eat where she sits. She was so pale, so emaciated, that tears would have come to our eyes though the agitator had not said, in a declamatory tone: —

"Is it not a shame to humanity?"

What could we reply, if not that when the strike came this human wretchedness would not have even this bone to gnaw?

January 15. — About eight o'clock in the evening, a fellow journalist of New York, Richard Harding Davis, came with two friends to take me to the Bowery for a nocturnal expedition to succeed that by daylight. This remarkable author, one of the first short-story writers of young America, is a man of less than thirty years, with a strong face, square and hard-featured, burned red by the sun, a snub nose and a square chin. It is a typical face of this side of the water, beardless and forceful, with the fine-cut features of a strong physiog-

o

nomy.   There is extreme nervous tension, almost exhaustion, in the lines around the mouth and the expression of the eyes. And yet the dominant look is of youth and health.   Back of the overburdened journalist and romance-writer you can detect the near presence of the "Princeton man," the student who, six or eight winters ago, was captain of some great football team!

On leaving the University, Davis became reporter on a great Philadelphia daily.   This singular calling having put him in touch with the lowest rabble of the worst parts of the city, the picturesque qualities of these refractories awoke the artist within him, and in a series of short stories he has pictured a number of these socially doomed characters, of which one, to which I have already alluded more than once, Gallegher, is a masterpiece.   In him, with a few strokes, of matchless precision, he has painted the Gavroche of this country, the untamable boy with nerves of steel and indomitable will, whom you see in the tramways and railroad cars, rushing in by one door and out at another, crying his wares, newspapers, novels, or fruits, in a high-pitched voice.   There is both humor and tragedy in the fifty pages of this story, to which I refer the reader who may be curious as to American customs.   It is the result of an observation terribly keen and yet pathetic, darkly realistic and yet light-hearted.   A sort of untamed whimsicality works out in healthiness all that might have been atrocious in this etching from nature, and on this January evening, when we were rolling in a carriage toward the Bowery, the paradise of those whom in Paris we call *escarpes*, and in New York "toughs" and "roughs," Davis was the very talker of his story, a fanciful humorist, full of the freshest anecdotes of these grotesque figures of vice and crime.

For example, he told us how the original boy who posed for him as Gallegher went to the newspaper office in which the sketch appeared, to demand his share of the author's rights.

He described himself, going out from his father's house in Philadelphia, in evening dress, and meeting a thief with whom, for the purpose of study, he had fraternized incognito in a low gambling-house. The thief approached him with a wink: —

"What are you doing here? Are you butler in this house?"

And as the writer amused himself with answering in the affirmative, he went on, —

"When you rob it, don't forget me. I'll be in with you."

On this good promise, with a hearty hand shake, the two parted.

While he was charming us thus with his rendering of a coarse conversation, mimicked with a sort of genius which explained to me his success as an author, that gift of his for making his words flow and almost gesticulate, we arrived at the central police station, where the other morning I had seen Mr. Byrnes smile into the face of the courageous Mr. Clark. We were to take another detective this evening, who, however, showed the same broad shoulders and the same quiet intrepidity as the former. Social species in these singular callings work out a uniformity of type not to be surpassed by natural species.

This one, like his colleague, professed an idolatry for Mr. Byrnes and a passionate love of his calling. As a hunter of big game never spares you a single one of the lions and tigers that he has shot, and spreads out before you skin after skin, showing you the bullet hole, so the policemen would have us look over hundreds of photographs of criminals arrested in New York during the last few years. The predominant characteristics of these heroes of robbery and murder are a wandering or a maniacal expression, and sadness. You can count the laughing faces — and what laughs they are! insolent, defiant, sneering. Still less numerous are faces that reveal intelligence. When it occurs, it is so concentrated, so visibly turned in upon itself, so armed and defiant, that it frightens you even in this impotent reflection, emanating from these inert pictures. I think that if ever I meet them in life I shall recognize the eyes of one of these photographs among others, those of a man of thirty, condemned for forgery, whom the detective gazed upon with undissembled admiration, murmuring, "He was a great man."

As in memory I compare this collection of portraits with a similar one of French criminals, which I have had in my hands in Paris, it seems to me that those of this country are more bitter, more sinister, more entirely unclassed, more implacable, and especially more perverse. I sought in vain among them for the features, so common in Latin countries, of the man who has fallen through weakness — the near neighbor of him who remains respectable through circumstances.

Are these things really so, or have I, in this view, taken up with general theories, so natural to a traveller? Neither did it seem to me that the collection of confiscated articles tending to prove criminality was made up as it would have been made with us. Roulette tables alternated with revolvers, night sand-bags with burglars' tools, counterfeiters' moulds and dies with engraved plates for counterfeit bank bills. One would say that thieves were more industrious here and — how shall I express it? — less *occasional* in their criminal acts. The detective showed us a saw with which a celebrated criminal had dismembered the corpse of his victim. To wring from him a confession of his crime, another detective conceived the plan of walking by night clothed in a shroud, and moaning, up and down a corridor, which we also visited, on which the criminal's cell opened. The murderer believed he saw the ghost of his victim and confessed his crime.

"For all that," said one of our companions, in disgust, "it was not fair play."

That is the true Anglo-Saxon cry, with all the innate horror

of the race for subterfuge and falsehood.   Hearing it, I recall
to mind a similar indignation experienced by a young girl, in
whose presence was related a story of the delightful hypocrisy
of a Sicilian prince of the last century.   Sick unto death, he
vowed to build a Chartreuse if he should recover.   He did
recover, and to reconcile his devotion with his avarice he
hit upon the device of building in his park, at the gates of
Palermo, a pavilion in the form of a monastery, which may yet
be seen.   The word "Certosa" still adorns the entrance, and
the half-score of cells are inhabited by the figures of monks,
but in wax, among which is found an Abelard occupied in
writing to Heloise!

"What a shame!" was the only word which this charmingly
humorous anecdote called from the American girl's lips.   She
saw in it only a want of conscience, and ignoble insincerity.
Our friend of this evening is not far from the same judgment
of the perfidy used in the matter of the dissector of corpses,
and I am sure he will not willingly give his hand to the inventive policeman who devised this cunning trick.

Upon this discussion we went downstairs to the street, and
this time we went on foot.   It was nine o'clock, and already
all the houses were closing.   Nocturnal life exists only in
Paris.   In New York, as in London, all the house-fronts are
dark long before midnight strikes.   Only the "saloons" continue to blaze forth from the ground floors of buildings, large
and small.   On the counters are prepared by the score such
ingredients as were wittily defined by a Bacchic poet of Louis
XIII.'s time, "spurs to much drinking."   There are salted
biscuits and smoked fish, ham, and fried oysters.   A betting-
machine stands in a corner, like the swivels that decorate the
wine shops of Paris, with this difference, that here they only
play for whiskeys or cocktails, and also that the ball is here
replaced by a whole poker deck.   One of those ingenious
inventions which the American is never weary of inventing

causes these cards to come and go under glass each time that a silver dollar falls into a slot arranged *ad hoc*. A "full" appears, or a sequence, or two pairs, or a flush, or some other figure, and this suffices to give the poor devils who are playing thus their evening dissipation, the illusory mirage of such a game as they like.

They are standing in the blinding light of gas or electricity, already, at this hour, so drunk they cannot move. Almost all of them, even in this low part of the town, have that air of being *all but* well dressed, which gave me the first day an impression as of a whole city dressed from a shop of ready-made clothes. How many have I seen, Americans of all classes, dressed in this *all but* good style, carrying a tiny valise of leather paper, with a change of collar and cuffs! In the morning they go to the barber's, after taking a bath in the dressing-room of their hotel bedroom. One negro brushes their boots, another their hat and clothes. A narrow line of white linen at the wrist and neck, and above the large Ascot necktie which hides the shirt another line of white linen, and you have a gentleman whose neatness will hold good till the midnight bar.

They end by going into one of these bars. From eight to a dozen "gentlemen" of this type were discussing matters over their glasses, in which preserved cherries were floating between slices of lemon. For the moment they were intensely interested in comparing the chances of the Californian, Corbett, and the Englishman, Mitchell, who were to have a match at Jacksonville, Florida. A number of portraits of celebrated athletes, in fighting costume, which hung on the walls, bore witness to the admiration of the saloon-keeper and to his secret business. No doubt he arranges those clandestine matches which Davis has so accurately described in his Gallegher, tickets of admission to which cost a hundred, or two hundred, dollars. He was a German, and with his crafty bluish eyes, set in his broad, pallid face, he glanced at the detective, who seemed not to know him, though he knew him very well. Both indifference and a feeling of equality spoke in that glance. With the secret history of elections in the United States, who can tell whether a simple saloon-keeper is not one of the chief suborners of votes for the party in power? Was there some consciousness of this strength in the calmness of this German, as also in the attitude of the infamous customers of this obscure patron, who smoke great cigars at half a dollar apiece, with all the serenity of the gods of Lucretius? They appear to be little disturbed by the moral campaign announced in the last few weeks. Two new visitors came into the resort, and talked German with the liquor-dealer. Decidedly, New York is not only the true Cosmopolis of the idle and the dilettante, but a monstrous crucible in which all the adventurers and the needy of the whole world meet, mingle, blend together to form a new people. What people?

Blend? Does this intimate mixture of elements, so far from solvable, which we call "race," really take place? As far as the yellow race goes, we can boldly reply, no. What strange power keeps these people so unsusceptible to surroundings, so capable of abstracting themselves from those around them, — *insulating* themselves, if we may so speak? I received a new proof of this that very night, as I left that den to go to the Chinese theatre, a few steps distant.

Upon the stage the actors, men disguised as women, all painted and dressed, — painted in bright colors that lacquered their faces, dressed in heavy stuffs, embossed, embroidered, stiff and shining,— act or rather mimic, with slow, infrequent gestures, a scene in an interminable play. A stringed instrument, harsh and monotonous, accompanied this phantom-like representation with a moaning, creaking sound. What did I say about gestures? During the half-hour that we spent there the seven actors did not make twenty motions between them.

The scene represented the interior of a pagoda opening upon a garden, and called forth, no doubt, action enough to sustain the interest of a public who utter not a word, and neither laugh nor applaud.

There are five hundred of these copper-colored men in the audience, motionless, in their working clothes, every one like all the others, in his round hat, his braided queue of black hair, his ample blouse of dark blue, and those everlasting serpent faces, spanned by long, shining, inexpressive eyes. Not one of them appears to observe our presence, although we must have made some noise as we went down the passage between the seats toward the stage. You feel them to be foreigners, to a degree inconceivable — impenetrable and above all unintelligible. These unresolvable differences show themselves in their choice of amusement and its quality; for our amusements are ourselves, our individuality, our tastes, whereas our labor often only interprets to us the slavery of our surroundings.

This theatre, and the hypnotic automatism of the play, had nothing in common with the sort of diversion which we seek for in a play. And in the same way, the coarse and mechanical drunkenness on alcohol — our drunkenness — has nothing in common with the intellectual poisoning by opium, which is ever the favorite vice of these people. One must see how some of them abandon themselves to the delights of this terrible drug, immediately on leaving the theatre, to understand how this mania for stupefactives corresponds in these natures to profound, and doubtless indestructible, instincts. The two impressions complete one another with singular power.

On leaving the theatre, twenty steps brought us to the door of one of the cellar rooms which serve these maniacs as dream caverns. By the light of a half-lowered gas-burner, we saw an emaciated Chinaman lying on a matting which covered a stone bench running around the wall. With supple fingers he felt about in a pot filled with a blackish substance. With a stout metal needle he adroitly and surely rolled up a thick pellet, which he warmed at a flame. Then, with the point of the same needle, without haste, with the same adroit and accurate motion, he inserted the burning pellet in the metal bowl of his pipe, and drew a few whiffs. The pipe was smoked out, and he began operations over again, his eyes swimming in a luxurious languor. Twenty such operations, and he will be like the stout man whose figure is visible in the depths of the cellar, bloated, livid, and motionless, deep in visions, from which no human force could ravish him.

A smiling and supple personage—the keeper of the cellar—runs hither and thither, preparing pipes and opium for other customers, who are awaiting their turn to abandon themselves to the charm of this mysterious and deadly ecstasy. The solitude and taciturnity of this dissipation make the place almost tragic. No loud voices, not even a word. There is a solemnity as of initiation in the attitudes to which the devotees of this artificial paradise abandon themselves, and this debauch appears at once less vile and more criminal, less disgusting and more incurable, than that on whiskey or brandy. Certainly it is so different that a shudder, as of a nightmare, creeps over us, and we leave this den with a sense of relief.

Chinese lanterns light up the lower end of the street with their fantastic light. A turn of the corner, and they have again given place to gas, and opium to alcohol. Now "saloons" follow "saloons." A gigantic and obsequious policeman, whom the detective had picked up to guide us through the opium dens, suddenly stops before a tall building, which he points out with a gesture of pride.

"Well," he says, with most comical emphasis, "you may

be globe-trotters, but you will never find any place like the Bismarck of New York. Do you want to go in?"

We assent, and he explains — Oh irony of human glory! — that the Bismarck is simply a lodging-house at twelve, ten, or seven cents a night. Immediately entering a dark passageway, we saw him conferring with the doorkeeper of this dormitory of poverty. The latter, after some affected objections,— the prelude to a tip only too intelligible to one who knows the lack of conscience of the American policeman,— permits us to ascend a badly lighted staircase, pervaded with an abominable odor. A door opens on the first landing. We parley again, and enter an immense room, heated almost beyond the breathing-point by a colossal iron stove.

There, in a vapor hardly pierced by an occasional lamp, we dimly see a double row of beds of rubber cloth, literally heaped with human beings, some draped in remnants of rags, others entirely undressed. The wretches were all plunged in that death-like sleep in which life yet renews its deepest energies. We could see by the position of their limbs that they had not lain down, but fallen down, sunk down, exhausted as they were. The soles of their feet, black with the mire of the streets, told of aimless wanderings by sidewalk or street. The emaciated faces of those who had unragged themselves — one must create words to describe the nameless divestment of these nameless tatters — followed us with their eyes, passively, stupidly. We seemed to them the apparitions of a dream, seen through the double vapor of this heavy air and of their overwhelming lassitude.

Yet these sleepers are the favored ones. The sort of hammock in which they are reposing must be a singular luxury, since to procure such ease they have spent two cents extra. Two cents' worth of bread! Two cents' worth of whiskey, of tobacco! The lodgers of the floor above sleep on boards. Those of the third story, on the floor — hard indeed, in its pestilential promiscuity. But it is not the street, it is not the January night, so cruel to poor exhausted flesh. This is the thought that I distinctly read on the delicate, weary face of a white-bearded old man, who had taken off his jacket, seated on the floor of the last of the three dormitories, a veritable phantom of human want, never to be forgotten, with the anatomy of his emaciated body, with tufts of grizzly hair on the projecting ribs.

Looking at him, I recalled to mind that this very evening I had been invited to a ball in one of the palaces on Fifth Avenue. Without regret I had sacrificed that festivity to this visit. The house rose up before my mind, decorated with roses at a dollar apiece, illuminated by the dress of women who bear on their persons twenty-five, a hundred, two hundred thousand francs' worth of precious stones. The champagne which is poured out at the buffet costs five dollars a bottle. And the roses will fade before any one has so much as taken the time to inhale the sweetness of their perfume, and not one of those diamonds and rubies has dissipated a sad thought of those who wear them, and these lovely lips will barely have touched the cups in which sparkles the monotonous beverage. These contrasts between the frightful reality of certain sufferings and the useless insanity of certain luxuries, explain, better than the most eloquent theories, why, at certain times, a rage simply to destroy such a society takes possession of certain minds.

The extortionate policeman, who might have been detailed to mount guard over that ball, as he has been charged to guard the Bowery lodging-houses, is as proud of the excess of poverty into which he initiates us as his Fifth Avenue colleague would be of the ostentation of the festivity. He jocularly repeats his former remark : —

"Well, have you seen anywhere in the world such a place as the Bismarck?"

And standing on the threshold, breathing the free night air with all the breadth of his robust lungs, he adds: —

"Now you know, gentlemen, how much a breath of fresh air is worth."

Decidedly, this humorist is determined to earn his fee; for perceiving that we are moved by the sight of that inauspicious hostelry, he invites us to dispel these visions of sadness by a descent into another cellar, inhabited by an Italian. "There is always some *jollification* there," he says.

The word is untranslatable, like the *jolly* from which it is derived, and which signifies good-humored gayety, good-natured practical jokes, a certain rough grace of good health. Upon this, I ask him of what nationality are most of the inhabitants of the Bismarck. According to him, Germans and Irish predominate. Americans, properly so-called, are rarely found there. For that matter, one might almost think, on exploring the lower quarters of the city, that there are none in New York, or else that they are all rich, so many are the foreigners we have met to-night and the other night. We find more foreigners in the nocturnal *trattoria* to which our guide introduces us. But the promised jollification is limited to a sight of an evidently embarrassed patron, irritated under his constrained politeness. While the three compatriots with whom he was conversing went on smoking their long cigars of chaff, and emptying their fiasco of Chianti, without looking at us, the big haggard man, with crafty eyes, assured us, in a tone which suggested the penitentiary: —

"You may see everything in my house. I have nothing to hide." He repeated "nothing to hide — nothing to hide," four times over. What act of conspiracy, smuggling, or prostitution had we interrupted by our entrance? The policeman must have known, for he drew us out of the cavern with as much eagerness as he had before used in urging us in. He claimed to be at the end of his beat and we left him, to finish this night of low investigation in a series of public balls and beer-gardens.

January 18.— This morning, D——, K——, and I paid a visit to the two islands in the East River, Blackwell's and Ward's, where are the insane asylum and the penitentiary. We were to meet Mr. Clark, the detective, who accompanied us the other day, at the door of the Tombs. This is the municipal prison of the city, containing also a police court and a court of special sessions. New York slang has baptized it with this funereal and symbolic title because of the large and heavy Egyptian columns of the peristyle.

The calling of a detective does not lend itself to punctuality in keeping appointments, and Mr. Clark is on duty. He sends us word by one of his "policemen" that he will join us later "if he gets through in time," which signifies that the worthy bloodhound is on the scent; who knows, perhaps only a few steps away, in one of these streets? Perhaps the criminal that he is tracing is still hurriedly treading these sidewalks with despairing step, casting searching glances over the houses which seem to us so insignificant, but which to him may prove an asylum or a place of destruction.

They stretch out in long rows, commonplace, enigmatic, betraying no secrets that they may have, while another "car," then an elevated railway, then another "car," carry us to Bellevue Hospital. Close by, a small wooden wharf serves as point of departure for the ferry-boat, which daily carries to the islands the men and women under sentence and relatives of the insane persons. A cell-like wagon arrives almost at the same time as ourselves, bringing its load of convicts. The people give it the classic nickname of "Black Maria." Its occupants, who will not return until after months or years, if ever they return, get down carelessly. They are swallowed up in rooms arranged in the sides of the boat, while the deck is crowded with poor folk, women especially, carrying baskets filled with provision for some unhappy being, to whom this is all that remains of joy!

The boat puts off. It is operated by men in brown uniform, many of them negroes; they are working out here their purification from a long sentence.

We begin to converse with the "boss," while the strange floating house glides over the curling waters, that wash against the boat with loud surgings. We pass other ferry-boats, tugs, merchant vessels. A sharp wind is blowing, the sky seems as if contracted by the cold tension of a black snow-cloud. The shore line of the city is a shabby, so to speak soiled, coast, with a leprosy of mean buildings and dark beaches, where are collected the unclean refuse of the approach to a capital. The "boss," whose trade it is to transport poverty, folly, and crime along this scene of buildings and rubbish, is a jovial old man, who serenely chews his quid and ejects his streams of saliva while watching over his crew. He opens for us two cabins, into which he has bolted the guests of the "Black Maria."

That of the men contains about ten individuals. Their debased and unexpressive faces do not even speak of the resolution of "tramps," as they call the wayfarers whom one sees trailing along the New York streets, picking up ends of cigars with pride. The women seem more vivacious and more tragic. There are seven: three Irish, three Germans, one negress. The seventh alone is a true American. Of the unhappy creatures who compose the crew, those who are not black are also all Europeans.

The "boss" points out a Frenchman who has strayed in among the others. He is from Picardy, and came to the United States after the war. Why? He does not confess this any more than the crime that brought him first to the penitentiary and afterward to this boat.   He tells us of his arrival here, the first few years, his solitude, the too hard work — he was a slater — the too implacable people.   He is probably telling the truth on these points; you feel that, by the severity of his words.   No trace of his fine national humor survives in him, not even the mocking flattery by which the Latin takes his last and useless revenge, when he is vanquished by too severe civilization.   He is really too thoroughly vanquished.

Perceiving his wretchedness in infamy, I regret less that the figure of French immigration into this terrible country is so low.   Statistics figure it at fifty thousand four hundred and sixty heads in the last ten years.   On the other hand, America has received during the same period, a million four hundred and fifty-two thousand nine hundred and fifty-two Germans. What a formidable sum of certain temptations, of probable crime, is represented by such an afflux of adventurers!   One shudders at it, when one examines some authentic examples taken from life.

There is the same singular collection of foreigners, male and female, between the walls of the two asylums for the insane which we visited; the first on the more distant island, Ward's, the second on the nearer, Blackwell's.   But for this peculiarity, which proves how disastrous is the over-pressure of American life to nervous systems not native to the country, these buildings are like others of the same kind in all lands. I shall long see before me among the men a German from Koenigsberg, who believed himself to be the old Emperor William; with his curled moustache, he talked and swore, marching up and down with threatening gestures.   And among the women I shall not soon forget a Norwegian, with soft, sea-colored eyes, who sat at the piano and played a vague air, a thousand times repeated.

Both buildings are kept with that perfect adaptation of material convenience which distinguishes America and England.

The principle here, as I had already observed when visiting the Boston hospitals, is to assure autonomy to each establishment. Each, from the least to the greatest, must suffice for itself. Each must have its own bake-shop, its own laundry, and its own laboratory for preparing its own medicines.

With this independence of each establishment there is much more freedom of initiative. If there is an experiment to try, an invention to apply, there is no need of going through administrative red tape and awaiting an order from the central power. Each one makes its own conditions, and this absence of official supervision, so much admired by people so highly centralized as we, may well have its disastrous aspects. We received that impression from a few words which one of the doctors said to us with an air of triumph. We had asked to see the violent cases.

"We have none here," he replied.

"How is that?" we asked.

"We have none," he repeated.

"But if those who are not violent should become so?"

"Oh," he replied, "we should soon quiet them."

"May we see your appliances?"

"We have no appliances," replied the physician, proudly; "we believe that physical constraint is degrading to the patient; we prefer to use chemical restraint."

"They drug them to death," whispered K——.

Was he right? After this we always imagined that we saw in the eyes of those we met the numb stupor of opium or morphine, although the doctor affirmed that both these substances are forbidden. A gloomy terror seemed to reign over the asylum for men, while in that of the women we were touched by an air of pleasantness, almost of gayety.

The halls and corridors were hung with flowered paper; Christmas trees, with their fruits of stuffed cotton, still remained from the festival of the preceding month. Bananas of yellow cloth alternated with oranges of red plush. The tender home instinct, imperishable in the heart of woman, and that maternal instinct that abides even through insanity, had suggested to the inmates a graceful and touching thought — that of placing around the Christmas trees large dolls, dressed in warm garments, to take the place of the children for whom they had imagined themselves to be preparing their gifts. And yet, with all the care they had taken thus to adorn their place of confinement, they were truly prisoners, and they knew it. All of them said in thought what one of them said aloud,— a white-haired negress who was giving a warm cloak to another. The latter laughed with pleasure at the warmth of the garment.

"How happy she is," said one of our party. "What more can she want?"

"To be free," replied the old blackamoor, and both paused, the one in her kindly adjustment of the garment, the other in her laugh, and looked toward the window, with the longing eyes of a caged animal.

And how sad a reminder of liberty was the view from that window! the broad island plain, sterile and bare. Sorry trees grew here and there in shapeless fields, greenish with a scraggy, worn-out turf, across which meandered the gray lines of unused paths. The clouds hung low in the sky; in the distance were two barrack-like buildings. One is the workhouse, the charity building, the other is the penitentiary.

We finished our day by a visit to this prison. Mr. Clark was now our guide; we found him waiting for us outside the insane hospital. How did the police watch-dog know that we were there — precisely there and nowhere else? We did not particularly wonder at this small proof of his professional scent, any more than at the carriage which he had found for us — where? — in this desert plain.

P

We had not been ten minutes in it when we began to see convicts laboring in some earthworks. But for their uniforms of white, with broad dark stripes, we might have taken them for workingmen at their ordinary task. Absorption in work is so essential a characteristic of American life that these convicts seemed not different from free workmen. Their countenances were not more sad than those of engineers on their locomotives, or smelters in their foundry.

The prisoners became more frequent as we drew nearer to the huge building on the height. Arriving there, we had no need to parley, as at the door of the Bismarck. Our guide felt himself quite at home in these great barracks, of which he is one of the most skilful purveyors. We followed him through them, especially interested in the rows of cells, in which we again perceived the spirit of the country. Their strong iron gratings opened upon a broad passageway, affording the greatest facilities for surveillance. They are narrow, high, and so arranged as to admit of two superimposed beds, like those of a steamer cabin. A placard above the door bore the names of the inmates.

I read a few of these, corroborating my recent observations; most of them are not of this country. The terms are short, — six months, a year, two years at most. In general, a fine is added of one, two, or five hundred dollars. When the convict has no money, he works out his fine at the rate of a dollar a day. The fare is decent, almost comfortable when one thinks of the bitter poverty of the Bowery. The men are called up at half-past five; at half-past six they have bread and coffee, at noon they have meat, at half-past five bread, soup, and coffee. At six they are locked in, with permission to read until ten.

Their librarian was seated at a table in one of the galleries, classifying tickets. Even in his convict's dress, his intelligent and serious countenance, his white hands and quiet application, attested the "gentleman." He, too, was a foreigner, an Englishman of excellent family, guilty of having enjoyed club life, sport, gaming, and general elegance, by means of checks too dextrously made. He was here employed in the work for which he appeared to be best fitted, and this is the case with all of them.

The workshops were, therefore, filled with workmen, who do excellent work at a low cost. In pavilions surrounding the central building there was a forge and a cabinet shop, a shoe factory and a locksmithy, and so on through the whole range of trades. We saw rows of tailors, painters, bookbinders, clockmakers, peacefully at work. They would have needed only to have lived this way in their time of freedom to be happy. And yet if their freedom were given them, not one of them, Mr. Clark assured us, would maintain in the slightest degree the habit of work which they now seem to have formed. Most of them are recidivists who have taken, quitted, and taken again the road to the disciplinary workshop, without this active use of their hours of servitude in the least affecting their perverse wills.

What part of their internal machinery is it that is so radically perverted? In this land of all enterprises they have tried to create, not very far from here at Elmira, a reformatory, a sort of rural hospital, precisely that they may reach this hidden spring. It appears not to have had much success, and hence they are coming to the pessimistic conclusion that the best solution of these problems, as of all that touch upon social maladies, is simply an efficient police force. The thought is too terrible, and yet it seems to be only too much in keeping with human nature. Some men are born foxes, wolves, and tigers; others are born watch-dogs. I came to this view of the fundamental duality of the human race while walking the streets of New York behind Bazarow and Mr. Clark. It struck me again as I heard the latter say aloud : —

"Ha! There is my quarry!" And he pointed to a turner, a young fellow of twenty years, broad-shouldered and sturdy, with a coarsely vicious face.

"I arrested him with this hand," said Mr. Clark, opening and closing his hairy hands. The convict leaned over his work without appearing to recognize the detective, but he turned as soon as Mr. Clark had walked on, and followed him with an expression of mingled fear and hatred, speaking at the same time a few words to his neighbor. But Mr. Byrnes's bulldog cared no more for that than the dog that ran down one hart and is chasing another cares for the former's furious or suppliant glare.

I might extract hundreds of such pages from my travelling-journal. Will these suffice to make concrete the objection urged by my New York friend against the somewhat official and determined optimism of the two great Catholic archbishops? At any rate, they will suffice to throw a full light upon the fact which appears to me to dominate the entire history of the social movement in the United States, and to explain its apparent contradictions.

This fact is the presence in the lower classes of a foreign contingent so considerable that at certain times the American, born in America, of American parents, seems to be a sort of aristocrat; too proud to serve any master whatever, too intelligent to subject himself to small details of business, naturally destined by virtue of his inventive genius, perseverance, will, to draft into his service these hordes of immigrants whose labor he unfeelingly uses and pays for.

This paradox hardly overstates the truth. To be convinced of this it needs only to examine a table of statistics — in one of the almanacs issued every year by the newspapers, for example; and these incontestable figures give a still more significant import to this foreign contingent when one has just visited the parts of New York where Italians, Germans, Irish, Poles, Jews, and Chinese swarm and struggle in poverty.

In the first place, observe that this formidable immigration is entirely of recent date. From 1789 to 1820 hardly two hundred and fifty thousand colonists left Europe for the United States, or only nine thousand men a year. The newcomers of this period were very soon taken up into the American organism, which still possesses a remarkable power of assimilation. But assimilation has its limits. And figures show the gradual rising of the flood which by degrees passed these limits.

After 1820 the number of immigrants increased year by year tenfold, almost a hundredfold. It reached twenty-three thousand three hundred and twenty-two in 1830, eighty-four thousand and sixty-six in 1840. The result of the events of 1848 and 1849 was to carry these figures in 1850 to three hundred and sixty-nine thousand seven hundred and eighty-six. The Franco-German War and the Commune reacted still more strongly upon this invasion of the New World by the desperate inhabitants of the Old. In the year 1872 four hundred and five thousand eight hundred and six, in 1873 four hundred and fifty-nine thousand eight hundred and three expatriated men came here to seek — what? They themselves did not know.

We must look at totals in order to gauge as a whole the astounding phenomenon of a tide of men, or rather of nations, breaking upon this continent. In the two decades before the present one, the United States received from Europe, between 1871 and 1880, more than three million immigrants; between 1881 and 1890, more than five and a half millions. The population was therefore increased one-twelfth in these last ten years, by means of foreign accession, and this accession was solely, exclusively composed of workingmen.

Look through any guide-book you like, you will find that in Chicago, out of about eleven hundred thousand inhabitants, there are four hundred thousand Germans, two hundred and twenty thousand Irish, ninety thousand Norwegians, Danes, and Swedes, fifty thousand Poles, fifty thousand Bohemians. In Milwaukee two hundred and five thousand, or more than half the population, are Germans. There are a hundred and fifty thousand Germans in St. Louis. Denver, which in 1880 had thirty-five thousand inhabitants, now has a hundred and fifty thousand, an increase of, say, a hundred and fifteen thousand, all minors and foreigners. St. Paul and Minneapolis are Scandinavian cities, and San Francisco is entirely peopled with immigrants from all parts, including twenty-five thousand Chinese.

In the face of such evidences of an interior invasion so impetuous and so recent, we must see that the majority of the newcomers cannot possibly be Americans except in name. The United States did, indeed, assimilate the newcomers with marvellous rapidity so long as work was chiefly in the fields, while the great modern cities did not yet exist; before 1840 there was not a single city in America of more than five hundred thousand souls. Especially when these newcomers, immediately scattered abroad upon farms, did not form a compact, almost solid crowd, as irresistible and formidable as one of the elements.

This assimilating power was still miraculous thirty years ago, when the War of Secession recreated and strengthened American self-consciousness in a community of discipline and danger. One proof among a thousand may be given, — very slight but very remarkable. Before this war the Germans, under pretext of athletic meetings, had founded a group of revolutionary societies with the title *Socialistischer Turnenbund*. Before 1860 they were all radical, international, and Germanic. At the close of the war they had all, very naturally, become national and conservative, in a word, American. But in the last thirty years by what means can this assimilation have been exercised over these serried masses hastily engulfed in the labor of great industrial cities?

All these, landed but yesterday, may, indeed, dye themselves with Americanism, which for them generally means to drop off the feeble remnant of moral prejudice which clung to them from their previous life. They even learn to speak the language brokenly, though the greater number of them continue to use their native tongue. The proof of this is, that always in the courts accused and witnesses are interrogated through interpreters. It would be folly to suppose that their ideas have changed, their deepest aspirations been modified, their soul, in fact, metamorphosed. Once upon the soil of the United States, they remain the violent, desperate folk that they were upon the steamer; all the more that, in this country of their last illusion, they have met the same necessity for work as in the Old World, and a still sharper competition. They landed with all the moral dispositions of which revolutionaries are made, and they have remained revolutionaries, ready to follow those of their number who have brought hither from Europe their fierce and feverish Utopias, their furor for agitation, and their methods of organization.

Thus is explained the sudden development in this free democracy of a socialism most incompatible with all the past of the United States, with all their tendencies and their constitution, bursting out in disorders as formidable as the recent strikes of Chicago and California, in adventures as grotesquely threatening as the formation of the Coxey army and its march upon Washington. Look closely at it. These episodes presage not a social war, but a war of races.

The true American workingman — for he exists — is just such a man as Monsignors Gibbons and Ireland depicted, respectful to law, proud, above all, of the Constitution which he loyally obeys, and without hatred of capital. At his side swarms the immense crowd of workingmen of foreign race, ignorant of the history of a country which is to them only a last card to play against destiny, not understanding this country, — I might say hating it for all the disappointments they have undergone.

A few months ago, going along the Missouri, I was gazing upon the former America of other days, through the America of to-day, and the first struggle for extermination between the redskins and the Anglo-Saxons of the last century. This first outgrowth of civilization ends again in a conflict between men of alien blood. Will the Grand Republic, issued from the first Massachusetts colonists, so closely, so necessarily Anglo-Saxon in language and laws, uprise, be broken and destroyed by these foreign elements, these last few years, seeing that she seems no longer to absorb and transform in the same way as formerly? Class struggle is here only an appearance; at the bottom is an ethnic duel, and one may follow its motions in the history of the "labor movement," as they say here, detail by detail, almost year by year.

One of the best-informed economists of this country, Professor Richard Ely, has written this history with much conscientiousness and impartiality. Although he has placed himself simply at the point of view of an analyst, the succession of facts, as he gives them, shows at once the alternation of one current with the other, the American current and the foreign, in this vast flood of the laboring inundation. Thus also, at their confluence, the two shades of color in the waters persist long without mingling.

Would you, first of all, see the American soul at its work? See it struggling with those first experiments in communistic organization which it attempted, and which in madness of principle exceed the worst Utopias of the most extravagant collectivism. You will find this soul here like itself,—all will and in consequence, first of all, occupied with problems of responsibility; — all action and in consequence, deeply, thoroughly realistic in the details of its enterprise, even when the final aim is a chimera.

For example, there is the community of Perfectionists at Oneida, senseless as it was in its first conception. A graduate of Yale founded it, in company with other graduates of the same university. These young men were so exhilarated with their absurd logic that they included free love in their scheme, on the ground that exclusivism is no less culpable where the person than where property is concerned. When you study the practical regulations of a society whose principles are so contrary to the most profound instinct of human nature, you are thunderstruck on seeing men, of doctrines so Utopian, become psychologically most wise and accurate in their application. To cite only one illustration, you will find *mutual criticism* an organic feature of this singular community, the right of public and reciprocal criticism, "in order," they say, "to utilize the wasted power of observation which in the world is squandered in gossip and useless slander." Look into the financial result of their experiment, and you will be convinced of their sagacious administration by the balance-sheet of their final settlement. Having, in 1881, abandoned their plan of reform and resolved themselves into a simple co-operative society, their assets were found to be six hundred thousand dollars for two hundred persons, or three thousand dollars apiece. They had begun with the most insignificant capital.

So with another community, not less exceptional in its principles, the *Shakers* of Mount Lebanon. Under their religious mysticism, their ruling characteristic is a wise and practical acquaintance with the true conditions of human life. Daniel Fraser, one of the oldest of the brethren, used continually to say: —

"The two bases of morality are the cultivation of the soil and hygiene."

Regular habits, a scientifically arranged diet, well-drained houses, well-ventilated rooms, and a carefully supervised temperature,—to these minute details their ethic condescends, and to still more humble ones. "At Mount Lebanon," says Professor Ely, "I learned to close a door so softly that no one could hear the slightest sound. 'That is a lesson in Shakerism,' Daniel Fraser said to me; 'it is Shakerism reduced to the finest point.'"

Here you recognize, under an artless form provocative of smiles, a scrupulosity, a watchfulness over self, which is itself only one instance of their acute sense of responsibility. You find in it also the same innocent realism of conventual life by which monks so quickly became rich from the smallest beginnings. Everything holds together in such communities, and such a degree of discipline can hardly exist without a superior degree of the virtues of order and economy. Is not this pretty far removed from the sphere in which modern revolutions have broken forth?

But the social experiments of the Perfectionists and the Shakers were entirely isolated and arbitrary. The characteristics of the popular soul in the United States are more clearly marked in the development of the simple labor associations. For these associations have really been the work of the laboring men, a sort of stock of civic implements made by themselves for their own interest and according to their profound needs.

Here the two currents are the more clearly visible, because the second appeared at a considerable time after the first. Until after the War of Secession, the societies founded by workingmen, almost without exception, manifested the distinctive features of the Anglo-Saxon race, in its American variety. First, there were the trades-unions, entirely professional and local, like those of England; for instance, the typographical union of New York and that of house carpenters in Boston, founded in 1812.

The programme of the latter society falls into the line of those minds of which Robinson will ever be the ideal type, perfectly indifferent to vast general theories, but positive, moral, with a very individual power of initiative in the service of their own interests, and with ardent Christian convictions. The charter of the carpenters shows that they combined with intent themselves "to govern their own affairs, to administer their own funds, to study the inventions peculiar to their art, to assist the unemployed by loans of money, to support the sick and their families."

If one had talked with these fine fellows of a universal reform, if one had advocated a forcible reconstruction of the relations of employers and employed, a crusade of labor against capital, they certainly would not have understood the meaning of such dangerous words. They desired, as laborers, to improve their condition as laborers, because, in fact, that is the only practical and moral way, at once conformed to the precept to render to Cæsar the things that are Cæsar's, and at the same time truly useful, with an immediate certain utility. As to that, is not this the complete statement of the social problem: to improve the rich man as a rich man, the noble as a noble, the commoner as a commoner, the workingman as a workingman?

This spirit of Christian realism and patient progress continued to inspire the larger unions, which, after 1825, bound together the men of the same trade in different cities, or the men of different trades in the same city. In 1833, Ely Morse, the president of the general trades-unions of the city of New York, in a remarkable address, which was the first utterance of American socialism, spoke only of "elevating the intellectual and moral condition of the workers, diminishing the line of demarcation between workman and employer, and better administering the pecuniary interests of the poor."

Still this general trades-union society already foresaw the

danger of violent means, for one of the articles of the agreement forbade that "any trade section should enter upon a strike for higher wages until the motives of such strike have been investigated by the central council." Such, indeed, was the nationalism of American workmen at that period, that one of their chiefs, Stephen Simpson of Philadelphia, in a manual which at once became very popular, condemned with a thoroughly puritan indignation European ideas and literature as the source of all the errors of the United States. Another prominent labor leader in the same way announced the necessity of "checking foreign encroachments, and hindering their pernicious influence upon the moral and political health of the country."

In fact, the associations, which rapidly increased until 1860, were almost all thoroughly, zealously patriotic. · They were such not only in their names but in their claims, which never looked to be anything like an overturning of existing conditions. A more humane limitation of the hours of labor, a more generous distribution of aid, greater facilities for education, a more equitable scale of wages,— ideas as moderate and reasonable as these continually appear in their constitutions.

To realize these, the workmen always relied upon the most practical means and those most in conformity with the true Anglo-Saxon spirit of free action and liberty; they asked for individual subscriptions, they advocated clever electoral methods, they founded newspapers, they studied technical questions. Thus the American hatters' association, founded in 1854, is chiefly interested in the question of apprenticeship. It undertook to limit their number, in order at the same time to limit the number of workmen among whom work must be divided.

Following the various lines of their effort and their propaganda, one feels inspired with profound respect for so much conscience in the search for the better, for so manly an acceptation of their lot, for such constant and clear-sighted energy. One sees how much the Yankee of good stock was worth, is still worth,— he upon whom the strong tradition of the early New England colonists is imprinted; and one becomes clearly aware of the sudden astounding deviation of this movement by the second current, that which has made possible such speeches as those of Mr. Debs at Chicago, denouncing one of the great companies of the country, as a barbarian chief might denounce a city to be sacked: "We will side-track Pullman and his cars together," and accusing the government of military despotism for a mere calling out of the police!

Immediately after the War of Secession foreign influence began to make itself felt, and at the same time immigration began to increase from year to year. Even during the war, all Americans by birth or affection being in the army, foreign labor began to replace native labor. This substitution went on during the period that followed, which was marked by an enormous revival of industry. More and more hands were needed, and, as the means of transportation were becoming more and more easy, immigrants came in flocks. The Atlantic became the great conduit through which flowed all the malcontents of old Europe, especially of Germany.

The latter country, the true fatherland of revolutionary socialism, had already, after 1848, sent to America the first agitators who had sowed upon this soil of realistic individualism the seeds of an absurd overturning and a bloody Utopia. They were not destined to germinate until twenty years later. A tailor of Magdeburg, Wilhelm Weiteling, imprisoned in his own country for carrying on a revolutionary propaganda, came to New York. Aided by Henry Koch, another German, he immediately founded a German revolutionary society, the *Arbeiterbund.* A third German, Weidemeyer, a friend of Karl Marx, was not long in joining them. These three men may be considered as

very remarkable specimens of a type now common in the
United States, the cosmopolitan agitator, who imports into a
country of which he knows nothing revolutionary theories
which he has constructed with reference to the abuses of
another.

Both the convictions and the characters of all three were
entirely matured when they arrived. Weiteling was forty years
old, Henry Koch thirty-two. Weidemeyer had passed his whole
youth in conspiring in his native land. None of their ideas
were American, and none of the manifestations which they
stirred up, without immediate result however, were American.
Thus it was that a club of communists being founded in New
York, under their direction, in 1857, they decided to celebrate
the next year — what anniversary? That of the insurrection
of June in Paris! Several thousand men and women took
part in it; they belonged to all countries except America.

This society, this festival, and this club were the prologue
of the great drama of internationalism which is being played
to-day from Boston to San Francisco. The very word international had hardly been pronounced then. Now, and especially since in 1872 the grand council of the International
Association of Workingmen was transferred to New York, it
may be found in hundreds of programmes and in thousands of
articles published by newspapers which are printed in several
languages.

Even when the word is not there, the international spirit may
be recognized by the essential alteration of the principles on
which the truly American societies rested. In the first place,
there are no longer any religious declarations. Whether the
leagues bear the name Socialistic Labor Party, or International
Workingmen's Associations, whether they are called International Working People's Association, or Central Labor Union,
the S. L. P., like the I. W. A., or the I. W. P. A., and the
C. L. U., are all alike in the absence of Christian ideas. In

the chief, the arrogance of materialism has taken the place of the half-mystical solemnity of the workingmen still imbued with the spirit of the " Pilgrim Fathers." " The Church," they say roughly, " seeks ultimately to make complete idiots of the mass, and to make them forego an earthly paradise by promising a fictitious heaven."

With Christianity, humility of heart has taken its leave, and with it, the noble submission to the fundamental laws of human life, formulated once for all in the Decalogue. No doubt, certain orators still repudiate violence in the means, though holding up revolution as aim. It is enough, however, to look at their practice to understand that the foundation of every man's thought conforms to the terrible expression of the Pittsburg manifesto, " Destruction of the existing class law, by all means: that is, by energetic, relentless, revolutionary, and international action."

From this point there is to be no more slow and wise solutions, no more of that intelligent and purposed positivism which is the very essence of the American soul. From any traditional point of view we have had the last of these calls to the grand War of Independence which brought together both poor and rich in a common pride of belonging to the freest of peoples. The spoiled children of the party expressed the sentiment which the others scarcely concealed, when, unfurling the black flag at Chicago in 1884, they cried : —

" This is the first time that this emblem of hunger and despair has appeared upon American ground. It proves that this people has come to the same conditions as other peoples."

The *Freiheit*, one of their organs, put into brusque words what the Internationalists think of America : " Judge Lynch is still the best and least costly tribunal in this country."

In all these tendencies you recognize the obscene and violent socialism of Germany, from which issued Russian nihilism and French anarchism. This it is that three million Germans have brought with them within thirty years; this is the spirit that effervesces in monstrous strikes like that of Chicago. This is what flowed like a destroying metal into the moulds of the associations so solidly and practically formed by the first Trade-Unionists. Thanks to German socialism, these associations are bloated and deformed. Veritable armies, whose soldiers do not know one another, have been organized under the pretext of labor federations. The generals who manœuvre them are foreigners or the sons of foreigners, perfectly indifferent to the happy future of the country whose hospitality they have received. Even societies like the Knights of Labor, which keep the grand tradition of Christian idealism, have been urged by their new chiefs in the direction of international revolution, and Mr. Debs could exclaim a few months ago, with a pride which was at least American in its conception of the " record " : —

"We are going to have the greatest railroad strike that the world has ever seen."

This perverse ranter had a hundred and twenty thousand men behind him.

Sometimes it happens that a newspaper artist sums up in the happy hit of a caricature a whole political or social situation. Thus a picture in *Fun,* toward the end of the Chicago strike, brought together in three figures and a legend the entire significance of the strike and all its lessons. The traditional Jonathan is standing beside a rocking-chair, his hand in his pockets, a dead cigar in the corner of his beardless mouth. He has even forgotten to finish his glass of whiskey and soda which he has set down upon the counter. His thin melancholy face with its high cheek bones, lengthened by the legendary goatee, is profoundly meditative. On his waistcoat are the thirteen stars representing the thirteen original States, which are also seen on his silver coins. Facing him, a colossal policeman has by the collar a personage who might be a Russian peasant or a Bavarian workman, in a flannel shirt, trowsers tucked into his boots, and a soft felt hat: " I was obliged to arrest you, Debs. It was not a strike ; it was a revolution."

Jonathan utters this remark with the serious phlegm of one who understands and wills. What does he understand but that the newcomers are about to carry on in his country a work irreparably hostile to all his ideas, his conscience, and his past. What he wills, is to hinder at all costs, were he to die in the attempt, such a disintegration of his country. The formidable movement at Chicago may have been so far good. The problem had been stated with such tragic clearness that it was necessary indeed to affront it ; and it is to the honor of Mr. Cleveland that he acted with regard to this Western affair, in proportion to its importance, as Mr. Lincoln firmly acted with the South.

This first episode is probably only a prologue. Looking upon the map of the United States, and reflecting that between Chicago and the Pacific all the cities of this immense country are peopled with these newcomers, one sees the menacing possibility of a scission between the two parts of the vast continent which will have nothing in common, neither memories nor ideas, nor aspirations, nor even a language. Again the image of Lincoln arises, with face like that of Jonathan in the caricature, and you think that if he were to return to that Chicago whence he went forth, and which has become so terribly Germanized since his death, he also would utter the word of conflict : —

" Obliged to arrest you."

Just as the question of slavery was only a battle-field for the clashing of two contradictory civilizations, of the South and of the North, it sometimes appears as if, at the present time, the East and the West were also about to seek a field in which

Q

to measure their strength, or, rather, the America of Americans and the America of foreigners. The Silver Bill was one of these fields. The Chicago strike was another. The social question is a permanent one, upon which, perhaps, the decisive battle will be fought. The grand formulæ of social reforms have no more meaning nor any more sincere adherents in the United States than in France. The infinite complexity of a civilization is not modified at the bidding of even the most justified of our revolts, or the most intelligent of our theories. Except a few insane people, everybody in his inner heart admits this too evident truth, though almost every one says the contrary.

Under these problems, which every one knows are insoluble, throb other forces, real and not to be resolved. The day when excessive immigration shall have truly created two Americas in America, the conflict between these two worlds will be as inevitable as that between England and Ireland, between Germany and France, between China and Japan. Not against his employer will the American workman of New York and Philadelphia be led to make war, his employer and he will end by acting together against the foreign workman.

To sum up, in this vast democracy a very peculiar form of civilization has been elaborated, Anglo-Saxon in its origin. Another is in process of elaboration, through cosmopolitan associations, with nothing in common with the former. If the second form comes, by way of too widespread strikes and too violent illegalities, to a weakness of the whole national life, a civil war will break out.

Pessimists insist that such war is very near. Optimists point out that immigration, on the one hand, appears to have diminished; on the other, that assimilation, though become more slow and very difficult, yet goes on in an irresistible way, and that foreigners are becoming fewer and a little more Americanized every year, almost every day. They demonstrate that Christianity continues to dispute possession of the revolutionary masses with materialism, and that the Protestant pastors rival our Catholic bishops in zeal when it comes to the people. Was it not a Reform minister who uttered this fine exclamation, which was at first attributed to the generous heart of Monsignor Ireland: —

"Theologians say that the problem is to bring the masses into the Church. As for me, I affirm that the problem is to bring the Church to the masses. The Church is the leaven. The masses are the dough which it will leaven."

Optimists add that in America all the capitalists are still men thoroughly penetrated with the primitive energy, and that, in case of need, they will know how to defend their own interest, with a personal vigor very different from the spiritual weakness of the nobles of 1789 or the indolent cowardice of the small European landowners in 1894. As to the psychology which perceives in American society an experience without analogue, the years to come will be more interesting here than anywhere else, because, after having established the truth of all the novelties of this New World, we remain astonished on perceiving that fundamentally it is going, under particular forms, through the same crises as the ancient world endured. If the social problem in the United States was only a question of nationalities, is the political problem of Europe, armed to the death, to end in anything else? So true it is that thoughts and constitutions, doctrines and systems, are only appearances, under which are hidden a number of facts, always the same since the world was made, always real and indestructible, like duration and extent, first and last; conditions of our whole being and activity, our triumphs and disasters. And perhaps among the facts which are most indestructible, most real, the most essential is that of Race.

II. *Farmers and Cowboys*

To estimate more accurately the revolutionary strength of
international socialism in the United States, we must know
which side the immense agricultural population of the West
would take, in case of a decisive conflict — the farmers who
produce the wheat by which all America and all Europe is
fed, the drovers who feed the gigantic packing-houses of
Chicago with such a continual procession of cattle.

Here the foreign element is indeed found, but entirely surrounded, diluted, corrected by the national element. When
an Eastern man goes West, it is seldom with the intention of
becoming a workingman. He prefers to take the chances of
a more speedy fortune with the independence which inheres
in the cultivation of such fertile land, such productive horse
raising,[1] or in prospecting for gold. He becomes farmer,
cowboy, or miner. Thus is explained that abandonment of
the rural homes of New England, of which I have already
spoken. But if it is difficult to divine the real thought of the
workingman, even when we know the plan of the associations
to which he belongs, the newspapers he reads, the speeches
he makes and listens to, the leaders whose influence he is
under, how much more difficult is it to fathom the mind of
the gold-digger in his *placer*, the horseman in his tent, above
all, of the farmer in his circumscribed life, his long medita-
tions, and the almost vegetative darkness of his own consciousness?

We should, at all costs, understand this last, for he forms
the very basis of this immense population. But by what processes shall we attain to a knowedge of him? We know that
his lot is hard, worse than that, exhausting and murderous.
Travellers who have studied the laborer of Kansas, Missouri,

---

[1] The average of births, which is not more than 50 per cent in a state
of civilization, reaches 70, 80, and 90 per cent in the prairie.

Iowa, in his log-house, agree in describing him as put to the severest strain of all the much-tried inhabitants of the New World. The log-house, the little house of ill-squared trunks, is built in a corner of the prairie, his vast domain, burned by a torrid sun in summer and buried in snow in winter. The principal ornament of the room is an engraving of the death of Lincoln,— the last episode of a life begun like this, and which went, according to the popular play upon words, "from the log-house to the White House," from a hut like this to the ·little white palace in Washington, by way of how many severe efforts, continued struggles, hardships continually renewed!

The farmer, for his part, nourishes no such ambition, not even for his sons. He wants to live and to have his farm pay. He wears himself out in this struggle, and his wife dies of it. The courageous creature has long kept to herself the palpitations that rent her heart whenever she climbed to the garret in the cold mornings, the cracking of her joints when she lifted any burden, the shivering fevers of her sleepless nights.[1] The doctor lives several miles away, and each visit costs from five to ten dollars. She goes on trying the patent medicines advertised in her newspaper, following the advice of the neighbors, above all, hiding her sufferings from her husband, till she drops at last, and goes away, leaving him alone with his children on the little demesne covered with mortgages.

And yet these farmers, who labor under such cruel conditions, appear, when they have occasion to bring forward their private opinions, to be as wise and as respectful of the rights of others as the strikers of Illinois and California are unreasoning and fierce. The widespread association by which they guard their common interests, "the Grange," has always kept itself sedulously outside of political movements. It assumes, as its name indicates, to be at the service not only of agricul-

---

[1] Cf. in *Scribner's Magazine* for March, 1894, a striking picture of such an existence, "The Farmer in the North."

tural laborers but of the entire agricultural class,—"the Grange, or the patrons of husbandry." To say all in one word, its merits are such that in the book by Aveling, already cited, appear the following significant words:—

"It may in time become leavened with the leaven of the general working-class movement, but as it is at present constituted the Grange is more likely to be a hindrance to that general movement than a help."

What shall we conclude, if not that once again the land has done its moralizing work? It has given man the great, the unique virtue, in teaching him to *accept himself*, as he accepts the order of the months, the slow growth of the harvests, the rain, the snow, the wind, the sun, all the apparent and necessary wrongs of the seasons.

One characteristic of these Western farmers may be discerned at the first approach; it is a thirst, a hunger, almost a fever of desire, to know, an intense, even violent, passion for the things of the mind, which explains how so many remarkable men in the United States have been farmers' sons. This shade of character is so completely unexpected in these rough men that at first one does not believe it when the Americans tell you of it, some of them in complaint, some in admiration. The former deplore the excessive seriousness of the national character, which ends they say in a constant excess of work, an absolute incapacity to enjoy anything, "to enjoy himself," as they say. The others see in it the presage of that sovereignty in the civilized world which is the secret dream of all full-blooded Yankees.

Whatever conclusion may be drawn from it, the fact remains. I have assured myself of it, not once but twenty times, thirty times, only by studying the crowd which thronged around the Exposition buildings in Chicago — now burned, because to take them down would have been too slow a process. When I visited them they were in the splendor of their

whiteness and their fleeting glory.   With their capitals copied
from Rome and Athens, their slender domes, the chaotic
medley of their composite architecture, they gave the idea of
a dream city, a city of vision suddenly appearing on the borders of Lake Michigan vast as a sea, whose bright green
waters dashed against the columns of a gigantic portico.   Yes,
it was truly a glorious scene in the fine days of early autumn,
raised up as by a wish, for the pleasure of this great nation of
toilers, called together there as to a meeting of joy and repose.

But, no.   The multitude scattered along these walks and over
these lawns was more than all striking to a Parisian by the total
absence of both joy and repose.   These people were neither
heedless nor lively.   They went about examining the interior
and the exterior of the Exposition with a sort of blank avidity,
as if they were walking in the midst of a colossal lesson in
things.

"I don't care about seeing folks.   I kin see folks to home.
I came to see what's made in the world." [1]

These words, overheard and reported by one of the chroni-
clers of this singular festival, were mentally uttered by all the
visitors.   They were, for the most part, just these farmers,
come from the four quarters of the immense plain that stretches
from Montana to Kentucky and from Arizona to Wisconsin.
You could see them about two o'clock sitting on the ground,
with their families, around their State building, leisurely eating the provision of cold food which they had brought in a
pasteboard box.   The coarse cloth of their garments, their
sunburnt faces, even their way of eating, without a table, and
with the ease of people accustomed to take their food in the
open air,— everything about them betrayed the fixed habits
of rural life.   Their lunch finished, they began again their
indefinite, indefatigable walk, not of pleasure but of instruc-

[1] *Scribner's Magazine*, March, 1894.

tion, application.   How many of these rustic visitors have I followed, as they went from the Hall of Mines to that of Electricity, or from the Transportation Building to the Woman's Building, attentive, patient, obscurely reflective, and, it seemed to me, even less interested in the machines, in the prodigality of positive and material invention, than in the exhibits that were more scientific, more useless, nearer to the wide field of abstract speculation.

As I write these words, I see three of these personages — a father and his two sons — motionless in a corner of the anthropological exhibit.   They were looking at the colossal mammoth, the enormous hairy elephant of before the deluge, copied from that of St. Petersburg.   All around them were gathered the forms of animals and men that formerly inhabited America,— races extinct or dying out, elk and caribous, bisons and grizzly bears, Sioux and Apaches in their encampments, cliff-dwellers, those Troglodytes of the Grand Cañon of the Colorado.

The farmer and his two sons took no notice of these things, absorbed as they were by the colossus, the history of which one of the sons was telling to his father.   The latter listened to the seventeen-year-old boy without taking his eyes from the formidable beast, the silent giant, with his long recurved tusks.   Did he feel the beauty of this ancient king of creation, so tall, so slight, so simple, nature's first success, very evidently superior to the shapeless masses of the monsters, his contemporaries, the plesiosaurus, the ichthyosaurus, the megatherion?   What was this witness of distant ages, this traveller in the forests of giant ferns, saying to the thoughtful colonist?   The boy ceased to speak; the three men stood there without exchanging a word.   The grave countenance of the ignorant father, the almost equally grave faces of the two better informed boys, were bent forward with an expression of insatiable curiosity.   Did they, in their rudimentary condition, feel that amazement, in view of the enigma of the world, which is not so foreign to primitive minds as we in our pride imagine, since it is these minds that have created the myths, the poetry of legend, and, to say all in one word, the religions?

Did they ask themselves the reason of the rhythm of creation and destruction, which will carry us away in our turn, after having carried away innumerable species? Why that world before our own, the attempts and new attempts of Nature, trying her powers, like a never-satisfied artist, in these new beginnings, in which the indefinite power to produce forever alternates with the impossibility of preserving? Is man himself the limit of this evolution? His roots are so deeply fixed in it, he is so distinct from it by the higher parts of his being! Thoughts, words, moral problems, what an abyss divides these things from those! What a miracle is the mere astonishment of the thought in face of the miracle of destiny? How new a thing, in this universe of blind instincts and unconscious needs! This gigantic elephant, but now the dispossessed sovereign of our planet, did he ever look at another creature with the thoughtful gaze with which this farmer and his sons have enfolded him?

They begin at last to talk, without taking their eyes from the admired animal, and I could hear in passing that they were speaking of the Bible, pronouncing the name of Noah. Then the squatter of to-day, like the men of a hundred years ago, in burying himself in the prairie, carries with him the old book, so dear to the Puritans, to be the companion of his solitude, his work, and his thought.

It was written that I should see again the serious faces of the father and his two sons, and that the same day I should collect some very unexpected and still more significant information about Western life. These vast fairs, which go by the pompous titles of Universal Exhibitions, have at least this advantage, that they bring about meetings elsewhere impossible, yet natural in this Babel of people from all parts. I shall, therefore, simply narrate both of these meetings, which, I may add, were purely accidental. I do this with all the more pleasure, because it gives me the opportunity to sketch, as if on the margin of this travelling-journal, a rough draught of the most singular spectacle which I have seen in America ; a session of the Parliament of Religions, where I again met my three friends.

This Parliament was held in one of the halls of the Art Institute which stands, as it is quite in keeping that the Chicago Museum should do, close by a railway station and a steamboat landing. I went there one morning, deeply moved with the expectation of a profound, religious impression. I received my impression indeed, but entirely through the public : the multitude of humble folk, evidently working people, who crowded the benches and chairs of the vast semicircle. With what touching attention they listened, ready to receive the good word —any good word. And with what surprise I recognized, seated about ten chairs from me, the three persons who had so much interested me by their way of contemplating the antediluvian monster ! I felt a certain vanity of the astute observer, in perceiving that I had not erred in attributing to these people a regard for religious things. Their rugged faces wore the same absorbed expression as before. Out of doors locomotive bells were tinkling, trains puffing, steamboats whistling. Not one of the fifteen hundred auditors gathered in this hall remarked the strangeness of such noises at the door of this palace, just as no one appeared to observe the astounding contrast which existed between the true, simple, devout fervor of the audience, and the sort of sacred parade that was going on upon the platform in the rear, opposite a gigantic photographic apparatus set up in the opposite side of the hall.

In fact, in spite of my good will, the feeling that it was all a parade forced itself upon me whenever I turned my eyes from the crowd to the speakers' stage. There were thirty persons sitting there that morning,—one of the last of the session: first a Japanese in a coat of embossed silk, a dog-like face with a pair of glasses across the flat nose and black moustaches against a shining yellow skin. He was busily cutting the pages of a pamphlet, without listening to what was going on, while at his side an Indian robed in white, with very gentle, very brown eyes in a face so swarthy that it looked burned, was vaguely smiling in the visions of a half-sleep. A Chinese in a blue robe, his body encased in a violet silk vest, and a black cap with a red button on his head, was scanning the audience; his wizened little face was pale and thin, with a not too straight nose. A Greek archbishop sat superb, with squared shoulders, his long brown beard spread out over his gray almost yellowish robe. Over it a black toga was draped, and the gold of the chain from which hung his cross gleamed between the two stuffs. He held a long, silver-headed cane in his hand, and his inexpressive eyes shone with the brightness of a magician, set as they were in a large face of a thick warm pallor and surmounted by the high cap of a professor.

One of his priests sat beside him, a *pappas*, with long, illkept hair, untrimmed beard, and delicate, sensual, ironical face. Then came another Indian, twenty years old, perhaps, selfsufficient in his ardent youth; his dress intensely red, and his turban intensely yellow. Around these Orientals were grouped English pastors, rosy and shaven; German professors, heavybearded and sharp-eyed under their spectacles. A Frenchman of delicate profile, but thin and worn, sat cross-legged, showing feet elegantly shod in patent leather, with white jean gaiters. A little in the background were two women: one, gray-haired and fifty, with the abstracted and modest air of a poor school teacher; the other, young and beautiful, very dark, with cheeks brown under their paint, her shoulders covered by a silk shawl of mingled brilliant colors.   Large gold circlets jingled on her wrists.   And to make this composite exhibition as vulgar as it was foreign, a fat, uncleanly man of forty-five, in the front row, was fumbling at his nose with his fingers ; while a chairman, with the voice of a showman, rose between two organ measures, to introduce the speakers, with all the graces of an impresario.

I was wrong in looking thus minutely into the accidents of this realization of a great idea, and my Western farmers were right, like the other auditors, in seeing that idea beyond and through these accidents.   There was a moment when the three heads were bent forward with more profound attention.   A speaker had risen, a celebrated minister of the Anglican Church. He was a small man of about fifty, very thin and ruddy.   The black of his straight-cut coat and the white of his all-round collar, without cravat, made his red face seem redder.   He began in a low voice, hardly audible.   With a monotonous, almost automatic, gesture, he indefatigably raised and lowered his arm.   By degrees, as he spoke, he warmed up, his body straightened out, his foot beat the floor, his color grew more purple, his voice deepened.   For me, too, the absurdities of the platform vanished.   Here was that frenzy of religious eloquence and passion which made Protestantism and its innumerable sects.   When the words "Church of England" occurred in his discourse, the orator's whole being trembled with profound inspiration.   You could hear it, could see it thrill to the tips of his toes, as he raised himself upon them in his earnestness.

"No!" he once exclaimed; "it was not the English people who made the Church, it was the Church of England that made the English nation!"

These words, uttered with furious emphasis, no doubt met in his hearers a previously formed idea, a conviction that national life must find its strength in religious life, for it evoked a tempest of applause.   I turned toward the father and his two sons; they were clapping their hands, enormous hands, that two hundred years ago would no doubt have applauded the Lord Protector, and thirty years ago Lincoln, when he uttered to the people the strange words announcing that the war would last

"Until every drop of blood drawn by the lash shall be paid for by another drawn by the sword."

These men, with their intense faces, have without doubt drawn their tragic vision of divine justice directly from the Bible. It alone explains their almost anxiously serious response the other day to the reminder of the deluge, and to-day to the representatives of their faith. If there are many like them, the socialistic atheists may conquer the villages, but they will never get any hold upon the fields of the West.

My curiosity with regard to these three men was so lively that I believe I should have followed and tried to speak with them if I had not myself been seized by the arm at the moment the audience rose at the sound of the organ. I turned, and found myself face to face with a celebrated Parisian physician, whom, if his name had been spoken, I should have fancied anywhere rather than at Chicago, — in his magnificent apartment in the Boulevard Haussman, in the clinic of the Lariboisière hospital, in his laboratory at the medical school. He had made the most of an official pretext of a hygienic congress to cross the Atlantic and see American civilization with his own eyes, object, as it had been, of so many capricious judgments. In two words he had explained his journey to me, and presented to me a great fellow of perhaps thirty-five, also a Frenchman, who accompanied him, and whom by his thin, clean-shaven face, his somewhat stiff attire, and the decision of his glance, I took for a civil officer.

I had not taken five hundred steps with my two compatriots before I found myself interested in this young man to such an extent that I no longer regretted the mischance which had made me lose sight of my friends of the anthropological exhibit and the Parliament of Religions. I learned from the doctor that the man before me was one of the most daring adventurers of the West, such as for several weeks I have much desired to see. M. Barrin-Condé — I will designate him by this name — had in fact left France fourteen years before, to start a ranch in the Rocky Mountains, and had lived there eight consecutive years. The accident of a short excursion having led him to Toronto, Canada, in the course of his exile, he there met a young girl with whom he fell in love. To marry her he had changed his mode of life, sold out his ranch in North Dakota, and taken root in the city of his fiancée, now his wife. He had founded a steamboat company, which he administered with the same superior good sense and energy as formerly his ranch; it had now monopolized the major part of the traffic of the great lake.

It is rare, indeed, and most pleasant, to meet in a foreign land a Frenchman in whom survives a spirit of enterprise equal to that of the Anglo-Saxons, one so loves to convince oneself by his presence that our race has kept the same qualities of enterprise that once made it the great conquering power; to talk over the country with a man who himself has seen its lower side is deeply interesting! In short, I did not leave the doctor and his companion the whole day long. I was never weary of asking the latter about his life at Lance-Head, — so his breeding-farm was called, from the sign with which his horses were marked, — about the folk among whom he lived, their manners, their ideas, and about his own ideas. He answered me quietly, simply, with that accuracy of speech that belongs to the man of action. There was in him something of the wild dignity that Cooper gave his "Leatherstocking." But it was a Leatherstocking who had kept up with our literature, having been careful, through all his rough life, not to fall behind in intelligence.

I remember that we finished this day—which on my part
had been one long interrogation, and on his a long response —
by an hour in an orchestra chair of one of the great Chicago
theatres. As if to make the occupations of this evening a
perfect contrast to those of the morning, chance would have
it that we saw *Tartufe* given by Coquelin and his troupe. I
had been proud of my country while talking with M. Barrin-
Condé, and I was again proud on seeing this admirable piece
played as it was, even before a half-filled hall. And what
spectators! Almost all followed the copy in a translation,
and we could hear the leaves of the pamphlet all turned over
at one time. But what mattered that to Coquelin! The great
artist seemed not even to know that there was a public. He
evidently played for himself, with the conscientiousness and
the care for his art which he would have displayed on the
stage of the Rue de Richelieu at his first performance. He
was still studying it, still studying himself, ever applying himself to reveal more clearly the moral anatomy of his character.
And in Chicago, where all extravagances, all improvisations
prevail, *Tartufe* appeared finer than ever by its strong and
true simplicity, by the genius for moderation and delicacy,
which always kept itself at the level of a man, if one may
say so, neither above nor below, neither on this side nor
on that. There is something of Philippe de Champaigne
in Molière, something of the vigorous but sober, ardent but
judicious painter in whose portraits you ever find something
to admire more deeply, and which never leave you anything
to take back on reflection. Although the doctor and I
had seen this piece thirty times, and had seen Coquelin in
this part at least ten times, we were as much taken by the
dialogue and the play as at the first time. As for the former
"cowboy" of Lance-Head, as he called himself, he entirely
ceased to speak during the whole play, between the acts included.

"You do not know," he said, as we went out and walked along toward Michigan Avenue, "no, you do not know how much, how painfully, those who live as I have lived feel the want of the intellectual stimulus of the theatre, and how we value an evening like this. See here," he added, turning to me, "you were laughingly asking me, after dinner this evening, if I had not some time raided a train in the West, and I did not answer you. The fact is, my friends and I did attempt nothing less one day, or, rather, one night, than to carry off from one of the great transcontinental express trains — guess whom? Sarah Bernhardt herself! She never knew anything about it, however."

"And how many may you have been for such an expedition?" I asked.

"Oh, very few; but you need not think it is hard to stop one of these important trains. When we were planning this fine scheme, we tested it,— rehearsed it,— forgive the word, since we are speaking of an actress. We learned that Sarah Bernhardt was to pass through Green River, Wyoming, a week later. We wanted to know if it would be possible to stop a train long enough to carry out our project. There were eleven of us knights of the 'round up' as they say out there, all well mounted, all with that sort of ardor for danger which in youth so easily leads to a misuse of strength. We posted ourselves, in broad daylight, at a place where the line made such sharp curves that the express was obliged to slow up. It appeared in sight. One of us galloped alongside of the locomotive, guiding his pony with his knees, covering the engineer with his rifle. I did the same on the other side. The engineer stopped his train. Our comrades dismounted and went through the train, with revolvers cocked, crying 'Hands up!' We risked a terrible scrimmage if there had been a man there plucky enough to draw his weapon. Luckily there was not. While the terrified travellers were hurriedly opening their valises to buy their liberty, the pretended robbers had already remounted, and away we went, firing our pieces into the air."

"How about the police?" I asked.

"They were represented," replied M. Barrin-Condé, "by a sheriff who lived eighty miles off, and who, I think, is still investigating the matter. And besides, — for everything in the West has its grotesque side, and it all seems natural enough when one is carried along by this life, — we were all masked, or at least our faces were muffled in handkerchiefs. Though the experiment was successful, we perceived one danger. We wanted to play a joke, which I leave it to you to qualify, but we did not wish to run the risk of killing or being killed. We decided, therefore, to carry off Sarah Bernhardt from the station itself. Her train was due at Green River at eleven fifty-two. We were to rush into her car, carry her out by main force, put her in a buggy, and gallop off at full speed. Some of the party were to protect our retreat with their revolvers. One of us, a certain Sarlat, who is now a captain of infantry in Africa, was charged to board the train at the preceding station. It was understood that he was to wave his handkerchief at the door of the parlor car in which the great actress might happen to be, for it would be necessary to act promptly and to the purpose. Such an operation is always a little dangerous in a village.

"Sarlat, therefore, set off, as it had been arranged, and we waited patiently at the station, grouped on horseback around the buggy. Perhaps if you had heard our remarks, you would have decided that this unreasonable attempt was even more ingenuous than unreasonable. No doubt our illustrious guest would struggle. She would have hysterics. We should have to bind her. But once at the ranch, we should make her amends by our respect. She should be received like an empress. We should obtain her pardon and would live over again a few days of France, getting her to recite for us the finest

R

passages in her repertory.   The train did not arrive till midnight, and then we saw Sarlat get down, with no handkerchief in sight.   Sarah Bernhardt had passed through the town
an hour earlier, by the Salt Lake City express."

This extraordinary story was told so naturally, it represented
customs so peculiar to the country, it showed such a curious
medley of delicate civilization and savage life, that I did not
rest until I had extracted from M. Barrin-Condé a promise to
send me some of his notes regarding his residence at Lance-
Head, his journal, if he had kept one, a few recollections at
least.   He promised, but several weeks passed before I received the papers I asked for, or even any news of the young
man.   He had gone back home, and I went on travelling over
the vast Republic.   I was persuaded that the documents of
which I had so unexpectedly learned would never reach me.
They found me, however, when I had given up expecting
them.   Whether it was the pleasure of an agreeable disappointment,—we so seldom enjoy one!—or whether it was
really the originality of his confidences, it seemed to me that
they were worth transcribing just as they were, without commentary.   What analysis could be as valuable as the testimony
of the man of action, who has seen that of which he speaks,
not, like a learned man, in the pages of books, not in the
amateurish way of one who travels for pleasure, but as one
who could do no otherwise.

Perhaps, also, the place where I received the packet with
a Toronto stamp made me more than ever sensitive to the
picturesque quality of these pages.   It was in October, in a
quiet, deserted hotel, among the fallen leaves, beside the
Falls of Niagara, which are still, in spite of the declamations
of guide-books, one of the noblest and most striking spectacles in this world.   All that men may build around it, of
bridges, stairways, balustrades, all the paths they may make,
or the advertisements they may stick up, cannot affect the

inviolable and mighty beauty of these two great cascades. How I loved the slow, soft slide, the monotonous fall of the tremendous current over the edge of the rock, that here forms a sharp right angle! How I loved the deep wail, the complaining murmur,— so much sadness in so much power,— and the wavering mist, that cloud of humid incense that floats above the lowest fall, rising, transparent in whiteness, above the great green mass. Yes, and I loved it, in that season of the year, the autumnal softness, the golden woods of Goat Island, without a bird, with only this strange sobbing sound to fill them and speak of the irrevocable end of summer,— symbol of the inevitable flowing away of life!

As I walked about in these groves, so dishonored by advertisements, I regretted the coming of the white man, the civilized being, who is so much more destructive than the savage. I thought of the cruel but simple-minded Indians, the yellow, tattooed warriors, who respected nature and did not mutilate her. I cursed the civilized man for having defaced this admirable landscape with those factory chimneys, that pour forth their black smoke toward heaven, and those wrought-iron elevator towers. I felt the need of calling up before me, in this scene of grandeur, a freer, more hardy existence, more conformed to the mysterious and tragic beauty of this great river, so suddenly precipitated into this gulf.

The narrative of the colonist adventurer of Lance-Head doubtless met this wish. Nevertheless, reading the manuscript over in cold blood, I still think that it does not need such a setting, and I have no hesitation in copying it here, hardly modifying it in any respect. The reader will judge whether it would be easy or difficult to engage in revolution men who live in the atmosphere of danger and conquest which exhales from these unquestionably true notes. He will also, it seems to me, more easily understand the reasons why energy and will are here developed, even to hypertrophy. And perhaps the incongruity of the circumstances under which these pages reached me, and which I have reproduced at the risk of breaking the apparent unity of my own study, will give a truer picture of all that is chaotic and arbitrarily connected in American life.

You visit an exhibition where antediluvian monsters are lighted up by electricity; you attend meetings where religious fervor alternates with charlatanism; you see plays by Molière given by fine actors to an audience of barbarians, next door to a theatre where Shakespeare's plays are given by English actors; you rub elbows with Kansas farmers and Parisians; you go in a Pullman car to scenes of nature, such as Chateaubriand described, — and all these madly complex impressions group themselves at last around a story told by a former volunteer, once garrisoned for a year in some little provincial French town, of his adventures in an unexplored valley of the Rocky Mountains !

A COWBOY'S STORY

My ancestors were originally from Florence, whence, about 1270, they, with several other Ghibellines, emigrated to Dauphiny. We were then called Barberini, though without ever having had anything in common with the noble Romans of that name. From Barberini we became Barberin, then, by some means, Barrin. About the end of the twelfth century a certain Raymond Barrin headed a troop of young men to hunt out certain brigands that infested the district. "He fought like a Condé," every one said. The name stuck by him, and we have kept it ever since.

Whether it was that I heard much in my childhood of the ancestor whose name I bear, or whether it was simply the inheritance of a restless race, always ready for action, certain it is that while yet a youth I began to dream of adventures. When, on quitting the regiment, I found myself once more in my father's house, with no other prospect before me than to grow old there, indolent and useless, the thought of such a fate became physically insupportable.

Yet I loved my family, I loved our house, I loved Dauphiny, its rugged mountains, its clear sky, its peasants and their accent, and, above all, the past which they represented to me. I had always been a man of the former time, a devotee in every sense you may choose to give to this word. You might have seen me on the eve of departing for the United States going to our village cemetery, kneeling upon our family tomb, and picking up some of its pebbles ; I have them still. But nothing could prevail against the appetite for action which consumed me, urging me, though so young, to cross the seas.

I must add that being a Royalist by tradition and conviction, it would have seemed to me a crime to serve the Republic. I had no commercial acquaintance nor any capital that would enable me to set up in business, while to think of marrying an heiress was revolting to my pride.

In short, in November, 188–, I returned as a volunteer to my regiment. By December my resolution was taken ; I would seek my fortune in America. In February I embarked at Liverpool with a friend of my boyhood, an Englishman, the Honorable Herbert V——, who had decided to go with me. We took with us four stallions, two percherons, two Arabs, and my regimental groom. We were going to set up a little stud farm in the Black Hills of Dakota, and had been in correspondence with a ranchman of that country, named Johnson. Our entire capital for this enterprise was the support of this man, whom it happened that some of Herbert's friends knew, our four horses, and a draft for thirty thousand francs. I forgot to mention our youth and energy. Many people have begun under worse auspices.

The steamer, which from motives of economy we had chosen, went partly by the aid of sail, so that we were seventeen days in reaching New York. The passage was pretty rough, but I do not suffer from the sea, and as I had not only to take care of my comrade and my groom, both of whom were very ill, but also of the horses, I had no leisure for melancholy thoughts at the beginning of my exile. The first heartrending sense of expatriation took possession of me in the tumult of the great American city, amid the crowd whose language I did not know, and whom at first I found so uncouth, so hostile, more than all, so different from what I was used to. We were lodging in Brooklyn, at the recommendation of the ship's captain that we might find good stabling near the railway stations. Several days we spent in visiting the town, which with its hastily-built houses, some so high, the others so low, with their tall iron chimneys, and the fever of its populace, gave us the impression of something wild and monstrous. To fill up the measure of our wretchedness, our hotel was a veritable den of drunkenness and prostitution, where we came near losing all we had the very first week of our arrival, as the result of a stupid adventure.

Herbert and I had spent the first four evenings at the theatre. The fifth, proposing to go to bed early, we had gone into the bar-room to smoke awhile after dinner. Some women and a few men were there. One of them, a great hulking fellow, a former soldier, red-haired, wall-eyed, with a bulldog face, took upon himself to talk loud to one of the girls, looking at us the while. A coarse laugh that followed would have irritated me even if Herbert had not at my request interpreted the fellow's imbecile joke. He had said to the girl : —

"Get that Frenchman to take you. He must be a —— They all are."

I omit the insulting word he made use of. I sprang up, roughly shaking off Herbert, who would have detained me, and walked straight to the man. Seeing me coming, but trusting to his strength, he began to defy me with a smile which I can still see, with the shining of a gold-plugged tooth which he had on the left side of his mouth. I gave him a blow of my fist full in the face with such strength as to bring the "claret," as they say in America; that is, his face was bathed in blood. I had practised boxing in the regiment and was very nimble, and I had the good luck to avoid his return blow — he was slightly drunk — and to hit him a second time in the stomach, throwing him to the ground. I expected a scuffle, and drew back to face the others when, to my surprise, they uttered a murmur of admiration. The singular audience were applauding my pugilistic talent. They carried off their friend, but that very evening the proprietor of the hotel said briefly to Herbert : —

"The gentleman would better change his quarters. Jim Russell is not the man to put up with that without taking his revenge."

Although neither Herbert nor I was easily frightened, the idea of being hindered at the very outset of our enterprise by a low quarrel like this seemed to us so absurd that we decided not, as our host had advised, to change our lodgings, but to take our departure. The very next morning we took the continental express-freight train, with our horses and our luggage. It would take seven days — a whole week — for us to reach the town of Sydney in Nebraska, where we had appointed to meet Johnson. It would have been easy to send our horses by this train and ourselves to take the regular express train. But our first impression of American life had thus been so disagreeable that we thought ourselves in a barbarous country, and would neither separate from one another nor lose sight of our stallions for a minute.

We made the whole journey then, in the same car as the beasts. This method of locomotion was so uncomfortable that we paid no attention to the country through which we passed. I remember nothing of this singular journey across the immense continent as wide as Europe, except that at Chicago we

had to resist by force four " tramps," who entered our car in-
tending to hide behind our horses and " steal a ride " — that is
their expression.　These wayfarers of the United States have
the habit of passing over incredible distances crouched on the
floor of a freight car.　At the entrance to the towns they jump
off — a tramp must necessarily be something of a gymnast —
and get aboard of some other train just going out, having, if
possible, joined some more productive rapine to their theft of
a ride.　In general, these poor fellows are inoffensive ; but not
being familiar with the picturesque features of American vaga-
bondage, we supposed ragamuffins who could board moving
trains to be dangerous robbers.　I could laugh yet at the memory of the way they hopped over to the bank beside the track
at sight of the six revolvers that we pointed at them.　We
should have deemed ourselves imprudent to have had only
one weapon apiece !

Johnson, advised by telegraph, was indeed awaiting us at the
Sydney station ; but we were in fact only one stage nearer the
real end of our journey, — Custer City, two hundred and fifty
miles beyond.　These miles we must cover on horseback, and
the seven days in the freight car had so shattered us that we
had not the courage to set forth at once.

At that time Sydney had the name of being one of the most
dangerous nests of thieves in the United States.　The five
hundred inhabitants of the town — a veritable mushroom of
the railroad, which would have disappeared with it — spent
their time in a series of real battles, arming themselves with
guns and revolvers.　We did not know this.　But our new experience in Chicago had made us so wary that we resolved to
sleep on straw across the door of the stable where our Arabs
were lodged, for they had been quite too much observed as we
brought them in.　It was well for us that we took this precaution.　Toward midnight, in spite of weariness, I was awakened
by a strange sound.　I struck a match and distinctly saw the

end of a saw in the act of cutting the wood around the lock that fastened the barn. I wrapped one of my hands in a handkerchief and gripped the end of the saw, cocking my revolver with the other, and uttering the only English oath that I knew — you can guess what it was. The saw remained motionless, and on the other side of the door I heard a click like that which I had just made with my own weapon.

I aroused Herbert and my servant. Our three voices made the robbers understand that we were in force. We heard retreating footsteps ; our horses were saved. But how could we go to sleep again after this new alarm? Our anxiety was so great that we resolved to leave Sydney as we had left Brooklyn, and not the next morning, not an hour later, but at once. We saddled our horses with our own hands. We drew Johnson's wagon from its shelter, put in our baggage, and harnessed the horses. Thus equipped, we went out into the street to call up to him in the hope of arousing him from his first sleep. He had been playing poker and drinking whiskey all night, and having by good luck won several hundred dollars, he was more accommodating than we could have hoped. Besides, like many Americans, he had a sentiment of national hospitality, and was ashamed for his country of the robber-den where he had met us. He was willing to go with us, and before dawn we were on our way.

Our ride across the prairie lasted two long weeks, and I owe to it the first pleasant impressions which I had experienced since my departure from Dauphiny. This portion of the broad territory that extends between Sydney and the Rocky Mountains was not then the civilized country that it has since become. At the present day several lines of railways furrow it ; farms abound and the embryos of large and small towns. At that epoch, from Sydney westward the vast prairie of Nebraska presented no other trace of human life than passing cowboys, driving before them some scattered herd. Ranch succeeded ranch, with no road leading from one to another. The immense extent of desert through which our cavalcade was moving appealed to us with a sort of savage charm, in which our feeling of youth and of an unlimited future counted for much. The desolate solitude inspired instead of saddening us, as our contact with the foreign multitude had done. We no longer felt ourselves weary, and we even drank with light hearts the abominable alkaline waters that we scooped up from the crevices of the ground — creeks, as they call them — to water our horses.

Our excitement increased as we drew near to the mountains and entered the great forests of Douglas pines. The first spring flowers were peeping through the grass. Transparent running waters gushed out everywhere from fissures in the quartz. The sky was blue and high above our heads; and besides, we were drawing near to Custer City, the town of whose magnificence Johnson had been boasting ever since we set out. We were looking forward to it as the Hebrews to the Promised Land. Many a year has passed since then, years of bitter struggle which count double and triple. Not one of their sensations has effaced the intense strain of expectancy of that April afternoon when our worthy friend led us up a hill at a gallop, that he might proudly point us to the end of our hard pilgrimage. He checked his horse, made signal to us to do the same, and extending his arm he said : —

"There is Custer City."

I looked, my heart beating hard with hope. Why should I blush to own to one moment of cowardice, the only one that I knew in all my prairie life? Tears that I could not restrain suddenly gushed from my eyes — tears not of hope, but of despair, tears wrung from me by atrocious disappointment, the sudden collapse of all my high dreams.

A wretched mining-camp lay on the other side of the valley, more miserable than the poorest hamlet in the Alps. And it was to live there, in one of those hovels, in this remote corner of the world, to struggle there, to die there, perhaps, that I had left three thousand leagues behind me our little château in Dauphiny, with its three square towers and its square donjon, and in the château my mother, my sisters, everything that I loved and that loved me !

Then I looked at Herbert, and was ashamed that I, a Frenchman, should have shown such weakness before this impassible Englishman. He was lighting his short pipe with the finest possible coolness, although I saw well enough, from the trembling of his hand, that the shock had been severe to him, also. I have told you that I have always been a little religious. I called to my aid the innermost forces of my soul. I offered to God a prayer of thanksgiving for having protected me since my setting forth, and asked him to protect me still. I put myself into his hands, like a little child. My horse, El Mahdi, pawed the ground, and neighed. It was his way of saying, " Here is Custer City." I gathered up the reins, and, pressing my knees against his flanks, set out at full speed for the city, leaving my childish tears to be dried by the wind of my headlong course.

So, under a glorious sunset, at the foot of Mount Calamity Jane the " tenderfoot " Raymond died, on his first arrival from Europe. And in his place arose the cowboy Sheffield, — so named because of his knife-blade face, — he who wrote these memoirs.

Some time later, about a month, I was quietly breakfasting in Miller's bar-room, situated in the principal street, — Main Street, — when a well-known miner, Big Browne, began to quarrel with a cowboy who had left his ranch, Eddie Hutts.

Both drew their revolvers and fired at the same moment. Browne fell stone dead. His opponent's ball had gone through his head. But his ball had taken me square in the jaw, breaking the bone, and stopping near the artery. Miller, who professed a particular esteem for Browne, has often, since then, tried to excuse his friend, with the plea that the unfortunate man had that morning taken a few too many "corpse revivers." The Americans have a jolly lot of names for the various alcoholic mixtures with which they delight to poison themselves: "a widow's smile," "a sweet recollection," "an eye opener." The most potent of all was the one used by Miller, the "corpse reviver." There was some irony in the circumstance, since the intemperance of that brute Browne nearly caused two deaths, his own and mine.

I had sprung up when I found myself wounded, but I had not strength to take a step. Everything seemed to turn around me, and I fell as if struck down by a blow. Consciousness quickly returned, with that sort of lucid and unavailing attention that we have in dreams. I was lying on the ground near Browne's dead body. I could have touched it by reaching out my hand. Half a score of faces, all automatically moving in the act of chewing tobacco, were gazing curiously upon me, without any one thinking of coming to my aid. My blood was still flowing upon the floor, and I was suffering cruelly. I asked for a priest, but I spoke in French and no one understood me. For that matter, the nearest was a hundred and fifty miles away, and what need had I of a priest, to die like Browne? One more or less doesn't count on the prairie.

Seeing that not one of the men around me so much as shifted the quid in his cheek, so indifferent were they to my appeal, I began to shout, or rather to gurgle, the names of Herbert and Johnson. Within a quarter of an hour my friends both arrived, accompanied by an ill-favored personage in a frock coat, with a ten days' beard, a battered silk hat, a white necktie streaked with dirt, and diamond studs shining in his frayed shirt. This was the celebrated Dr. Briggs, the principal physician in the Black Hills, a somewhat skilful surgeon, though even the Americans thought him "rather fond of the knife, you know." He was usually drunk at ten in the morning, but by good luck he was now sober. I had abundant leisure to note the details of the picturesque dilapidation of his costume; for having caused me to be laid upon the billiard table he began to probe the wound, very gently, I must admit, while drops of tobacco juice fell from his lips upon my face.

"Well!" he concluded, with a coolness hardly reassuring. "The gentleman has had a lucky escape. The ball has just grazed the artery. The bones will soon knit, but, as to the ball, if he lets it remain it will by degrees wear through the artery, and will suddenly burst sometime, causing internal effusion and sudden death. If he prefers to have me remove it, I can try, but I will answer for nothing. It is for him to choose."

Herbert translated for me this redoubtable diagnosis. I mentally performed my act of contrition and said that the ball was to be removed. Before probing the wound, Briggs had cleared the room of every one except Herbert and Johnson. He now called by name six of the men who were standing around the door, who ranged themselves, grave and indifferent, around the billiard table.

"Why?" I asked Herbert, who was still acting as interpreter.

"Well," replied Briggs, "these gentlemen are the first citizens of the town, and they will testify that it is no fault of mine if death occurs during the operation."

With these words I fell asleep under the sickish odor of chloroform. When I awoke, I had a great slit in my throat and the ball in my hand. The best citizens disappeared, enchanted at having had this little morning "excitement." The doctor received three hundred dollars.

A month later my jaw was well, but I had lost so much blood that it was some weeks before I recovered strength.

As to Briggs, meeting him three years later at Rapid City, at the time of a hotly contested election, he dragged me up to the platform, exhibited me and my scar to fifteen hundred loafers, and secured a brilliant victory over his opponent. It appeared that I was his sole living witness to a successful operation!

This sample of the manners and customs then reigning in Custer City will convince you that this abode of idleness, intemperance, and assassination did not keep us long. For that matter, we could hardly make a living there. The smallest necessaries of life were horribly dear, as in all mining towns. For example, at Custer it never occurred to any one to ask change for a nickel. The five-cent piece was the unit of expenditure. It is hard to conceive of the ravages which such trifles made in small incomes like ours. We resolved, therefore, to return to our original plan, and select a ranch, a wide pasturage, watered by living streams, where we could devote ourselves to horse breeding.

We had the luck to find almost immediately such a place as we sought, and we named our little establishment Lance-Head, because in digging the foundations of our house we found an iron point, which had no doubt dropped many years before from some Indian's arrow. With roughly hewn beams, ill-planed boards, and wooden pegs,—nails were scarce in those parts, — we managed to put up a sort of barrack for ourselves and a stable for our horses. This work cost us no less than six months' labor, during which we were too busy to concern ourselves with the ranch itself. Now calculate: a fortnight's voyage, five days in New York, seven on the railway, two weeks on the prairie, come to more than a month. A month of expectation, a month of illness, a month of convalescence, make three months. Add to this six months devoted to our wretched little building, and you have nearly a year since we left our homes,— Herbert's in Derbyshire and mine in Dauphiny.   And in the course of this time I had nearly died, we had impaired our joint capital, and our sole acquisition was this "log-house," this hut built with our own hands!

And we held this property only on condition of defending it.   The stream and pasturage had belonged to a former proprietor, Bob, a well-known horse thief, called "Yorkey Bob," from his native city.   This rascal, by abandoning this property, had forfeited all his rights in it.   That, however, was no reason why he should not undertake to fleece the new occupants; and, in fact, having returned to Custer City, he loudly proclaimed in Miller's "saloon" : —

"I shall soon settle up with those two European tenderfeet. I'll teach them to enter upon my succession before my death!"

This reassuring remark was reported to us by Dr. Briggs, who lavished visits upon us.   When my "savior," as he freely called himself, had given us this so-called evidence of sympathy, Herbert and I looked at one another.   Each read in the other's eyes a desire to mount at once and be the first to settle accounts with this saloon bully.   On the prairie one soon comes to this theory of legitimate defence,— to attack first and not be attacked.   Very happily, we did not yield to this impulse of preventive indignation.   Herbert had the presence of mind to concoct a test which should forever safeguard us from all threats of this kind.   He took aim at an unconscious pigeon that was cooing on the roof of the stable fifty feet away, and brought it down with his revolver.

"You may tell Yorkey Bob what you have seen," he said to Briggs, "and add that if ever I meet him, wherever it may be, in a bar-room, in the street, or on the prairie, I shall do as much for him."

He turned his back upon the doctor.   This worthy stood for a moment as if nonplussed, then spat at a distant point. It is the American token of profound impression.   I have always thought that his purpose in coming had been to propose to the new proprietors, in the name of the old, a good and firm treaty of alliance, cemented by hard cash. However that may be, Herbert's pistol-shot and his little remark sufficed to discourage this intention. But for two whole months we were on the alert, sleeping out of doors every night for fear of a surprise. As to precautions by day, we could not have taken more. The times were so troubled that if two horsemen saw one another at five miles' distance on the prairie, each would turn in the opposite direction. Strange desert, which man sought to make still more deserted, and where he dreaded nothing but his own kind! This was the time when the Deadwood mail was looted about once a month, the time when the carriage of the Lead City receiver, notwithstanding its escort of six horsemen, was held up, and the one hundred and fifty thousand dollars that it contained — seven hundred and fifty thousand francs in gold bars — dispersed to the four corners of Dakota and Wyoming. A flood of adventurers, the scum of all countries and all races, had overwhelmed Deadwood, where a new lead of gold had just been discovered. Human life, which the Yankees like to say is "very cheap" among them, was really so cheap that to live in the Black Hills was to be on campaign every day and every hour. One soon adapts oneself to conditions that appear so extraordinary. It is surprising how soon one becomes accustomed to the thought of a violent death. It is the other death — by illness — with which the imagination can never reconcile itself, at least mine cannot.

As for Yorkey Bob, he no doubt thought differently from me on this subject, for he took great care, after the proof of address given by Herbert, to keep clear of the two tenderfeet from Europe. It was written that he should be killed, but in a different manner. He again stole so many cattle in the neighborhood of Custer City and near us, that the cowboys determined to rid the town of so dangerous a character. One evening, when he was quietly drinking in Miller's bar-room, a treacherous cowboy lassoed him from behind, and threw the end of the cord to a horseman who was waiting outside. The latter set off at full speed, and Bob was strangled in a few seconds. He had instinctively seized his left revolver (he carried one on each side), and through all the frightful consciousness of that mad flight across the plain his fingers never loosed their hold. It was necessary to break them to get the weapon from him. We happened by accident to be present at this last episode of our enemy's death. I cannot better explain to you the metamorphosis which this first awful year had wrought in us than by telling you that we remained indifferent to this summary execution.

Bob was regretted by one person only, a woman thief who kept a hotel at Custer City, and whose lover he was. This creature had a dexterity with the rifle of quite another sort than that of Herbert. I have seen her, not once but ten times, pierce a gourd at a hundred paces, sending her ball through a hole already prepared for the cork, without even grazing its edges. In every room of her hotel you might see the following inscription, written up with her own hand in enormous red letters: —

"*Don't lie on the bed with your boots on. Don't spit on the blankets. Be a man.*"

She had committed many murders, and with her man's clothes and her continual oaths she was a fit companion for Bob, whom she would certainly have avenged if she had known his assassins. But enterprises of this nature were always carried on with masked or muffled faces, as I have already said with regard to train robberies. For that matter, you can learn as much from the newspaper reports. This summary justice was more potent than legal justice as we afterward knew it, with its judges and lawyers, costing much more than executive committees such as the one which rid us of Yorkey Bob.

s

And take it all in all, the second sort of justice was much less just.

After this new experience, we resolved to live more closely on our ranch. No longer going into the towns but by way of exception at long intervals, we at last had no other society than that of cowboys, "grangers," and miners. Into these three classes all the inhabitants of the prairie are distributed. All three are alike in their aversion for civilized life, their energy in enterprise, and their familiarity with danger. Their ambitions differ so far as to make them at times enemies. Each class has its heroes, whose story is continually told with ever new complications. Buffalo Bill is the hero of the cowboys, Mackay of the miners, Lincoln of the grangers, because of his early life. These classes form the vanguard of America, between the ever-mounting tide of immigration on the one hand, and the last redskins on the other. Or, rather, they did form it in the recent and yet remote period of which I speak. For every year the Indians draw further back and disappear, the waste territories become more populous. In half a century, if I live so long, I shall certainly see immense cities occupying the prairie which I have known so vast and so free.

The proper domain of the great ranches is still at the present time limited only by the boundaries of the Indian Reservations. The "Home-ranch," with its wooden houses and its stables of earth, is built near a spring. A score of worthy vagabonds live there under the authority of a chief, a "foreman," who is naturally the strongest and most clever of them all — I do not say the most courageous. They are all equal in degree, or they would not be worthy of being cowboys. Fifty thousand horses, cows, and bullocks wander free over Uncle Sam's pasturage, and these boys pass the year in counting, marking, and despatching them by rail to Chicago.

It is not an easy task to conduct a drove of three or four thousand beasts across the prairie. A certain number of horsemen precede the drove, others keep watch on the flanks, others gather in the stragglers. They must keep away from the railroads, or an almost uncontrollable panic may set in. Returning from Colorado, whence I was bringing three hundred and fifty horses, it happened that I came upon a road just as a train was passing. My horses had never seen a locomotive. A terror seized them, scattering them in all directions, in a circumference of a hundred miles. It took me fifty-five days to get them together again. At another time a storm came up, one of those prairie tempests, like a cyclone. The enormous living mass of animals was driven into a single group, around which the cowboys galloped like a whirlwind. It was necessary to keep the animals in this circle, literally distracted as they were by the thunder and lightning. We succeeded by dint of discharging revolvers by the dozen over any head that should be uplifted. Had the rotary movement been checked, the enormous herd would have broken through on one side, and, like the wild bisons of a former day, they would have trampled men and horses under foot like so much chaff.

Such an occupation in such surroundings requires men of invincible energy, ready for anything. I may add that the composition of a ranch-gang resembles nothing more than that of a battalion of the foreign Legion of France. The refuse of the civilized world naturally finds refuge in it. At Lance-Head we had a German cook, one Italian and two French cowboys, and among Americans such unclassed men as Billy, the son of a Chicago pastor. He made us laugh till we cried, one evening, with stories of his youth, entirely passed in one of those mixed schools which have become the object of serious study by foreign authors who come to write up the country. I wish that one of those grave article-makers might have heard Billy describe the drawing class, and his girl classmates, busy with models of the principal masculine schools, while he devoted himself by preference to feminine anatomy.

Among us were enigmatical personages who never spoke of their past, — for example, another Frenchman, whose real name I do not know to this day. He called himself Jean Bernard. He was the most dextrous lasso-thrower on the prairie, and he had a real passion, almost a mania, for danger. One day, to make sure of not being thrown by an unbroken horse, he fastened the reins to his wrists by slip knots, and set off at full speed. Both his arms were broken in two places, and he would still have hung on if Herbert had not stopped the horse with a ball in the chest.

I never knew, either, the name of a Dutchman who went by the single name of Frank. One evening, being drunk on whiskey in a small Western town, he took it into his head to drive a score of travellers out of the hotel at the muzzle of his revolver; then he barricaded himself in the house and sustained a regular siege. The thermometer was twenty degrees below zero, so, having kept on drinking to keep himself warm, he ended by tumbling down behind the door like a slaughtered beast. Thus ended his desperate prank, without the cost of a drop of blood. It would have cost Frank dear if he had not been the best fellow in the world when sober, and particularly the intimate friend of another personage who also enjoyed legendary authority, the Count of La Chaussée Jaucourt. I one day met this Belgian gentleman, who had long been lost to the sight of his family, in the depths of the Indian Reservation. He was on horseback, escorted by his two wives, two veritable "squaws," who, like him, had their guns on their shoulders. He accosted me with an expression of vanity, singular indeed under the circumstances.

"You are the Frenchman of Lance-Head. I am the Count of La Chaussée Jaucourt, bachelor of letters and of science."

He looked like a highwayman, and I took good care not to betray the least surprise. All these trappers are infallible shots. But the apparition of this bachelor of letters between these two savage women, dressed in skins and with face tanned as yellow as those of his companions, long stayed in my memory. "Shall I ever come to that?" I thought, and such a singular result of my Western adventure appeared to me neither impossible nor to be dreaded, so much was I daily more and more overcome, saturated, intoxicated, with the charm of this free, primitive life. And I answered myself gayly, "Why not?"

Yes, a charm! Even now it is the only word — taking it in its original sense — that I can find to express the sort of witchery which this existence exerted over me. Through all the years it still exerts it. When I try to distinguish the reasons of this all-powerful attraction I find, first, — a singular enough feeling in a country where revolvers go off of themselves, — that I have never lived through days when I less feared the future. I knew then a sort of serenity, I might almost say, an incomparable security. I was fully conscious of my courage and my strength. I knew that my cowboys were as faithful as mamelukes. These desperadoes for the most part found in themselves — once they were free of civilization and of their past — a profound strength of personal honor.

Did a rancher send me word by post, according to custom, that such or such a mare had been seen two hundred miles from Lance-Head, I had only to summon Frank, for example, and beg him — we never give orders in the West — to hunt up the strayed animal. He would assure me that he would find it, and I felt no further anxiety. He would set out with three saddle horses, his waterproof blanket, and his six-shooter. I was sure of seeing him reappear one or two months later, and the mare with him. He had given me his word. As to where he had slept or how he had lived all this time, I never so much as thought of asking.

With men of this calibre I lost the idea of the impossible. I had lost it as far as I was myself concerned, so much did my whole being superabound with youthful fire, fed by the open air and by complete purity. The habits of this life were violent even to tragedy, and severe even to ferocity. But they were not corrupt. I found a sort of interior poetry growing within me, as I went about my solitary rides, poetry made entirely from a deep communion with nature, and untranslatable into words. I became animalized with the cattle, or they became humanized with me, as you prefer. I understood now the language of horses, who talk with their ears and their nostrils; of the cows, who speak with their eyes, their foreheads, and, above all, their tails; of the dogs, who speak with their whole body, and whose thought changes so rapidly that one can hardly follow it. I carried on real dialogues of signs with these creatures, once mute to me. I carried on a still more sublime and intimate dialogue with the great Being who is above all things and creatures. When, at sunset, seated in the saddle and about to set forth, I looked over the prairie, its billows stretching away as far as the eye could reach, like a motionless sea under a quiet breeze, I felt a sacred intoxication, an ecstatic ravishment that I was alive, that I felt myself strong, that I had within me this horizon of light and solitude. Almost involuntarily the prayer would break from my lips, "Our Father which art in heaven." I would thank God for the blessed gift of life, for the beauty of his visible work, for the favors of my lot, with a thrill of my whole soul such as I had never known before and have never known since.

After what I have lately told you I should stultify myself in claiming that such effusions were general among the coarse companions among whom I had been thrown. Nevertheless, they all in their own way felt this presence of God, which is nearest, it seems, in the midst of virgin nature. Whence comes that sort of elevation of heart that continually appears in the better ones among them, their fidelity to a promise, their firm friendship, their virtues of endurance and loyalty, if not from an influence like that to which we more consciously yield?   In any case, this was my way of feeling, and I should not have given a true notion of my life in those days if I had not reported these emotions as well as all the rest.

When you have galloped for months and months over the prairie, your free domain, the day comes when, passing near a well-known spring, you observe a disturbance of the soil not there when last you saw it.   Near it you see the framework of a covered wagon.   A plough, a few instruments of cultivation, and one or two lean jades picketed near by attest that an emigrant has arrived with his meagre possessions.   You urge your horse in that direction, and in response to your vigorous "hellos" you see a blanket thrown back that covered a hole dug in the ground.   A man's head emerges, and behind him the heads of children, with the timid and weary face of the mother in the background.   It is a "granger."   He must have come this way on horseback last autumn.   The place pleased him.   He went back East for his family and his goods, and here he is.   This hole in the ground, twelve feet by fifteen, will shelter them all till he gets his log-house built.

"Hello, stranger!" he says, "where are you from?"

"Where are you from, my friend?   You are the stranger!"

"I came from Nebraska — there are too many there to please me.   I shall be better off here."

The cowboy shrugs his shoulders.   One granger is nothing. But to-morrow there will be ten, and the day after a hundred, —in a year thousands.   However, he dismounts from his horse, and the two men begin to talk, coldly at first, then in more friendly fashion.   The cowboy tells the other where the best hunting-grounds are.   Both of them, squatted on the ground, are busily whittling bits of wood.   The woman remains in her hole.

How many of these human mole-hills have I seen thrown up on the prairie!   These hardy pioneers of the vanguard never

come from Europe ; they are Americans of the United States
or Canada, whom European immigration has pushed toward the
free West. Half farmers and half hunters, lean and taciturn,
bronzed as redskins, and hardly more civilized, they are flee-
ing from civilized life, from cities and factories. They precede
the armies of woodsmen, and hardly interfere with the cattle-
breeders. Only a day comes when others follow their example.
The best pasturages are taken up. Fences are built everywhere, on which the ranch horses wound themselves. These
people take possession of all the springs. It is not rare to see
in the spring their cows with five or six calves — a wealth not
surprising when they live near a ranch where there are five
thousand head of cattle. In fact, they are not at all bashful to
make the most of their powerful neighbor in all sorts of ways.
So much so that the foreman one day decrees their expulsion.
Sometimes his cowboys resort to threats, sometimes to fire.
Most generally they simply drive the granger's cattle off a
hundred miles in the night.

Next morning the poor wretch wakes up and finds himself
ruined. He understands the situation, and makes up his
mind to depart. Or else he sets off to look for his cattle,—
an endless search. The process, perhaps, appears somewhat
summary, but it must not be forgotten that the Old Testament
is the model of law in the West, and newcomers must submit
to it. Besides, when it is a case of life or death for the ranch,
it is a case of legitimate defence, in which measures of this
sort are permitted. At least so it seemed to me when I was
there. In fact, as soon as the number of arrivals becomes
considerable, the ranch has nothing for it but to give up and
move nearer to the Rocky Mountains. It has played its
part of vanguard and must begin over again, as far as possible
from the grangers, and as near as possible to the Indians.

As for the Indian, he is the cowboy's enemy only when the
war hatchet is dug up. This came near being the case a few

months after our arrival. The foreman of one of the ranches had sown the prairie with quarters of venison filled with strychnine, to poison the coyotes. Two Sioux ate one of them, and died in frightful convulsions. Happily, the foreman was the friend of Sitting Bull, the hero of the massacre of General Custer and his cavalry regiment. The chief kept his tribe from rising. They used to be very useful neighbors to us at the time when the county tax was levied. We would drive three-quarters of our cattle into the Reservation, and could then, in all honor, declare only a very small number of animals.

I shall later explain to you how this apparently unhandsome conduct was only a too legitimate way of escaping legalized robbery. The Indians obligingly lent themselves to this stratagem, having themselves much to suffer from the thefts of government agents. And besides, their dread is not the free cavalier, who lives on the prairie as they do, but the colonist and the engineer. I knew Sitting Bull well, myself, who, by the way, having given himself up, received a house from the United States. He always slept before the door, outside, and had never slept under a roof. I happened to be with him, on a hill, the first time the whistle of a locomotive resounded among the echoes of the Black Hills. He looked long at the strange machine, then he squatted upon the ground, his head in his hands. Two hours afterward, coming back to the place, I found him in the same posture.

"Sitting Bull is old," was his sole reply to my questions. "He would be with his fathers, on the other side of death."

It was impossible for me to get another word from him that night. Did he divine that these two rails, crossing the prairie as far as the eye could reach, must bring to his tribe, in this last remote refuge of their independence, civilization, and in its train a certain end? I think so.

He was a great chief, and his wish was not long delayed.

He was killed in the uprising of 1891, and I wish him all peace "on the other side of death." When I think of the Indians I knew in those days, his gaunt face, with its long jaw, comes first before me, and that of a young woman, a Utah, whom I met with her husband in the outskirts of Salt Lake· City. They asked me for tobacco, and devoured my cigarettes, wrappers and all. The brave, displeased with his wife, was proposing to kill her in some retired spot. In fact, she never reappeared. Although I did not then suspect the Ute's design, I have always reproached myself for not having continued my explorations in their company, either by good-will or by force. The thought of it did cross my mind in a sort of presentiment. I should doubtless have saved the life of that poor child. Her sad face, with its great, gentle eyes, resigned in advance, has followed me for years.

Such events are rare, as I have already said, most happily so. If the rivalries of sex were there to heighten the ferocity of the quarrels over play or in drink, which strew the saloons with corpses, the whole prairie would soon be depopulated. On the other hand, one temptation is not rare, that of gold or silver mines accidentally discovered in your neighborhood. You hear the news from a chance passer-by. You do not believe it. You remember having talked with the man to whom this good luck has happened. He has been prospecting for a mine for years. You have jeered at him, like others, and here he is, a millionaire. Other like cases come to your mind, and you say:—

"Why should I not try, too? Who knows? I might have the same luck."

It is the first attack of gold fever. However, the work of the ranch recalls you to reality. You have horses and cattle to sell. You must ride miles and miles. The fit passes over.

A few weeks later your cowboys are talking around the fire.

You listen to them. They are talking of another miner, who has discovered another lead. You are seized again with the same desire to go yourself to look for this gold that surrounds you, hiding itself here and there all about you, under your feet, perhaps.

After a few such fits the fever grows stronger. Some day you take your revolver, some pork and flour, and set off over the rocks, your eyes bent on the ground, your mind, heart, will, bent on the ground, bound, dragged, hypnotized by the magic word which you repeat to yourself along the wretched roads, under burning sun or snow, "Gold! gold! gold!"

It is a contagious madness from which few escape. I was affected by it like the others. I, in my turn, took up the prospector's pack and set out. One of my cowboys had just discovered a silver mine, and sold it for ten thousand dollars. On the morrow of that sale I succumbed! I can see myself now plunging into the mountain defiles, trying, trying, continually trying, the rocks with my eyes, my hands, my pickaxe. Miles succeeded to miles, and rocks to rocks. Everything disappeared under the mirage of gold,—fatigue and appetite, the sense of duty to the ranch I had left behind me, and of my dignity as man. To-morrow I should find it! To-morrow, and yet to-morrow! For six days I went on this way. I was "possessed." On the morning of the seventh day, as I was saying the prayers I had neglected during this whole week of possession, God in his mercy opened my eyes to my wanderings. If I speak of this solemnly, it is with purpose. I have known, I still know, minds of the finest, energies of the noblest, lamentably wasted in these desert depths, in pursuit of gold, which no disappointment, no reasoning, no trial, can cure of their hypnotism.

One of these, Hopkins, told me of weeks that he had spent among the crevices of the rocks, living on cold pork. The least smoke would have given the alarm to Indians, who were beating the prairie in all directions, searching for his scalp. None the less, he went right on with his chimerical search, during and after as before this time. When I became acquainted with him he was opening a new mine. His shaft had already gone down thirty feet.

"A very rich mine! There are millions down there, millions like those of Mackay in the Bonanza. I only need capital to develop the lead. I have written to Chicago, they will come —"

Poor old Hopkins! He already saw his millions, touched them, counted them. He was going to be rich, rich, rich! He would have giant machines, crushing the metal day and night. What rapture overspread this thin, wan face, that seemed to have taken on the color of gold by dint of dreaming of it, worn and hollowed by privation and pain, with his eyes of flame, the eyes of the believer and the visionary! The west wind blew harshly through the wretched hut whose leaky roof sheltered his dreams. And I, who for a moment had known the same fever, I pitied his madness, and went away softly not to recall him to reality.

If miners do not often discover mines like the Bonanza, they at least wash out a little gold dust in their "placers," and if they saved their earnings after the manner of French peasants, they could grow old in prosperity. But the West is not the country of savings-banks and small investments. It is the country of adventurers, gamblers, and of the all or nothing. Gold-seekers no sooner have a few hundreds of dollars, cowboys no sooner draw their wages, than they hasten to spend their money in the nearest town, a hundred, two hundred miles away.

As for us, once a year we went to Deadwood and treated ourselves to the luxury of the one box in the Gaiety Theatre. One had small comfort there, in view of the fact that the spectators in the orchestra applauded the fine passages by firing pistols at the singular pictures of the ceiling. I had already paid dear for the knowledge of how easily a ball may wander from its aim. The box offered fascinating attractions to the horrible dancing girls imported from Chicago, who assassinated us with winks while executing figures with their legs.

When we had thrown a sufficient number of dollars to them upon the stage, they would come up, according to custom, to kiss us and ask for a bottle of so-called champagne, which cost six dollars and was not worth twenty cents. Often a facetious cowboy would lasso them on their way from the stage to our box, and this would give the public new occasion for an explosion of applause, accompanied by a new fusilade, in an atmosphere so charged with alcohol that it seemed as if the matches with which the audience lighted their pipes and cigars must set the whole room in a flame, like an enormous bowl of punch.

The miner's life oscillates between pleasures of this order and a chain-gang life in the mines, — those at least who keep good faith in their illuminism. Others, more intelligent and more cunning, attain to great fortunes by swindling processes, the ingenuity of which would fill volumes. I shall content myself with relating the adventures of a certain Parker, who, in 1885, sold a mine for two hundred thousand dollars to Frissel & Company — great bankers of one of the largest cities of the West. Parker had sown his "placer claim" with gold dust over a stretch of two miles, having buried more than ten thousand dollars' worth of dust in the sand.

Never did capital bring in such interest. On the report of two experts, grave men who came expressly from Boston, the mine thus "salted" was pronounced to be of incalculable wealth. Frissel & Company deemed themselves fortunate to acquire such a treasure in exchange for the two-hundred-thousand-dollar check which Parker demanded.   The experts, with their fat recompense, returned to Boston.   Parker no less generously recompensed the citizens whose testimony had confirmed the existence of the placer.   The more honest among them had been content with holding their peace.   "Let him look out for himself!"   So says every one on the prairie, though only two steps away from a man who is being plundered.

As Frissel & Company never made a complaint, it is probable that they are only awaiting an opportunity to sell again this stream sown with gold, at double or treble what they paid for it, to a society which will scatter its stock, greatly reinforced by advertisements, among rich Europeans. It will all end with a failure, in which the weak will suffer. That is the law of life, as Americans conceive it.   As to Parker, his admirable bluff gave him even more prestige than fortune.   He is now one of the most influential citizens of Omaha,— "so smart a man!"— in a fair way to become senator.   He owns four entire blocks of houses in a new city, and has no doubt forgotten his own knavery, and also that cursed Frenchman, Sheffield, who gave him a ball in the thigh from his Colt, No. 44, one day when he was pouring forth in public all the turpitudes of Frenchwomen, which he claimed to have learned in Paris.   I had aimed low expressly, not wishing to kill my man, who, on his part, sent his ball on a level with my ear.

Three months later, that pistol-shot came near costing me dear.   Parker, who had lost sight of me after our altercation, met me one day in Custer City.   He immediately had me arrested for assault and battery.   The affair came first before the police justice, a certain Richardson, who happened to be my grocer.   I owed him more than two hundred dollars. Besides, I had supported his election.   I was honorably acquitted by a judgment thus conceived: "Seeing that the defendant's feelings received a more cruel wound than the plaintiff's leg."

Under other circumstances I might have been obliged to put in the hands of this same judge a large sum, which he would have divided with Parker; and this possibility brings me to speak of that which rules all business and hinders all success in this Western country, naturally so rich and free,— the bitter, implacable war between money and the foreigner, particularly under two forms, which our French habits lead us to look upon as protections, law and taxation.

The breeding of horses and cattle brought in my time thirty per cent net on the prairie. Good pasturages, as deserted as possible, where, like modern patriarchs, we let our innumerable flocks and herds increase and multiply; resolute cowboys, who never hesitated to hang a horse thief high and short, or to repulse grangers and Indians by force, — these would have brought us in sixty per cent on our capital if we had not had to reckon with these two leeches.

The tax upon capital forms the principal revenue of the States. Declarations naturally tend to reduce it, and it would be hard to reckon the number of false oaths given in the spring of every year in the Western Territories. A special commission then sits, and rectifies at will three-quarters of these declarations. Its decisions are based upon anonymous accusations, which abound there as elsewhere, and chiefly on the political affiliations of the tax-payers. If he is a friend, his declaration is at once received. If an enemy, his estimate is doubled, tripled, quadrupled. Finally, a surplus of five to ten per cent is added to the total, according to the deficit to be made up, which is the same as saying, according to the number of county treasurers who have succeeded one another in office. What must become of a foreigner who, being pledged to no party, is skinned by all? Only one ground of hope is left him, — the difficulty the assessors may find in counting his herds.   We had at Lance-Head an Arabian stallion, who had become a real wild beast in the midst of his wild stud.   He had half killed an inoffensive wayfarer who was crossing the prairie not far from his favorite pasturage.   These stallions set upon all persons whom they do not know, with the fore hoofs and the teeth.   The terror spread abroad by this animal saved us from assessment.   The assessors were forced to trust to my statements.

Not to perjure myself, as I have said, I sent my droves over into the Indian Reservation at the time of making oath, and I therefore had only a small number of cattle to declare.   Notwithstanding this precaution, our taxes were rated so high as to amount to half our profits.   For, three times during my career of cowboy, the county treasurer made off with the bank, so that in the end we had to pay a nine per cent surplus to balance the budget.   Am I right in affirming that false returns became a legitimate defence in such a case? –

As may be supposed, the ranchmen are not behindhand in this matter.   I can still recall the countenance of Fyffe, treasurer in 188–, — now in the penitentiary, — when the foreman of the Anglo-American Company solemnly declared that, in consequence of the rigor of the winter, he had not a single milch cow left.   As a fact, the company possessed over thirty thousand head.   It must be added, that the said foreman had had too many " corpse revivers " that morning.   Fyffe was petrified with admiration of such audacity.   " What pluck ! " he exclaimed, and at once accepted this astounding declaration. Then a large bonus, offered by a rival company, made him reverse his first decision, and with one stroke of the pen he raised the declaration twenty thousand times.   This roused the cowboys to a simulated lynching, where he nearly left his bad extortioner's skin.

How can one defend himself against persons of such a state of conscience ?   To what can one appeal ?   To the law ?   Every

little Western village has, side by side with its two or three
generals and twenty or thirty colonels, an equal number of
lawyers.

Ah, these lawyers! The scourge of a country that has an
elective magistracy! With their feet in the air, and their
cigars in their mouths from seven in the morning till nine
at night, they meditate on possible lawsuits. Not a quarrel,
not a difference, not a hasty word, but its echo reaches them,
and they throw themselves upon you with offers of gratuitous
services, with the enticing prospect of large damages. You
accept. The suit begins. Soon the confusion is such that no
one understands anything about it. Then your lawyer informs
you, with a long face and tearful eyes, that your suit is lost.
He tells you the reasons, which are precisely the opposite of
those that he brought forward to induce you to take this step.
The better to convince you, he takes you secretly to the judge,
who confirms the views of the estimable lawyer. However, a
compromise is possible. You subscribe to it, and leave this
hell. Costs, two hundred, three hundred, a thousand dollars,
according to your property. The amount is most amicably
divided between the two lawyers and the judge. I have seen
one of our compatriots, guilty of killing a robber who had first
drawn upon him, unable to secure the most just of acquittals
except by spending twenty thousand dollars!

You are indignant, are you not? I used to grow indignant over this frightful absence of professional honor. It has
exceptions, indeed, but very few; and one finally becomes
accustomed to it, as to rain in autumn and snow in winter.
It is with the magistrates in these small Western towns, as with
doctors and dentists. A few more anecdotes before I conclude.
Herbert came home, one day, from Omaha, where he had been
to have his teeth attended to, with his mouth full of little holes
that the operator had dug in his teeth, after putting him under
gas. He suffered from them so much, that he went back and

T

had them filled with gold at ten dollars a cavity ! One of my cowboys was wasting away in consequence of a course of treatment prescribed by a doctor who had diagnosed a disease of the stomach. He had been told to take daily a packet of powders that seemed to us suspicious. We had the powder analyzed, and found that the only object of this so-called remedy was to prolong the sick man's malady. He had already paid his poisoner a hundred dollars — two months' earnings !

These moral blemishes, and hundreds more that I spare you, are the inevitable consequences of the formidable conflict of energy and ambition carried on upon the prairie. I was aware of this necessity even when I was suffering the most from it. When we found ourselves clashing with some more powerful barbarity, Herbert and I would remind one another of a picturesque sign in which we had seen the symbol of this budding civilization. We had read in a railway station during a strike of railway employees : —

"Passengers, this line is boycotted. You'd better buy an insurance ticket, as this train will be run by a green engineer."

Everywhere on the prairie we came upon tokens of the "green engineer," and I would think of France, so beautiful, so pleasant, so complete, true land of love 'even in its faults ; and that it needed only to have left it to appreciate the charm of living there, the charm that an American so well expressed to me one day when I asked him what had most struck him in Paris.

"Well, the finish of it," he replied.

And I have not returned to that dear France, and I do not know that I shall ever return there. Where one's family is, one's country is, and mine is now in that Canadian city on the shore of that vast lake, stormy as a sea, where I went to repair the losses which the last Indian insurrection inflicted on the poor ruined ranch of Lance-Head.

And now that I finish this account, which I may well call posthumous, since the cowboy, Sheffield, is dead in his turn and and has given place to Francis Raymond, a feeling of homesickness for the prairie comes over me. I feel how deeply I loved that desert, so sad yet so attractive when one has passed there years of exuberant life, revolver in hand, rifle on the pommel of the saddle. I have my cowboy saddle before me. I seem to hear the wind of those nights that I spent out of doors; the wind that, as in the early days of the world, spoke to me so many mysterious words. I can see the immensity of the steppe, here and there cut by cañons where at noon the does hide with their fawns; the quiet streams where the pumas come to lie in wait for the frail, delicate antelopes. I feel my horse's hoofs rustling the tall, dry grass of Dakota. The wind brings me the fresh vegetal aroma of the sage brush of Wyoming. The whole great country lies outspread before me, wild and dangerous, but free; a country where I experienced that, take it all in all, life is less painful there than anywhere else; a country of high emotions, where I was so near to nature, so near to God! I touch with trembling fingers the tanned leather of this saddle, and I must needs conquer the insane desire that takes me to be seated in it as formerly, to plunge my spur into my brave horse as formerly, and to go farther, always farther, westward — I, the father of three children!

VII

EDUCATION

WHEN one has seen a certain civilization in some of its fully developed representatives, and has formed an idea, correct or incorrect, of its good qualities and its defects, its value and its insufficiency, it remains to test these notions by a counter experiment, if I may so speak. One must try to see in the formative state these individual men or women, whom one has already seen exercising their matured powers. To put it more simply, the indispensable corollary of the study of the life of a people is the study of the educational processes of that people. The nature of the instruction given by a country to its youth is doubly instructive; for on the one hand it reveals the educator's conception of men, — hence of the citizen, hence of the entire nation, — and on the other hand it permits you if not to foresee, at least to have a presentiment of what the future of the nation will be, when once the children and youth thus brought up shall become the nation in their turn.

For example, is it possible perfectly to understand England without having understood Oxford, and the sort of seminary of "gentlemen" established there many centuries ago? You seat yourself on the turf of New College, at the foot of the ancient ramparts of the city; in the close of Wadham, near the apse of the chapel built by Dame Dorothea, whose statue may still be seen, stiff and severe under the folds of her robe of stone; on the edge of the pool of Worcester, where De Quincey dreamed; in the grandly quiet park of St. John's.

Only to see the young barbarians, as Matthew Arnold called them, playing tennis in the beautiful setting which owes everything to the dead, only to follow them, as in their flannel suits they seat themselves in a canoe and glide along the venerable walls of these ancient cloisters; or on horseback, trotting beside the grassy graveyards scattered everywhere in this city, — all the future of this youth is unveiled to you. The boy who has been in such surroundings during his impressionable years must be, he cannot but be, just what in fact nine out of ten Englishmen are: healthy and traditional, capable of all endurance, of all physical daring, and deeply, thoroughly conservative, even when he believes himself to be a radical; respectful of the past in his most intense ardor for individual action, because he has felt it too deeply, too much realized its benefits, to be anything else.

On the other hand, you visit a French *Lycée* with its barrack-like buildings, its narrow, hemmed-in playgrounds, the promiscuity of its dormitories, the bare ugliness of its studios and class-rooms. What more is needed to show you that the young men there brought up must be physically impoverished, nervously overstrained, robbed of joy and spontaneity. Discipline, too little individualized to be intelligent, must inevitably either cow or irritate him. He comes forth from it either a functionary or a refractory, crushed or revolted, nearly resembling the man careful only of his own interests and the anarchist, two equally baleful types of the civilized man, wasting himself either in feeble platitudes or in destructive insanity. Such is the fatal end of a system of culture apprehended as the reverse of nature and tradition, first by the men of the Convention and then by the Emperor, the most ill-omened of all their ill-starred works, most calculated to dry up, at its source, the energy and virtue of our middle class. Here, as everywhere, education explains history, because it explains customs.

It is not always easy to grasp the influence of a whole social system upon the schools, and again of the schools upon the social system. In the United States, in particular, the very character of the nation makes it almost impossible to define its system of education, spread as it is over an immense extent of country and absolutely without central direction. The power of states, of cities, especially of individuals, to initiate action conspires incessantly to modify the innumerable centres of instruction which have spontaneously blossomed out upon this soil where social forces seem to have a plasticity very like the plasticity of natural forces in the youth of the planet. The chances are great that each educational building will be constructed on a different plan, for each educator is apparently a man with his own ideas, and each pupil even is an elementary personality.

I remember when I was in Newport being entirely nonplussed by the question of a negro who waited upon me in the hotel, a sort of black giant whom up to that time I had admired solely for his dexterity in carrying in the flat of his hand a tray loaded with six or seven entire dinners.

"Is it true, sir," he asked me, "that you are going to write a book about America?"

"Perhaps," I replied. "But why do you ask?"

"Because I should much like to have a copy to read this winter in college."

"The negroes are so vain," said a New Yorker, to whom I laughingly related this dialogue. "He wanted to make you think he knew how to read." And he added, "Since you are collecting anecdotes about the 'colored gentlemen' don't forget this one. The other week Lord B——, one of the first nobles of England, was travelling beyond Chicago. At a certain station one of the Pullman car porters approached him with the words, 'They tell me that you are Lord B——.' 'Yes,' replied the other. 'Would you give me your hand?'

asked the negro. The nobleman thought this request showed a touching humility. He extended his hand to the unhappy son of slavery, who perhaps had formerly been himself a slave. What did the darkey do but shake the nobleman's hand with the proud remark, 'You know, Lord B——, I am an American citizen and I propose to tell all my fellow-citizens that the British aristocracy is all right!'"

My witty interlocutor was mistaken. It was not in braggadocio that the waiter in the Newport hotel had spoken of his college. I had the proof of this when, in the course of the winter, being in a little Southern city in which the newspapers had made known my presence, I received a letter which I cannot refrain from setting down here in all its artlessness, so significant does it appear to me.

"I write you a few lines to let you know that I have succeeded in entering college as I hoped to do. I entered January 1, and am getting along very nicely with my studies. My wish was to take the full, regular course, but I am not able to do so as I must support myself while in school. I must therefore content myself with the normal and scientific course. I do not precisely know what I shall do next summer. I have thought of going back to the hotel in Newport, but nothing is decided. I am looking for a copy of your book when it is finished."

What can be the spirit of a college on whose benches a servant, twenty years old and more, may take his place for six months in the year, between two terms of service, and the fact not appear in the least exceptional? What must be our opinion of the man himself, his demands of life, the thoughts he exchanges with his fellow-students; what of an entire society in which such features are of daily occurrence? Once more measure the abyss that separates the Old World from the New. And yet the very exclamation that falls from a foreigner's lips on meeting such incidents — "How American that is!" is a proof that he recognizes a certain character common to all the manifestations of this singular country, however unlike they may be.

This unity it is that I would try to discover in the complex problem of education, having special reference to certain groups of very clearly defined facts. At the advice of some of my friends, I have chosen the schools of Boston as sufficiently representative types of primary instruction; Harvard as representing universities for men and Wellesley those for women; of technical schools, West Point, the military academy, the St. Cyr of the United States. The reason of this choice is easy to give. Massachusetts has been for many years the matrix, so to speak, of the figure from which the genius of America has taken its moral and intellectual stamp; it is therefore probable that the spirit and method of American teaching are more visible there than elsewhere. This is why the Boston schools, and the universities of Harvard and Wellesley, whether they are superior or inferior to thousands of other schools and hundreds of other universities, are doubtless more striking and illustrative to a passing observer than the others. On the other hand, West Point has this advantage over other technical schools, that the human product, such as is there made, must be pretty much the same in all parts of the world, for everywhere war resembles war and officer resembles officer. The similarity of the results to be obtained permits us to understand better the difference in methods. These are, if you like, four pretty strong meshes in the vast tissue of instruction thrown over this whole great country. Considering how they have been woven, the reader will be able to judge of the probable value of the stuff. If he wants more complete details, he will find them in the fully attested works of M. de Varigny, in the acute observations of the superior woman who signs herself Th. Bentzon, and finally in the clever volume of M. Pierre de Coubertin, *Les*

Universités Transatlantiques. Upon West Point in particular,
Count Louis de Tarenne has written very interestingly in his
work, *Quatorze mois dans l'Amérique du nord,* a repertory of
incomparably full and accurate facts concerning the United
States.   I myself make no claim of doing more than set forth
here a hypothesis which fits in well with very many of the
facts so carefully collected by these conscientious and distinguished observers.

Let us try to imagine a traveller who knows absolutely nothing of America and who lands in Boston with letters to a
prominent resident of that city.   It is the time of full activity
in this old New England metropolis, consequently, it is winter.
The Bostonian comes to the traveller's hotel in a sleigh which
glides rapidly over the frozen snow.   His first act is to take
him, with justifiable pride, to that central park which he calls
the Common, and which has the peculiarity little known in the
United States of dating from far back, — from 1636.   Next our
man takes his guest by a network of streets, the crookedness
of which speaks of relative old age, to the " Old State House,"
the scene of the Boston Massacre, the museum where, side
by side with a marvellous Japanese collection, are some very
singular relics, — a glass case full of boots and shoes, among
them a pair of boots worn by Napoleon at St. Helena.   The
Bostonian will not fail next to show the river Charles, where,
it is said, are seen the finest sunsets in America, — the athletic
club, with its gigantic swimming bath in the basement, fed by
running water, — Beacon Street with its fine residences, and
Music Hall, where more music is given during the season than
in all the Conservatories of Europe.
More than once during these comings and goings the traveller has questioned his guide as to one or another building
which has appeared to him larger, more pleasing, of newer and
more elaborate style than the others, and every time the Bos-

tonian has told him that it was a school. Without considering it a matter of much importance, the traveller asks how many of these schools there are in Boston. He knows already that they are public and free, for his companion has made much of these two points, but he finds it extraordinary indeed to be told that there are six hundred and seven of them. Upon this he is taken to the office of the superintendent of this immense educating machine. The gentleman is absent on one of the tours of inspection made necessary by his truly ministerial office. But his secretaries are there,—women, of course,—and they interrupt their playing on the type-writer to search the library for divers pamphlets bearing on all sorts of educational problems : studies of the proper height of chairs and desks from the hygienic point of view, reflections on methods of teaching, statistics and criticism of courses and examinations, statistical tables of teachers and scholars, calculations of expenses.

When the traveller on returning to his hotel, still pursued by that figure six hundred and seven, begins the reading of these apparently dry reports, he finds it impossible to stop. He is taken possession of by them as by a unique sort of romance. They are, in fact, the romance of a city, athirst to know, hungry for culture, and which desires to learn and understand through all its inhabitants, to saturate itself with intelligence. This is one of the American fevers — this fanatical, almost unhealthy longing for knowledge, but it is only a phase of that grand and noble fever with which this whole country is consumed, crude as it yet is, and chaotic and unformed; too recent, and yet homesick for civilization.

To measure accurately this effort after "more light" as the dying Goethe said, you must analyze into its component parts that figure six hundred and seven. These schools are subdivided into six grades, in accordance with the different ages of the children, and also with the different courses of study. First of all, at the very bottom of the ladder, if one may so speak, there are thirty-six kindergartens, attended by nineteen hundred and sixty children. Next come four hundred and eighty-one primary schools, with twenty-five thousand pupils; fifty-five so-called grammar schools, with more than thirty thousand pupils; ten Latin or high schools, attended by three thousand four hundred scholars; twenty-four special schools, twenty-two of them held in the evening, with an attendance of five thousand five hundred students; and finally a normal school, destined to the maintenance of the members of the teaching staff. This staff contains a thousand six hundred and fifteen men and women, who hardly suffice for the immense service which, during the first nine months of the present school year — 1893 — represented to the city an expenditure of two millions of dollars. Of seventy-three thousand one hundred and seventy-six children or youth between five and fifteen years, the total number in Boston, fifty-three thousand six hundred and thirty-eight were at that date receiving, without the cost of a centime, an instruction that extends from the first rudiments to a culture which we reserve for our middle class.

And the city does not find itself satisfied with this amazing result. Between 1889 and 1892 it built, furnished, equipped, and opened, at its own expense, a new Latin school, four grammar schools, seven primary schools; bought land for three others, and spent, besides its ordinary estimate, another sum of two million dollars in the work of improvement. Such progress did not hinder the committee who reported it from providing for new foundations in the year to come. One observation among many others gives an idea of the spirit with which these indefatigable propagators of knowledge are animated. Speaking of the normal school, a reporter wrote in entire good faith: —

"It will be understood how necessary is this addition when it is remembered that the building is in precisely the same state that it was in fifteen years ago."

These lines from an official pen show better than any commentary what the words "recent" and "old" signify on American lips.

Upon this you close the bulky collection of documents. Beneath the minute but indisputable details of these statistics you have perceived a great social fact which is too much in harmony with facts which you have yourself observed not to be correct; namely, the profound vitality of civic feeling in the United States. This prodigality of millions has no other principle. It expresses the conviction felt by all citizens in their inmost hearts,— that the community should spare nothing to furnish to all its members the opportunity to develop the gifts they received at birth. But what community? Certainly not America; the government that sits in Washington has nothing to do with these expenses. Not even the State to which the city belongs; but the city itself, the city which these youth see with their own eyes, which might be pictured as a being to whom they are bound by ties of flesh and blood. In consequence, these educational benefits are not to these youth an anonymous gift, for which they know not whom to thank, the studies they undertake are not directed by a remote superior council of functionaries whom they will never see. They see and know not only the administrators of this great system of municipal instruction, but also the generous givers, who, to their public contributions, are continually adding private gifts. All these direct influences contribute to develop and exalt in them the same civic feeling which impelled their elders to support and aid in the great work of their culture, so that, once rich and great, their constant care will be to aid their younger brothers in their turn.

Here, as in France of the Middle Ages, as in Italy during the Renascence, strong municipal life naturally produces strong municipal virtues, and it produces them in the woman as well as in the man, — a fact entirely in conformity with the genius of the country, with its strong sense of equality. In all this work of the schools it is curious to note to what degree the woman rivals the male citizen in spontaneity and generosity. To take only two or three most typical facts; it is thus that in 1884, a lady of Boston, Mrs. Quincy A. Shaw, submitted to the city authorities her project of opening some rooms for *manual training* in the schools. Her thought was to found cooking courses and lectures on the care of a house and its linen for the young girls and for the boys printing, cabinet-making, and shoe-making. She has spent a great sum in this work since 1884; the report tells us how much — a million and a half of dollars.

Under the impulse of this entirely personal good will, two cooking-schools were opened in 1885, and received one hundred and fifty pupils apiece, and as Mrs. Quincy A. Shaw was at this moment busy with the kindergarten, two other Boston ladies undertook to go on with these two experiments, "The first," says the report, with the pride of local patriotism, "which have been established in America." In 1886 a third cooking-school was opened under the same conditions. The city has since accepted the charge of all of these, and now the women are seeking for other enterprises to which to devote their energies, time, and money. The committee considered the experiment conclusive, and undertook to continue it in the name of the community for reasons which are worth citing, since they also are stamped with that civism which is at once so ardent and so sagacious. After showing all the advantages which the art of cooking may procure to the poor girl as well as to the rich, — rendering the one capable of making her home more comfortable, fitting the other the better to manage her servants, — the report takes a larger view of the question, and, speaking of the place of manual training in education, it concludes : —

"This training also serves to counteract one of the greatest evils which threaten the nation: the excessive disparity between the rich and the poor. This disparity often results from the scorn with which many people of means look upon those who work with their hands. This is a false conception, for which there will be no place if all children are brought up to work with tools under the direction of teachers in working-clothes, at the side of school-fellows who, rich and poor alike, work with the same tools. The result of this teaching will be *a higher citizenship.*"

This higher citizenship, — the expression is hardly translatable so little of the thing is found in centralized countries, — this impulse to love one's city and make it beloved, this pride in one's native place, and this care to make it ever better, — all these are the secret of such generosities in educational things. They sometimes attain really fantastic proportions. There is a citizen of Illinois who made a single gift of six hundred thousand dollars to the University of Chicago, on condition that others would increase the sum to a million. The required four hundred thousand were subscribed the same day. Thus a capital of five million francs was paid down in a day, which the first giver doubled, for his own share, — say ten more millions of francs. He desired, said a journalist, to secure to his city a superior "standard" of higher education. This American expression, which might make a companion to the "record," is also difficult to translate. The "standard" is the value of a manufacturer's mark, the tape by which you measure the quality of the product. You find there applied to the things of the mind, to literature and science, that which makes the very basis of this mercantile Democracy — that estimate by comparison, which these people still express by the verb "to beat." Of a hotel or a view, a fine book or a certain brand of champagne, of a great artist and a steamboat enterprise, they say equally that it "beats anything in the world." Perhaps this self-love, which we think somewhat childish, is the condition of the astounding vitality of the local centres from which comes the vitality of the whole country. Shakespeare somewhere speaks of one of those men each of whose thumbs is a man. America is a country whose cities are all prairies, a republic whose each city is a republic, an immense corps of which each city is a corps. This energy of the municipal unit may be known by a thousand signs. While studying the processes of instruction, we feel that we are close in touch with it.

Admitting that the school is an entirely local creation based upon the good will of individuals, the methods of instruction ought to be all alike conformed, not indeed to abstract and conventional theories but to the peculiar needs of the city, its individual and encompassing life. A short tour of investigation suffices to show the traveller that in fact education is minutely and systematically organized here with a view to the adaptation of the individual to his surroundings. The teachers are both men and women, but especially women. These zealous creatures earn nearly nine hundred dollars a year. Most of them are unmarried, and though in constant contact with male teachers "cases of scandal," as they say here, are extremely rare. These women teachers are, above all, moral persons. Their sense of responsibility enables them to exert an all-pervading influence over the children and youth whom they instruct. Perhaps we may find here one of the reasons for the peculiar respect in which women are held in America. They are a part of the strongest and most tender impressions of youth.

It is worth while to see these school-mistresses, most of them pretty, teaching their classes, especially in the primary schools, where girls and boys of ten to twelve years sit side by side. They proceed mainly by questions put to the school at large, the pupils asking permission to reply by raising the hand.

The mistress chooses one, then asks another question, looking up this or that one who is backward. It is very simple, very animated, very pleasant. The great variety in the exercises, none of which lasts more than half an hour, forbids fatigue. In the beginners' classes, as also in the grammar grades, the feature which most strikes a middle-class Frenchman, of grammar school education, is the constant use of the concrete and positive method. Modelling in clay plays an important part in this method of instruction. In almost every schoolroom that you may visit you will see a whole collection of figures modelled by the children of both sexes, who follow you with curious eyes,—simple objects made in the likeness of the humble realities that surround them, a carrot, a loaf of bread, a biscuit, a butterfly, a flower. Here are some busy with a lesson in which they must draw and describe a potato that lies before them. Others are busy copying some leaves. They must identify the tree and give some positive facts about it. Others have just finished some rather complicated woodwork, made after patterns drawn with chalk upon the blackboard ; pigeonholes, boxes, pieces of carved wood that might be adjusted to some machine. In all these details you recognize the same principle ; to make the eye, the mind, and the hand work together ; to train the child to observe, and to regulate his thought and actions in accordance with his observation.

After seeing these methods of education, you understand better certain peculiarities of the American mind,— its almost total lack of abstract ideas, and its amazing power of recognizing reality, of manipulating it in the domain of mechanics as well as in that of business. The aim is, to the most remarkable degree, to confront these awakening minds constantly, indefatigably with the *fact*. The exercises which they choose are the evident proof of this. Thus I have seen the pupils in a somewhat advanced class occupied by way of written exercise, in replying to a newspaper advertisement for employees.

When they are grown up, they will have such advertisements to draw up. These things are facts, and this education bows to facts. They will need to write letters relative to travelling, and here is a class of little girls of twelve who have just been dealing with the subject: "A trip to Europe."

I read two of the copies that the teacher is correcting. The first is the work of a child who has never been abroad. It is a very dry and meagre production, which, however, reveals a minute effort after accuracy. The child names the ship on which she is supposed to have made the voyage. She mentions the day of setting out, the length of the voyage, the number of miles made each day, the name of a hotel in Liverpool and one in London. All these details are accurate and real. She has heard relatives or friends mention them, and she has retained them. The little girl of the second paper has actually made the journey. She had observed and remembered each daily event, the incidents, the meals, the conversation of her mother and the stewardess. She had observed the small size of the London houses and the air of "refined gayety" of Paris. It is all told without effort and sometimes with a good deal of naturalness. It seemed as if I were tracing to its source that talent for conscientious and truthful writing which in America even more than in England has produced an enormous amount of feminine literature. The attention here is carefully directed to the daily current of events. Fifteen or twenty years hence this little girl will go to the poles or to Egypt and her notes of travel will appear in some magazine, if indeed she does not undertake some monograph on art or history, science or literature, or if again she does not try her hand at a "short story," that brief and sensational study of life, in narrative form, which is really the summit of excellence in American literature.

Returning from these visits, you must take up the report of the school committee, to read it with the picture before you

U

of these boys and girls with their spirited, resolute faces, these masters and mistresses with their lively, familiar ways, these light and well-ordered schoolrooms, these well-stocked laboratories — all this little world of study in which nothing calls up the thought of discipline or constraint. You will receive the fullest light on the whole system of instruction by reading the part of the report entitled "Examination Papers." This is a list covering pages and pages of questions put to the pupils in written or oral examinations. There is not one, from the simplest to the most difficult, which was not designed to put the child's mind in an atmosphere of positive action, to connect it with facts by a firm and sufficient tie. In the matter of spelling, for instance, the easiest dictation exercises contain facts of domestic life or counsels of practical utility.

"While I remain in the country this summer my time will be occupied in active recreation." "John, come here. Did you hear me quoting the old saying, 'A stitch in time saves nine'?"

If the examination is in composition, subjects like these are given: —

"Wanted: a young woman in a photographic gallery. Must have practical and artistic experience and good references. Address, Room 15, 154 Tremont Street, Boston, Mass. Write the letter that you would write if you desired this place."

"Write a letter to some one you know who has never been in this school. Describe the playground, the building, your room."

"Write to a friend, giving advice as to her health, telling her the things you have learned about the care of the body."

If it is geography, this is how they prepare children for their future travels: —

"Sail from Cape Ann to Cork, with a cargo. What goods would you take and what would you bring back?"

"Make an excursion from San Francisco to Paris. Describe the route. What articles would you bring back?"

Then follow an infinite number of questions upon climates and products, both vegetable and mineral, and the division of industries.

If the study is mathematics, mental arithmetic will occupy the first place, of course, and all the problems will refer to processes of buying and selling.

If it is history, all the questions turn upon the annals of the great Republic, and especially on New England.

"When and by whom was Boston founded? Describe the Tree of Liberty, the Boston Massacre,. the Boston Tea-party. Describe a New England village, a Sunday morning in colonial times. Give an account of the landing in Massachusetts Bay and a short description of the leaders of the first colony."

Evidently the pupil who is prepared to reply on all these points has been educated with a view to becoming a business man in a democracy and if possible, in a special city of the democracy. The citizens who manage this vast organization for civic instruction are finding, nevertheless, that in these programmes there is too little room for the workingman. The report sketches a project for a new school of mechanical arts, more complete than any other. It will be called — no doubt by this time it is already called — "The Mechanical High School." The prospectus is summed up in these words, which I transcribe textually: —

"For the first time in Boston the child who is to enter industrial life will have, at the public expense, the same opportunities for preparation which have long been given to those who are preparing for business or professional life."

Having reached this point, it seems to me that these people must have attained their ideal, which can be expressed in one word: *the complete identification of education and life.*

You find the same ideal on your first view of a university. I have taken Harvard for the type, precisely because, being the oldest, it seems best to show the persistent tendency of the American mind. In the first place, its history alone shows how essential a characteristic of this mind is faith in individual initiative and local vitality. It is the story of a constant struggle for an ever more complete autonomy. It would be interesting to put opposite it the history of an old French university — that of Paris, Montpellier, Toulouse — as a test of the degree of divergence between the two democracies. With us, the contrary work has been done; institutions once independent and powerful have been brought under the central administration, the service of higher education has become a state service. When there was a question, a few years ago, of giving back an independent existence to these *universities*, now absorbed in *the university*, one of the most eloquent orators of the Republican party, M. Challemel-Lacour, maintained, with the support of our Senate — like him Republican — that such a measure was opposed to all the work of the Revolution. His Jacobinism saw clearly in this matter, and no argument more strongly shows the wretched tyranny of the work of '89, essentially hostile to all liberty, destructive of all living energy.

As for higher education in America, it began where ours ends. When in 1636 the University of Harvard — then of Cambridge — was founded, the General Court of Massachusetts — that is to say, the State — establishing it by a vote, this Court — consequently the State — reserved to itself the right of control. The "overseers" or surveillants were at this date the governor and magistrates of the colony, by virtue of their office, and they had full power to administer the funds of the college. But in a few words of the charter was already indicated the future of the University: "All the funds," it ran, "including gifts, legacies, and donations" —

From the first the founders foresaw that the co-operation of private persons would be the principal support of their institution, and already in 1636 a Nonconforming clergyman, of the name of John Harvard, — thus becoming the godfather of the college, — made the first of a long series of gifts by virtue of which the University to-day has a capital of twelve million dollars — or sixty millions of francs.

The right of inheritance and possession carries as inevitable corollary the right to administer one's possessions at will. Therefore the first one hundred and fifty years of Harvard's existence saw continual efforts on the part of the president and professors or "fellows" to secure this second right. Not until 1814 did they obtain it, and then subject to the control of the "overseers." It remained to secure that these should themselves be incorporated in the University.

It is interesting to follow this attempt during these eighty years. They began by modifying the law under which the overseers were nominated. They thus became an independent and self-perpetuating body. This independence was already a guarantee of a sort of autonomy. A law was then passed that the State of Massachusetts should not have the right to modify the statutes of the University without the united consent of overseers and corporation. A new step forward was taken in 1843. The law of 1810 provided that the board of overseers must include fifteen clergymen, all of them Congregationalists. In 1843 it was provided that these might be of any denomination, and in 1851 the board was authorized to dispense with clergymen altogether. In 1854 a bill of still more liberal scope was introduced, giving all the graduates of Harvard a vote in the election of overseers; but this law was not passed until 1863. It contained, however, this restriction, that the overseers thus chosen must be residents of Massachusetts. This restriction clause was abolished in 1880 as the last vestige of injurious state supervision.

At the present time, being mistress of her funds, which she administers according to her own judgment, mistress of her methods of instruction, which she arranges at her own will, herself naming her overseers and professors, this University, which began by being doubly official, since it was under the government also of the Church, has no longer to reckon with any but her own members. She is free, in the deepest and fullest sense of the word, and the statistics are there to show that to this increase of independence corresponds an increase of vital force. The number of students, which was eleven hundred in 1870, was in 1893 two thousand nine hundred and sixty-six. There were forty-one professors ; there now are eighty-six. There were eighty-one tutors ; there now are two hundred and ninety-four. The aid extended to poor students amounted to twenty-five thousand dollars; it is now eighty-nine thousand. There were a hundred and eighty-four thousand volumes in the library ; there are now four hundred and twelve thousand. Now translate these figures into concrete realities; they show that within the fifteen or twenty years since the last thread was cut which bound together the State and the University the affluence of life has doubled in this organism, that its overseers have been more active, its professors more diligent, its students more in earnest. Let our French faculties to-morrow be thus masters of themselves, not nominally, but really, without minister or inspector or council to rule them ; let them inherit and possess ; let them modify their courses of teaching according to their own views and the needs of their region ; let the teachers, chosen by their own colleagues, feel themselves really in their own place, and the students, too, and with all this let the great central schools be suppressed, to leave to the universities their full range of influence, — and the same causes would produce the same effects, and the intellectual life of our provinces would suddenly awake. Alas ! we are not travelling in this direction.

Harvard University is composed of the college,—properly so called,—a scientific school, a graduate school, and six professional schools. Two of these—the schools of law and theology—are in Cambridge, like the college itself. The four others, those of medicine, dental surgery, veterinary surgery, and agriculture, are in Boston. The college students are about two-thirds of the whole number. It is therefore the college life that we must try to picture to ourselves in order to understand the soul of Harvard, and the social type elaborated during the four years of the full course,—the "freshman," "sophomore," "junior," and "senior" years. These are the names taken by the student from twelvemonth to twelvemonth, and they explain themselves.

Equality and activity, especially equality, are the essential characteristics which emerge, on a first glance, over the sort of life which these young people lead during these four years. If the English proposed to send sons of the nobility to Oxford, in order to create the complex type of the "gentleman," the Americans appear, on their part, to have proposed to bring together poor boys and rich boys in order to abolish, or even to forestall, that prejudice against paid work which is, in fact, the principle most destructive of democracy. To put our finger on the distinction, I may transcribe here a letter quoted by Mr. Frank Bolles, the treasurer of the University, which by itself alone will, better than any analysis, make the reader acquainted with the conditions under which the young Harvard men pursue their studies. It is the detailed account, year by year and figure by figure, of the methods employed by a poor student to pay his own way through college. It will be seen that the expenses of a student are pretty high, especially for a comparatively small town such as Cambridge. But here we see another American characteristic. Having the alternative of diminishing his expenses or increasing his work, the American always prefers to increase his work.

The poor student, whose statement Mr. Bolles reports, fixes his freshman expenses at three hundred and eighty-one dollars, his sophomore expenses at three hundred and sixty-one, those of the junior year at three hundred and ninety-five, and those of the senior year at four hundred and sixty-two. He had twenty-five dollars of debts when he entered Harvard. He was, therefore, obliged to earn money, and a large sum of money, during these four years, while at the same time pursuing his studies.

The details of the methods he employed are very significant. As freshman, he "made" three hundred and forty-six dollars, thus divided : a prize of two hundred and fifty dollars, a loan of fifteen dollars on his watch, seventy-one dollars earned by type-writing for his fellow-students, eight dollars by selling books, two dollars by tutoring.

As sophomore he used the same methods, except that, in view of the smallness of the prize gained that year, he decided to wait at table. His work as waiter brought him thirty-eight dollars. It may be remarked that this is not an isolated case. Many Harvard students gain by this means, especially during vacations, the small overplus of resources which they require. This student, in his second year, added to this business that of preparing the brains of sheep for the lectures of Professor William James, the great psychologist.

The third year, the junior, appears to have been easier. Tutoring brought him in more — one hundred and twenty dollars. He got work in the library that helped to set him on his feet. A large prize which he took in the fourth year put an end to his difficulties, and he left college at the completion of his studies, having met all his own expenses during the four years, and put aside a small sum of money.

This is a perfect specimen of the American student, and Mr. Bolles is right in concluding at the close of this letter: "A young man who has gone through all this is certain to succeed in any calling." He cites among possible careers, railway service, journalism, book-publishing, political life, and teaching. The elasticity of this programme of the future is simply in conformity with the genius of a country where a man finds it perfectly natural to change his profession at forty, fifty, or sixty years. One consequence of this facility of guiding his life in the most opposite directions is that the "poor scholar" is unknown in the United States. The students who wait upon their classmates, napkin on arm and dish in hand, and who will presently be sitting on the same benches with them, attending the same lectures and passing the same examinations, have, if one may so speak, taken and given a lesson of destiny. They know and they demonstrate that the man of energy accepts all and conquers all, if only he will. Neither he nor his fellow-students will forget the lesson.

Such letters give a sort of sketch, accurate though cold, of one kind of life. To give it color, to change these true though abstract details into a living picture, one must go himself to Cambridge, and see with his own eyes the setting in which such a career is possible and even normal. No excursion could be easier. Hundreds of electric tram-cars connect it with Boston by day and night. You cross the broad river Charles; then about two miles of a country all built up with small wooden houses, with verandas, where the eternal rocking-chair awaits the American's wearied repose.

The car is filled with young men and young women. Of the latter, in this suburb of a student town, not a single one would suggest the idea of a bad character. The *demi-grisette*, the half-venal, half-sentimental mistress, who abounds in our Latin quarter, does not exist here. The type that you have met in these cars is chiefly that of a girl from eighteen to twenty-five years old, thin and slight, with quantities of auburn hair, a delicate, freckled face, bright eyes, and a smile that has a sort of stern languor, telling of too much work, too much tension, too

much endeavor — not her own, but of her race, of a whole
long ancestry behind her. The well-kept teeth show white
between the parted lips, which droop at the corners. The
voice is harsh and slightly nasal. The neck is thin, and suggests a thin body, the frail anatomy of which you guess at —
for it is winter — under the double-breasted coat, the knitted
jacket, the flannels, and the "combinations." The whole person stands on india-rubber shoes, and is enveloped in india
rubber, suggesting the factory and the waterproof.

Where is this child going? Is she a student of the "Annex,"
the portion of the University reserved to women? Is she a
dressmaker going back to her shop, a salesgirl going to her
store, a doctress going to her patient, a clairvoyant about to
give a private *séance*, an actress returning from a rehearsal?
This creature might equally well adapt herself to all situations,
exercise all callings, except that of trafficker in love ; and the
youths who sit facing or beside her, with books, or racquets, or
skates under their arm, according to the occasion, are also prepared for all feats of daring, except an adventure of gallantry.
I am told that a certain number go into Boston for nocturnal
dissipation. It is possible. But in that case, this is a real
debauch, a lower phase of life, so coarse, so distinct from all
the rest, that the young man is degraded by it, and not cor-
rupted. The difference is great. The temporary household
of the Parisian student, with its daily intercourse and its
romanticism, bears witness to greater refinement, but it is far
more dangerous to the healthiness of future life.

The aspect of Cambridge on the winter day when I reached
it by the gliding of the rapid but commonplace car, was delightful to see. The great red University buildings looked all
the redder against the white snow. The little wooden houses,
in general the dwellings of professors, wore a pleasant look of
friendliness, gray and neutral between the white ground and
the red of the vast edifices reserved for libraries and museums

and students' rooms. The pines showed black against the cold blue sky, and so did the leafless branches of other trees, slender and fragile frameworks where sparrows were twittering. Purple berries gleamed in the shrubberies, making gay this peaceful, quiet scene of study.

There were students passing and repassing on the wooden sidewalks, swept clean from snow. They were simply dressed, and between their lips they held the short wooden pipe of a shape special to Harvard. They go where they please and do what they please. More independent than their contemporaries at Oxford, they are not even subject to the obligation to be in at a fixed hour, which is the first servitude of a Balliol or Christ Church man. The second is the necessity of presence at table. Harvard men know no more of this than of the other. They are not, like the English, set in a sort of lay monastery, part cloister, part club, and part gymnasium. The rooms in which they live in the buildings set down here and there in the neighborhood of Memorial Hall are subject to no supervision. They live there as at a hotel, giving no account of their actions.

There is a great diversity in the elegance of these rooms, as well as in their price. Most generally two students live together. One parlor serves them as study and two closets as bedrooms. Two desks, two bookcases, two sets of furniture, divide the study into two distinct domains. Everywhere are the inevitable rocking-chairs, and on all the window-seats of the guillotine windows are small mattresses with pillows, where they stretch themselves to read, to smoke, to look at the view. On the walls are hung the medallions of clubs and photographs that tell of the favorite pastimes of the owners of the room : football teams, yacht crews, theatre scenes, views of Europe, Egypt, the Holy Land. Almost all of them have been "abroad," and the rest are going. In the most expensive rooms which, like those in Claverley Hall, cost six, seven, eight hundred dollars, the student lives alone, and usually the two little rooms give the impression of a club man: almost no books, a slight desk with folding cover, steady enough to scratch off a note upon, but too fragile to support a dictionary or to work upon: everywhere mementos of races, balls, and hunting. In this inequality of expenditure so offensive to us, we really find the democratic spirit of America. What is equal with them is respect for the individual. He is left equally free to spend his money or not to spend it, to have it or not to have it. Any regulation, however wise, would encroach upon this vigorous freedom of action which to them appears to be the grandest of human qualities. On reflection we see that they are right. Our system, which makes rich children and poor children live in our schools under the same material conditions, has for its most certain result to develop the most furious envy when this identity of life suddenly ceases with the young man's entrance into the world. This disastrous influence has less chance of being born when there has never been any such identity.

One of the most striking features of Harvard life, giving the measure of the spirit of independent action, is the number of clubs or societies which the students maintain by themselves outside of all administrative control. There are no fewer than forty-nine of them, each one founded with a positive and definite purpose. To read over their lists and programmes is to pass in review all the interests of the American student, his labors and his pleasures.

Some of these clubs, like the Porcellian, are the precise image of a closed circle of New York or Boston. The club derives its name and emblem — a boar's head — from a celebrated dinner given in 1791 by one of its members, at which a whole pig was served as a roast. You observe, here again, in the fidelity with which these young men adhere to the comic surname, in the pride with which they show you some last century's reviews on the shelves of their library, the constant desire to overlay the present with the past. One of them, who had passed some time at Oxford, used a very singular and suggestive expression to describe how much in a new civilization is slight and superficial and thin.

"We feel the want of *density* so much here," he said.

The principal object of some other clubs, like the "Hasty Pudding," is to give dramatic representations. The name of this club, which also recalls a culinary whim, corresponds well with the character of good humor everywhere imprinted on the little house where it abides. Most of the pieces played on the stage of the ground-floor are satirical buffooneries composed by the students themselves. The spirit of these lively boys is shed abroad on the walls in grotesque programmes, drawn with a certain power of gayety. I am told that the club is expensive, each member being assessed fifty dollars a year. At the time of my visit a broad-shouldered young man, with the build of a boxer, his fine eyes hidden by spectacles, was seated at the piano, accompanying himself in singing a Yokohama song. He went to the Pacific islands last year, and doubtless his companions will go in a year or five or ten. There is quite a body of Americans in the extreme Orient. Japan is so near — thirteen days from Vancouver, fifteen from San Francisco. In this students' club I find a tiny trace of this exotic influence. I found it in Washington the other day when I sat at dinner beside a young girl who was all absorbed in Buddhism, and in Boston where a very distinguished doctor, who has been completely initiated, said to me, drawing two concentric circles on the table: —

"Christianity is to Buddhism what this small circle is to the large one."

And his conversation was filled with formulæ of Hindoo wisdom, which seemed all the more striking coming from those stern and decided Yankee lips.

"There are many roads that lead to the mountain," he concluded, speaking of the different religions, "but the landscape
around it remains always the same."   "We are all living on
the surface of our being," he said again.

The young fellows of the Hasty Pudding have not got so
far as to plunge into these formulæ beneath which lies the
abyss of the grand, but deadly metaphysical vision.   But I
shall not be astonished if there is some day at Harvard a
Buddhist club, as already, beside the circles for pleasure and
for the theatre, there is a Christian circle, the St. Paul, and a
philosophical circle, the Harvard Philosophical Club, whose
purpose is thus described in the prospectus: "A genial and
pronounced individuality is as great a requirement for mem-
bership as to be deeply versed in philosophy."

Then there is a whole series of literary and secret societies
that by an artlessly humorous pedantry are called by Greek
letters: the *Delta Phi* society, the *Delta Upsilon*, the *Phi
Beta Kappa*, *Pi Eta*, *Theta Delta*, *Zeta Psi*.   There is a
series of sporting societies, the *Boat Club*, the *Cycling Association*, the *Cricket Club*, the *Football Club*, the *Baseball Club*,
the *Photographic Society*, the *Camera Club;* there are political
clubs, the *Democratic*, and the *Republican;* musical societies,
the *Banjo Club*, the *Guitar and Mandolin*, the *Pierian*.
There is a series of associations for the publication of serious
or humorous periodicals, the *Lampoon*, the *Crimson*, the *Advocate*, the *Monthly*.   The youthful editors of these periodicals would not be American if these enterprises did not
become real business undertakings.   Last year, to give only
a single example, the *Crimson* brought in to its editor-in-
chief five hundred dollars, and a hundred dollars to each of
the other editors.   I have looked over some of these sheets.
They are, in fact, real newspapers, filled with news interesting
to the University.   I read in one of them an excellent criticism of *Le Mariage Forçé* given by the members of the *Cercle*

Français and a discussion of a decree of the overseers. Advertisements abound, filling two or three pages. In the *Advocate* I find a witty essay on "Feminology," which closes by a quotation from Maupassant: *"Cette canaillerie charmante, cette tromperie raffinée, cette malicieuse perfidie, toutes ces perverses qualités qui poussent au suicide les amants imbécilement crédules et qui ravissent les autres."*

This quotation and a poem entitled *Fleur du mal* with the last line "I hear the mocking laugh of Baudelaire," bear witness to the freedom of mind of these young men and the boldness of their range of reading. This admiration for French writers of the extreme Left is one of the features that most distinguishes America from England. But it suffices to converse with the men and women who profess it, to perceive that their interest is entirely in the sphere of the intellect and the will. It does not reach the deep sources of private life, which are still simple and somewhat primitive. The unhealthy complexity of our great artists is a subject of curiosity to Americans of both sexes, a sort of moral *bibelot*, to be looked at and handled like a cup of peculiar form which nobody ever drinks out of. Here, especially in this wholesome setting of Harvard, the difference of surroundings puts these young men in the same mental attitude toward our contemporary authors that they have toward the Alexandrian poets and the Arabian story-tellers. The realities of their own life, which preserve their hearts from being poisoned by the senses and their wills by dreams, are work and sport, good fellowship and athletics, the intense attractions of the gymnasium with its running track and its thousand appliances, which include instruments to develop all muscles, even to those of the fingers. They are safeguarded, too, by their precocious aptitude for organization, which enables them to administer for themselves such establishments as Memorial Hall, where eleven hundred of them eat daily at an expense of more than fifty thousand dollars a year. They handle these sums with the wisdom and the strict probity which they will one day apply to the management of their own property.

Again, we perceive that in the university as in the school the Americans have sought and have obtained the perfect harmony of education and life. Here again they have been guided by facts. Their good sense has preserved them from the too tempting imitation of European things. They have neither built up a false English university, as might have been feared, nor a false German university. But to look into the faces of the students, so energetic, so virile, with an expression of decided candor all their own, you feel that they have succeeded in producing just the stamp of man which their democracy needs. You feel also that they have not yet done away with that trace of stern harshness natural to the son of a recent and still incomplete nation. And yet Harvard is the most traditional of American universities, the most like Europe. How I wish I had leisure to test my observations of it by the others, above all those of the West, whose student cheers express a singularly untamed joy of living. Here, for example, is the " cheer " of the University of Illinois, " Rah-hoo-rah, Zip-boom ah ! Hip-zoo, rah zoo, Jimmy, blow your bazoo. Ip-sidi-iki, U. of I., Champaign ! " and that of the University of Indiana, " Gloriana, Frangipana, Indiana !　Kazoo, Kazah !　Kazoo, Kazah !　Hoop Lah !　Hoop Lah !　State University, Rah ! Rah ! Rah ! " and that of Denver, " U, U, U, of D, Den-ver, Ver-si-tee !　Kai Gar Wahoo Zip boom — D. U. ! "　The University of North Dakota follows with her cry, " Odz-dzo-dzi ! Ri-ri-ri ! Hy-ah ! Hy-ah ! North Dakota ! "

I doubt whether the roar of a lion is more wild and blood-curdling than these onomatopœan cries, issuing from broad chests and robust wide-open lungs, suggesting health that would suffice for years of hard work and bitter competition. Health is the first of conditions in a country without a middle class, where the *rentier* does not exist and where the student who is rich to-day will to-morrow, by a freak of fortune, be the poor engineer, the needy journalist, the business man in straitened circumstances, the doctor without patients; in fact, the man compelled to struggle for life, as though he had never been either freshman or sophomore, junior or senior. Let us not be anxious about him. He is ready.

And they are ready also, the freshmen, the seniors and the juniors of that woman's college, which rises at the edge of the little Lake Waban, at Wellesley, near Boston, its great red building in the shape of a Latin cross, with its brick villas and its wooden cottages. A college ! How inadequately that word, so sad and dreary in French, represents the freshness and poetry of this oasis ! It is most truly a young girl's university, a sort of realization of that fantasy of Tennyson's, "The Princess," concerning which Taine has written, "No jest is more romantic or more tender. You smile to hear weighty, learned words issuing from those rosy lips. . . . Clad in lilac silk dresses, with golden girdles, they listen to passages of history and promises of social renovation."

But that the toilettes of the lovely Wellesleyans are more modern, these lines of the great philosopher might be placed at the head of the catalogue of this singular institution. I say singular, involuntarily taking the Gallo-Roman point of view, which admits of no other means of education for women than the convent or the paternal roof. The girls' school with us is but a lay convent, without that which alone corrects its seclusion and monotonous discipline; namely, confession and communion. In vain it bears the name of academy, after the fashion of boys' schools; it is radically, unalterably different. Nowhere is the radical inequality between the two sexes, which forms the very foundation of our society, more perceptible than in the difference between the methods and the results of the

x

two modes of teaching. I have elsewhere tried to show for
what infinitely complex reasons Americans uphold the truly
democratic dogma of absolute equality between man and
woman. True to their great principle of accepting all the
practical consequences of the truths in which they believe,
they could not but make the education of both identical. In
the mixed schools that reform has already been realized so far
as primary and secondary education is concerned. Wellesley
is one of the most complete attempts to realize it in higher
education.

This attempt — like all those which the traveller finds in this
country, where the State is nothing — was due to private initiative. At the risk of being monotonous we must not weary
of repeating this observation. All things grow clear in the
United States when one understands them as an immense act
of faith in the social beneficence of individual energy left to
itself. This, so to speak, is the mystical basis of their realism,
the message that they bring to the world, and above all to us
French people, whom the most retrograde of revolutions has
for the last hundred years made the slaves of a centralized
state. Nor must we weary of telling of the moral dramas of
which those generous foundations are nearly always the outcome. Here is the one to which Wellesley owes its birth : —

In 1863 there lived in Boston a distinguished lawyer, Mr.
Henry Fowle Durant. His portrait gives one the idea of a
face most refined, radiant, with an expression at once gentle
and bright. The somewhat stern line, observable in the faces
of so many Americans, is seen at the corner of the nostril.
The chin is rather long and prominent, the face absolutely
smooth, with that expression of fixed intensity which we find
among all who are compelled to self-restraint and self-com-
mand, such as doctors, clergymen, and actors. Those who
have known Mr. Durant speak of him as having a body so thin
and frail, so delicate in its motions, that he reminded them

invariably of the words of the apostle, " He will be raised a spiritual body." We may imagine from such details and from small photographic likenesses one of those too sensitive organisms which life touches very deeply, and which cannot support it unless they interpose between themselves and reality an abstract faith, in which they wrap themselves for protection. In the year 1863 this tender-hearted man lost his only son. The trial was so severe that instinctively he sought refuge in religion. He became, says the biographer from whom I borrow these details, the most intense of evangelical Christians. It was in this crisis of mysticism that the vigorous spirit of positivism, always present in the American, showed itself. He abandoned his profession as a lawyer, which no longer seemed to him to be in accord with the ardor of his new convictions. His wife and he began to consider what use they could make of their fortune. Debating the matter, they conceived the scheme of founding a university for women, the basis of which should be the Bible. "Mr. Durant," adds the same biographer, "said strongly both in public and private, that the object of his college was to form learned Christian women, Christian wives and Christian mothers."

In 1871 the first stone of the college was laid. It has now had twenty years of activity. The sum expended by the founder was more than eight hundred thousand dollars. Other persons added to the endowment, and at the present time this succession of private munificence has brought the property of the college to the sum of $1,636,900.

When modern Americans talk of Christianity we are haunted by the recollection of puritan fanaticism, but we err. They understand thereby simply a rather small number of essential principles which must be taken "for granted." This is the expression which they constantly make use of, when they are questioned regarding their moral or religious education. Their fundamental realism causes them to consider as useless any

discussions which call into question these first postulates. So
far they are all naturally Christian, if we may say so. But
these doctrines once admitted, their tolerance is infinite. I
observe, for example, in the list of professions of faith represented at Wellesley sixteen different sects ; Congregationalists,
Presbyterians, Baptists, Methodists, Unitarians, Reformed,
Quakers, Lutherans, Universalists, even Swedenborgians. This
diversity of beliefs goes to show in what spirit the Biblical
programme of Mr. Durant has been developed. One of the
teachers in the College has written : "What we should like to
suppress in this world is the frivolous and the ascetic woman."
Visiting the College yourself, and rectifying your observations
by conversation and the reading of the catalogue, you perceive
that everything here is arranged with a view to this double
result, — on the one hand, to form the minds of these young
girls by a thorough instruction equal to that of the young men
of Harvard or Yale, and on the other to adapt these girls to
the habits of elegance and comfort common to the prosperous
class in their country. If the religious life is hidden beneath
this free régime it is only as the regulator of a machine is
hidden.

You enter the principal building and you find yourself in a
hall, resembling, with its green plants, its pictures, its statues,
its lacquered furniture, the interior of one of those sumptuous
New York hotels, in which entire families pass their seasons
year after year. You mount the wooden staircase, wainscoted
like that of a club. All along the corridors, which are also furnished with statues, pictures, and plants, open the students'
rooms. They usually live two together, like the Harvard students. They have two little sleeping-rooms and a common
sitting-room, which does not differ in the least from the sitting-
room to which every American woman who is at all refined is
accustomed. Photographs, flowers, furniture of light wood,
and lounges with cushions of chintz, printed in fanciful pat-

terns, show off the elegance of these dainty little chambers, the occupants of which, by the way, have nothing monastic about them. They are constantly asking one another to tea. They also invite young men. Every Saturday evening the gymnasium ceases to be an athletic club and is transformed into a ballroom, to which they invite their friends from Boston and Cambridge, as if they were living at home with their parents. They go and come, in and out of the house, without giving account of their conduct. Some are rowing on the lake, others riding on horseback, others driving phaetons. Others have gone by train to Boston, alone, of course. They merely said that they were going into town. No surveillance is exercised over them during their absence. No questions are asked of them on their return. Since they intend entering on life, to become individuals capable of defending themselves, they must be educated with this end in view. And, moreover, a most equitable law which punishes the seducer equally with the forger and the thief, would protect them even were their own characters and those of the men whom they met insufficient.

This Draconian code appears to us in France to savor strongly of Pharisaism. It seems to us, also, that it must give room for the detestable practice of blackmailing. The value of laws is measured by their results, and the States where these laws are in force are certainly those in which the personality of women is developed with the greatest amount of energy and happiness. Surely this shows progress beyond countries like our own, where the relations of the sexes are still so grotesquely unequal that when a case of seduction occurs it is the woman who is dishonored, and the illegitimate child must be wholly cared for at the expense of the mother, since the search after paternity is forbidden. We shall have changed our régime several times yet before we shall dare on this point, as on so many others, to attempt one of those moral revolutions which are as fruitful as political and social revolutions are vain and criminal.

Are the girl students whose youthful grace is sheltered in this elegant and comfortable Wellesley equal to the men, and are they as well protected? Are they contented with their lot, or. do they long for still more liberty? Surely, if they wish to criticise the system to which they are subjected, the habit of public debate, as well as the quality of their instruction, admits of it.   Nothing is more curious than the contrast between the severity of their studies and the coquetry of those palaces and cottages standing on the shores of that little lake in that beautiful park.   The entrance examination requires a considerable knowledge of English literature, history and geography, mathematics, Latin, Greek, and of one of the two great living languages besides English — namely, French and German.

There is no limit of age for this examination, so that pupils of sixteen years may enter the college at the same time as those who are much more advanced in life. They gave me one example of a student of sixty years of age, already a grandmother, who presented herself and was admitted. In this country, where so many begin the work of life over and over again, young girls do not consider it extraordinary to have a companion of that age. There is no exclusive principle as. regards the entrance of students. They may be poor or rich, daughters of millionaires or of very humble parentage. So long as they are morally honorable, no one asks how they find the means to pay the three hundred and fifty dollars per annum, which is the cost of board. It often happens that a young girl, quite ready for examination, takes a place as a cashier or saleswoman in a store, as secretary in a hotel, or as copyist, in order to make up the sum. Others serve their classmates as dressmakers or milliners, take care of the rooms or carry messages. Here, as at Harvard, this extra work is not only tolerated but esteemed. It is a species of instruction in equality, given by those who undertake the service to those who can do without it, but who must nevertheless treat their less fortunate companions with unvarying politeness and sympathy. For that matter, after a very brief journey in the United States one is no longer astonished at the consequences which the democratic idea carries with it when constantly, indefatigably applied. Among the significant facts given to me by the former cowboy, whose story I have transcribed, I neglected to note this: One of his friends and he had hired a cook while staying in a Western city, and this woman stipulated in her engagement that once a week she should have the use of her master's sitting-room to receive her friends.

A simple little fact of this kind proves well enough how very intact mercenary occupation leaves the spirit of individual pride among those who undertake it, even when they are by extraction and education really inferior; all the more so when there is really no inferiority. On the other hand, one wonders when these Wellesley girls find time for supplementary work, so full and so many are the courses. Here, for example, is the Greek course, which a pupil in her first year must have passed in order to become a sophomore, — certain speeches of Lysias, the *Apology* and the *Crito* of Plato, five hundred lines of the *Odyssey* of Homer. In Latin she has studied the works of Cicero, the *Germania* and *Agricola* of Tacitus, and one or two books of Horace. In German she has mastered the general history of literature, the first part of *Faust* and the dramas of Schiller. In French her studies include *Le Cid*, *Horace*, *Andromaque*, *Le Misanthrope*, *L'Avare*, and, among modern works, *L'Abbé Constantin*. As regards philosophy, I cannot resist translating some of the lines from the programme of a class: "Types of ethical theory; psychological investigation of the laws of the human mind as a propædeutic basis for theories to account for moral experience and to justify ethic methods. The doctrine of evolution applied to account for the motives of individual conduct and the history of social and civil institutions, customs, etc.; the various types of ethics in the phases of moral conduct as they are revealed by literature and art."

Consider that to this work is added what may be called the work of the clubs. All the students are members of some club or association — musical, like the *Beethoven;* literary, like the *Shakespeare,* the *Phi-Sigma,* and the *Zeta-Alpha;* political, like the *Agora;* or for the study and practice of painting or sculpture, like the *Art Society.* Finally, nearly all of them take physical exercise, as it is understood in America — that is to say, as a calculated and carefully studied training. In the last report of the president I notice six tables of a strange description, which reveal in all frankness the tremendously realistic spirit by which this College, in appearance so paradoxical, is animated. The first is entitled "Girth of Chest." It is a series of comparative columns showing the average development of the chest obtained by twenty students, taken at random, after five months of training in the gymnasium and on the river. From thirty-one inches these young athletes passed to thirty-three. Two parallel columns show at a glance the cessation of development of those who have not exercised their muscles. The second table gives similarly the capacity of the lungs, the third the strength of the arms, the fourth the strength of the back, the fifth the depth of the chest, the sixth the breadth of the shoulders.

At first this manner of treating the physiological development of young girls, as trainers might treat that of their horses, appears strange. Then you reflect that these young girls who come here for instruction, are also destined, for the most part, to become wives and mothers. It is, therefore, advisable that they should be injured as little as possible by cerebral overwork and that their physique should remain sound in spite of intellectual effort. That object being admitted, the Americans employ the most efficacious method simply and quietly. All that remains is to collect statistics of the weight of the children to which these young women will give birth when married. I seem to hear one of the woman doctors who have made those instructive tables answer, "Why not?"

Between a woman's university like Wellesley and a military academy like West Point there should be, one would think, the same difference which exists with us between the Convent of the Sacred Heart, for example, and the School of St. Cyr. *A priori* we say to ourselves that one should be strictly watched over and the other but little. The Americans think exactly the contrary. Accustomed as they are, not to deal in words, but to see things as they are, they have said to themselves that independence being, in their world, the condition of woman's life, the colleges for young girls should accustom their students to the practice of independence. Inversely, discipline being the essential condition of military life, it has seemed to them that a school of officers should be governed with very strict severity, and it is for this reason that the cadets of West Point have the right to only two months' holiday in their four years of study. It is for this reason also that the list of "offences" punishable by bad marks is as large at West Point as it is small at Harvard and at Wellesley. There are no fewer than eight categories of these. Twelve of the first receive ten bad marks each, forty of the second receive seven, seventy-six of the third receive five, one hundred and five of the fourth receive four, and so until we reach the forty-three faults of the eighth category, which receive one bad mark each.

This apparent want of logic in a system which shuts up the future soldiers to a discipline such as is applied to children, while it leaves the future housewife with unlimited latitude, is in truth logical, and, if you wish to trace the ideal portrait of the officer of a democratic army, you will find that the Americans have succeeded in ascertaining and applying with incomparable common sense the laws that apply to formation of that personage so abnormal in an essentially pacific and commercial republic.

And, first of all, it is necessary that each officer should be deeply, closely attached to the democracy, and that the entire corps should be permeated with the democratic spirit. There are numerous examples to prove that an army, large or otherwise, has always a tendency to insulate itself in the country, to detach itself from the nation and to make itself a thing apart, and the possibility of a military despotism is always in the future. The Americans have foreseen this danger, and have warded it off by such a singular method of recruiting their military school at West Point that at first sight it disconcerts common sense. On reflection one understands its wisdom. They began by absolutely suppressing all competition for entrance. Each electoral district which nominates a Congressman has a right to name a candidate for a cadetship, and to that Congressman belongs the right of designating the candidate, whom the War Secretary nominates on that presentation. Ten places "at large" are added, which the President of the United States fills at his will. He reserves them, as a rule, for the sons of soldiers or sailors. On this list of candidates an entrance examination, or rather one of qualification, exercises a kind of weeding out. Is it necessary to add that politics almost wholly determines the choice of Congressmen? Vainly do they try to escape therefrom, as, for example, by offering for competition the place of a candidate which they have at their disposal. In fact, one-third of those places remain unoccupied, in consequence of the deficiencies of the youths whom the Congressmen present.

The person from whom I gather these details and those which follow, one of the most remarkable officers of our army, was astonished on visiting West Point at such an anomaly, evidently so harmful to the service.

"'There are in it two advantages," was the reply made to him. "In the first place, this recruiting answers to the spirit of equality which forms the very foundation of our democracy; each district of the country shares the expenses, and it is, therefore, right that each should share the benefits. If admission to West Point were thrown open to competition, the candidates coming from New England would necessarily beat the candidates from the South and West, where the average of development is feebler. In the second place, the present procedure singles out in the lowest classes, if only as an electoral bait, boys who, without this, would otherwise remain destitute of instruction. It is a means, among thousands of others, of giving the poorest the same facilities of culture as the richest. And the statistics of the callings exercised by the parents of the pupils testify that the method has succeeded. We count since the foundation, eight hundred and twenty-seven sons of farmers and planters, four hundred and ninety-five sons of merchants, four hundred and fifty-five of lawyers, two hundred and seventy-one of doctors, only two hundred and forty-six of officers, then the sons of all trades — butchers, innkeepers, footmen, detectives, house servants, washerwomen. There are many chances that an army commanded by chiefs who to such an extent are the issue of the people, will not become an army of pretorians; there are great chances also that those officers, thus aided by the Republic in the struggle for life, will remain faithful to the Constitution. The written oath of allegiance which they take on their entry to serve the federal power in preference to their native State — without doubt as a provision in the case of a new war, like that of the North and South — will cost them

nothing to keep. The United States have done too much
for them.''

This democratic method of recruiting was, however, not
without its peril. If the aristocratic officer is a danger to
liberty, the officer without education is a danger to the army.
He destroys and dissolves it by his mere existence — at least
in time of peace, when he is not even placed in a position to
secure for himself the credit of personal valor. The Americans have well understood this difficulty of origin, if we may
so say, and they have not overlooked it. Their self-respect
is too deep for them to accept, without trying to change, a
too evident inferiority, and they have remedied it, always
.after their habitual method of accepting facts. Which is the
strongest of the influences that can induce a rather coarse
youth to control himself, and to train himself in the direction
of refinement? It is feminine influence. They have therefore asked themselves by what means they could bring woman
into the life of the cadets, and have bethought themselves of
constructing a hotel at the doors of the school, in that admirable landscape which is formed by the Hudson and the mountains — the river with its deep waters flowing at the foot of the
plateau on which is West Point, and turning round it almost
at right angles, the mountains spreading themselves out
behind, their slopes covered with wild forests, and in the
distance the vast plains where Albany lies. Quite naturally
the beauty of the site, the comfort of the establishment, the
facility of access, and the purity of the air attract a great
number of gentlemen and lady visitors, the principal amusement of whom is to watch the cadets going through their exercises and taking part in the entertainments which they give.

You arrive. The sound of military music draws you to the
esplanade. The young pupils of West Point are executing a
manœuvre in their elegant uniforms of light gray, with a triple
row of gold buttons. They go and come, while a number of

ladies watch them coming and going, and in the intervals of the exercise you see them leaving the ranks to salute those they know. The grass lawns, shaded with trees and gay with flowers, where this parade, at once military and social, takes place, give this scene the appearance of a garden party of a unique kind. Those same ladies which grace it will be found this evening or to-morrow at the dances which the cadets themselves organize three times a week in summer and twice in winter.

The observer whom I have already quoted, whose official position prevents me from naming him, thus described one of those balls to me: —

"An invitation was sent to all the visitors at the hotel. I took care not to miss it. The entertainment lasted two hours, from eight to ten. I was standing in the alcove of the window, by the entrance, and, thanks to my incognito, I heard the conversations of the cadets, who came to cool themselves, without paying any attention to me. Not a dubious word was uttered. The cadets introduced one another to the girls. When one of them did not dance a member of the committee wearing a red sash, the badge of service, went and fetched a disengaged youth and brought him to her. From time to time a cadet and a young girl would leave the hall and promenade in the dark for ten minutes or so. It seemed quite natural, and no one smiled at it. Everything went on with ease and dignity."

Respect for woman and the refinement caused by that respect, — these are the means which the Americans have boldly employed to make those youths, recruited at random, the "gentlemen" that officers must be. Regarding technical instruction they have followed their habitual method, which consists in bringing the mind into direct contact with the object. Thus they have reduced theoretic teaching to a minimum. During three years out of four there is not a single class of that kind. Each pupil receives in September, the period at which the scholastic year commences, pamphlets containing the matters which he must study. He prepares these tasks by himself, and then the professor questions him. There are eight or ten pupils in a room, with a master who knows them all, and who is with them from week to week. The exercise regularly done, the youths are enabled each evening to apply what they have studied, and thus the abstract work of the day is completed. As soon as the fine weather comes, that is to say, from the first days of June to the first days of September, even the abstract teaching ceases. The cadets camp out. It is an object lesson which they receive for three months in the open air and under conditions as analogous as possible to those which would exist in real war. Of their four years at West Point they have, therefore, spent one entirely as though they had been with a regiment, but in a regiment without promiscuity, without dangerous companionship, and without the fetters of discipline. With great wisdom the "adjutant" has been suppressed at West Point; to the future officer he is nothing more than a semi-superior. Graded cadets or real officers command with a fulness of authority which carries with it at once more rigor and less minutiæ. Thus, though the code of offences is, as we have seen, extremely strict, punishments are rare.

When the question is of those machines for forming a certain kind of man, which we call a special school, the result gives the measure of the value of the method. With its strangely varied recruiting, with its individual education, with its instruction, which would appear very commonplace to one of the ordinary pupils of our schools, West Point turns out, according to the best judges, an excellent corps of student officers. Whatever be the arm of the service chosen, the young man who leaves the academy must pass through a school of application. But he arrives there sturdy and balanced, trained to bodily exercises by gymnastics, fencing, riding, and, above all, by camping out in the open air, well prepared for a superior education, by the positive apprenticeship which he has served. His teachers have taught him nothing which he has not understood. Instead of making him, as in many of the military schools of Europe, a scholar, whom they will afterward ask to descend into practical details of artillery and engineering, they have made him a manipulator of cannons and a worker in the trenches, knowing that he can become a scholar later, if he have the tastes and aptitudes, which, however, is scarcely probable. On the other hand, if the United States found it necessary to organize once again an immense improvised army as it did thirty-five years ago, they would find in the former pupils of this democratic and living academy precisely the kind of officers whom they would need to put the machine in motion.

American patriotism has one of its centres in this College, the only one in the country which works in the opposite direction to universal decentralization, and in the direction of a deep federal unity. This displacement of object and method, which testifies once again to American adaptability, shows also to what a degree these great realists are exempt from the evil of doctrines, so pernicious to countries where traditions obtain, and how much the servitude of ready-made ideas is repugnant to them. Here again you find the great feature of the national character, that active will, which holds itself in the face of the social world as it will hold itself face to face with the physical world, fearless in assertion and in daring. It is the necessary rhythm of all effective resolution — the exact " lucidity " of a glance over given conditions and their acceptance and adjustment in view of a no less lucid project. Be it a question of a bank, of a bridge, of a railroad, or of a school, American energy proceeds always in the same manner. And the success attained shows that the procedure is good.

In the word "lucidity" we sum up this short inquiry, which can evidently be generalized, but only with much reserve. Lucidity being the aim, and the means, it is very probable that these same characteristics would meet in all the other enterprises of public or private instruction, and in consequence there would be that fundamental identity of education and life which forms the common foundation of the four groups of instruction, of which I have sketched the plan. If you search a little into this formula, it seems that many of the qualities and the defects of this civilization are illuminated, and also several very deep and too little known laws of human nature. And in the first place, this identity of education and life explains the prodigious development of the whole of this vast country, in which each new generation on reaching maturity has no further apprenticeship to serve. It is a common saying with us, heard even in the speeches at the distribution of our prizes, that for collegians a second period of education is about to begin with their liberty. In fact, a youth of twenty years in France, who has brought his literary and scientific studies up to such a point that he is enabled to take his degree, is in no way equipped to earn his living, still less to make his own fortune or that of his family. Quite a new moral and intellectual drill is necessary to train him to face the realities of his surroundings. The decadence of our secondary education — to speak of nothing else — is enormous. In America that decadence does not exist. It cannot exist, and the type of the *déclassé* is as yet such a stranger to Americans that he is, I think, quite incomprehensible to them. When his eighteenth or twentieth year has been reached, a man in New York, Boston, or Chicago is a made man. He will, without doubt, after fifteen or twenty years of struggling, have more experience, a wider scope, and a greater authority. But it will be only a difference of degree. From the day he leaves school or the university he is complete, prepared for the struggle of life.

The woman is in the same condition; and this is why you seldom meet in the United States those really young faces, in the sense in which we understand the term, those faces in which there is uncertainty, something unfinished, a beginning, a mere sketch of the individual, who is, as it were, being fashioned and modified.

Age is recognized in the freshness of the skin, the brightness of the eyes and the teeth, the growth of the beard, the slenderness of the figure; and one says, "That young man is not twenty-two years of age, that young girl is not twenty years old." But the faces of both these young persons are those of persons who are thirty or forty years old, and their practical activity is just as mature.

This precocity of initiative is indubitably one of the benefits of the method, at least from the social point of view. Another, which I have noted in the course of this analysis, is the greater elasticity of the local centres, each town raising its future citizens according to its needs, and, so to say, according to its measure. With us a cabinet minister, taking out his watch, could tell you what all the rhetoricians in all the academies of France were doing at the time.

In America you have as many systems of education as you have towns; and it is certainly due to this fact that towns quite near to one another, such as New York, Boston, Philadelphia, and Baltimore, each retain that originality which is so distinct and that patriotism which is so separate. Therein lies, for a democracy, a condition which is a *sine qua non* of political health; and from that point of view, again, American education, by working in the direction of local vitality, shows itself a superior machine for producing this healthy state. Democracy is, in fact, according to definition, the government of the people by the people; that is to say, it is the empire of the majority. In centralized countries the power which such a majority gives to its representatives is too great, too absolute. They are

Y

capable of penetrating too deeply into individual life; and past and contemporaneous history proves that in fact they have always so penetrated, and that republics thus established are Cæsarisms of long or short duration, but always Cæsarisms.

The tyranny of a ministry two months in power, or that of an emperor who reigns eighteen years, is always a tyranny. One of the greatest thinkers of France at the present moment, and one of the least known, M. Louis Ménard, has given its formula in the following admirable aphorism: "A centralized republic is not capable of living. Monarchy is the only logical form of unity."

The federative system, which tends always to scatter the power of the local authorities, has the advantage of giving to the individual a far larger number of probabilities of independence and of rendering almost impossible the rise of a dictature. If the organization of socialism continues to extend in the United States, as is very probable, one of the surest obstacles to its despotism — for the fact that it is collective does not render its despotism any less hateful or iniquitous — will be the vigor of the municipal centres.

It is, therefore, true to say that among the causes which contribute to augment that vigor, and which tend to preserve the country from revolution from below, as well as from subjugation from above, the school, such as it is understood in America, represents perhaps the most powerful.

It is a conservative force, upon which the country will lean in the day of danger; and as the government of America is at one and the same time an instrument of progress and conservatism, we can say that this is one of the most wonderful machines of this country which has invented so many.

There are, however, in this system of education some very serious inconveniences, which are to be recognized in the most conspicuous defects of that society. Words fail to express them well, so deficient in certain delicate shades is the psychological vocabulary, made, as it is, for common use and observation. For want of more intelligible words I will say that this education does not give a large enough place to the unconscious. It is too precise, too positive, too clear. It lacks uncertainty and, to put it in a word, it is too utilitarian. The result is that this immense civilization has the appearance of having been manufactured, of being maintained by an effort — in fact, of working after the manner of a machine continuingly wound up. We do not feel instinct enough, the almost involuntary expansion of a force which ignores itself. It is a strange thing that this country, in which everything is done by the people and for the people, has none of the characteristics which we are accustomed to consider as the mark proper of the popular soul. *Naïveté* and timidity, clumsiness and credulous simplicity, are never found in this civilization. It seems to have no undercurrent, nothing taken for granted, for the reason that everything is actual, realized, and grown up. This is why, in spite of that immense culture, and what is better still, that appetite for culture, there is as yet no purely American art, no purely American literature, no purely American poetry. The great artists, the great men of literature, and the great poets in the United States — their names are known — remain exceptional and solitary. They do not form part of the national life, precisely because that life is too voluntary, too self-conscious, too intense, and education is constantly at work rendering still more intense that self-consciousness and that will.

Looking into it more deeply we recognize that in this the Americans illustrate one of the most inevitable yet most unlooked-for consequences of the democratic idea. With all nations, poetry, to take that word in its broadest sense, has always drawn its sap from the hearts of the people. What a Homer, an Æschylus, a Virgil, a Dante, and a Shakespeare express is the ideal elaborated during centuries by the ignorant and the illiterate, by sufferers too, by the great unknown crowd of workers ; by artists and soldiers, laborers and sailors, country women and women of the suburbs. Giotto painting his frescoes, Michael Angelo carving his marbles, were sustained by an obscure Italy beneath them, which did not know itself, which did not understand itself, but which had a distant glimpse of the unattainable, a far-away and vague ideal. It is the " mystery " enveloped in that unconscious life of the people, which completes itself and takes form in the consciousness of these great men — mystery made up of misfortunes and errors, of blind efforts and baffled ardor.

There is a deal of individual suffering, of defeated aspirations, an immense and tragic failure of countless life-histories in that embodiment of a shade of feeling, sublime or delicate, tragic or touching, which we call a work of art. Those sufferings, those failures, that ignorance, are just what democracy is striving to do away with in the world. It desires that all should have their part in the joy of living, of understanding, of expressing themselves. It is a legitimate, a generous ambition, but it seems irreconcilable with the development of a certain idealism which is but the revenge of the mutilated desires of a race. Nemesis, the goddess of fatal compensations, is found here again, as in all phases of human life. When we try to define the intelligence too closely we mutilate it. When we limit facts too severely, restrict them too much, handle them too learnedly, we identify ourselves too much with them, and the power of pure thought is by so much diminished. Purposing too strongly, we destroy in ourselves instinct and replace it by mechanism. Making instruction and education too general, we interfere with the deep sources of the soul of the people, whose reserves of unconscious poetry form the mystic aliment of the future masterpieces of art and letters. If American civilization has up to now lacked that æsthetic geniality, it certainly seems that the fault of it lies here, and that by one of those ironies in which nature delights, this colossal effort at self-cultivation, this fever of education, account for a great deal of it. The future, however, may give a denial to this hypothesis.

The Americans have the right to say that they have at least realized, through a most beneficent audacity, the most legitimate purpose of democracy, the indefinite multiplication of the chances of well-being and education. A Cambridge professor expressed this in a touching manner one afternoon when we were in his library looking at the engravings of the "Job" of William Blake, the remarkable painter-poet, the precursor of Rossetti and of Morris. Outside the snow was falling over the pines, with their black boughs, and over the bare branches of the other trees. Around us a score of scattered engravings and as many pictures brought dear, sunny Italy into that dim and silent Northern corner. My host had just expressed to me in the presence of those objects — silent witnesses of past years of travel — his longing for a land of beauty, where there are fewer machines, fewer factories, fewer newspapers, fewer schools, but touches of art everywhere, and everywhere traces of that innate poetry which you find on a sunlit morning on a quay in Florence, on a street in Pisa, at a turning of a road in Sienna.

"And yet," he said, "I would not be ungrateful to my country. I meet with many things which shock me." (He employed the more delicate expression, "which are offensive to me.") "But in return I feel that a great number of people are well off. I think that on this immense continent there are few lives which have been absolute failures. That is an incontestable benefit of our democracy, and it is well worth while to accept all its conditions."

VIII

AMERICAN PLEASURES

HAVING exaggerated his nervous and voluntary tension to the pitch of abuse, almost to vice, it is impossible that the American should amuse himself as we Latins do, who hardly conceive of pleasure without a certain relaxation of the senses, mingled with softness and luxury. The human animal remains the same in those manifestations which are apparently most opposed, and in our amusements we merely extend that which makes the ordinary foundation of our life. The anecdote of Napoleon at St. Helena has often been quoted — that he could not sit down at the whist table without at once trying to win a rubber. With the cards in his hand he was once 'more the audacious and reckless player who said one day, "The prince was in me, in my indomitable spirit, which, in its ascendency, put all Europe at my feet. The chances of destiny, it is true, placed me on the throne. But even in a cloister I should have always been the Emperor." He was so still, in the unconscious fever of domination which impelled him to take all the tricks on the pitiful green cloth of his house of exile. It is the symbol of pleasure of all people and in all races.

This profound unity of national character is not recognized at the first glance, but a little analysis quickly reveals it. In France, for example, the dominant feature of national character appears to be excessive sociability. It began by creating among us the misuse of drawing-room life, and consequently the misuse of conversation, and then the taste for subtle, ingenious, and abstract ideas. An entire modification of political spirit followed, and, through the sad bankruptcy of 1789, arose a system founded on pure logic, in which the State devours all the living force of the country, absorbs all its individuals, and exhausts its impulse to action. As a result of this same excess of sociability we find a very low order of popular amusements and a habit of lounging in the cafés, which is so striking to one arriving from an Anglo-Saxon country, and the privation of which was for Vallès the most insupportable form of his exile in London. This same taste for sociability makes us like theatrical pieces which are light, flimsy, and easy to understand, and which touch in an easy and clever way upon the manners of the day and the petty social follies which have already been commented upon in the conversations of drawing-room and clubs. This sociability is found again in our better newspapers, filled with chatty literature, if we may so call it; in our popular fêtes, with their open-air balls and their gossiping familiarity, and at another pole, in our conception of gallantry.

The "woman of the town" with us is not only the paid creature who ministers to the lewdness of man. If only she is in the least witty, graceful, and lively, she very soon becomes the comrade in whose company the man lingers with pleasure, whom, if he is free, he installs in his home, and whom he will end by marrying. All these phenomena, taken together, reveal the close and secret tie which binds them to one another.

An essayist, knowing the United States thoroughly, would have no trouble in establishing a similar co-relation between American ideas, labors, and pleasures. Their pleasures seem, in fact, to imply, like their ideas and their labors, something unrestrained and immoderate, a very vigorous excitement, always bordering on violence, or, rather, on roughness and restlessness. Even in his diversions the American is too active and too self-willed. Unlike the Latin, who amuses himself by relaxation, he amuses himself by intensity, and this is the case whatever be the nature of his amusements, for he has very coarse and very refined ones.   But a few sketches from nature will explain better than all the theories that kind of nervousness, and, as it were, fitful sharpness in amusement, if we can here use that word which is synonymous with two of the least American things in the world, — unconstraint and repose.

The most vehement of those pleasures and the most deeply national are those of sport.   Interpret the word in its true sense, and you will find in it nothing of the meaning which we French attach to it, who have softened the term in adopting it, and who make it consist above all of elegance and dexterity.   For the American, "sport" has ever in it some danger, for it does not exist without the conception of contest and daring.   Thus with yachting, which to us means pleasure cruises along the coasts, means to him voyages around the world, braving the tempest and the vast solitudes of the Atlantic, or else rivalries of speed in which everything is taken into consideration except human life.   While I was visiting one of the private yachts at Newport at anchor in the harbor, I noticed an entire arsenal of guns and pikes hanging in one of the state-rooms between decks. "It is in case we should go into Chinese seas and should meet pirates," said the proprietor of this dainty travelling toy.   Another, discussing before me the probabilities of speed between the *Vigilant* and *Valkyrie*, two sailing yachts whose names were for weeks last autumn the subject of every conversation, said, coolly, "We had to make the bulwark too low; we shall be lucky if we do not lose several men."   There was no more emotion in that statement than vain boasting in the other.   It was the natural expression of an energy that instinctively likes to associate the idea of a play with that of a peril, and to which a little tragic risk is as the necessary condiment to its most innocent festivities.

Among the distractions of sport, none has been more fashionable for several years past than football.   I was present last autumn, in the peaceful and quiet city of Cambridge, at a game between the champions of Harvard College — the "team," as they say here — and the champions of the University of Pennsylvania. I must go back in thought to my journey in Spain to recall a popular fever equal to that which throbbed along the road between Boston and the arena where the match was to take place. The electric cars followed one another at intervals of a minute, filled with passengers, who, seated or standing, or hanging on the steps, crowded, pushed, crushed one another. Although the days of November are cruelly cold under a Massachusetts sky, the place of contest, as at Rome for the gladiatorial combats, was in a sort of open-air enclosure. A stone's throw away from Memorial Hall and the other buildings of the University, wooden stands were erected. On these stands were perhaps fifteen thousand spectators, and in the immense quadrilateral hemmed in by the stands were two teams composed of eleven youths each waiting for the signal to begin.

What a tremor in that crowd, composed not of the lower classes, but of well-to-do people, and how the excitement increased as time went on! All held in their hands small, red flags and wore tufts of red flowers. Crimson is the color of the Harvard boys. Although a movement of feverish excitement ran through this crowd, it was not enough for the enthusiasts of the game. Propagators of enthusiasm, students with unbearded, deeply-lined faces, passed between the benches and still further increased the ardor of the public by uttering the war-cry of the University, the " Rah! rah! rah!" thrice repeated, which terminates in the frenzied call, " Haaar-vard." The partisans of the " Pennsy's " replied by a similar cry, and in the distance, above the palings of the enclosure, we could see clusters of other spectators, too poor to pay the entrance fee, who had climbed into the branches of the leafless trees, their faces outlined against the autumn sky with the daintiness of the pale heads in Japanese painted fans.

The signal is given and the play begins. It is a fearful game, which by itself would suffice to indicate the differences between the Anglo-Saxon and the Latin world — a game of young bull-dogs brought up to bite, to rush upon the quarry; the game of a race made for wild attack, for violent defence, for implacable conquests and desperate struggles. With their leather vests, with the Harvard sleeves of red cloth, and the Pennsylvania blue and white vests and sleeves, so soon to be torn — with the leather gaiters to protect their shins, with their great shoes and their long hair floating around their pale and flushed faces, these scholarly athletes are at once admirable and frightful to see when once the demon of contest has entered into them. At each extremity of the field is a goal, representing, at the right end, one of the teams, at the left the other. The entire object is to throw an enormous leather ball, which the champion of one or the other side holds in turn. It is in waiting for this throw that all the excitement of this almost ferocious amuse-ment is concentrated. He who holds the ball is there, bent forward, his companions and his adversaries likewise bent down around him in the attitude of beasts of prey about to spring. All of a sudden he runs to throw the ball, or else with a wildly rapid movement he hands it to another, who rushes off with it. All depends on stopping him.

The roughness with which they seize the bearer of the ball is impossible to imagine without having witnessed it. He is grasped by the middle of the body, by the head, by the legs, by the feet. He rolls over and his assailants with him, and as they fight for the ball and the two sides come to the rescue, it be-comes a heap of twenty-two bodies tumbling on top of one another, like an inextricable knot of serpents with human heads. This heap writhes on the ground and tugs at itself. One sees faces, hair, backs, or legs appearing in a monstrous and agitated *mêlée*. Then this murderous knot unravels itself and the ball, thrown by the most agile, bounds away and is again followed with the same fury. It continually happens that, after one of those frenzied entanglements, one of the combatants remains on the field motionless, incapable of rising, so much has he been hit, pressed, crushed, thumped.

A doctor whose duty it is to look after the wounded arrives and examines him. You see those skilled hands shaking a foot, a leg, rubbing the sides, washing a face, sponging the blood which streams from the forehead, the eyes, the nose, the mouth. A compassionate comrade assists in the business and takes the head of the fainting champion on his knee. Sometimes the unlucky player must be carried away. More frequently, however, he recovers his senses, stretches himself, rouses up, and ends by scrambling to his feet. He makes a few steps, leaning on the friendly shoulder, and no sooner is he able to walk than the game begins afresh, and he joins in again with a rage doubled by pain and humiliation.

If the roughness of this terrible sport was for the spectators only the occasion of a nervous excitement of a few hours, the young athletes would not give themselves up to it with this enthusiasm which makes them accept the most painful, sometimes the most dangerous, of trainings. A mother said to me, speaking of her son, who is not fourteen years old: " He adores football. He is already captain of his eleven. I should not be anxious if he never played against any but little gentlemen, but they have a mania for playing against common people. It is in such struggles that dangerous accidents are always to be feared." " What will you have? " replied one of the professors of Harvard. " In the frenzy of the game they deal each other some hard blows, it is true, and it is true, above all, that the heroes of matches like that of to-day are victims. The training is too intense. The nervous system cannot bear up against it. But the feats of the champions keep the game fashionable. Hence all the small boys in the remotest parts of America take up this-exercise, and thus athletes are formed."

He was putting into abstract form that which is the instinct of the American crowd, an instinct which does not reason and which shows itself in very strange ways. During the contest, which I have attempted to describe, I heard a distinguished and refined woman, next to whom I was seated, crying out, " Beauty !" at the sight of rushes that sent five or six boys sprawling on the ground.

No sooner are such matches as these in preparation than the portraits of the various players are in all the papers. The incidents of the game are described in detail with graphic pictures, in order that the comings and goings of the ball may be better followed. Conquerors and conquered are alike interviewed. From a celebrated periodical the other day I cut out an article signed "A Football Scientist," wherein the author sought to show that the right tactics to follow in this game were the same as those used by Napoleon. What can be added to this eulogium, when we know the peculiar position occupied by Napoleon in the imagination of the Yankees?

It must not be thought that such intense enthusiasm for so brutal a sport does not often arouse strong opposition. The same spirit of initiative which urges entire crowds of Americans to bow down in front of these semi-gladiators and to idolize this violent display of physical energy drives other Americans to raise a campaign against this uncontrolled and uncontrollable violence. Leagues have been formed in favor of and against the game. It is very possible that too numerous accidents will cause certain States to pass legislative restrictions against the terrible game. When one has closely followed a really ardent game, "with plenty of life and ginger," as the reporter of a newspaper said, one can notice that at a certain point of excitement the players are no longer masters of themselves. As I write these lines I see once more the figure of one of the champions of Pennsylvania after a disputed point and the gesture of rage with which he threw the

ball which he had to give up.   Between that display of anger
and a bad action there was too little distance, too little psychological breadth — to employ a pedantic and very exact scientific formula.

However, such restrictions will no more cure the American
public of the passion for football than they have cured them
of the passion for boxing.· When, last winter, Corbett and
Mitchell were to meet at Jacksonville, it was necessary to run
special trains to carry the partisans of one and the other boxer
to that fortunate city of Florida.   There was not a newspaper
in which the physical condition of the two rivals was not mentioned morning after morning, hour after hour.   The names
of the relatives and friends who assisted them, the furniture
of the hotel rooms in which they resided, the menu of their
meals, their reading and their thoughts — what details did
one not find in the columns of the newspapers!   When I
went to Jacksonville a few weeks later, the fight was still the
subject of every conversation in the trains which ran through
the pretty little town, and people only stopped speaking of it
in order to discuss the next fight, which was proposed between
the Californian champion and Jackson, of Australia.   Even
the election of the future President will not excite more popular feeling.

To obtain an idea of what such encounters must be, these
"prize fights," as they are called, wherein the fight only ends
when it becomes impossible for one of the boxers to continue
it, one must witness some contest regulated by an athletic
club, that is to say, in which the rounds are counted and the
blows are limited.   The most interesting among those, the
details of which I followed, took place in Washington.   It
was also the first at which I was present.

On the third floor of the club, in the gymnasium, a platform
was built at the height of a man's head, closed in with ropes.
All around a thousand spectators were waiting, some seated

on chairs, others standing in the gallery. Along the walls were
hung gymnastic implements, giving the scene a most appropriate framing.   The electricity — it was nine o'clock in the
evening — lighted and chiselled the outlines of the impatient
faces of the votaries, and on the square platform a man was
nervously pacing up and down, the "referee," the arbiter of
the fight. He wore one of those jackets that are made here
which exaggerate the fashion and have a cut so ample, so
round, that it makes them resemble the shell of some vast
coleoptera.   At last a murmur of satisfaction rises.   The first
two boxers arrive with their trainers.   They are covered with
big bath-cloaks, which they cast aside as soon as they get upon
the platform, and their bodies appear quite naked, thin, and
with knobs of muscles.   They seat themselves upon chairs and
give themselves over with a singular passiveness to the care of
their trainers, who wash them, comb them, rub them like animals, while the personage clothed in the ample jacket an-
nounces the order of the fight, its duration, the number of
rounds, the weight of the champions, their names and their
country.

One is from Philadelphia and the other from Wilmington.
The first shows a black face, almost that of a mulatto, in the
centre of which is flattened out a broken and crooked nose.
The other is fair, with a square face, the nose also broken in
two places, making a mark on his face somewhat resembling
a death's head. He has extended his two arms, which he
rests on the two cords crossed behind him at an acute angle.
His muscles of marble gleam under the massage, which does
not even seem to move them.   At last the toilette is finished.
Both men draw on their gloves. A gong sounds.   They rise,
walk toward one another, shake hands, and the contest commences. A sort of gurgle of pleasure escapes from the audience, an interrupted gurgle which will change by and by from
a sigh to a howl, as the fight becomes brisk or quiet. The

Philadelphian attacks with more vigor than his opponent, but he is too nervous. His legs do not keep their balance. He dances and hops, his arm moving in a mechanical and irresolute manner, like a pair of hesitating pincers, advancing, retiring, then advancing again, indefinitely. His adversary has a better guard. He advances, he retires without moving his body, and his cruel face, in which his eyes gleam, as it were, from two blue hollows, is really like that of death. The blows fall more heavily as the fight progresses. The bodies bend to avoid them. The two men are furious. One hears their breathing and the dull thud of the fists as they fall on the naked flesh. After several blows of harder delivery, the "claret" is drawn, as they say, the blood flows from the eyes, the nose, the ears, it smears the cheeks and the mouth, it stains the fists with its warm and red flow, while the public expresses its delight by howls, which the striking of the gong alone stops.

It is the pause between two rounds. The boxers, again seated, give themselves up, as before, to the care of their trainers, who rub them like ostlers grooming a horse. The seconds spring upon the platform, taking off their coats, and, once in their shirt sleeves, begin to fan the unfortunate pugilists, who are half faint from loss of blood, from blows received and given, and from the intense nervous effort of the fight. Another sound of the gong and the next round begins.

There were four such fights that evening, one of six rounds, the second of eight, the third of five, the last of eleven, and during the two hours and a half that this terrible scene continued not a spectator left his place. Not for a second did the passionate interest, which fixed every face on the ring, seem to be suspended. Scarce was a protest raised, when, on the referee calling for the champions of the third contest, two lads of sixteen appeared, the one broad-shouldered and lithe, the other so meagre and slight of body, poorly developed and fragile.   A voice cried, "They are girls, not boys!" but that did not prevent frenzied applause when the thin, undeveloped boy was struck down at full length, the blood dripping from his boyish face.

Merely time enough to carry him away, and another duel began, this time between two old boxers, who seemed the incarnation of two physical types; the one short and heavy, almost fat, with red hair, the blood on the surface of his too white skin; the other lank and very tall, all gall and nerve. The sinister face of the latter, green under the blue of a shaved beard, with the sly eyes of a tricky servant, relaxed in a ferocious smile.   I saw him towering above the other, towering above us all, while the agile and vehement precision of his movements gave the idea of an invincible energy.   After eleven rounds, this olive-colored athlete was as dry as when he put foot on the platform, while sweat, mingled with blood, flowed from his adversary.   It was a series of surprising attacks and returns no less surprising, and when the two champions had completed the eleventh round without either having been "knocked out," there ran through the assembly an irresistible stir of sympathy for the feebler fighter, for the short one who had defended himself with so much pluck.   To the giant was awarded the victory with loud acclamations; and in the handshakings given to the other, there was admiration and friendship.   The vanquished but courageous fighter might have asked anything of those men and they would have given it to him, so greatly did they respect him for having so well held an impossible position.

This term of "respect," applied to professional boxers, will seem very strange, and yet it is the only one which describes the prestige with which those heroes of pugilism are surrounded in the United States.   One of my lady friends here, to whom I spoke of this enthusiasm, told me that she owed her life to one of the most famous boxers of the West, and under circumstances so singular that it is worth while to report them in detail. She had dined and spent the evening in one of the suburbs of the large town, which was then her home, and was returning in her carriage when she had to cross a street which was full of dangerous characters. She had fallen into the turmoil of a monster demonstration after a prolonged and unfortunate strike. Her horses were compelled to stop. She put her head through the window out of curiosity, and an overwhelming clamor at once saluted her appearance. The gleam of electricity which lighted the streets had just struck on some large diamonds which sparkled in her hair. This sign of luxury, added to the aspect of the brougham, the livery of the coachman and the footman, and the turnout of the whole establishment, raised the indignation of this famished crowd. Fists were extended, faces approached with insulting words. "I had taken a long gold pin," said the young woman, "and I was resolved to strike at the eye of the first one who came too near."

At that moment, when she believed herself to be in extreme danger, having only so feeble a weapon, she saw with terror a colossal form break through the ranks of the crowd, pushing people aside with so much authority that she took him for one of their chiefs. "Don't be frightened at those foolish people," said the man when he was near her, "I will see to it. Tell your coachman to drive on." The young woman once again leaned out of the window, but this time the terrible shout was not raised, and she gave her orders to her servants, who sat motionless on the box, overcome with fright. The brougham started, escorted by the unknown, who simply rested his hand on the ledge of the window, the crowd separating to let the equipage pass. Once beyond the strikers, the unknown saluted the lady. The coachman whipped up his horses and started off at full speed. The footman was still trembling all over as they reached the door of the house.

z

"You may imagine that I was anxious to know by whom I had been saved," she continued, "but the two servants were Irishmen, who had just arrived from Europe, and knew nobody. The description which I gave to some of my friends who were acquainted with the personal appearance of the leaders of the strike did not answer to any of them. I had, therefore, given up the hope of knowing the name of my mysterious protector whom in fancy I saw continually, with his thin face, haughty and martial, his domineering look and the ease, at once strong and supple, of his movements.

"But fancy, seven or eight weeks later, as my mother and I were in a shop buying furs, a disturbance broke out at the door. I saw my coachman off his seat and one of my horses on the ground, and a man, totally drunk, fighting with the police. I recognized my rescuer, and at the same time learned his name and the wild exploit which he had just accomplished. It was John M. V——, the celebrated boxer, who, under the influence of alcohol, had bet that he would fell a horse with his fist. Chance had it that this absurd wager brought him in front of this store, and that he just happened to strike one of my horses. I was able to acquit myself, at all events to a certain extent, of my debt toward him by preventing them from prosecuting him for his act, although there was little risk of his being rigorously dealt with. He was too popular."

Beside the pleasures of sport we must place those of the theatre. The two are not so far apart as might at first sight appear. A passion for the play which results in respect for the actors is general among the Americans, and we know what reception Mme. Sarah Bernhardt, Mme. Eleonora Duse, M. Coquelin, and Mr. Irving have had among them — to mention only the names of four famous artists, and not to speak of singers. Not only the playing of these great actors interested the public, but also their personality, and, above all, their ideas about art.

In every town in the United States there is a group of amateurs whose study and delight it is to discuss the more or less intelligent rendering of such and such a play or musical work. I have said study, for even here the evidence of purpose is visible. At Boston, for instance, you will find that the programmes of each of the celebrated concerts is accompanied by a technical commentary, so accurate, so lucid, and at the same time so erudite, that the pamphlet is in truth a chapter in the study of musical history. At Chicago, when Coquelin was giving the representation of *Tartufe*, of which I have spoken, the newspapers of the following day contained dissertations on Molière's comedy which were as scholarly, as analytic and as critical as could have been the *feuilleton* of the *Temps* or the *Journal des Débats*. And yet, besides these evidences of a fastidious taste and a superior dilettantism, you find this same public accepting the most astonishing oddities.

I remember a gala night at the opera in New York, when the music was sung by one of the actors in German and by another in French, while the chorus replied in Italian, and no English was heard. But is there not a secret harmony between such apparently contradictory manifestations? If you go to the theatre for pleasure, if you are a voluptuary of music and an epicure of harmony, such things shock and annoy you. All your enthusiasm cools in that displeasure, and you have the uncontrollable desire to take up your hat and walk out. But if you are conscious that you are studying the genius of a master or the talent of an artist, you accept the performance, though mutilated. You accept it, above all, if you are devoured with that need of European assimilation which takes possession of intellectual America not less than fashionable America. Not being able to have the whole opera and all the Comédie Française from the other side of the ocean, these people take what they can — the very best, it must be acknowledged — and they enjoy it, as the English can enjoy the frieze of the Parthenon, which is in broken fragments and without cohesion. But their double passion is satisfied, — that, in the first place, of cultivating themselves, and, second, of having all the best actors of London and Paris in New York.

We must look for the original American genius and the true dramatic pleasure of the people in performances of quite a different kind. The play which the authors of this country excel in writing and the actors in playing is a kind of comedy, almost without affectation and intrigue, entirely composed of local scenes and customs, and mixed with pantomime. If the now antiquated expression, "a section of life," could ever have been applied to plays, it may be to these. They show all the peculiarities of the different States, — sometimes the singular customs of the South, as in the *New South*, which I have already analyzed; at other times those of the West, as in *In Mizzoura*, or those of the North, as in a play called *A Temperance Town*, which I saw in New York. In the sub-title of this last play — the most typical, perhaps, of all — we are told that it "is intended as a more or less truthful presentation of certain incidents of life relating to the sale and use of liquor in a small village in a prohibition State." The great curiosity aroused by this comedy lies in the fact that the sympathetic personage is a drunkard.

"Is it worth while to destroy the abuse of drink in order to install the triumph of hypocrisy?" asks one of the heroes in the last act. Therein lies all the moral of this singular work, in which, besides pathetic scenes, almost melodramatic buffooneries of this kind are to be found. It is Christmas night. The daughter of the minister, expelled by her father, is dragging herself along the walls of the church in which her father is preaching. Meanwhile a facetious drunkard places, on the steps of the church, a large plank covered with snow, over which, one after the other, all the members of the congregation fall as they come out. It is in such extraordinary contrasts

as these that the public seems to take wild delight. Laughter
is not, as with us, excited by the witty and somewhat free joke
with double meaning. It is cold-blooded and totally unexpected drollery which excites it. All of a sudden and in a
tragic moment, one of the artists accomplishes a clown trick.
He raises the hat from the head of his interlocutor with a kick,
as he performs a dangerous jump over a table. Then the scene
continues, these extravagances having done nothing more than
raise the wild laughter of the audience. To the eyes of the
stranger, unaccustomed to this mosaic out of real life, scenes
of local customs and of extravagant gambols, this epileptic
gayety savors of the bar, of the intoxication of alcohol, and of
incipient madness.

The oddest thing is that these players, who are in a measure
gymnasts and clowns, are extraordinary in the accurate simplicity and realism of the serious portions of their parts. In
one of these comedies, which was called, I think, *The Country Circus*, I witnessed a scene of theft acted with incomparable perfection by three chance performers. One represented
the manager of the circus at his ticket office, the second was a
negro asking for a ticket at that office, the third was a policeman guarding the entrance to the theatre. The negro gave a
ten-dollar bill to the manager, who returned him only five dollars' change. The negro complained. The manager bent over
toward the opening, cried, " Officer ! " and accused his victim
of theft, upon which the policeman collared the poor black,
and pushed him by force into the circus. Then, having
returned to the ticket office, he received two dollars from the
manager. The startled passivity of the negro, the cutting
banter of the Barnum, who was " letting him in," the brutal
and sordid duplicity of the policeman — the features were
marked as in an etching, the pantomime was rendered almost
intolerable by its truthfulness.

The negro and the policeman are, moreover, two of the favorite personages of the really popular farces ; another is the chivalrous blackguard, whom I have already outlined. But the unrivalled character is the "tramp," the professional vagabond, in the toils of his two enemies, the policeman and the brakeman. The struggle around a freight car, wherein the tramp wishes to have a seat, or whence the brakeman expels him, is the unfailing theme which lends itself to all sorts of tricks and jokes. The tramp is, in fact, the great popular humorist. It is he who gives their nicknames to the railroad companies, who, for instance, baptizes the Baltimore and Ohio, the "B. and O.," "Beefsteak and Onions." In one of the theatres in Washington I have known an audience rise in wild laughter at that joke. The large box in front of the stage, one of the only four in the hall, was occupied that night by a spectator who had placed his feet on the velvet of the balustrade, and of whom one saw nothing but the patent leather of his boots shining beneath the electric light, and his swinging hand, a big, hairy hand, loaded with rings. He manifested his delight by knocking his heels against the red velvet, which served him as a support in his comfortable position. Probably this man, who must have paid fifteen dollars for his box, was one of those newly enriched Westerners, who have tried twenty vocations, have made a fortune several times, and have kept company during their adventurous existence with people of all classes and of all descriptions. Such individuals, and they constitute the foundation of the American public, have too complete an experience of human life not to expect exact observation in a comedy, and real pictures of manners. On the other hand, though often without scruple, they have retained, through their Odyssey of business, a certain youthful, almost infantine, *naïveté*, which is traceable everywhere here. They are, besides, honest enough, and even scrupulous in questions of love.

These local studies, interlarded with buffooneries, from which all obscenity is eliminated, correspond to these various features.

And notice that the managers understand it well. Read this puff which I copy from a programme : " The actors of this troupe propose to act only native plays by native authors and this one [follows the title] is essentially American in its scenery, in its action, and in its aim. The characters are essentially American, and the play breathes everywhere an American freshness which is in keeping with the greatness of America. There is not in the piece a single bad character, man or woman. Not a syllable is uttered which could bring a blush to the most modest cheek. This piece attacks the vices of dissipated society and the miseries which are the outgrowth of the concentration of civilization in the great towns. No soiled dove beats its soiled wings here ; there are no brigands in dress clothes flying round in search of prey. . . ." All was true in this announcement, which was only incomplete on this point, — that the piece ended without any reason having been given for the exhibition of a family of acrobats.

I have turned over the leaves of a great number of illustrated comic newspapers, those which friends in New York have pointed out to me as the best. The Americans dote on these publications, which are to be found in all the halls of the hotels, in all the railway carriages, and on the club tables. Without exaggerating the importance of these pamphlets, we must recognize in them, in every country, a certain documentary value. They characterize the humor of the race and its delight in mockery. Besides, you will find in them a thousand details of habits, described off-hand, their exaggeration rendering them still more perceptible to the traveller. On running through a collection of several numbers of some of these papers, a first observation is forced upon one ; namely, the entire absence of those nude drawings which form the perverse prettiness of similar periodicals in Paris, and the no less remarkable absence of allusions to marital misadventures. One might believe, in noting this absence, that neither gallantry nor adultery existed

in the United States, or that, if they exist, it is in such a shadow
of secrecy that they escape even satire. Do not suppose, however, that the caricaturists profess to be particularly prejudiced
in favor of marriage. But when they see its defects, it is especially from the point of view of the budget, as is fitting in the
country of the " almighty dollar."

Family life is too costly and the men must work too hard.
This is their principal grievance. Here, for example, is a
wedding reception. The drawing-room is full of people who
are complimenting the newly married couple and the parents.
" I congratulate you on the marriage of your daughter," says
one of the visitors. " I see you are gradually getting all the
girls off your hands." And the father answers, " The misfortune is that it costs so much to keep their husbands." " Your
men work too hard in America," said a foreign count to a girl.
" Yes," she replied, " they have to maintain their titled sons-in-
law." When it is not the father who works himself to death, it
is the husband. Here on a Christmas night appears a certain
Popleigh, aged before his time, thin and bent, his arms full
of presents, which tell of his numerous family. A gentleman
wrapped up in a comfortable fur coat, a cigar in his mouth,
gazes at him sarcastically. " It is Mr. Singleton," says the
legend, simply, " who was a rejected suitor for the hand of the
present Mrs. Popleigh." Even aside from the question of
money, this nation does not seem to believe that an American
marriage is a very fortunate operation. Listen to this dialogue
between a husband and his wife. *She:* " After all, what
have you at the club, you men, that makes it so attractive to
you, and which you have not at home?" *He:* " My dear,
we have not at the club what we have at home. That is the
attraction." It is the bankruptcy of the happiness of the man.
As for the happiness of the woman, she herself does not expect
it. " Yes," replies an engaged girl, with her eyes dreamily
fixed on the skies, " I am very happy. At least, I suppose so.

There is but one great bother.   Once married, I shall no more
be able to flirt."

This mocking remark is but a commentary on a very real
fact, which I have attempted to explain; namely, the social
sovereignty of the young girl in the United States, and if a
thousand little signs had not pointed out that sovereignty to
the traveller, he would find the proof of it in the caricatures.
The young girl appears as often in these papers as Lorette in
the albums of Gavarni, as the fast woman in those of Grévin
and as the *marcheuse* of the opera or the sidewalk in those of
Forain.   As those three great masters have felt the graceful-
ness of the Parisian woman at three different epochs, so the
American artist feels with an incomparable delicacy the beauty
of the young girl of his country.   There she is, smiling,
dreaming, talking, on horseback, alive, in fact, with her fine
figure, her well-developed shoulders, her daring elegance, her
white teeth, her eyes wide open on the world — too wide open,
for they see too clearly.   Listen to the conversation which
the artist attributes to these admirable persons, and you will
be edified by their intelligence.   Here is one of them who
has seated herself on a deck chair near a young man as beautiful as herself.   With deep emotion, she clasps her hands and
says, replying to a question which one can guess: "Yes,
but you are very poor, Tom, and I have no money.   With me
my face is my fortune."

Another is taking a country walk with an adorer who is saying with bitterness, "If I were rich you would marry me at
once."   "Ah, George! George!" she replies.   "The devotion which you show me breaks my heart."   "What do you
mean?"   "That you have often praised my beauty, but until
now I did not know how much you recognized my good sense."
These realistic girls, just as the most realistic men, know
that marriage is an association where their partner will ask
them to bring money — a great deal of money.   Two of them

are chatting, doubtless on the Newport landing-stage, for one of them wears a yachting-cap, the other a sailor hat with a colored ribbon. Vessels are passing out at sea. "I heard that your father had sold his yacht?" queries one. "Yes," replied her friend; "in these hard times it is a rather heavy expense." "Then," replies the indiscreet friend, "the news that you are going to be married is doubtless not true." Further, the handsome young men, companions and accomplices in the flirting of these pretty children, do not conceal from them their interested motives.

"Would you have loved me had I been poor?" asks one of them of a fine young fellow of twenty-two or twenty-three years of age, who replies, clasping her to his heart: —

"Ah, darling! I should not have known you."

And you do not feel over-indignant at seeing money constantly mixed up in affairs of the heart. The heart is so little in question. The caricaturist takes care to let you know it. Engagements which are tied and untied so easily do not enlist the hearts of the elegant dolls which the society man and girl are.

"Ah, dear," murmurs a Perdita, raising her beautiful, half-veiled eyes, with their long lashes, to the lips of an elegant cavalier, "tell me truly how much you love me."

"You are my favorite betrothed," he replies, seriously, "the only one that I love."

And there are a great many chances that she will see a delicate flattery in this singular declaration, for she herself does not attach a very deep significance to the word "betrothal," at least if we are to believe this other dialogue between two young girls who are exchanging confidences.

"They told me that you were in love with him," says one.

"No, no," replies the other, quickly; "it was not so serious as that. We were only engaged!"

She has doubtless heard — or he has heard — that the stocks

held by his father — or by her father — have gone down considerably and everything has been broken off. Had they acted otherwise, society would have thought them very silly.

"Do you know that Mr. and Mrs. Brown-Smith must find things very amusing?" says Perdita to her friend, Penelope.

"Why?"

"Why? Both of them wished to marry for money, and neither of them has a cent. They have lots of fun laughing at each other."

"Lots of fun." There is the best summing up, not only of the situation, but of all these caricatures. Nothing less resembles the sharp and grim acerbity of our own humorists. In this chaffing of young girls, which might so easily be cruel, there is much jovial good-humor. The same may be said in regard to the caricatures of the lower classes — notably, the tramps, the negroes, and the Irish. Indeed, poverty is more intolerable in the United States than elsewhere, in a climate so severe in winter, so burning in summer, and amid crushing competition. Listen, however, to this vagabond, whom a piece of money, given by a generous passer-by, has enabled to enter a bar, where he is standing in front of a free-lunch table : —

"Haven't you eaten enough?" cries the proprietor, overcome by the sight of the ham, salted fish, bread and butter, and fried oysters disappearing in the abysses of that rag-bedecked stomach.

"Do I look like a man who has eaten enough?" replies the vagabond, sneeringly.

One of his feet is shod with a slipper and a gaiter, the other with an elastic boot. A check scarf is bound round his chin and protects the swollen cheek, the eye at once insolent, jeering, and knavish like himself. This impertinent joke shows the tone of the replies ascribed by the caricaturist to these tramps, whom he willingly shows us, one smoking, another reading a newspaper with spectacles on his nose. Their idleness amuses him without making him indignant, and he does not consider it right to characterize them with sinister legends such as Gavarni found for his Virelocque.

Nor does the caricaturist develop the worst and most atrocious features of the negro, — the criminal sensuality, ferocity, and perfidy of the former slave. No. He makes merry joyously over his vanity and his familiarity. He has drawn one, for instance, entering his master's room wearing a pair of check trousers of the same material as the coat of his master. And the latter says to him : —

"Look here, Tom, I have told you already not to wear on week days those trousers that I gave you when I wear the rest of the suit."

And Tom replies : "Why, boss, are you afraid they will take us for twins?"

We can imagine the happy smile which parts the big lips that show the jester's white teeth. He is about to say, as one of his brethren said to one of my friends who had been stopping in a country house where he was the servant : —

"Come soon again to see us, you are such a palatable gentleman."

So in regard to those terrible Irishmen, so astonishing with their poetry and their cruelty, their patriotic flame and vindictive rage, their eloquence and drunkenness, their spirit of enterprise and disorder, it is noteworthy that the caricaturists only show the drunkenness and disorder. One time it is an Irish servant-girl whom they depict, saying in her brogue to the inspector of immigration : —

"Oi'm a French nurse." At another time a maid of the same race, whose mistress asks : —

"Have you swept the room?" replies, "Yes, ma'm, I've swept everything under the bed."

We can see that the space beneath the bed has become a

perfect cavern of refuse, where all the leavings of the house have been dumped. Sometimes it is an Irishman coming home perfectly intoxicated, whose state the sketcher represents by multiplying the head of his wife seven times, as she looks at him and out of her seven mouths says: —

"If you saw yourself as I see you, you would be very much disgusted."

"And if you saw yourself as I see you," replies the drunkard, "you would also be very much astonished."

Sometimes it is domestic quarrels, in which everything gives way, the man assaulting his wife with a chair and she retorting with a flat-iron. And policemen, themselves Irishmen, preside at this carnival of tramps, negroes, and Irishmen, drinking hard and hitting like the others, and shouting, "Take that!" as they progress with their game of head-breaking.

No bitterness spoils the joviality. One would imagine that for these observers life in the streets and in the drawing-room is really a clownish pantomime. With that they are very exact — their drawings without imagination come very close to reality. Scarcely do they change the phiz of the tramp, the mouth of the Irishman, the big mouth of the negro, the self-importance and vacuity of expression of the "dude," to employ their slang word. One guesses that they are good-humored people, very lucid, very positive, writing and sketching for lucid, positive, and good-tempered readers. The dark misanthropy of a Gavarni or a Forain makes you suffer as you laugh. It entails long reflection and nerves worn with thought and powerless for action. The American belongs to a world which is too active, too hasty, and on certain sides, too healthy for such poisoned irony.

It is curious to compare the sarcasm of political caricatures with the innocent and altogether indulgent gayety of the caricature of manners. These same sketchers, who show themselves simple and light caricaturers of the ridiculous characteristics and vices of every-day life, develop, when it becomes a matter of party, a species of frenzy, and of hatred which can hardly be surpassed. The nomination of an ambassador who does not suit them, the adoption of a bill against which they are carrying on a campaign or the rejection of a bill which they are upholding, a hostile candidature, a stirring speech, — these are to them occasions for severe blows, the hardness of which contrasts in the most unexpected manner with the good temper of the sketchers of manners. You suddenly feel calumny and its bitterness, anger and its insults. From amusing and easy fantasy you fall into the depths of the harshest polemic, without wit, and without fear of making personal allusions of the most grossly insulting kind. It seems to me that both phenomena are logical and well in keeping with what may be seen everywhere among Americans. So far as regards the affairs of every-day life they are good fellows — amiable, open, easy. But as soon as they have to do with a business question, they are as keen and energetic in the defence of their interests and in the conquest of yours as they were found easy and generous before. The reason is that then they were amusing themselves; now they are fighting.

Politics is one of the most important businesses of a country where each triumph places all public offices at the disposal of the party. It is a matter which interests not merely a small number of ambitious people, but an enormous number of citizens enrolled under the republican and democratic banners. Their antipathies must be gratified, their enthusiasm stirred, their passions served.

In all countries where universal suffrage is the rule, it becomes necessary to speak to the people by means of pictures. They see everything as a whole, and naturally like coarse and striking things. The colored caricatures which are set forth on the first pages of the illustrated newspapers satisfy their taste. As the editor of a Chicago newspaper said to me, they always like a fight.   The fight here takes the form of pictured burlesque, but the burlesque is ordinarily so exaggerated and so plainly unjust and prejudiced that it becomes offensive. Wishing, for instance, to lampoon a perfect gentleman, who was simply guilty of having been nominated to a high position by Mr. Cleveland, the caricaturist represented that distinguished man with grossly travestied features, writing underneath such phrases as "Cleveland's nominee for ——"; or again, "If Abraham Lincoln were to meet Mr. So and So in the flesh, his first impulse would be to take him by the collar and throw him into a mud-hole."

Such means of combating an adversary may succeed with electors of the lowest class.   They are far from clever; for, according to Talleyrand's profound remark, "Everything exaggerated is insignificant."   For this reason, the Americans succeed well in caricaturing social customs, treating them lightly and inoffensively, and, for a like reason, their political caricatures, with few exceptions, are but commonplace.

The American goes into all recreations — sport, the theatre, burlesque — with the same spirit which we have seen him bring into society, into social problems, into education.   He shows himself clear-headed and positive, with a singular mixture of good fellowship, tenacity, practical realism, and exuberant social health and spirits.   Students of human nature, who have reflected upon the laws of the equilibrium of human faculties, will not be astonished that in this country, where the practical spirit is so developed, there should be a place for other pleasures, which, for want of a better expression, I shall call the pleasures of mysticism.   In no country more than in America do spiritual mediums find a better reception, nowhere do the occult sciences gain more adepts, nowhere is there a larger number of persons ready to be initiated into their mysteries. One of the most celebrated professors of Cambridge, who has

made special study of the reason why his countrymen feel this
interest in the supernatural, said to me: —

"There are among us many minds who have no interest in
science, but who believe in direct and personal communication with the unknown world. Science teaches that truth is
one, and always the same, independent of the individual; these
people, on the contrary, are convinced that there is a constant
revelation by Providence proportionate to the needs and
merits of all. When I made their acquaintance, brought up
though I had been in orthodoxy, I thought them mad."

"And now?" I asked him.

"Now," he replied, "like Hamlet, I think that there are
many more things in this world than are dreamed of in our
philosophy."

This frame of mind in a truly superior man, who ended by
telling me that he believed in the possibility of communication between the living and the dead, is not exceptional in
America. A traveller, interested in psychology, would find in
the large number of those whom they call here spiritualists, and
who really are mediums, a most interesting subject of study.

Here, in place of that analysis, which would furnish the
material for a volume, is a sketch of a visit to a woman who
is one of the most celebrated in the United States for the gift
of double sight. Mrs. N—— lives in the outskirts of Boston,
in a condition of ease, which she owes to her singular power.
How far is that power imaginary? How far is it real? How
sincere is it? How much is charlatanism in this strange
creature? These are questions which I cannot answer. Since
a great number of Americans believe in her, it is worth while
to describe a visit to her house, as a contribution to my inquiry into the habits of thought of this country, so fruitful in
surprises.

My companion in this visit was Mr. H——, an Australian,
who is particularly interested in questions of this nature, and

who himself believes absolutely in the good faith of Mrs. N——. We met on a cold winter's morning at one of the stations of Boston. Nothing was more American and less in accordance with the character of our expedition than the restaurant which we entered, to warm ourselves before setting out, with its hot soups, its large plates of fried oysters, its atmosphere of tobacco, and its population of smokers and chewers making themselves drunk on cocktails at eight o'clock in the morning!

The aspect of the car which we finally took was not more appropriate as a preparation for spirituality. It was full of people of all conditions, who had come to Boston to work, and who were dressed in such a way as one sees only here, which makes it impossible to guess the social rank of the man. With small movable tables before them, they were all playing cards "for fun," as H—— told me,— "for the pleasure of passing the time." Thirty games of whist were played, while the train was running through a snow-clad country, all white, and studded with small wooden houses with wooden verandas, the charm of New England. This harmless gambling-room on wheels gives you the idea of a people who have time to spare, a great deal of time. The faces of the players wear an expression at once of freedom, fatigue, and strength. The moment is one, so rare in America, when the foreigner feels a lull, an apathy, beneath the apparent fever. There is always apathy beneath all activity; but to perceive it one must be in sympathy with it. Paris to a Frenchman coming from the country, seems to be a town of intensest movement. To a Londoner, on the contrary, the Place de la Concorde and the boulevards give an impression of luxurious, semi-tropical idleness. But one who goes from New York to London, finds the old English city, in its turn, strangely tame, strangely peaceful, and, I was going to say, strangely backward. These expressions, however, correspond to a reality less real than we imag-

AA

ine.   We cease to be aware of what we always feel; that is,
what we know very well, but had forgotten; once aroused to
a certain degree of energy, we maintain ourselves there without effort.   So these hard workers amuse themselves, between
two crises of hard work, as calmly as a French *rentier* in a small
town, who spends the whole afternoon, between a morning
and evening of utter idleness, in front of the green cloth, at a
game of "piquet voleur"!

Mr. H—— and I alight at a country station.   Low hills, all
covered with snow, close in the horizon around the shed
which serves as a station house.   A sleigh awaits us, drawn by
a shaggy horse, which is driven by an old man, accompanied
by a large dog.   It is the vehicle which the "seer" sends for
her clients.   There is no sham about her, nothing which
savors of humbug or advertisement.   Her *séances* are a profession with her, and she practises it with a *bourgeois* simplicity, with the same absence of surprise, which is one of the
most striking characteristics of the American.   Whatever may
be the strangeness of his fate, he accepts it without seeming
more surprised at it than he is at yours.

Here we are, then, gliding in this sleigh, up one slope and
down another.   We slip along over the snow between the
scarce-awakened little wooden houses, to the last one, separated from the street by an asphalt path, a sort of black abyss
hollowed out in the whiteness of the snow.   Footprints indicate that more than one person must that day have knocked
at the door of this modern sorceress, to whom we in our turn
are coming.   Still the *séance* is expensive,— ten dollars.
But of all passions, that which reasons the least is the supernatural, when it has possession of us; and we cannot but believe that this passion is in the blood of the race, since we
are close to Salem, that little seaside town, the theatre, just
two hundred years ago, of a terrible persecution for witchcraft,
in which twenty persons were condemned to death!

Heaven be praised, contemporary manners and customs are gentler, and Mrs. N——'s quiet home runs no risk of being troubled by a like inquisition to that of the terrible Protestant ministers of 1692. A little girl receives us, all smiles, and conducts us into the parlor, saying that her mother has had a great many sittings during the past few days, and that she is very tired. The furniture of the room is just the same as that of hundreds of others of the same class which I have seen. On the wall a picture of Christ bearing the Cross, on the table a Bible, bear witness to the owner's religious sentiments, and volumes of poetry — Tennyson's *Princess*, Scott's *Lay of the Last Minstrel*, Moore's *Lalla Rookh*, — testify to the purity of her literary tastes. She appears presently, — a woman apparently thirty-five years old. The outline of her features seems almost elastic, doubtless owing to the extraordinary suppleness of the muscles of her face. Her complexion is fair, bloodless, pale, and lighted up by eyes so strangely bright and so fixed, that on looking into the contracted pupils, so dark and brilliant, you feel an undefinable uneasiness. She is, however, very unaffected, and when she speaks it is with a soft and languid voice.

She tells you that she is not equal to the demands upon her, that her trances tire her too much, also that she has given a great number of ineffectual sittings, so greatly are her nerves overtaxed. And, in truth, when one sees her entering into her "trance," as she calls it, it is easy to understand what such an organism must expend in vitality under such an experience.

With the shutters closed, and every light extinguished, except a candle under the table, she unfastens her hair, settles herself at ease in her loose garment, and takes the hands of one of us. Some minutes of silence and expectancy pass, and then she begins to wail and twist her fingers, which escape from the grasp and wander into her hair. She sighs heavily, deeply, with sighs that seem to come from her innermost being; her bowed head bends forward more and more, her entire body is contorted, as though she were fighting against an attack. Then comes a pause. She sleeps. Her open palms reach out to feel the face, the shoulders, the arm of the person in front of her, and she begins to speak in a changed voice, with an Irish accent. Her veritable "self" has disappeared, giving place to another. She has ceased to be Mrs. N——, living near Boston, Massachusetts, and has become a certain French doctor, who died at Lyons.

"A strange man, that doctor," said some one to me, who had attended several *séances* of this Yankee pythoness. "You know him, he knows you. He is useful to the last degree, pleasant, always at your service. He is a parasite, who seems to wish to excuse himself for living at the expense of another, and at the same time he is something of a fraud."

I never could find out whether the person who said this was serious or joking. I imagine that the American who interests himself in these phenomena of double sight, does not himself know. What attracts him in such experiences is the satisfaction of that need of excitement which follows him through all the vicissitudes of fortune, and which is ever as intense as upon the first day. Then there is a certain nervous want of balance, from which many persons suffer here,—a reaction of the inveterate realism of the world around them; above all, it is the undying instinct of the heart of man — more alive in these natures, more genuine and more intense than in others — to pierce that veil of mystery with which human life is enfolded. By a sort of compensation, wherein a philosopher would recognize the great law of the correlation of forces, the sense of mystery becomes more acute in a country where everything is too evident, too definite, too voluntary.

One of the most striking traits in the psychology of men of action is the presence in them of a vein of superstition, the more evident as they are more resolute and thoughtful. Napoleon was a startling example of this. Men of action such as the Americans are, and of action so intense, could hardly fail to have their own kind of illuminism, and why should I not acknowledge that, in the course of *séances*, such as Mrs. N—— gave us that day and on another occasion, it is impossible not to admit certain phenomena, which, in fact, remain entirely inexplicable from the purely natural point of view.

A traveller's diary such as this is hardly the place for a discussion of problems so complex as the question whether it is possible for thought to communicate with thought without the intermediary of a sign. Mrs. N—— was holding my hands, and at the same time touching a small travelling-clock, which had belonged to some one she could not possibly have known, —a sculptor, who killed himself under particularly sad circumstances of temporary madness. How did she know this, how learn even the profession of the former owner of the clock, and of his madness, and even of the details of his suicide? Was there a communication between my mind and hers, united by the personality of that mysterious Lyonese doctor? Did my hands, which she held in hers, reveal by shakings perceptible to her hyper-acute nerves what my impression was after each of her words, and had she in her sleep preserved a power of being guided by these small signs? Or, rather,— for it is always well to reserve a place for scepticism,— was she an incomparable actress, who guessed my thoughts solely from the tone of my questions and answers?

But no. She was sincere. The psychologists who have studied her in her trances know too well the character of magnetic sleep by mechanical means, which do not cheat. All that I can conclude from the really extraordinary details which she gave me, a passing stranger, about one who had disappeared, and of whom I had spoken to no one with whom she was acquainted, is that the spirit has methods of knowledge unsuspected in our analysis. I remember that one of the American Buddhists whom I had met here said to me:—

"In Europe and the East you give an enormous, immoderate, and unique importance to demonstration, which is but organized sense vitality. There is something else."

.. When he spoke thus, we were seated at the table of a club, toward the end of a repast which had been prolonged by the conversation of twenty guests. Around us were bottles of Apollinaris and whiskey, green mint in glasses with cracked ice, and boxes of cigars, all symbolizing that which is least ideal, least mysterious in civilized life; and this strange man went on to speak of the far East, of its religions, with their atmosphere of dreams, of the wisdom of those people, and of their inaction. Who knows but that certain powers of mysticism, to-day almost abolished in the modern world, will again wake up, and certain faculties of the mind temporarily paralyzed, begin to work again; who knows whether our humanity will not see again a period analogous to that of the Alexandrians and the Gnostics, or, more correctly, of the Brahmins? It would be one of the greatest ironies of nature if a future awakening of the so-called occult sciences should have one of its starting-points in America.

At all events, researches in morbid psychology have nowhere been pushed further than here, and for this reason alone it is worth while to tell of this visit to the hermitage of Mrs. N——. When she awoke from her sleep, she seized my companion and myself, each by the arm, with a tragic gesture. Thus she remained some seconds, clearly without recognizing us. Then a kind of pale smile came over her tired face. The "seer" gave way to the simple person of New England, who offered us tea with a voice which had become soft again. She seemed to have completely forgotten — indeed, she had completely forgotten — the singular doctor with the

Irish accent, who had gone into some country far from ours.
Vanished, but where? Chimera of her imagination? Invention of her will? Supra-sensible reality? Who can unriddle
this enigma?

It would be unjust, in these few notes on American recreations, not to mention the lively interest which the cultivated
people of this country — and they are legion — profess for the
pleasures of the intellect. I have already tried to note, as
regards conversation in society, the part their intelligence
has to play in it, how much the will has to do with it, resulting
in what I have called the "point of view." When Americans
turn toward the intellectual side of life, then the words of the
anchorite of the Middle Ages become true. Their ear is
really not satisfied with hearing, just as their eye is not satisfied with seeing.

Through his intense and ever-active curiosity, the American, that son of a recent nation, has reached that condition of mind which we are in the habit of considering as the
supreme vice and the last refinement of a century of decay,
namely, dilettantism. I have found this condition of mind,
which consists in entering through thought into the most difficult and contradictory forms of life, adopting them in order
to study and understand them, in a higher state of development
in the United States than anywhere else. I have concluded
from it that we moralists of old Europe are very wrong in
attributing to this condition our sentimental degeneracies and
the maladies of will, which really belong with the senility of
our society. Everything is pure to the pure, says a proverb,
often incorrectly interpreted. It is also true that in the moral
domain everything is healthy to the healthy and unhealthy
to the unhealthy. This is a conclusion most frequently forced
upon me in the course of this journey. It is at once consoling and cruel,— consoling because it diminishes our own and
our fathers' share of the responsibility for the maladies with

which we see Europe afflicted, and cruel — but do I need to say why?

This dilettantism of the cultivated Americans is recognized more particularly in the literary clubs, clubs which they like to call Bohemian, although between the true Bohemianism and these organizations, with their practical comfort, there is all the difference between a hotel of the new style, with electricity, hot water, and elevators and a *pension bourgeoise* of the rue de la Clef.

One of the most representative clubs which I saw was the Tavern Club, of Boston. It occupies three floors of a small house, the interior partitions of which have been knocked out, in order to form large rooms. The ground-floor serves as a smoking-room and ante-chamber, and the first floor is a dining-room. Above is a kind of hall where music is played and private theatricals given.

This club corresponds well enough to certain societies that formerly existed in the Latin Quarter, — such as the Hydropaths, whose founder, the poet, Émile Goudeau, has written a clever and lively history of it in a small volume entitled *Ten Years of Bohemianism*. I may remark in passing that this book, which has attracted little notice, is, according to my mind, a most exact contribution to the history of the habits and the ideas of our literary youth between 1870 and 1880. The literary youth of Boston, young writers, young painters, and young musicians, founded this Tavern Club. The following are some of the features of difference which I have noticed while frequenting this club and similar ones in New York and elsewhere; they appear to me to characterize well enough the particularly healthy state of American dilettantism: —

1. The respect of the young for their elders, and also the respect of the elders for the young. The president of the Tavern Club, for instance, is the distinguished Professor

Norton, of Cambridge, and when the club gives its monthly dinner, white-haired judges, bankers, doctors, are there, seated at the table with all the youngsters. The American who is concerned with intellectual life no more hesitates in the pursuit of novelty than one engaged in business in the pursuit of fortune. You will hear an aged collector of pictures discussing with a stripling about to start for Paris the works of Degas or of Gustave Moreau, with the same suppleness of intellect which another will develop in speaking to a writer of romance of Flaubert, of the brothers de Goncourt, or of Maupassant. There is a great deal gained by this intercourse of men of various ages with one another.

But is it not rather an effect than a cause? The oppositions of taste and the disagreements between men of different ages which exist among us arise from the totally different ways of living of these classes. I imagine that the young Parisians of to-day are not very different from those whom I knew when I was under thirty. We were in a revolt against our elders in all that concerned sentiments and habits. It is not so in America, where literary and artistic tastes are purely intellectual. I have already remarked, in regard to Harvard, that a liking for French writers of the Extreme Left is both frequent and innocent. Just so we see one of Chéret's advertising sheets, representing the Moulin Rouge, decorating the walls of the Tavern Club, alongside a copy of "The Spinners," of Velasquez, that picture in which a woman's throat is painted with such power. The little figure of the Parisian gutter woman has here just the value of those pretty little Greek courtesans who have become the statuettes of Tanagra!

2. The profound knowledge of foreign literatures and arts. The few names which I have quoted are so celebrated, that to mention them alone proves a certain amount of reading, but these people utter these and twenty others, with references which reveal not a superficial reading acquaintance with

them, but serious and conscientious study,— I will not say a complete comprehension. For the best-informed dilettantism is often a little uncertain when it applies itself to writers of a foreign country.

I thus heard at Oxford one of the most exquisite critics of our age, the regretted Walter Pater, speaking to me in the same sentence of Flaubert and Feuillet, as the two French prose writers that he liked the best, associating in similar admiration and for the same reasons two styles, the difference between which, absolute as it is, he did not perceive. At other times these impressions of foreigners are singularly suggestive, and show us unexpected depths in the works of our own country.

At a dinner at one of these clubs, a guest had just quoted the witty saying of old Professor Jowett, of Oxford, the master of Balliol: "It is not *lasciate ogni speranza* which is written over the door of hell, but rather, 'here they read French novels,'" when another guest rose and proposed a toast to Zola, with the sentiment that sympathy for the sinner is the soul of that great romance writer's works, and describing this as one of the most beneficent and humane sentiments in an era in which the influence of surroundings on the development of personality has been recognized by science as a fundamental law.

"If we do not join to justice pity for those who are the victims of it, what place do we give to justice in our universe?"

I wish that the enemies of the admirable author of *Germinal* and *La Débâcle* who reproach him for giving foreigners a bad impression of French literature, had been present at that banquet and heard that defence uttered amid the applause of all, in one of the most respectable cities of New England.

3. The absence of every element of libertinage in conversation and in the mind. This is the true sign of great intel-

lectuality. This quality admits of breadth of apprehension, as may be seen by the example which I have just quoted. I am sure that the very sincere severity shown to certain French writers by excellent judges in France is owing to the fact that sexual life occupies an exceptionally prominent place in our habits. We very rarely find an inhabitant of the Latin countries who can consider a book which treats of the passion of love with absolute independence of judgment. His imagination is either tickled or disgusted. When, on the contrary, an Anglo-Saxon can free himself from hypocrisy and cant, all serious study of the human soul, daring as it may be, seems to him legitimate. I had noted this feature, so little observed and yet so logical, while talking of Baudelaire with the youths of Harvard. But I could quote twenty examples of it, derived from a quality which is entirely to the honor of that great democracy, at times so coarse, namely, the worship of talent.

Though it is by no means exceptional, I have nowhere recognized this rare and delicate sentiment more than in Boston. It is the contrary which is the exception; namely, that spirit of disparagement evinced by derogatory anecdotes in which so much envy is concealed. I could mention certain houses that are veritable museums of literary piety, one, among others, all the windows of which open out on the Charles River. The aged lady who lives there, the wife of an editor, Mrs. F——, has made her house one of the most significant museums which I visited. I saw there a portrait of Dickens as a young man with long, flowing hair, a feminine face, almost the pendant of the admirable head of George Sand, painted by Delacroix, with deep black eyes, which used to light up the severe cabinet of old Buloz.

Letters and manuscripts of the great man lay around, showing one of those cramped and nervous handwritings which revealed the abuse of "copy." The mistress of the house described him to me as he sat in that same room after his reading, exhausted by his nervous effort, merry, however, and full of anecdotes.

The last time he came to the United States nothing amused him so much as the artless form of flattery devised by a mother of a family who had asked him to dinner. He arrived and found a child in the first room.

"What is your name?" asked the writer.

"David Copperfield," replied the little boy.

"And yours?" asked Dickens of another who entered.

"Oliver Twist," was the reply.

"And I am Little Dorrit," said a small girl.

"And I am Florence Dombey," said another.

Dickens was very much out of health when this adventure occurred. Gout made every movement painful, and the results of overwork had already begun to make his remunerative readings very arduous. However, in relating this story he showed all the gayety of his first visit to the United States.

Opposite his romantic head, is the lined and thoughtful face of the powerful analyst, Thackeray. A slip of paper is fastened below, on which we read, traced in microscopic characters, this brief adieu: —

"Good-bye, Mrs. F——, good-bye, my dear F——, good-bye to all. I go home."

He had been a month in America, occupied with engagements of extreme importance. Toward Christmas the desire to see his children got the better of him, and this note tells of the abruptness of his departure. On the walls is also a portrait of Carlyle when young, and it is very like Carlyle when old, in the depth of the eyes below the curve of the brow, in the shape of the forehead, and the firmness of the jaw. That forehead and that chin is all Carlyle. There is a lack of human nature in that strong physiognomy, too set, too self-willed. This is one of the faces that offend those who look at them, that defy the spectator, and arm themselves with outward arrogance to conceal the feeling of inward security.

For my part, I prefer the high and serene beauty of Tennyson, that Virgil of the Isle of Wight, who has so well known how to collect its waters around his garden of dreams. The fairy of this little museum of relics told me of a promenade she had had with the poet in a real garden in Surrey, where, having inhaled the sweet aroma of the violets, he said to her in his deep voice : —

"Down on our knees, these are violets."

And he did as he had said, in order that he might religiously gather the fragrance of the flowers without picking them.

I like also the portrait of noble Emerson, with his thin face lighted up by his high ideal — and what writing is his, passionate, inspired, from one end of the line to the other! Other autographs in an immense collection showed the writing of Longfellow, half slanting, very firm, very clear, always the same; and the simple and strong handwriting of Lowell. In thought I go back ten years, and again I see his face, with its long beard and simple expression, as it appeared to me at the Rabelais Club, in London. Little did I suspect then that he would die so soon, and that I should be turning over his manuscripts in his native town, chatting about him the while as of one whose recollection is piously preserved, among many others.

That piety, that literary cult impressed me, touched me. I find in it a desire to have celebrated men for friends, but, after all, such a desire is in a measure right. It is legitimate to love glorious men, whose superiority we feel through their reputation; especially when one does not maliciously draw attention to their faults for the petty pleasure of humiliating that superiority. Americans may have many faults, but they are certainly neither small nor mean.

Another feature of intellectual dilettantism, in the particular
phase which it takes in America, is the search for sensations
by travelling, and by travelling in a large and audacious way
bewildering to our European imagination—at least it would
have been so if Pierre Loti had not somewhat accustomed us
to the most distant journeyings. But Loti remains alone
among us. I am not sure that criticism would permit even
him those wanderings in Japan or Oceania, if the great writer
had not the excuse of his calling to offer for those expe-
ditions, which he tells of with the grace of a poet sensitive
even to painfulness and delicate almost to morbidness. To
an American artist, on the contrary, those journeyings through
the vast world in quest of a little fresh beauty seem so natural
that neither the public, nor himself, even thinks of noticing
their dangers and eccentricities. I remember hearing an
American writer say to me : —

"I shall return to Japan next year for the flower season,"
just as simply as he would have announced to me a trip from
Paris to Saint-Germain.

This passion for long journeys is so common that it has
modified the system of holidays for professors in the most
unexpected manner. They have every seven years a full year
of holiday, which they call the "Sabbatical year," and which
they employ in visits to Europe, to Africa, or to Asia, according to the needs of their studies or their curiosity.

Nowhere have I more strongly felt the influence of travel
upon the intellectual American than in New York, in the studio
of the admirable painter — who is too little known among us
in spite of his French name — John La Farge. The man himself, who is no longer very young, with his refined face and
white skin, as though dried up by internal heat, with his restless eyes in strongly outlined, drawn eyelids, gives a good
impression of one of those nervous activities which no effort
satisfies, which no experience appeases, and which are ever

searching and in motion. He has invented a new process for stained glass; he has exercised himself in decoration and illustration, in painting in oils and in wax, in vast altar pieces, such as the grandiose and delicate "Ascension" of the Fifth Avenue Episcopal Church, and in pastels, and only a few months ago he was travelling about through the Pacific Islands — Samoa, Tahiti, the Fijis.

"We wanted to go very far," said he to me. "Japan is too near. They have the telegraph there. The Pacific always means two months without news."

That is the longing of the artist, tired of conventional life, tired of the railroad, of the telephone, of all that facilitates business and saves time, hungering after novel sensations, and above all devoted to his art; valiantly, heroically resolved to live only for his thoughts, during days and days; and while that cold, snowy January afternoon was freezing the town, those islets scattered on the map became alive, bright, and green for me in pictures and water-colors of this refined painter, whose smallest works show him to be of the race of Fromentin, the visionary, who thinks his feelings — a rare power. Here are branches too green, at the edge of a too blue sea; the veins of the leaves seem saturated with water, and tell of the eternal humidity of the air. Banana trees rear their straight trunks, bearing their long supple leaf-blades. Cocoanut trees wave their palms in the ceaseless Pacific wind, the wind that goes, like the immense swell of the wide ocean, from one pole to the other. The burao, a large tree with a knotted trunk, spreads out its broad leaves like those of our fig trees. Flowers everywhere, above all, the flat-petalled, full-blown corollas of the strange hibiscus. In this scenery of nature low hovels are seen, with thatched roofs and open sides, along which fall flexible mattings.

Men and women pass between those trees at the edge of the sea; some dancing with crowns of roses; others, hidden by branches, cowering on the earth in wait to commit murder; others carrying on their shoulders light skiffs ; others embarked in similar boats going forth to fish.   And around them is that trim landscape, cleaned, almost combed.

"The savage," says the painter, profoundly, "is the old-fashioned gentleman, the gentleman of tradition, who does everything according to custom, and who does not wish to change his habits;" and, showing a young girl, who is shooting a canoe across an apparently fearful cascade, he adds: "She is not frightened; for there is not a turn of the ground which she does not know, not a pebble which has not been in the same place for centuries, out of the water and under the water.   In that country, when you hurt your foot, you say, 'Sure enough, my grandfather told me there was a stone on that road!'"

Above all, the bathing scenes are charming to behold. Wide rivers flow through the woods, and women throw themselves into the water, blue with the reflection of the sky, with noble, antique immodesty.   Children play in the surf of the ocean.   The wave breaks on reefs, and, in places where it drags along the coral bottom, its green shade becomes so pure and so intense that it takes the coloring of a precious stone. At other times, at sunset, it is quite rosy.   The brown and lissome nudity of the savage is outlined on this blue ocean with the fineness of an antique bronze.

You feel the soft and caressing atmosphere, where the human animal is happy in an almost vegetative felicity, where it is languid as a plant.   Tahitian women, sitting around the fire, which lights them up fantastically, their bodies clothed in long dresses of light material, with straw hats on their small heads, seem to be playing at winter, while other groups make up scenes of Biblical or Hellenic grandeur: a blind and naked old man, led by a child; a dark youth galloping on horseback, at the edge of the sea; dances,—bacchanalian, I

was about to say,— where the thick foliage of the wreaths worn
by the wild female dancers recalls the festivals in the ravines
of Taygeta, celebrated by the poet:—

> . . . et virginibus bacchata Lacoenis
> Taygeta. . . .

The joy of the artist as he shows these studies is pleasing to
witness. His eye warms, delighting itself again in that light,
his mind goes back to that primitive life with the delight of
second youth and of initiation. He raises the stole of the
Buddhist priest, which veils an unfinished picture, and with
the action reveals a figure painted in wax, with colors so
blended as to be almost indistinguishable. A woman is
seated, her feet crossed, her arms folded, her eyelids lowered,
clothed in material of a marvellous tissue, so diaphanous that
it seems about to melt away in the light of an aureole which
she herself seems to project. A cascade falls at the side of
this enigmatic form, the water flowing endlessly, symbol of
time that passes in eternal flight.

The young goddess, nevertheless, remains motionless in
her youth, whose serenity seems to have been attained
through storms. She is the Goddess of Meditation, "the
being who sees sounds," as the artist tells me. Silent, dead
to life, absorbed in her dream, she spreads peacefulness
around her. The grand lesson of the nullity of human
activity comes from the farthest East to this country of intense effort. The fever of culture, with which these men are
possessed, makes them capable of understanding through
innumerable experiences, and of translating into palpable
form, the poetry of meditative passiveness, so contrary to
their race. As after reading certain novels by Henry James,
so, too, on leaving John La Farge's studio, I have the impression, nay, rather the evidence, that the American soul,
when once it sees the beauty of being delicate, reaches acute

shades of analysis and unequalled visions.   But the painter,
like the writer of romance, is solitary.   Neither forms a
part of a school or even of a group.   Personality, the un-
changeable individuality of their culture, is still a feature of
this country, and one which does not admit of the prediction that there will ever be any American art.   Nevertheless,
there are, at the present day, very great and admirable American artists, and that is enough, after all, for the glory of a
people.

IX

DOWN SOUTH

I. *In Georgia*

The author begs the reader to look upon this narrative as a "short story," all the facts in which are true, but in which the author, for personal reasons, has been obliged to make several alterations. — P. B.

THE misfortune of a somewhat prolonged journey in the United States is that you begin to recognize at each fresh halting-place that the country is really too vast, too complex; that after having amassed mountains of notes, there are still mountains to amass; that after having lived in this or that town a month, it would be necessary to live there a year; that after having studied this or that class of people, thousands of other classes remain yet to be studied.

I especially felt this immensity, this complexity, during the course of an excursion through the South, of which I retain memories that I shall not attempt to connect with the preceding notes. This is perhaps the best way of making this travelling journal conform to reality. For, indeed, Charleston passed, a fresh country begins. The flora changes as well as the sky, the fauna as well as the people. The real reasons which precipitated these two worlds at each other's throats, using slavery as a pretext, appear to you as clear as do those which caused the war of 1870, when you cross the Rhine. But the wounds of our ancient Europe, like those in a poisoned body that has lost the power of creating fresh cuticle, have not closed; while, in the American nation, they have not only healed, but have been forgotten. The difficult task has been entered upon of finally mixing, blending, and amalgamating these two portions of a vast empire, this North and this South, so naturally, so radically antithetic.

You open a chance newspaper, in the train that carries you toward Charleston, and you see that the present Speaker of Congress, corresponding to our President of the Chamber of Deputies, was formerly an officer in the Confederate army. Prisoner of war for a year, he began the study of law immediately peace was concluded. He has had a career as a lawyer, and is now one of the important leaders of the Democratic party. Mr. Wilson is another illustration of the same state of affairs,— the Mr. Wilson who is so popular, the applauded author of a celebrated bill, the man whom I saw the other day in Congress carried in triumph upon the shoulders of his admirers, after a speech, with a basket of roses in his arms.

The flow of life has resumed its course in this powerful organism; and of a terrible war, lasting several years, — a war of races, a war of climates, a war of principles, a war of interests, a war of pride, — there remains no other trace than that contained in the list of pensions inscribed on the budget. This list, a fact almost incomprehensible to one not initiated in the hidden workings of American politics, increases in amount as the war period is left behind.

The soldiers of the North and the soldiers of the South meet and fraternize, just as though the slaughters of Chancellorsville and Gettysburg had never taken place. No, I am mistaken. The heroic struggle has left more noble traces than a shameful abuse of war pensions. It has left the memory of a common bravery, a proof that American industrialism has not diminished the energy of the race. It has left the legend of Lincoln, of one of those men who, simply by the propagation of their example, mould in their image the conscience of an entire country. This personage, so American by the composite character of his being, humorous and pathetic at one and the same time; this politician, acquainted with all artifices and trickeries, and yet so capable of idealism and mysticism; this half-educated man, with his magnificent simplicities of eloquence; this former woodman, his face embittered with disappointment and luminous with hope, enfeebled by trial and yet so strong; this statesman, close to the people, and yet gifted with such amplitude of vision, — is the most modern of heroes, one whom the United States may safely compare with Napoleon, with Cavour, with Bismarck. To-day the South recognizes his grandeur, as well as the North. He had the good fortune to be just the workman that was necessary for the task he undertook, and to die immediately his task was accomplished. Great destinies are made up of such timely hazards.

In selecting as the first stopping-place in my Southern travels a little town in Georgia, I was trying to realize a desire to meet an old officer of the Northern army, a particular friend of the great President. His name I must also keep secret. I will simply call him Colonel Scott, a disguise that will not hide him from his acquaintances. A mutual friend, who had given me a letter for him in Washington, described him to me. "Prepare," he said, "to meet one of the most complicated of men, a many-sided man, as we say. You will see for yourself. He comes originally from Massachusetts and there is the Puritan in him yet. He has been through the war, and he is still a soldier. He has studied medicine, and he is something of a scientist. Then he went into business and directed a large company manufacturing uniform and livery buttons, so that he is somewhat of a tradesman. Besides this there is in him a little of the landed proprietor, of the gentleman farmer, ever since he purchased a large plantation in the South on account of his daughter's health. And he is, above all, a charming personality, charitable and honest, full of curious memories of Lincoln, Grant, Hooker, Sherman. Certainly you must have a chat with him."

I arrived, then, at Philippeville — that is the pseudonym I shall ask the reader to accept for this little city in Georgia — toward the middle of the month of March. My first step was to ask the address of Mr. Scott. I was told that he lived only about two miles from the town, but that I ought to write to him in order that I might not make the journey uselessly.

"He is passionately fond of hunting," added Mr. Williams, the hotel proprietor, who gave me these details. "He sometimes remains out three or four days without returning to the house. You know, sir, that we have the best hunting in America here; deer, duck, wild turkey, partridge, quail, and not a single wild animal, not a bear, not a puma. Ah, Philippeville beats every town in the South."

"Not a wild animal?" said I. "And the alligators and the rattlesnakes?"

"Oh, they're all down there in Florida," he replied. "Why, my dear sir, I've been here for twenty years during the winter and spring, and I've never seen a bigger snake than an adder."

The worthy Mr. Williams neglected to add that, during these twenty years of residence, he had not quitted his hotel a hundred times, a hotel which, by the way, realized an ideal of comfort for travellers. He treated all travellers like friends, as careful of their well-being and recreation as though he had really been the host of some country-seat where was gathered a group of invited guests. I do not think you will meet anywhere in the world, save in America, this type of hotel proprietor, a man perfectly well-mannered, a man who dines in evening dress every day in the common dining-hall, opposite his wife, who is also in evening toilette, and who then passes the evening in the drawing-room, chatting and listening to an orchestra engaged for the season. I engaged a small light carriage on the morrow of my arrival in Philippeville; and passing down the long route, bordered by wooden cabins and populated by negroes, went with my black coachman through a great forest of pitch pines, strewn with honeysuckles in full bloom and as high as ourselves, and finally arrived at a large open turnstile upon which were written the simple words: "Scott's Place."

I can see myself again, as though in a dream, alighting from the little carriage and walking up a winding path, bordered by trees of odorous fragrance, and I again see, at the end of the path, the large, low house which was evidently that of the master. It was built of wood, like those of the negroes of Philippeville, but of varnished wood, lacquered yellow, with the roof painted a sombre red, and surrounded with a wooden veranda painted a bluish white.

I had not to take the trouble of ringing and asking for the master of this Southern country-seat, so peaceful and so coquettish, with its one story, and with its garment of clambering roses. A troop of fifteen or twenty negroes, men, women, and children, clustered before the staircase, ranged in a circle round a man of about sixty years of age, very tall, very red, but still robust and slender, in a huntsman's costume, with high leather gaiters and a striped velvet jacket. The Colonel, for it was he, did not perceive my approach any more than did the negroes who surrounded him, regarding him with breathless attention, so absorbed were they all in some strange task. Colonel Scott was bending over a rather large wooden box of open lattice-work, that appeared to contain some singular animal in a state of extreme irritation, to judge from the sounds that issued from it — sounds that resembled a file rubbed furiously on some extremely hard substance. He held in his right hand a stick, at the end of which he had fixed an enormous wad of cotton, and he worked this stick about through the interstices of the box, while he poured in it with his right hand the contents of a large bottle full of a water-colored liquid. I recognized almost immediately the sickly-sweet odor of chloroform. What was the animal the Colonel was trying to stupefy in this way? The filing sound became more and more feeble. You could hear it dying away like the moaning of an invalid succumbing under the influence of some powerful anæsthetic.

A negro said, "He's asleep now." The Colonel emptied the remainder of the bottle into the box, stirring around, meanwhile, the baton — I suppose to make all sure. Then, taking up a pair of pincers, he tore off one of the planks at the top and turned the box upside down. Out of it, I first saw issue the monstrous head of a serpent — a head as big as my hand, triangular and flat, with swollen glands hanging limply from the end of a long neck, of which I could see the throbbing throat, with its white, soft skin. The long body uncoiled and rolled out to the length of about eight feet, thicker than my arm, and terminated by a little tail composed of a dozen rings, looking as though cut out of gray horn. The sight of this rattlesnake was so hideous, so worthy of the surname, *atrox*, given by the naturalist to this variety, — *Crotalus atrox*, — that there was among the negroes a hurried attempt to retreat from the animal, which was, nevertheless, so defenceless at this moment.

The Colonel, with the rapidity of a workman who knows that every instant is precious, forced a stick into the mouth of this formidable monster. The raised jaw revealed the inside of the mouth, a horrible red of living flesh, with the thin, bifurcated tongue looking as though glued to the palate. I saw him with his free hand take up some metal instrument — one of those forceps that dentists use. He grasped, with the pincer, one of the fangs in the jaw, which was beginning to bleed. A little effort, and he dropped upon the ground one of the teeth of the monster, then a second, then a third, then a fourth — four long, curved, hollow needles, horrible and delicate biting instruments, which at that very instant contained enough venom to cause death, even with a scratch. The animal, nevertheless, continued to sleep with a bloody foam upon the borders of its closed jaw. The Colonel seized it by the middle of its body, with his hairy hand, and threw the inert mass into the box, renailed the cover with three strokes of his hammer, picked up, one by one, the dangerous defences, and placed them carefully on the wooden block of the steps devoted to the use of the horsemen, and called a negro.

"This big fellow will be a little astonished when he wakes. Take him away and don't get into the habit of bringing me a new one every morning."

As he pronounced these words, his eyes met mine. They were gray eyes that glistened in the ruddy face with a singular brilliancy of youth. He did not hesitate about my identity any more than I had hesitated about his. The letter of introduction that I had sent him in the morning, announcing my visit in the afternoon, left him no room for doubt. He saluted me by name while shaking my hand, and said, in French, without any further preamble, with the immediate familiarity of the American: —

"That's the sixth that I've operated upon in two years, and the third this year. That's why I spoke to them as you heard me. Jim Kennedy is the proprietor of a collection of monsters that he is taming, I don't know how. He is going to show them from town to town, from village to village, and to earn, in a few weeks, sufficient to enable him to live for months without working. That's the character of all these blacks," he continued, shrugging his shoulders; "as soon as they have enough to eat, they won't move their little finger."

"But suppose that they're happy thus, Colonel?" I replied.

"Happy?" he repeated abruptly. "Happy! They're only too happy, but it's a brute's happiness, and it degrades them more than slavery.   Yes, sir," he continued, with an insistence in which I found the Puritan that I have spoken about. "They were worth more when they were slaves, you may believe me.   I was one of those who served under Lincoln with the utmost enthusiasm, and I don't dispute the truth of the principles we fought for.   No, I do not dispute it.   He is not a man who admits that there can exist a single slave in the world eighteen hundred years after Christ.   Unfortunately, we imagined that we had finished when we had freed them. But that was too simple.   Our troubles only began then. We didn't realize that a being of an inferior race, like the negro, could not pass at once to a superior condition without danger.   You will see some sad things in the South, sir, if you travel.

" But here I am, keeping you out in this afternoon sun, which is nothing to me and which is suffocating to you.   Come into the house, and be presented to Miss Scott.   It's only a modest little house, but it will give you, for all that, an idea of what the house of a slave proprietor in Georgia was forty years ago. All around it, you see, were the negro cabins.   I have left three or four of them standing.   The cooking was done in that little building out there.   Here were the stables.   I have only repaired those which the Chastins left.   That's a French name, isn't it?   It's the name of the family that lived here.   The last member of it has been dead about nine years.   They came from New Orleans.   Would you believe that after the war, ruined by the emancipation of their slaves and having nothing to live upon except this land, they remained here for several years almost without leaving it, without cultivating it, killing a pig now and then, hunting a little, eating tomatoes that were grown for them by a poor negro who would not leave them? They were good people and kind masters, and yet that had not prevented them from selling one after another the seven children of that very negro.   He opened the gate for you, did he not? "

"What ! that little comic personage, with hair and beard like
gray moss, like lichen, with a parchment face?"

"That very man," said the Colonel. "Now, just see what
slavery makes of a man. He has never hated his master for
those sales. He found, and he still finds, it quite natural that
they should sell his sons, just as they would sell calves or suck-
ing pigs. He loved his masters, and his masters loved him !
Such inhumanity is inconceivable. But be seated. I will go
for my daughter."

An oil painting, about one-fifth life size, somewhat clumsily
but sincerely painted, showed Mr. Scott at twenty years of age,
wearing his cloak of cavalryman in the Northern army. He
was recognizable, even after half a century, with his rude figure
of improvised officer, just the parallel, in his indomitable
energy, of the generals of our first revolution. I had not time
to make a more minute examination of this salon, nor to read
the titles of the books arranged in the low bookcase ; for the
sliding door opened and I saw the Colonel enter, pushing
before him, with all the delicacy of a sick-nurse, a wheel-chair
on which was seated a young woman of about thirty years of
age.

The sight of an irremediable infirmity, particularly when
this infirmity is allied to youth, stirs some profound chord in
the soul. When youth, thus attacked in its very flower, is found
embodied in a perfectly beautiful and perfectly good creature, this pity becomes still more poignant. Miss Ruth Scott,
if you considered nothing but her face, had those large, delicate features which resist the action of years. Her color had
all the brilliancy given by magnificent blood ; she had a finely
curved mouth, in which a smile disclosed very large and very
white teeth — like those of her father. Her eyes were clear
blue, a little lighter than the Colonel's, telling of a very loving
woman's heart, proud and delicate. Above her noble forehead
grew the most opulent hair in locks of a tawny gold, thick and

luxuriant — hair with which one might weave a glorious shimmering mantle for the shoulders of a goddess.

Alas ! the most humble and the most implacable of maladies, — almost too ridiculous to name for a girl of this age and of this splendor, — rheumatism, had deformed and knotted the feet, which one could not see under the shawls, in such a way as to render futile even an attempt at walking. Without any emotion she showed her hands swollen at the joints — poor, infirm hands which could neither guide a pen nor hold a needle. And, yet, a smiling resignation — nay, more than that, a serious, serene joy could be read upon this face, which one would think ought to have expressed all the melancholy of one destined to martyrdom. It was not long before I understood whence came this serenity of mind under so great and so incurable a misfortune. Miss Ruth had not spoken ten phrases before she had revealed to me the secret of her inner strength. Like her father, she was possessed by the idea of the responsibility of the people of her race toward the negroes. And I recognized in her at once that fervor of proselytism which is so difficult for a Latin to consider without some little suspicion.

The history of the Anglo-Saxon race would, however, be inexplicable without this hereditary instinct of the missionary. Miss Scott was only an example of this instinct, a more touching example than many others on account of her infirmity. I can still hear her slightly hard voice in which trembled the reproaches of a conscience always striving toward apostleship. And I can hear her say to me, speaking about those poor negroes whose happy heedlessness I had just been praising : —

" They are not always so. There are racial tragedies even to-day that you would never suspect. About ten years ago I was studying in Boston. One day a colored girl presented herself at our college. The president had strong ideas about justice. She assembled us all and asked us to promise that we would treat the newcomer as though she were one of ourselves. Otherwise she would not receive her. She gave us an hour in which to make our decision as to whether we would give her this promise or not. We deliberated together. As opinion was divided on the question, we decided to vote and to submit the matter to the decision of the ballot. The result was favorable to the stranger.

"Would it not have been cruel, I ask you, to deprive her of a little culture on account of her blood, particularly as her father was a very distinguished doctor? She remained among us for four years. She was intelligent, as the negroes very often are, and scrupulously honest, which they are not always. We liked her very much, and even those who did not vote in her favor kept their promise and never let her feel that they considered her other than as white. I suppose she was happy. Her father, however, died and left her without fortune. She had to return to Savannah to the family of her grandfather. There this girl, accustomed to live in the best society in the North, could not find a single respectable person who would receive her, who would even recognize her. She was compelled to mix solely with the people of her race, inferior, brutal, coarse, knowing themselves to be such, beings without instruction and without education. She suffered so much that she finished by a crime. She committed suicide — threw herself into the water. Isn't that a tragedy, as I told you? Is it not frightful?"

"But why did she not remain in the North?" I asked. "Would she not have been able to marry there?"

"Ah, no," said the Colonel in turn, "and I understand the reason. Marriages between negroes and whites are not permitted in the United States, and that is right. God has not willed that these races should mix. The proof of this is that mulattoes have almost always an evil nature. No, it will not do to corrupt the white race by the mixture of the black. One must make of the negro, so long debased, a race of men who will be men, of citizens who will be citizens, something other than children or animals."

"But are they not already Christians ?" I interrupted.

"And good Christians," replied Miss Ruth. "You should hear them sing their hymns in which they speak of Paul and Moses as of people whom they had once known. Sometimes these hymns are most exquisite poetry. Do you remember, father, that about the bones, with the air that so well fitted the beautiful words ? Suppose you sing it for Mr. ——."

"I will try," said the Colonel. He seated himself at the piano quite simply. When had he found leisure to learn music enough to play and sing so pleasantly? He began with a little prelude, seeking the notes with the supple fingers that had held the officer's sword, the doctor's lancet, the administrator's pen, and that I had seen only half an hour before plunging a pair of forceps into the mouth of a rattlesnake. He played a soft and gentle air, one of those subdued melodies that suggest the echo of a monotonous measure beaten upon a stretched skin during the warm nights, and the words were something like this: "I know that these bones are mine, that they are mine, and that they will be raised again upon that morning."

What a touching phrase and how singularly significant, when one considers that it was invented and sung by slaves, by poor slaves, who, as a matter of fact, owned only the skeleton, which it was impossible to tear from their body to sell ! What wretchedness and what hope !

"They used to crack their heels and their knees together in the evenings when they sang those words around our house," went on Miss Scott. "If you like the songs, we will find you some more of them."

"There is one song that I have never heard," I replied, "and that I am sure you know, Colonel ; one which, I am sure,

the negroes must have sung, since it was the hymn of their
deliverance — I mean John Brown's march."

It was not unintentionally that I asked my host, seeing that
he was so complaisant, to sing this admirable war song, which
has always appeared to me to be so impressive in its vigorous
simplicity : —

> John Brown's body lies mouldering in the tomb,
> But his soul is marching on !
> Glory, glory, hallelujah !

I meant this Marseillaise of the Northern army to serve
simply as pretext for the telling of battle stories, such as old
heroes love to recite. I had mistaken the amazing simplicity
of this hero. He appeared a little surprised at my request,
but turning again to the piano he sang the Warrior's Hymn.
It is a clear-cut, bright, almost gay melody, expressing superb,
almost jovial self-confidence and the courage that comes from
serving a just cause. I gazed at the singer while he uttered the
words associated for him with many a bloody memory. But
he sang the air just as it was written, with a countenance which
showed that he liked to sing it. My mind was, nevertheless, somewhat confused at his offer immediately afterward to
sing the Southern march, "Dixie." A genuine dance air is
this one, bright, agile, and frivolous. The Colonel evidently
took great pleasure in recalling both marches, so much was the
civil war a thing of another age to him ; one might say merely a
picturesque memory of the past.

Leaving the piano and swinging his great form in a rocking-
chair, he said : —

"You ought to have heard those two songs sung by thousands of soldiers on march ! They were brave men, on both
sides, and perfect soldiers at the end. I saw the armies made,
built up, day by day, hour by hour, like a new town. I remember, toward the end, that a French officer who had wit-

nessed one of our parades, asked : ' Now that you have this fine army, where are you going to begin? In Canada, or in Mexico?'"

"'We shall begin by sending them all back to their work,' I replied to him ; and that was the truth. At the end of the war we had twelve hundred thousand men ; six months afterward, only fifty thousand," and he laughed aloud in the strength of his national pride. He was prouder of this disbanding than of twenty victories.

"But," he said seriously, returning to his old point of view like a true American, " all the same, we have not done enough for the negroes. We ought not to have given them what we have given them, nor yet, on the other hand, have left them to themselves so completely."

"Do you think that one can improve a race?" I broke in. "While I was in Canada, of which you were just speaking, near Montreal, I visited a village of converted Iroquois. Their priest assured me that it was impossible to instruct them beyond a certain point. There is, as it were, a limit of culture prescribed in advance in the blood of all of us."

"Well, one can attain that limit at least," said Miss Ruth, quickly. "You may change your idea perhaps, when you have seen the school that we have founded at Philippeville. I will show it to you one of these afternoons if you remain here a few days."

When I left the Colonel we had made an appointment for this very visit. I was to take lunch with him, and we were to go to the school in company with his daughter, an ingenious invention perfected by him permitting her to be removed from her couch to a carriage. He told me his plans for the afternoon, as he conducted me, through his park, toward my carriage. We took a different road from that by which I had arrived, and, as we passed before a little enclosure full of trees and surrounded by low walls, he said : —

"That is the cemetery where all the Chastins have been buried for one hundred and fifty years. Would you like to see their tombs? Places like these are the remains of that old America which travellers forget so often in their studies of the new."

We entered the cemetery. The luxuriant Southern vegetation transformed these thirty square yards into a great mass of flowers. Wild jasmine, hawthorn, honeysuckle, narcissus, grew there in glorious confusion. Glycins climbed up the trees, and yellow roses, those miniature roses that are called bankshires, grew in large tufts among the dark cypresses. The gravestones were worn away by time in this garden of youth, of springtime, and of perfume.

I parted the fresh branches and sweet flowers to decipher some of the epitaphs. The latest of the stones, put there no doubt by the care of Mr. Scott, was decorated with a carved sabre. I read the inscription on it, and saw that it was the tomb of the last of the Chastins, and that this last heir of the name was also a colonel, but in the Confederate army. Near by, upon another tomb, nearly hidden by vegetation, I could distinguish the date 1738, and the words "New Orleans." I at once understood that the successor of the former owners had had the pious idea of placing in their last repose, side by side, the founder of the demesne and his descendant.

It was a pathetic thought what humanity lay in this enclosure. The race which here slept in its entirety had once been all powerful, and no one now remained to pay it homage except the generous enemy who had come into its inheritance, and the changing seasons that showered their splendors on the sad resting-place with that calm indifference of nature so hateful to us when we are young, and that we love when age begins to creep on. The consciousness of our littleness enables us to meet the inevitable defeat with a tranquil soul. Although as an active man, and one who has been through the war, the Colonel, perhaps, did not feel the same sort of emotion as I

cc

myself, this little mortuary oasis, which the murmur of bees
filled with music on that sunny day, did not leave him indifferent.
He became as silent as myself, and it was only when we had
left the place that he recovered his spirit, and said : —

"You noticed that the cemetery is still cared for? One of
their old slaves has undertaken the duty. They call her Aunt
Sarah. You will see her at our school. She looks after the
children. Her fidelity is a tribute to the Chastins, and it
makes the place dearer to me. Naturally there is some pleasure in the thought that one occupies a house in which have
lived none but noble people for four or five generations. It
makes one feel as though there were no unfortunates around.
As a matter of fact, there are none. When you have been to
the school, you shall visit a few of the cabins. You will see
the happy faces of these people. A little salt pork and some
fruit, and they are as comfortable as though they had all the
millions of all the cottagers of Newport. However, here is
your carriage."

My little carriage, in fact, awaited me almost at the door
of the cemetery. I recognized in this delicate, hospitable
attention the graceful foresight of the invalid. The Colonel
gave a few instructions to the coachman, and said to me.
"On Tuesday, at one o'clock," as he shook my hand. I had
to repress the temptation to reply to him, "Tuesday? What
a long time!" so great was my desire to see him soon again.
The originality of his character, the nobility of his daughter's
face, the picturesque aspect of their residence, had inspired
in me one of those sudden interests that professional novelists are probably the only ones to feel. The imagination is
as if entranced with a passionate desire to know all about
some one, to breathe the same air, to live the same life, to
think the same thoughts. While I was travelling along the
sandy roads toward Philippeville I hardly noticed the beauty
of the scenery, so absorbed was I by my reflections upon these

two persons, who were unknown to me a few hours before. I admired the puritanical ardor which had distinguished their ancestors, and which still burned in them like an inextinguishable flame. I found in their fervor of proselytism the influence of the pilgrims of the *Mayflower*.

I was surprised at the race prejudices which, notwithstanding this missionary zeal, made them regard as pollution the marriage of one of their race with the best of their black protegées. I thought of the wealth of this man's nature, a nature which five or six trades, and sixty years of work, had not exhausted; of the sadness of his daughter's life; of the peculiarities of this country, even; of the astonishing apparition, for example, of Mr. Scott busily engaged in wrenching out the fangs of a chloroformed serpent. In fact, fifty motives made me desirous of seeing again as soon as possible the man whom I had met to-day. I little thought under what different circumstances I should see him on Tuesday, very far from the family lunch presided over by Miss Ruth, nor that I should take part in his company in a stranger battue than even a rattlesnake hunt would have been for a Parisian writer.

It was on a Friday that I paid my visit to the Colonel. During the following three days, there fell in Philippeville one of those rains which in hot countries seem to fill the atmosphere with muggy vapors, rather than to refresh it. Imprisoned in the hotel, I had no other distraction than to watch the water falling in inexhaustible cataracts and to talk with the hotel-keeper. I had been mischievous enough to tell him of my visit to the Colonel and of my encounter with one of those formidable reptiles of which, I believe, he would have obstinately denied the existence, even if he had seen one lift its head in the middle of his tennis court.

"Oh, those niggers must have gone into Florida for it," replied Mr. Williams, without hesitation. "They have a perfect mania for catching them alive, in order to sell them to

some zoölogical garden." He said a "zoo," by way of abbreviation. · "Mr. Scott, who is a fine fellow, ought not to render
them such services. He only encourages them, without taking
into account that the serpents might awake during the operation. But the Colonel has always been too good to the colored people. He has been ill requited several times for his
kindness. Did he tell you that at this moment a certain
Henry Seymour, one of his old servants, whom he had dis-
missed for robbery, is in Philippeville prison, after having
ravaged the entire country? He took refuge in the woods,
after a murder, and stayed there with his Winchester.

"He was such a good shot that he terrified all the other
negroes, and the cowards furnished him with food, brandy,
and cartridges. Finally he was taken. A false friend mixed
some opium in his whiskey and delivered him up. He was
tried and condemned to death. Would you believe it, Mr.
Scott was indignant at the idea that the man had been cap-
tured by such means, and managed to obtain a postponement
of the execution. He even went to Atlanta to obtain a reprieve. He was not successful, and on Thursday this rascal
will be hanged."

"But the Colonel must have had other reasons, apart from
this treachery?"

"Oh, of course; he insisted that Seymour had been put on
the chain gang while too young. You have seen those men,
in white and brown suits, who work on our roads, with chains
at their feet. Those are our convicts. And this youth has
gone through that experience. I remember him well. It is
true he was only seventeen years of age, but he had already
committed two robberies, without counting that for which
Mr. Scott discharged him, although he would not have him
arrested."

"Only seventeen years!" I replied. "It's very young, all
the same. At that age one is very impressionable, and such

company is not calculated to improve a character that has gone wrong."

"Well," answered Mr. Williams, "there are many who remain in the chain gang for a year, or two years, and even then begin their life afresh. When a man has paid his debt, we Americans regard it as really paid. This Seymour could have paid his in work. If he preferred to carry on in a way that he would have to pay for by hanging, why, all right! By the way, would it not interest you to be present at the execution? In Georgia we have not adopted electricity. We just stick to hanging. You can compare it with France; for there you have the guillotine, have you not?"

"I have never seen it work," I replied, "and I doubt whether I have sufficient moral courage to stand by and see a man hanged."

"In any case, I will get you a ticket from the sheriff," said the hotel-keeper, "and you can use it or not, just as you choose."

He kept his word, and two days later — that is, on Monday — he announced to me that I should have the ticket. But on the evening of the same day he approached me again, in the hall of the hotel, wearing the anxious countenance of a good citizen who has learned bad news, and of a hotel-keeper who foresees some unpleasant occurrences for his guests, and said:

"What do you think? Have you heard the news? The ticket that the sheriff has given us is no good. That damned rascal, Seymour, is not going to be executed."

"Has Mr. Scott obtained his reprieve?" I asked.

"No; the man has escaped. They gave him too much freedom in his cell. He received too many visits. Some one passed him a knife, and this afternoon, when the jailer took him his food, he took advantage of the moment when the man stooped to put the tray on the floor and planted the knife right between his shoulders. The jailer fell dead at once.

Seymour took his revolver and his keys, freed seven negroes or mulattoes, prisoners like himself, but for slight offences, and the eight scoundrels escaped by the back door of the prison, which faces the country. They had the good luck to get away without being seen, so that their flight was only known two hours later. By this time they are in the woods, and there can be no traces of them on the roads after the heavy rains. Heaven knows when they will be retaken! Now was I not right in saying that the Colonel is too easy with those people? If he had not demanded a postponement, Seymour would have been hanged last week, the jailer would still be living, and I should not be afraid of losing my guests. A family is to come next week, but if they read in the papers about this adventure, they will be afraid and go to St. Augustine. They will get the idea that it is not safe in Georgia."

I was sufficiently accustomed to the newspapers so dreaded by Mr. Williams, and to their extraordinary accounts of daily happenings, to feel some astonishment at the change of plans of which he spoke. Apart from the larger cities, America still continues to be a country of daring exploits, executed with an audacity that recoils before no danger. On the other hand, I had not expected to find myself, I, a peaceable Gallo-Roman literary man, taking part in such a tragic history as this of the jail-breaking bandit. I passed the evening following Mr. Williams's revelations in wondering how I could bring the Colonel to speak to me of his old servant during our luncheon, on the following day. I had divined from a few words the hotel-keeper had let drop, that the philanthropic owner of Scott's place was very sensitive on this particular point. As things turned out, the Colonel spared me the trouble; for on the Tuesday morning, about nine o'clock, his card was brought up, with the message that he was downstairs and wished to speak to me. I found him wearing his hunting-costume, as on the first occasion that I had seen him, his legs thrust into stout leather gaiters, and with enormously thick-soled shoes. He carried a rifle in his hand.

"I came to beg you to excuse me," he said, without any preamble, "and to ask you to put off our luncheon to another day. I daresay you are aware that several prisoners have escaped from jail, and among them one who was condemned to death — in fact, a man who was formerly one of my servants."

"I have heard of it," I replied, "and also that you had formerly been very good to the wretched creature." /

"That is not true," he responded; "but in any case it is of no account. The important thing just at present is to recapture them, in order that they may not terrorize the country. Immediately on their escape, we telegraphed to Atlanta for bloodhounds, dogs specially trained for man hunting. I have collected about ten of the citizens for the work, and I have brought you a horse, so that if you choose to come with us — "

"Why not?" I replied, after a few minutes' hesitation. "At least, so long as there is no — "

"You are afraid of some lynching scene?" interrupted the Colonel, who had read the fear in my eyes. "Make yourself easy on that point, for while I am present they would not dare. Have you your gun?" and, upon receiving a negative response, he added: "However, you will not need it. You don't belong to the country, and you will naturally only be with us as a spectator. Besides, only one of them is armed, this very Seymour, and he has only a No. 48 Colt. If he had his Winchester, I shouldn't take you along; for he would never allow himself to be taken without bringing down five or six of us."

Twenty minutes later, and without any further preparation, I was following the Colonel along one of the roads which traverse the immense forests of pitch-pines planted around Philippeville. My horse, a Kentucky animal, was trained to

go at that gallop the Americans call "single foot," a kind of
swift trot that covers the ground very rapidly, and which I have
never met anywhere else. As I learned afterward, our little
party was composed of simple shopkeepers. Except for their
gaiters, they were dressed just as though at their counters, but
they all wore a singularly energetic expression, and displayed a
not less singular skill in managing their steeds.

It was very evident that they had all at some time been
occupied in some business which had not been without its cares
and worries, before establishing themselves in this remote corner
of Georgia, as grocer or as saddler, as dealer in ready-made
clothing or as undertaker. With the exception of the Colonel
and myself, the whole caravan was chewing tobacco. I could
see the regular motion of the jaws, and the barrels of the rifles
— each of them carried one — gleaming close to the faces,
stirred with this automatic movement. Eight dogs, rather
small in height, and undistinguishable to a novice from the
ordinary hunting dog, went on ahead of us, around us, to right,
to left, sniffing the air, hesitating, running, taking up the scent,
and losing it again.

The storm had ceased on the preceding evening, and the
morning, after many days of torrent-like rain, was made lovely
by a moist, bright radiance. Although the forest roads passed
through a sandy country which had already swallowed up almost
all the rain, so much had fallen that the low-lying portions were
still full. The tiniest of the watercourses which descended
toward the neighboring river had overflowed, and we had almost
constantly to clear some brook transformed into a pond, in
which our horses waded up to the chest.

Almost continually, also, we had to leap over trunks which
strewed the road. In the great forests of Georgia and Florida,
the negroes are accustomed to draw the resin from the pitch-
pines by notching them. The notch they cut is so deep that
a wind storm of very slight force is quite sufficient to break

the tree, and a veritable tempest had been raging all through
the region during the last two days.

"The negroes call these fallen trees 'hurricanes,'" said the
Colonel, in explanation of this newly felled mass, an explanation which, however, did not account for the old trunks, the
innumerable rotting stumps, between which grew a rich, thick
vegetation of tiny palms, showing themselves bravely or lying
crushed to the earth. Out of this carpet of large flat leaves
sprang great honeysuckles and flowers such as I had admired
the other afternoon, a luxuriant mixture of pink and white,
freshest pink and most delicate white. Colossal yellow jessa-
mines were interlaced in the trees. Violets as large as pansies
peeped out among the grass. The barking of the dogs, who
were now following the trail, began to fill the spring landscape
with a clamor that seemed to me exceedingly fantastic.

Not being charged with the civic duties whose trace I could
see printed upon the faces of the horsemen, who were now
walking their steeds, their bridles twisted round their wrists,
their eyes wide open, and their rifles in their hands, I had
time to dream, and I was oppressed with the thought that the
vehement bark of those ferocious animals was being heard
with terror by seven or eight unfortunates crouched motionless in the woods, or, perhaps, crushing, in their furious course,
flowers similar to those which surrounded me; casting the
branches to one side with frenzied arms; breathless with fear
and panting with fatigue. At this moment the pack, which
had again been at fault, took off along a cross road with such
fury that they were soon lost to our view. The Colonel halted
us. He listened for a few moments with the close attention
of an old warrior accustomed to interpret distant sounds.
"The dogs have stopped," he said at last. "They have got
one of them. We had better spread ourselves out fan-like in
order to surround them and the man."

Acting upon his instructions, the little troop disappeared in a few seconds among the trees. I saw the horsemen, one after another, dive deeper into the gloom, the bridles hanging free now, and the rifles ready for use. The shrewd, intelligent horses appeared to go in the right direction by sheer instinct. The horsemen had merely to press with one of the large, wooden stirrups, decorated with leather, in which the foot was fixed in the Mexican manner, and the knowing animal turned, passing with sure and firm tread, through the pools of water and crossing the obstacles formed by large, fallen trees, which lay on every hand, without even brushing them with the hoof. The Colonel and I remained alone. We began to advance in the direction whence came the barking, but we had not ridden in this way more than two hundred yards before we had to slacken our pace. The river, one of these little watercourses, almost without name, of which hundreds flow in that region, and which are about as large as the Adige or the Po, had over- flowed its banks. Its muddy waters flooded the portion of the forest where we were now marching. The Colonel went on in front of me. "I know the route a little," he said, "and there's less chance that my horse will break its leg in some hole."

I could see him about a neck in advance of me, his body so supple, notwithstanding his age, upon his stout steed. Now and again he would turn and stoop as though to gather up into one ear the full significance of the disturbance coming from the place toward which we were riding. I could see his profile at such times, a resolute, serious profile, but wearing an expression of sadness that I was beginning to read both by the light of the hotel-keeper's indiscretions, and by that given me by his own character. At that very moment, engaged in doing his duty as a good citizen in hunting down a brigand, he could see again, without doubt, that same brigand just as he was when in his service, a mere boy, almost a child. The contrast was too great between the day that he had discharged Seymour from his house, after a first escapade, and the pres-

ent time, when he was conducting a troop charged with the
duty of tracking his old servant, now an outrageous malefactor,
through these inundated woods. With the idea of responsibility proper to the old Puritan, it was impossible that the
Colonel should not contrast these two episodes, impossible
that he should not say to himself, "I might, perhaps, have
averted this destiny if I had been less severe."

I could read the cares of a troubled conscience upon that
strong countenance, side by side with the natural tension of
the soldier lying in ambush. All at once the complex expression of the martial visage became more intense. The Colonel
again stopped his horse, his hands again gripped his rifle,
which he brought to his shoulder with terrible deliberation.
I stooped almost to the neck of my animal, and through the
foliage of the pitch-pines I could see the shore of the river,
recognizable in this enormous flood only by the abrupt cessation of vegetation. I could see the dogs swimming upon the
sheet of reddish water. I could see their three wide-open
jaws collected threateningly round the head of a man. With
one arm the unfortunate creature was swimming, with the
other he held a pistol out of the water. Slowly, almost im-
perceptibly, he advanced, fighting against the current and
trying to reach a submerged bridge, of which the iron cable
was still visible five or six yards away. It was the only chance
that he had of crossing that terrible river. You could measure
the force of its current by three logs that went drifting by.
It was a miracle that the swimmer had not been struck by one
of them; a miracle that he had gained even that little distance. He must have been fighting in this way a long time,
and yet he did not lose courage! When the pack surrounded
him too closely, terribly united and howling, but without
biting him, he would strike at the muzzles of the dogs with
the butt end of his revolver. The furious blow would drive
back the living barrier of implacable jaws and would thus

leave him sufficient room to enable him to make a little more headway. It was easy to see that he was keeping his weapon intact for a more important occasion, if he was compelled to abandon his one hope of safety.

There was in this desperate combat against such opposing forces, against the elements, against animals, against men, something so courageous and so hopeless that it oppressed the heart. We were so close to the man that I could see with extreme clearness the expression of his face. It was a mulatto's face, rather yellow than brown, a nearer neighbor of white blood than the negro's. His hair was not kinky, it was even hardly curly. The nose, instead of being flat, was aquiline. What family had bequeathed this aristocratic face to this robber, this murderer? From whom had this Henry Seymour descended? For it was Seymour. If any doubt had remained in my mind after the description the hotel-keeper had given me, the Colonel's agitation would have dissipated it. His rifle continued to remain at his shoulder, but his finger did not press the trigger. Even had it touched it, it is not probable that the ball would have struck the mark, so great was the trembling of the old man's arm, now that he was aiming at his old servant. Finally the rifle barrel was raised without having been fired, and I heard Mr. Scott say aloud, as if he had been alone: —

"No, I cannot shoot him so!"

He spurred his horse. The water was so deep now that the Colonel was in it to above the knee. He could go no further without swimming, but he was upon the edge of the forest and there were no trees before him. He cried out, and the swimmer turned. I saw the revolver that the fugitive continued to hold out of the water aimed at the Colonel, and then begin to rise just as the Colonel's rifle had done. Seymour had recognized Mr. Scott, and he did not fire. This hesitation to commit murder was so completely unexpected in a professional murderer, and under such circumstances, that even at that moment and in the fever caused by such an adventure I could not help feeling astonishment. The man must have felt for his master a very strange sentiment of veneration to refuse to fire, he a man who had already spilled so much blood. Or could it be that he had seen the Colonel's gesture of a few minutes ago, and, being certain that he would not fire, thought it was useless to waste one of his five shots? Or, again, could it be that this excellent marksman recognized the impossibility of aiming accurately while swimming as he was? I shall never know the secret motive that prompted this scene, which passed with such tragic rapidity.

Standing up in his stirrups, thus making a still more prominent target of his huge frame, the Colonel cried, with a voice that dominated the furious barkings of the dogs, the tumult of the water, and the rustling of the forest: —

"Come, Henry, my boy, you see it's no use! You'll have to give up. There are seven other rifles after you, and they'll be here in five minutes."

The man shook his head without replying. Then, as though the presence of his enemies had given him new strength, he fired at one of the dogs with the muzzle close to the animal. It howled with pain, and the other dogs hung back. Then, judging that his weapon could not serve him any longer, he dropped it into the water in order to dive and swim with both arms.

"He's going to escape," said the Colonel, whose clear eyes became fixed.

He again shouldered his rifle, and I felt that this time he would not hesitate. This heroic effort of citizenship was, however, spared him. When Seymour's head came up in the river, he was quite close to the bridge, sufficiently close, in fact, to seize the cable. In another moment we saw him dive and reappear on the other side of it. Perhaps if he had once got upon the bridge and had gone on diving while walking, he might have escaped. But the instinct to stretch his limbs after such an effort made him stand erect the instant he felt his feet posed upon the planks. His chest appeared above the water, and that very moment two shots went off at our right, fired by two of the hunters: One of the balls struck the mulatto in the shoulder, and we saw his arm drop limp and inert. The other crashed against the iron cord of the cable, glanced off, and struck the fugitive in the head. He raised his unwounded hand to his forehead and then reeled. The few movements that he made to grasp anew the iron cable were a mere convulsive, instinctive effort. He felt himself fainting, and disappeared under the water. But the Colonel had already forced his horse into the stream and had begun swimming. He gained the side of the wounded man, whom he raised with his powerful arm and brought to shore.

A quarter of an hour later the entire troop, attracted by the shots, had assembled with us around the still fainting man. The dogs slipped between the legs of the horses, trying to smell and lick the bloody cloths with which Mr. Scott was wiping the two wounds, which were but slight, received by the unfortunate wretch. We learned later that, in the hope of putting off his execution, he had pretended to be ill, and had refused to eat for several days. That was the real cause of his defeat. Had he been more robust, he would not have been so much retarded. He would have crossed the bridge, as his comrades had done, two hours before our arrival, and once in the other part of the forest he would have found, as they did, a line of railroad, and like them, without doubt, would have clambered on to a train in motion, like professional tramps.

Before long Henry Seymour began to recover his senses. At the first effort he made to rise, one of the men drew his revolver, while two others seized the wounded man by the legs and tied them firmly. He, however, did not make any fresh attempt at useless resistance. The ball which had glanced off the cable had struck him in the arch of the eyebrow, and had cruelly wounded all the left side of the forehead and the eyelid so that only the right eye was capable of being opened. But the furious glance he gave with this single eye was so ferocious as his gaze wandered around our circle that one of the huntsmen replied to his silent defiance by a word involuntarily spoken aloud : —

"It's too late, man," he said simply.

Seymour did not appear to have heard him. It was the Colonel he was looking at now, with quite another expression. The brown eyes had taken on again their look of soft, humid sweetness. I expected, from the nature of his look, to hear some strangely touching expression, but I had misread the animal simplicity of such a nature. All that the wounded man felt in the way of sentiment for Mr. Scott resulted solely in this demand, which he addressed to him directly, as though he would not deign to speak to any one else : —

"Give me something to drink, Colonel; I am so thirsty. Won't you give me something to drink?"

There was something so coaxing, so almost infantine in the voice with which he spoke to his old master, that it recalled the petting of which he had once been the object. Mr. Scott drew a flask from his pocket, uncorked it, and put the mouth to the lips of the prisoner, holding up his head as he did so. Seymour swallowed several mouthfuls greedily. His eye began to glisten more caressingly, and, with that versatility of feeling which equals in those singular beings their suppleness of movement, he smiled with pleasure as if he had quite forgotten his rage of only a few minutes ago, his crime of the preceding evening, his wild flight of this morning, his wounds and the certainty of his dark future.

"Ah! It's the same whiskey that we used to drink when hunting together," he said, smacking his lips. "He beats everybody, does my Colonel."

"And now," responded the latter, "you're going to be quiet and let me dress your wounds."

"Will you give me some more whiskey afterward?" asked Seymour.

"Yes, you shall have some."

"And one of your cigars, Colonel?"

"And one of my cigars."

"All right," said the mulatto, holding out, without any resistance, first his head and then his arm. Mr. Scott had brought with him a complete little field case of surgeon's instruments. He displayed all the skill of an old surgeon in cleansing and binding up the two wounds, while the soldier in him was displayed in a desire to clear up a certain point that had remained obscure to him, a desire that made him ask : —

"How is it that you did not cross the river yesterday?"

"Because we went to the Georgetown bridge, Colonel," replied the other, "and the waters had carried it away. There was only one of two things to be done — either to go down the river to the Berkeley Farms bridge, twenty miles lower down, or to come up to this one. As we knew the roads better, we chose this route, but we were wrong. How is it, though, Colonel, that you thought we should come in this direction?"

"I knew the Georgetown bridge had been carried away," said Mr. Scott, "and I calculated that you would reason exactly as you have done. You said to yourself, 'They don't believe that we would be audacious enough to come so close to the town.' But it's not daring you're short of, Henry, or courage. Now that the dressing is finished, is there anything more I can do for you?"

"Send me a bottle of your whiskey to the prison," replied Seymour. "And get permission from the sheriff for me to finish it before I have to swing."

Events such as those I had just witnessed are not very extraordinary in Philippeville, in a city where they do not recollect having passed a year without one or two lynchings. Ordinary life, therefore, resumed its course at once, and on the very evening of that dramatic day, when I went to buy some Richmond tobacco, I recognized in the grocer who sold it to me one of the horsemen with whom I had scoured the forest in search of Henry Seymour. He was chewing his quid with the usual impassible phlegmatic air, and we made no more allusion to our adventure than two Parisians meeting again at their club in the afternoon would speak of the bows they had exchanged at the Bois in the morning.

In fact, the incident appeared to have made a profound impression only upon Mr. Williams; for he did not hesitate to display a pleasure that appeared to me almost indecent, although he justified it by a quaint, business-like admission.

"Those people from New York, of whom I spoke to you, will be here the day after to-morrow. I telegraphed to them the moment Seymour was recaptured. They must have received the news of his arrest as soon as they heard of his flight, and they replied to me in this telegram, announcing their arrival. Ah, I was rather afraid. By the way, it appears that Seymour is not wounded so badly as to prevent his execution to-morrow (Thursday), as it was previously decided."

DD

X

DOWN SOUTH

II. *In Florida*

BETWEEN Jacksonville and Lake Worth, along that low peninsula — often lower than the sea itself — with all the lagoons, lakes, and rivers lying between us and the Everglades, and further away the Antilles, I saw landscapes filled with an almost tropical vegetation of a never-to-be-forgotten luxuriance. An entire civilization is delineated in this country, whose first possessors, the Seminole Indians, had not been conquered half a century ago. The massacre of Dr. Henry Perrine on one of the islands or keys — those breakwaters of the peninsula — occurred on August 7, 1840, and the first traveller, a New Yorker, who explored the Okeechobee, one of the great lakes of the interior, reached there in 1880. Even now an expedition off the railway lines which lead to Tampa, on the Gulf of Mexico, and to Palm Beach, on the Atlantic coast, would entail immense difficulties. This does not prevent a large number of young North Americans, fond of hunting, yachting, fishing, and, above all, of free life, from visiting each spring and winter these almost inaccessible parts of the peninsula with the floral name. The reader who may wish to follow the tourist's diary in which I here transcribe the various trips, will find in it the description of a perfectly easy and modest excursion. Had I possessed the talent to evoke in these pages the horizons on which I feasted my eyes during the three weeks of spring which I passed in this astonishing country, I should have given the impression which I still retain of that Eastern America — the impression of a mosaic, of a sudden change from the land of the factory and of industry to the most untouched and the most virginal realm of nature ! What must that Western shore be, that Southern California which stretches from San Francisco to Los Angeles and further south? And how am I to console myself for not having had, in these ten months of travel, the time to go there? The Americans are indeed right when they talk of the large scale upon which their country is established. It is but too large !

JACKSONVILLE, Easter Day, 1894.

A town of quite small houses, with dusty streets, and all along their wooden sidewalks trees of magic and exuberant verdure, a lavish leafage which the dust has been unable to sully. Persian lilacs, like those whose perfume I breathed in the East, stand in the very street, gigantic, in full bloom, and perfuming the heated air ; then there are overladen orange trees, Japanese medlars, also yellow with fruit, bananas, palm trees, all of which foreshadow a different world from that of Georgia. A subtle aroma seems to pass through the sun which shines in the intensely blue sky, like that which overhung the Dead Sea last year, when, on leaving the grim convent of Mar Saba, I perceived that still water and the soft line of the mountains of Moab. But history and legend were mingled yonder with the feeling of nature. Here it is nature alone with which I come in contact, nature with its murderous fauna, its violent flora, its atmospheric phenomena, rather its cataclysms, charm and danger, at once perceptible in the very air one breathes, in every small detail which we meet at the corner of the street, in the sudden alternations of temperature, in fact, in the entire life of this small town, so peaceful on this Easter morning.

Negroes and still more negroes. It seems as if the town belonged to them entirely, so densely do they throng on the sidewalks, the men in Prince Albert coats, with flowers in their buttonholes and wearing trousers of light shades, the women clothed in outrageously bright-colored dresses, among which those of apple green, poppy red, and light pink predominate. Their bodices are cut in "Figaro" fashion, their hats are decorated with ribbons and enormous flowers, and their hair is plaited in plaits which are very thin and very tight, the object being to diminish or destroy the natural crinkling. They smile, showing their white teeth between their thick lips. The white teeth of the men are displayed in a similar smile, and they all salute and approach one another with that ceremonious familiarity, that sort of natural affectation which is peculiar to this strange race. A group dressed in white pass along an avenue. They are converts who have just been baptized in the river! All these people are glad that they are alive on this warm April Sunday. I follow some, who press forward toward a crowded church, and through a door I see the usual mixture of conflicting colors in the dresses of the women as they listen to the sermon of a famous preacher. The voice of the black clergyman, standing at the end on a platform, comes to me over this multicolored sea. He is in a fever of excitement, his eyes showing their whites and rolling convulsively. He has just depicted hell with the eloquence of an untaught visionary, and now he is announcing salvation and offering Christ as a quack offers a remedy: "Do you take Christ?" The costumes, the religion, the smiles, the attention, suggest to me by strong contrast what these people were in their savage state, and I am impressed with the singular game of fate, the amazing irony of events which makes us all workers together for results that we never purposed. In contrast with this American town, filled with those happy negroes, those "ladies" and those "gentlemen" of color, as the whites call them with polite irony, who benefit by the railroads built by the whites, by the tramways invented by those whites, by the telephone organized by those whites, and by the justice and the laws elaborated by those whites, a vision rises up before me of far-away torrid Africa, fifty or a hundred years back, with its leaf-huts under a burning sun, its kings practising human sacrifice, its bestial, idolatrous, and perilous existence. Then comes the negro dealer, and the next step is taken in the transportation of the grandfathers and the ancestors of these folk in the hold of a ship! Those ebony wood dealers have proved to be the benefactors of the families whose founders they thus transported to this Southern country before the war ruined their traffic. They thought they were making slaves, and they were making citizens of free America. From time to time history shows such double-faced ironies, as though to prove to us that we are puppets in the hands of an invisible Author, who constructs the tragedy of the universe according to His own ideas. Our good intentions end in miserable results, just as was the case with those worthies of 1789, who believed that they were decreeing fraternity, but who were really preparing the "Terror."

ST. AUGUSTINE, March 30.

The hotel life of America does not resemble any other. You should go to St. Augustine if you would understand to what extent these hard workers enjoy it, how much they expect of it, and how much it meets their innermost personal characteristics. At this moment, although the end of the winter season is at hand, the traveller can scarcely find room in these palace-like buildings, one of which resembles the Alcázar, another the Alhambra, a third the Escurial, a fourth a vast house of the colonial period. And all is on a scale of extravagant luxury which all the travellers visibly enjoy. Unlike casual visitors in the large hotel of a European watering-place, these people feel as much at ease in these sumptuous halls, in these magnificent palaces, amid these plushes and these paint-

:ngs as they would at home — even more than at their own homes. Many come from new towns in the centre and on the border of the West. Their fortunes, recent as those towns, have roused in them a desire for luxury and comfort which this hotel satisfies grossly but easily. The grossness they do not feel, and they delight in the ease. You should see them during the day, rocking themselves on their chairs to the sound of the orchestra, which, from one to three o'clock and from eight to ten, makes the vast building vibrate. After dinner a ball is organized, and they all dance.

You see men of seventy taking their places in the quadrille, a grandmother polkaing beside her granddaughter, and young people waltzing with the incomparable lightness of the young people over here. The movement of these dances, the rapid rhythm of the steps, which are really danced and not walked, betray a physical ardor, an ardor for pleasure equal to the ardor for work. All these people are in full dress; young men are introduced to young ladies by other youths; laughing groups gather everywhere — on the stairs, on the terraces — there is in the air a good fellowship that would make you believe that these people have known each other for years were it not for the introductions continually taking place around you. The "very glad to meet you" of these travellers, who cordially shake hands, though this morning they did not know one another, gives you the impression of a railway station, at which the tourists of an entire train have been suddenly introduced with no distinction of persons.

ROCKLEDGE, April 2.

Almost immediately below St. Augustine the landscape changes. The palmetto, which crept along the ground as undergrowth, becomes higher. It first reaches the height of a child, then of a man, then twice that of a man. Its colonnades close up. Strange trees appear, the trunks of which spring

from huge bulbs like that of a gigantic orchid. The orange
groves multiply, becoming vaster and broader, and the burning
atmosphere reveals the near approach of the tropics. But
American energy does not seem to be affected by the climate.
This South has nothing of the South in it, except its vegetation
and its light. The stern, energetic race is just as intent as ever
on the great struggle. Cars loaded with fruits follow one
another on the railroad, as numerous as were the cars filled
with meat in the neighborhood of Chicago. Here, however,
they are ventilated, while the others were frozen. One sees
the plains brought under cultivation and covered with oranges,
not indigenous to the country. Not much more than twenty
years ago the people bethought themselves of planting them on
this soil, and already the orange trade of Florida threatens that
of Spain and Sicily. As in the West, small towns spring up
beside the railway, and land speculation extends all along the
line. I am told that at Lake Worth, where I shall be the day
after to-morrow, one of the magnates of this company suddenly
built in the wilderness a hotel which is a palace, and then
extended the line to reach his hotel, and that a winter resort is
in-course of growth out there as by enchantment. Here again
you find that infatuation for Europe, which in this people
always mingles with the intense originality of their spirit of
enterprise. The idea of giving to their country a Riviera
haunts these great Florida speculators, and they have succeeded, but without being able to give their coast that dainty
flower of cosmopolitan worldliness, that which forms the charm
of our Provence, nor the beauty of the environs of Genoa, that
home of the finest museums and churches of divine Italy. But
if Florida has not the elegance of Cannes, nor the fêtes of Nice,
nor the enchantment of art, what landscapes, what nature she
has !

I walked this evening on the edge of the Indian River,
which I shall descend to-morrow. It is a long lagoon, six

miles broad in certain places and fifty feet at others.   A slip of
land, stretching out indefinitely, separates it from the ocean,
and it thus extends along the entire peninsula, lapping the quiet
beaches of the winter resorts, such as the one at which I have
stopped to-day.   It was five o'clock.   The sun was sinking in
the west, enveloping the luxuriant vegetation in a sort of quivering luminous dust.

I was following between the palms the path which leads
along the shore.   Those beautiful trees were growing up on all
sides, not in clumps as in the oases of the East, but like a forest,
the gigantic trunks ending in large full green sprays, which the
wind moved with a metallic murmur.   Between those immense trunks, which looked as though padded with a woven
bark, immense plants of a scent unknown to me rose out of
thickets covered with full-blown flowers, red and bluish, — flowers twice as large as a lily, that looked as if made of cloth or of
silk velvet.   Green oaks were mingled with those flowers, in-
terspersed with palms smothered in a network of pale green
creepers.   At times, at some spot during the walk, a vista
would suddenly open up and reveal an orange grove, with the
golden fruit shining amid the lustrous leaves.   The water of
the lagoon quivered under the movement of the tide which
through a neighboring gully made itself felt even here.   It
rippled against the shore amid those standing trees and against
the fallen trunks, with a rhythmical monotony in which was
a palpitation like the breathing of the ocean, out of sight
behind yonder protecting slip of land.

They call it " Fairyland," a term calling up old recollections
of the lands of fogs — of Ireland, of Scotland — whence have
come so many of the colonists established here.   Light yawls
glided about on the surface of the lagoon, broad of hull and
high of sail; they were full of wind now — a warm wind, a
languid and ardent breath.   All along the road was a succession of cottages, their covered verandas all facing the forest.

Here a sick woman was swinging in a hammock. There a youth with a faded complexion was reading and dreaming. It was a scene of nature where one could die gently, not caring to fight any more, longing to be absorbed, rocked, put to sleep.

Thinking of the sharp winter of Boston and New York, with its snow and sleighs, I felt how large this land is, how it touches at both extremes of climate. Realizing the vastness of this continent, I asked myself again if, the conquest once established, — it is so recent, — the American will allow himself to be impressed with this diversity of climate, and if he will create for himself a gentler civilization in these States, one more analogous to this light and beauty. And, as though in ironical reply, I perceived at a turn in the road a drawing-room car going at full speed among the trees, and on the trunk of a palm tree, lighted up by the rays of the setting sun, I saw a board upon which I read that a certain mineral spring is the " Czar of Table Waters ! "

On the Indian River, April 3.

I resume this diary on a boat of singular form which is descending toward the military post of Jupiter, whence the railroad takes me to Lake Worth. The lower part is a sort of raft, manned by a unique crew composed entirely of blacks. Piles start out of it, supporting a kind of deck, and above that is a bridge. In the space between the deck and the bridge there is a large dining-room. Small cabins open out from it on both sides. The wheel, which slowly propels this construction, is behind, made both for these waters, which are deep, and for others where the flat bottom of the raft rubs constantly against the sandy bottom. I shall without doubt be one of the last to descend the lagoon in this fashion ; for the railroad will soon be opened between Titusville and Jupiter, so that we shall be able to go from New York to Lake Worth without changing cars. The captain, an American of the Southern States, who has much Spanish and French blood, with the clever little face of an inhabitant of Tarbes or of Pau, and with inexpressibly aristocratic, yet simple, manners, shows me the rails on the banks, and says to me: "Whenever you see a railroad sleeper, you see the tomb of a steamboat man." The railroad will go quicker. The traveller will avoid a long day of eight to ten hours on the turns of the river. But the railroad will never give him the same knowledge of the river.

First of all, immediately after embarking at Fort Pierce, there is a broad expanse of water shut in on the left by the narrow, wooded strip of land which separates it from the sea. Scarcely a trace of cultivation is to be seen either to the left or to the right, where the mainland stretches out, but in most places is that luxuriant vegetation which has increased continually ever since we left Rockledge. The closer the banks, the more we perceive the inextricable matting of the branches. There is a certain tree, the trunk of which serves as a crown to roots exposed above the water, which are twisted like an enormous knot of serpents. One might say that they were the motionless feelers of a monstrous animal, the body of which would be formed by the trunk of the tree, which was pumping the water greedily, insatiably, by its fifty parched mouths. Beside it are palms, nearly all burned and reddened. Grasses and briers interlace and form colossal thickets twice the height of a man, where one would imagine the most formidable beasts must lie in wait. At the place where the river becomes narrow, the great voice of the ocean is heard. All at once it appears above the line of trees, immense and blue, a sapphire blue, a lapis blue, with a trace on that intense azure of a large almost purple vein, so violet is it. It is the Gulf Stream, that mysterious flow of hot water through the cold depths of the Atlantic. Enormous waves break in crests of white foam upon the beach, all of which we see from the bridge of the boat, so thin and low is the preserving slip of land at this point. It is broken, and a gully appears, through which the high waves hurl themselves, stopped at once by an island of yellow sand, upon which there are thousands of sea-gulls and pelicans. The noise of the wheel of our approaching boat frightens them away. A whirlwind of scattered wings whitens the sky, where the black spots made by the long-legged waders disappear less quickly. I hear the prolonged cry of the seagulls, like that of a sick child, a wail so human that it is painful.

LAKE WORTH, April 4.

I arrived at Lake Worth yesterday evening after nightfall. Here, again, is one of those impressions of contrast, such as America alone can give — a corner of the world. A corner of a peninsula very far from towns large or small, without villages, without cultivation even, the whole extent a dangerous and inaccessible solitude, until, all at once, through the whim of a railroad owner, a hotel is built which is a palace. I see the one, of which much had been said, filling a break on the horizon with its enormous and luminous mass; beyond it a large sheet of water, wherein trembles the reflection of a sky brilliant with stars. The train has stopped at the edge of Lake Worth, this vast salt pond which bathes Palm Beach yonder, the beach of palms where that fantastic hotel is situated. A pleasure boat, a trim steamer, furnished with extraordinary caprice, comes to meet us, and, after some manœuvring, executed somewhat at random on this dark water, to avoid here a sand bank, there the piles of a future jetty, we see the palace, as luxurious as though it stood in New York on the sidewalks of Fifth Avenue, with its colonnaded entrance, lighted by electricity and perforated with elevators. Its hall is filled with men and women in ball dresses, who are dancing wildly, and who show complexions burnt by the torrid sun of the day, by the long hours spent on the sandy beach, and the baths in that surf, which is so close by and which the Gulf

Stream warms like the Mediterranean in summer. From time to time a couple of dancers come upon the terrace to breathe in the soft, tropical night, and lazily they suck oranges, which everywhere fill large baskets, perfuming the atmosphere with a sweet aroma, while the breeze coming from over the gardens wafts on to the terrace and into the hall the odors of countless flowers.

What a country to be happy in, after the manner of a plant that grows in the sun, unmindful and without desire to be elsewhere! In opening my window in the morning, I see, between the lake and the house, a forest of cocoanut trees. The fruit appears in the middle of the leaves, hung in bunches, and each is as large as a child's head. In going toward the ocean just now, I inhaled the perfume of a rose-laurel wood, which a tramway, drawn by a single horse, crosses for a mile. The carriage in passing brushes the beautiful trees with their flesh-colored flowers, and, as the people have not even trimmed the branches, we tear and destroy living flowers. But this vegetation is so rank that the damage will be repaired to-morrow. A warm odor and a sense of growth which inebriates, exhales from these trees and from these grasses, from these fields of pineapples, and forests of cocoanut trees. Nature is at one and the same time too violent and too soft. The sea at the end of this alley of rose-laurels is too blue. It is no longer the wild ocean, it is the Mediterranean, the voluptuous, the feminine —. But no. We look closer, and the colossal swelling of the waves shows that it is the great and powerful Atlantic. Over that azure there passes again the great dark artery of the Gulf Stream, and we notice gigantic forms of fishes as they sport in the blue and violet tints of the billows. They are sharks. Their presence does not prevent the young Americans from bathing on that free beach. I hear one say to another who hesitates, "Go, and run your risk."

That saying contains an entire philosophy.

I am going to leave to-morrow, at sunrise, this adorable oasis of gardens thrown in between this lagoon and the Atlantic, being bound for New York; thence, by one of the "ocean greyhounds" I shall go to Liverpool and then to France.

XI

HOMEWARD

AT SEA, ABOARD THE ———, April, 1894.

ANOTHER fifteen days in New York to classify my notes, to verify some of them, to revisit places which I had visited before, to speak with people whom I had already known,—in short, to bid an adieu, not without regret, to this land, which is really so captivating, since one breathes here at every moment the breath of liberty,—all this has been done, and here I am once more on the Atlantic, on board an English steamer this time, and one which is quicker than the steamer in which I "crossed the pond"—as the Yankees familiarly say—last August. We left New York on Saturday morning; to-day is Wednesday, and to-morrow, Thursday, we shall be at Queenstown, in Ireland, and the day after to-morrow, Friday, in Liverpool. When the Anglo-Saxons take upon themselves to vie with one another, their keenness of competition knows no impossibilities. The other boat was 11,500 tons register; this one registers 13,000 tons. The engines of the other were of 20,000 horse power; the engines of this one have a horse power of 30,000. The former was 580 feet long, this one is 620 feet.

And just as, on the other, we were practically on American soil, so, on this, we are already in England. I recognize it by twenty small signs; by the politeness and the exactness of the attendants; by the somewhat heavy and dark look of the drawing-rooms, which have no resplendent gorgeousness of plush and nickel; by the economy of the table, not weighted

414

with the innumerable dishes of American prodigality. But
when we are returning from so long a journey, we no longer
have the heart to take pleasure in observations of this description. The harvest of strange sensations is reaped. What
germs this journey to America may have sown in me; what
profound modifications contact with that civilization, so full
of life and so different from ours, may have made in my
thoughts, I know not. In turning over this diary, I find that,
above all things, I was going to seek in the United States
light as to the future, foreshadowed by those three great and
inevitable powers which are transforming the Old World,
namely, Democracy, Science, and the Race question. I have,
in fact, seen at work an immense democracy, which has caused
a scientific spirit to penetrate, in the form of industry, into the
smallest detail of life, and, in the form of education, into the
soul of its soul. I have seen living, side by side, blacks and
whites, Germans and Irish, Chinamen and Scandinavians,
Italians and Anglo-Saxons. What hypotheses has that sight
induced me to form, by analogy, as to the morrow of our own
civilization?

By analogy? But can any analogy be established? Has
what we understand among us by democracy anything in common with the form of civilization which the Americans have
established in their vast Republic? Yes, if we merely busy
ourselves with that vague programme which Lincoln — and
Napoleon, also, by the way — formulated in these terms:
" For the people and by the people." No, if, on the one side,
we look at the general spirit of the country, and, on the
other, at the customs which that spirit is working out in
France, that country among the great States of Europe which
believes itself to be the most advanced on the path of reform,
we shall find that the word "democracy" signifies that all the
powers of the State are delegated to the representatives of
the people, that is to say, to the majority. And, however

oppressive, however unjust, may be the measures taken by those representatives, the moment that they meet the desire of the greater number, we consider them not only legal, but democratic. Thus conceived, democracy consists in the constant sacrifice of the individual to the community.

But. it is precisely in the contrary sense that American democracy works. It is toward the more intense, the more complete development of the individual that it has striven until now, to the diminution, to the suppression, if it were possible, of the influence of the State. On arriving at New York, what strikes the stranger? The individual energy, the spirit of enterprise, manifested everywhere, and visibly without control. If he begins, as I did, the study of the country from the top, from that part of society which entertains and amuses itself, what characteristic strikes him first? It is the application of the same energy to social elegancies, the result of which gives the European visitor that continuous feeling of "too much," of abuse, of exaggeration. It is, again, the energy and the robust development of the individual which form the characteristic of the American woman and the young girl. It is also by energy and individuality that the man of business is distinguished in this country, and the feebler individualities of his employees, in their struggle against him, have no other resource than to associate themselves for the purpose; or, in other words, they can do nothing but defend themselves, without asking anything of the State.

It is again by energy and individuality that the people of the rough and savage West maintain themselves. The energy of individuality and the spirit of enterprise are taught in the schools of the most refined part of the country,— in other words, in New England,— and these schools, moreover, are all founded by individual generosity or municipal generosity, which comes to the same thing. This feature is so essential that it is found again in the pleasures of the Americans, all of

which are in harmony with purposed and personal action, and
it is so profound that it resists the weakening influence of
climate. Constantly, in the South, you meet with a living
testimony of that Northern activity, and you find that it is
invincible even near the tropics. Such, at least, is the résumé
of the brief inquiry which I made in my too short journey
through that immense Republic. Conceived and practised in
that way, democracy results, not as with us in a perpetual
levelling, but, on the contrary, in bringing about astonishing
inequalities between individuals, who forcibly devour one
another. The vital law of competition is at work there, as in
nature, to such a point that, at times, this democracy gives
the impression of an aristocracy,— I had almost said a feudal-
ism. The president of a great railroad, the proprietor of a
great newspaper, the master of a great factory at New York,
at Chicago, at St. Paul, has more real power than a prince.
Only, he is a prince who has made himself, and a similar
conquest is within the reach of all, provided they have the
strength. Equal social possibility,— such is the democratic
formula in America. Equal social reality,— such is the
formula in Europe, and particularly in France, since the
Revolution of 1789. I know nothing so contradictory.

There is a second difference which does not permit of an
analogy between the democratic ideal United States and ours.
The United States, even after allowing for the socialistic demon-
strations of German immigrants, appears to the traveller to be
the least revolutionary of countries ; the one where constitu-
tional problems are the most definitely and stringently regulated. It is a conservative democracy — that is to say, exactly
the contrary of ours. This is because the country has instinctively put into practice the maxim which dominates the lives of
nations, as it dominates those of individuals. Things maintain
themselves by the same conditions which brought them into
existence. In giving full play to his individual energy, the

EE

American has conformed to the law of his origin. Who made this country what it is? Exiles, rebels, adventurers. They came to this new land to recreate for themselves an existence of adventure, of daring, and of feats of will. A social compact, fixed enough to prevent those wills being turned into tools of disorder, broad and flexible enough to mutilate nothing of ·them — there, in an abstract form, is the programme which the doctors of social science would have given to this country, and which it has by instinct realized. They did not reach democracy through reasoning; they found themselves established under that system. Thence results that sort of ease in liberty which is one of the striking features of America, and that absence of defensive laws.

As a result of their origin, all the countries thus built up have that same profound unity, and, as a consequence, the same plasticity, whatever may be otherwise the nature of. their government. Aristocratic England is a proof of this. It is a lesson which we can take from the American democracy, but to practise it, it would be necessary for us to work in a direction opposite to that in which the democratic party has been working for a hundred years. We should have to seek what remains of old France and attach ourselves again to it with every fibre, and first of all we should have to restore the province with its natural and hereditary unity, instead of the artificial and parcelled-out "department"; municipal autonomy instead of administrative centralization; local and fecund universities instead of our official and dead university; then we should have to reconstitute the landed family by allowing complete liberty in the disposal of property by will; we should have to protect labor by the reconstitution of corporations; we should have to restore to the religious life its vigor and dignity by the suppression of the budget of public worship and by giving religious associations the right to own property freely; in a word, on this point, as on the other, the task before us would be the systematic undoing of the murderous work of the French Revolution. This is the advice which, for the impartial observer, stands out from all the remarks made upon the United States. If their democracy is so vigorous and strong, it is because the individual is free and powerful in a State which is reduced to a minimum of action. If it unites all wills in an immense harmony, it is because it is truly national. Our own revolution has so completely dried up the sources of French vitality, because it has established a régime in which the State centralizes in itself all the vital forces of the country, and because it has violently cut asunder all historical links between our past and our present. This criticism is not new. The three most lucid analysts of contemporary France, — Balzac, Le Play, and Taine, — starting from very different premises, have nevertheless arrived at the same conclusions. It is not without interest to note that it is also the conclusion formed from a visit to the country which is most often used as an illustration by the partisans of that revolution.

Thus I have learned to translate in America the word " democracy " into realities quite contrary to those which it represents in Europe, and consequently to fear it less. For if democracy is reconcilable with the most intense development of individuality and personality, all the objections launched against that form of civilization prove groundless at once. It is for us to lead it in that direction by every means in our power. I have learned there also to recognize the social benefactions of science. It is a common idea among us, and one to which I have for my part adhered too often, that a principle of nihilism is concealed within it, which renders it incompatible with the higher needs of the heart of man. Even those who do not go so far as to condemn it thus in the name of the ideal, are inclined to believe that it is a bad educator of the people. They consider that many of the moral maladies of the present moment are caused by the intoxication which those results, imperfectly understood, produce in ill-prepared brains. The pages in which these objections have been formulated and commented upon during the last twenty years, and in which minds less competent than well intentioned have proclaimed the bankruptcy of that science which has excited, for forty years, such enthusiasm among its devotees, the Renans, the Taines, the Flauberts, would, if collected into volumes, fill a library.

The enthusiastic hope of these great literary men in the future results of positive methods was not entirely justified. For the reaction of to-day the justification is not greater. A visit to the United States, where these methods have most constantly and most powerfully penetrated into the pettiest details of life, puts things back into their true place. We recognize, first of all, how incorrect are the statements of our moralists in regard to this general nihilism of science, since it exists yonder side by side with the most fervent Christianity — all New England is a proof of it — and neither does Christianity stand in the way of scientific development, nor does that development lessen the Christian faith. In an essay devoted to a celebrated article of M. Taine on "The Church in France," M. l'Abbé de Broglie, one of the most enlightened apologists of the time, very justly remarked that the word "science" long signified with us two very distinct ideas, — on the one hand, a group of positive notions acquired by experimental procedure; and on the other, the hypothesis of pure metaphysics constructed upon those notions. In truth, the group of positive notions alone constitutes true science. The American mind, with its distributive lucidity, appears to have seen this from the beginning, since religious and scientific life have grown as though in parallel lines without stumbling against one another. Its schools and universities have thus shown, as an object lesson might do, the exactness of the theory put forward by Herbert Spencer at the opening of the First Principles in regard to the possible reconciliation between religion and science through agnosticism.

The first having for its object the unknown, that is to say, by definition, the domain of research which escapes the second, all that is necessary in order that these two powers, equally necessary to the human soul, should work side by side without touching one another, is not to allow the two empires to become intermingled. That agreement, which America has succeeded in, we, in our turn, can and must succeed in, and it is one of the duties to which her example invites the best of us. This land of initiative also points out to us that this same science, in spite of all the prejudices to which I made allusion just now, is an excellent educator of the lower classes. But it is on the condition that it shall be taken really as an educator — that is to say, that it shall appeal to the will through the intellect. The Americans have only obtained the vitality of their industrial civilization by submitting to this rule. All culture is duplicated in their schools with a corresponding activity; all knowledge tends to practice; and the most scientific of teachings, understood in this way, produced neither degraded people nor rebels.

On one point, my visit to the United States has not modified my ideas; I mean in regard to the opinion which I have conceived of the irreconcilable antagonism of races. I had left behind me a Europe all rent asunder, even in time of peace, by that antagonism. I have not found that the New World has escaped it to any greater degree. When we strive to guess the future of America, it is always, as with that of Europe, from the side of this problem of races that we end by looking at it. If one day a conflict between the West and the East should break out, — and so many signs seem, at times, to point to it, — the true principle will be there, in this influx of elements of the Germanic and Scandinavian race, so abundant that the civilization of Anglo-Saxon origin is no longer able to assimilate them.

This is, however, but a hypothesis, and the majority of Americans refuse even to discuss it, so great is their confidence in the method adopted by their Republic for the settlement of these differences of race.

That method is very simple, and in conformity with the deep respect of individualism upon which all their democracy is founded. It consists in multiplying indefinitely the centres of local activity, and consequently in continuously breaking up, by means of localized action, the forces which, massed in groups, would be too powerful.

It is to be remarked, in fact, that the grave troubles from which America has suffered during these past years arise from the very centralized associations which have been built up contrary to the tradition of individualism. True, Europe, bound as she is by historic necessities, cannot borrow this method and break the unity of the great countries of which she is composed. There is to be found, however, in this example, an indication of general policy. It is a return to the theory of little independent States — replaced, alas! by that of nationalities — which, systematically applied on the morrow of the First Empire, assured us so many years of such fruitful peace. The solution of the problem of races will be found in a recast geography, which, without hindering hereditary tendencies, parcels out the fields of activity. When the crisis of acute militarism, which the most brutal and the most clumsy of annexations forces upon us, is solved, either pacifically or otherwise, that theory will impose itself upon those who will construct the new map of the Old World, and it will be a first step toward the United States of Europe, which was the dream of King Henry IV., and which remains the ideal of true civilization, reconcilable with all forms of government and all the interior traditions.

Twenty-four hours have passed since I lingered over the details of some of the salutary teachings which the New World can give the Old. I have said enough, in the course of my traveller's diary, of the defects which have shocked me in that New World, of its incoherence and its haste, of the crudity of the streets of its big towns, of the excesses of its fashionable life, and its lack of equilibrium, measure, and taste; of the too artificial tension of its culture, which gives to its women, as to its flowers, the artificiality of hothouse plants; of that abuse of energy which results in a sort of ferocity in the competition between business men, and which reduces the beaten — the lower classes — to a too cruel extremity of misfortune; of the corruption of its police, its magistrates, and its politicians, that indefinable something which excessive consciousness mixes with education; and finally, of the absence of relaxation and abandonment in its pleasures. But what then? All the defects of this society are summed up in this, — that it has dispensed with time. The sudden transplanting of the most energetic and the most unfortunate children of Europe to this new country has produced too rapid a movement. But why rake up these defects afresh? The more I proceed, the more I understand the justice of the phrase of Goethe, "When we do not speak of things with a partiality full of love, what we say is not worth being repeated," and, at the moment when I am setting my foot on European soil, it is truly with an emotion of gratitude that I say adieu to America — of gratitude, because I have received precious, incomparable teachings; of gratitude, because I feel that France is loved there; of gratitude, finally, because it exists, and its mere existence represents for the future of civilization an immense possibility.

In this last night, and within a few hours of Liverpool, all the ideas gathered in those long months of exile come back and stir me again most deeply. Toward five o'clock, a soft, vague vapor having risen, all the outlines of· the coast began to melt and sink away. I saw but the water, dead and green,

green with a greenness as of emerald and milk. A gentle
shivering ripple ran over the water as the steamer advanced.
Low in the sky was a large, broad band of mauve, and in that
mauve was the birth of a rainbow, the base formed on a point
of light cast — toward where? The sun, which was setting
yonder, threw its rays on the level of the water and struck
straight upon a light-ship painted red, which seemed aflame.
A sailing vessel was approaching, which took such dark —
nay, quite black — shades, that it seemed a mourning boat,
as it glided onward, with a motion tenderly and peacefully
funereal. It was a dream landscape, such as we meet in this
fairy-like climate, a landscape in which one might expect to
see the feet of the Saviour, of the celestial Friend, walking
toward us, toward the humble men whose hearts the beauty of
such evenings at once pierces and overwhelms. I turned to
the other side, and I saw the sun about to die. It was red,
like flowing blood, hemmed in with black — the black of night,
the night which pressed upon it, and engulfed without being
lightened by it.

A bar extended across it. Then it diminished until it ceased
to be, in that darkness of the sky in which there brooded over
a red-brown sea nothing but a purple point which flickered
out. Then there remained nothing but the clouds, just as we
imagine sometimes, in these days of threatening wars and revolutions, that other clouds, those of a new barbarism, are about
to veil the little point of light which is civilization. And here
I began to consider over again, in thought, the course which
the steamer had just travelled across the ocean. I said to myself that back yonder, at this same hour, that sun was at the
summit of the sky, half way in its course, lighting the towns,
the country, an entire universe. The harbor of New York
appeared to me in its enormous activity, then the avenues and
the crowds of passers-by. I saw again in a flash Boston, Philadelphia, Baltimore, Chicago, St. Paul, Minneapolis, so many

cities in which I scarcely stopped, yet in which I sojourned long enough for their names to conjure up vivid pictures; and the consciousness that that other world exists beside ours, that humanity has yonder so colossal a field of experiment in which to continue its work, fills me with a sort of mysterious exaltation, as though an act of faith in human will had declared itself in me, almost in spite of myself, and I opened my heart quite fully to this great breath of courage and hope that has come to me from " outre-mer."